AF631559

SOVEREIGNTY, TECHNOLOGY AND GOVERNANCE AFTER COVID-19

This book imagines how Europe might re-organise and re-group after the COVID-19 crisis by assessing its effectiveness when responding to it. For this purpose, it directs its focus on: 1) sovereignty challenges; 2) technological challenges; and 3) governance challenges. These three challenges do not present hermetic legal problems, they intersect and connect on many levels. The book shows this by examining the relationship between public and private power, and illustrating how the rise of technocratic authority is deeply connected to the choice of technological solutions. It illustrates how constitutional decisions taken during states of emergency give rise to private governance challenges related to cybersecurity and data protection. Experts from the fields of EU governance, data protection and technology explore these questions to provide answers to how the EU might develop in the future.

Sovereignty, Technology and Governance after COVID-19

Legal Challenges in a Post-Pandemic Europe

Edited by
Francisco de Abreu Duarte
and
Francesca Palmiotto Ettorre

•HART•
OXFORD • LONDON • NEW YORK • NEW DELHI • SYDNEY

HART PUBLISHING

Bloomsbury Publishing Plc

Kemp House, Chawley Park, Cumnor Hill, Oxford, OX2 9PH, UK

1385 Broadway, New York, NY 10018, USA

29 Earlsfort Terrace, Dublin 2, Ireland

HART PUBLISHING, the Hart/Stag logo, BLOOMSBURY and the Diana logo are trademarks of Bloomsbury Publishing Plc

First published in Great Britain 2022

Copyright © The editors and contributors severally 2022

The editors and contributors have asserted their right under the Copyright, Designs and Patents Act 1988 to be identified as Authors of this work.

All rights reserved. No part of this publication may be reproduced or transmitted in any form or by any means, electronic or mechanical, including photocopying, recording, or any information storage or retrieval system, without prior permission in writing from the publishers.

While every care has been taken to ensure the accuracy of this work, no responsibility for loss or damage occasioned to any person acting or refraining from action as a result of any statement in it can be accepted by the authors, editors or publishers.

All UK Government legislation and other public sector information used in the work is Crown Copyright ©. All House of Lords and House of Commons information used in the work is Parliamentary Copyright ©. This information is reused under the terms of the Open Government Licence v3.0 (http://www.nationalarchives.gov.uk/doc/open-government-licence/version/3) except where otherwise stated.

All Eur-lex material used in the work is © European Union, http://eur-lex.europa.eu/, 1998–2022.

A catalogue record for this book is available from the British Library.

Library of Congress Cataloging-in-Publication data

Names: Duarte, Francisco de Abreu, editor. | Ettorre, Francesca Palmiotto, editor.

Title: Sovereignty, technology and governance after Covid-19 : legal challenges in a post-pandemic Europe / edited by Francisco de Abreu Duarte and Francesca Palmiotto Ettorre.

Description: Oxford ; New York : Hart, 2022. | Includes bibliographical references and index.

Identifiers: LCCN 2022022117 (print) | LCCN 2022022118 (ebook) | ISBN 9781509955985 (hardback) | ISBN 9781509956029 (paperback) | ISBN 9781509956005 (pdf) | ISBN 9781509955992 (Epub)

Subjects: LCSH: Covid-19 (Disease)—Law and legislation—Europe. | Human rights—Europe. | Data protection—Law and legislation—Europe. | Public health laws—Europe.

Classification: LCC KJC6178.5.C68 S68 2022 (print) | LCC KJC6178.5.C68 (ebook) | DDC 344.404/362414—dc23/eng/20220705

LC record available at https://lccn.loc.gov/2022022117

LC ebook record available at https://lccn.loc.gov/2022022118

ISBN: HB: 978-1-50995-598-5
ePDF: 978-1-50995-600-5
ePub: 978-1-50995-599-2

Typeset by Compuscript Ltd, Shannon

To find out more about our authors and books visit www.hartpublishing.co.uk. Here you will find extracts, author information, details of forthcoming events and the option to sign up for our newsletters.

To whom we lost.

ACKNOWLEDGEMENTS

This book was written during one of the world's most difficult moments: the COVID-19 pandemic. Many of us lost friends and relatives during this time. When we asked people to imagine a brighter future, there was none to be seen. We do not forget this.

This makes our gratitude all the more important. Our profound thanks to all of the friends and colleagues who decided to join this project and imagine a world after Covid-19.

A special thanks is due to Professor Deirdre Curtin. Her care and support – many times through weekly zoom calls – inspired this book to exist. We could not have mustered the strength to engage in such an endeavour were it not for her belief.

A final thanks to all the young researchers who shared the difficulties and successes of these past years. This book is for you.

TABLE OF CONTENTS

1

Introduction

FRANCISCO DE ABREU DUARTE AND
FRANCESCA PALMIOTTO ETTORRE

In the film *The Day After Tomorrow*, Hollywood presents a daunting picture of what the world will look like if global climate change is not averted. Tornados, massive blizzards and global distress are some of the many challenges portrayed in the film which warn audiences of the cost of environmental idleness. This kind of apocalyptic film portrays the near future as a world of chaos, in which civilisation is put to the test only to come back stronger in the end. It leaves us with two contradictory feelings. On the one hand, there is a sense of urgency. The day after tomorrow is, after all, *just after tomorrow*. Action is needed as soon as possible. On the other hand, as we exit the cinema, there is a sudden sense of relief as we return to the safety of reality. That sense of safety, we naively thought, would last for a long time.

The COVID-19 pandemic represented the arrival of one of such unthinkable day. The *day after tomorrow* was suddenly upon us, and humanity had to face it unprepared. Its consequences remain to be assessed to this day. We know that COVID-19 has impacted every level of governance, and its scope – geographical dissemination and a dire need for cooperation – has undoubtedly put globalisation to the test. On the one hand, COVID-19 has changed how states relate to one another and to international organisations. Managing the pandemic requires an extraordinary coordination effort and has placed multilateralism and global cooperation under new tensions. On the other hand, individuals and businesses have had to reinvent social interactions, with prolonged confinements imposed in every country where the pandemic has hit. This combination of unprecedented global coordination and individual restrictions to freedom will have a long-lasting effect on our society.

By now, a great deal of scholarship has aptly described the challenges of the pandemic from different legal perspectives. Virtually every area of the law has had to grapple with the consequences of the COVID-19 pandemic. As the crisis hit all the different levels of governance, it also raised transversal questions across legal disciplines. Contract lawyers, for example, had to revisit classic doctrines to help businesses worldwide as they struggled to comply with their obligations.

Constitutional lawyers debated the limits and boundaries of the executive power, as they faced continuous declarations of states of emergency, which limited fundamental freedoms. Privacy and tech lawyers discussed the dangers of the new 'Zoom Society' and the collective surveillance of tracing applications and facial recognition technology. Criminal lawyers had to deal with new crimes related to the violation of restrictions and new forms of enforcement tools, such as the use of drones for monitoring compliance with the quarantine. We wish to build on such work by providing a fresh perspective on the topic in this volume.

In times of emergencies, a fast and effective decision-making process is imperative. In the words of the historian Yuval Harari, these are 'fast-forward historical processes'.[1] The risk is, however, that many emergency measures, initially temporary, can then become 'a fixture of life':[2]

> When choosing between alternatives, we should ask ourselves not only how to overcome the immediate threat, but also what kind of world we will inhabit once the storm passes. Yes, the storm will pass, humankind will survive, most of us will still be alive – but we will inhabit a different world.[3]

As we now face the conclusion of this unprecedented chapter of global history, we want to look at Europe after the storm, imagining what the post-COVID-19 world will look like. The *Day After COVID-19* is likely to have a different legal landscape altogether. As legal scholars, we must be ready to assess what impact the current legal solutions may have in the future. How will the pandemic affect the legal field as we move ahead? Are some of the emergency measures taken during COVID-19, or some technological developments made throughout the pandemic years, simply going to disappear as we exit this dark time? Or are they going to last? This edited volume looks at COVID-19 as an opportunity to rethink EU law. The contributions of this book all aim at answering, from different perspectives and backgrounds, the following question: What challenges will the EU face after COVID-19?

For this purpose, this volume addresses the central question from three perspectives: (i) sovereignty challenges; (ii) technological challenges; and (iii) governance challenges after COVID-19. As will be made clear throughout the book, these three challenges do not present independent or hermetic legal problems. Rather, they intersect and connect on many levels. The relationship between public and private power, for example, and the rise of technocratic authority profoundly connect with the choice of technological solutions. It is often constitutional decisions – for example, during states of emergency – that open the door to private governance challenges related to cybersecurity and data protection. It is precisely

[1] YN Harari, 'Yuval Noah Harari: The World after Coronavirus' (20 March 2020) www.ft.com/content/19d90308-6858-11ea-a3c9-1fe6fedcca75.

[2] ibid.

[3] ibid.

this connection between the many dimensions of the COVID-19 emergency that one ought to study to understand the future. This is precisely what the present book attempts to do.

Deirdre Curtin's chapter, 'Opening Executive Technocratic Bubbles: Gusts of Transparency in a Turbulent Europe', opens the first section on *sovereignty challenges* with an analysis of transparency and accountability of executive powers. The chapter firstly shows the phenomenon of the intensification in these uncertain times of government by experts, especially by medical scientists (government by experts) and through collaboration with private tech companies (government by shared data). The author then raises the critical theme of secrecy or lack of transparency of much of the data and discussions by the (medical) experts, and focuses on the efforts made by other accountability forums – courts and the (European) Ombudsman – to shed light on scientific black boxes. Tailwinds of transparency, activated by specific accountability forums, help anchor expert executive power in turbulent times but by no means fill actual accountability deficits.

Francisco de Abreu Duarte then turns the attention to expanded corporate power with his 'The New Providers on the Block'. There, the author focuses on the power obtained by big digital companies during the sanitary emergency and questions what it might mean for a post-pandemic world. The author argues that COVID-19 constituted an ideal opportunity for these companies to ascertain power and obtain a new type of legitimacy in the global community. By analysing the reaction of big tech players to the pandemic, namely Twitter, Facebook, Google and Apple, the author discusses the blurring between private and public power. The author concludes that Big Tech are assuming increasingly more relevant public-interest tasks. This transformation of the public–private divide is a long-lasting feature of the post-COVID-19 world, whereby communities start to rely on Big Tech to address public needs.

The section concludes with the contribution by Luisa Marin, where she addresses the question 'What Did the COVID-19 Crisis Teach Us about European Solidarity?' The chapter reflects upon solidarity as a legal principle in the context of European integration, considering COVID-19 as a crucial moment for the EU. The author compares the present emergency to previous EU's crises as all the solutions have been designed and based on the principle of solidarity. In all these contexts, the principle of solidarity has proved to have the crucial flexibility needed to address disparities consolidated by integration. The chapter concludes by reflecting upon this corrective flexibility dimension of the principle of solidarity for a transnational polity such as the EU.

The second section is dedicated to *technological challenges*. Technologies have been widely employed in the fight against the virus and represent a vital aspect of the legal challenges that might remain, hence profoundly changing post-pandemic Europe.

Francesca Palmiotto Ettorre opens this section by 'Tracing Transparency' of contact tracing apps. The aim of the chapter is to propose a governance model of technologies used for public purposes. The author uses the experience of contact tracing apps in the EU to test the concept of algorithmic transparency empirically. Using European contact tracing apps as a case study, this work investigates how transparency has been translated from theory to practice and whether transparency was beneficial. This work will also show that transparency can represent a suitable model for the governance of technologies used for public purposes, such as protecting public health. The author concludes that transparency, as resulting from the experience with contact tracing apps, can represent a suitable model for the public governance of algorithms in post-pandemic Europe.

Mariavittoria Catanzariti continues the technological analysis by exploring the management of health data processing during and after COVID-19. The analysis is based on a sociolegal approach that tries to transversally examine the main legal and regulatory challenges for surveillance from the perspective of citizens, data subjects and public health. After scrutinising the techno-legal models of app tracing, it analyses the main legal issues at the crossroads of the European approach. In particular, it explores the advantages and shortcomings deriving from data protection concerns in light of policy options that are oriented towards the interoperability of health data. It finally reflects upon the type of obligation underlying app tracing – whether moral or legal – and its adequacy to contrast the pandemic.

The third chapter in this section focuses on one of the most controversial applications of AI, namely facial recognition. Natalia Menéndez González, in her chapter 'Brave New (Normal) World', analyses how facial recognition technology (FRT) has been used during and will be used after the health emergency. The widespread employment of this technology has given rise to a vast concern over the privacy implications of FRT systems. Additionally, some voices claim that such technology would be difficult to withdraw once deployed. This could result in FRT strongly conditioning our future. Consequently, the author aims at ascertaining whether the COVID-19 health crisis might serve as an excuse to increase the surveillance state and ponders the impact of FRT technology in post-pandemic Europe.

Finally, Tommaso Fia concludes the section by reflecting on access to and ownership of data to tackle COVID-19. The main focus of the analysis is on IP law and on how the experience of data access during the pandemic can influence this field of law in the future. The fight against the coronavirus needed (big) data to orient decision-making and healthcare policies. However, the success of data-driven policies mainly depends on how data is managed. During the COVID-19 crisis, two main tendencies have emerged in this respect. On the one hand, there is a data management system resting on (access) barriers that restrict data access. Conversely, an alternative data management system is founded on open data access approaches valuing data availability amongst many actors. Fia's chapter presents the main tendencies which have arisen during the COVID-19 pandemic. Accordingly, it concludes with some policy arguments on the role of IP and other areas of law to foster data access for public interest purposes in post-pandemic Europe.

The volume is completed with the analysis of the *governance challenges* brought by COVID-19. In this final section, and in continuity with the previous section, the book opens with a chapter by Francesco Godano and Galileo Sartor. The authors analyse the governance model of technologies that emerged during the emergency, focusing mainly on techno-surveillance clusters in Asia and Europe.

The subsequent chapter, by Nicolas Petit, focuses on the role of Big Tech during the pandemic. The chapter looks particularly at how Apple and Google's efforts to assist European policymakers in supplying contact tracing apps backfired, in a paradoxical exercise given the substantial degree of business model adaptations that both firms initiated to cooperate with public authorities.

The third chapter in the section, by Maria Magierska, explores the role of data protection authorities (DPAs) at both national and European level during the pandemic. The author shows the extent to which these authorities participated in adopting COVID-19-related surveillance measures and asks fundamental questions: were they consistent in their positions on governments' actions? What was the role of the European Data Protection Board in that regard? What does the way the DPAs reacted to the EU-wide restrictions to the fundamental right to personal data tell about their role as quasi-ombudsmen?

Sarah Tas completes this final section on governance challenges with a piece on the rise of cybercrime and the increasing monitoring role of the EU. The chapter sheds light on the impact of COVID-19 on cybercrimes and on the role of the EU in monitoring the situation. The author ultimately proposes some solutions for the post-COVID-19 world and underlines the need for more coordinated legislation in the EU with regard to cybercrimes.

2

Opening Executive Technocratic Bubbles: Gusts of Transparency in a Turbulent Europe

DEIRDRE CURTIN*

2.1. Introduction

Europe's state-of-emergency politics was accentuated in the second decade of the twenty-first century,[1] with considerable environmental turbulence unsettling governance in Europe. Turbulence can be described as surprising, inconsistent, unpredictable and uncertain, and it adds additional layers of complexity to an emergency.[2] Turbulence may need to be met 'with robust strategies where creative and agile public organisations adapt to the emergence of new disruptive problems by building networks and partnerships with the private sector and civil society'.[3] In terms of timing, it corresponds with what Moyn has called 'the greatest crisis of expertise in living memory'.[4] The failings in expertise during the 2007–08 financial crisis, coupled with the ensuing rise in support for anti-expert movements, led to people to become 'weary of guardianship that failed in domain after domain even before epidemiologists took their turn'.[5] The paradox regarding the visible global reliance on experts from the very beginning of the COVID-19 crisis was that, on

* Professor of Law, European University Institute. I would like to thank Francesca Palmiotto and Hilary Hogan for excellent research assistance and Michal Krajewski and Anniek de Ruijter for valuable comments. Email: deirdre.curtin@eui.eu.

[1] For the wider existing context, see J White, *Politics of Last Resort: Governing by Emergency in the European Union* (Oxford University Press, 2019).

[2] C Ansell, E Sørensen and J Torfing, 'The COVID-19 Pandemic as a Game Changer for Public Administration and Leadership? The Need for Robust Governance Responses to Turbulent Problems' (2021) 23 *Public Management Review* 949. See the discussion in KH Goetz and DS Martinsen, 'COVID-19: A Dual Challenge to European Liberal Democracy' (2021) 44 *West European Politics* 1003, 1012–13.

[3] Ansell et al (n 2) 952.

[4] S Moyn, 'The Irrelevance of the Pandemic' in MP Maduro and PW Kahn, *Democracy in Times of Pandemic:Different Futures Imagined* (Cambridge University Press, 2020) 107.

[5] ibid.

the one hand, governments had no choice, but, at the same time, there was no build-up of scientific knowledge or consensus on that, nor any certainty as to what the virus entailed or its likely trajectory and how to manage the pandemic globally or nationally.[6]

In Europe, there were two basic lines of reaction to the COVID-19 crisis. One involved declaring a state of emergency in certain Member States of the European Union.[7] The other involved not declaring a formal state of emergency, either because it was not possible legally speaking (Germany, the EU) or because a decision was taken that it was not warranted.[8] The focus of this chapter is on those states in Europe that are in emergency mode but not necessarily in a formal state of emergency interlinked with the supranational EU.[9] In both lines of reaction, the intensification and accumulation of executive power is striking. In both instances, secrecy and a certain amount of legal informality or rushed decision-making was evident, certainly in the initial reactions.

Authorities at the national level, as well as European institutions and actors, have adopted various legal and regulatory measures in order to meet some of the challenges of the health emergency.[10] Many of these measures, from national lockdowns to border closures and new purchasing funds or furlough measures, were conceived to be temporary and highly exceptional. European actors quickly took measures to support economic aspects, such as exceptions to the state aid rules,[11]

[6] See, in general, JW Richards, D Axe and WM Briggs, *The Price of Panic: How the Tyranny of Experts Turned a Pandemic into a Catastrophe* (Regnery Publishing, 2020); A Monti and R Wacks, 'Science and Power' in A Monti and R Wacks (eds), *COVID-19 and Public Policy in the Digital Age* (Routledge India, 2020).

[7] Globally it appears that a majority of countries have declared a state of emergency, see C Bjørnskov and S Voigt, 'The State of Emergency Virus' (*Verfassungsblog*, 19 April 2020) https://verfassungsblog.de/thestate-of-emergency-virus. In the European Union, 17 out of 27 Member States formally declaring either a state of emergency as such or another type of (health) emergency by mid-March 2020. See further J Grogan, 'Analysing Global Use of Emergency Powers in Response to COVID-19' (2020) 22 *European Journal of Law Reform* 338; Symposium on State of Emergency (*Verfassungsblog*, 26 May 2020) https://verfassungsblog.de/category/debates/covid-19-and-states-of-emergency-debates/. For a general overview of EU Member States that declared a state of emergency, see O Marzocchi, European Parliament Directorate-General for Internal Policies of the Union, *The Impact of COVID-19 Measures on Democracy, the Rule of Law and Fundamental Rights in the EU* (Briefing PE 651.343, European Parliament, 2020). For details of specific countries, see the four reports by the European Parliamentary Research Service, *States of Emergency in Response to the Coronavirus Crisis: Situation in Certain Member States* (Briefing PE 652.002, July 2020).

[8] A number of countries had the option of declaring states of emergency but chose not to do so. See European Parliamentary Research Service, *States of Emergency in Response to the Coronavirus Crisis: Situation in Certain Member States* (Briefing PE 649.408, June 2020) www.europarl.europa.eu/RegData/etudes/BRIE/2020/649408/EPRS_BRI(2020)649408_EN.df.

[9] As argued by Meyer-Resende: 'By mid-March, all EU member states were in a state of emergency, whether they officially declared one or not.' See M Meyer-Resende, 'The Rule of Law Stress Test: EU Member States' Responses to COVID-19' (*Verfassungsblog*, 24 May 2020) https://verfassungsblog.de/the-rule-of-law-stresstest-eu-member-states-responses-to-covid-19/.

[10] A Alemanno, 'The European Response to COVID-19: From Regulatory Emulation to Regulatory Coordination?' (2020) 11 *European Journal of Risk Regulation* 307.

[11] The European Commission introduced the temporary measures for state aid on 19 March 2020, and activated the general escape clause the next day. For the timeline, see further Commission, *Timeline of EU Action*, https://ec.europa.eu/info/live-work-travel-eu/coronavirus-response/timeline-eu-action_en.

but held back on public health-related measures as EU competence is limited in the field of public health.[12] The main responses in Europe were from the national governments. In the emergency, governments closed borders, imposed restrictions on domestic and international travel, ordered and enforced lockdowns by closing schools and workplaces and banning public gatherings, conducted widespread COVID-19 testing, commandeered private hospitals and facilitated the adoption of tracking apps.[13]

From the early days of the crisis, the role of the EU was different. It was a largely supportive one to the Member States, attempting in various fields to coordinate action in several critical respects, from tracking apps to travel lists and vaccination campaigns.[14] This action has, later, hardened into a number of specific measures that have called into being new highly significant instruments with considerable power for the Commission.[15] In addition, the roles of the Council and of the European Council have been reinforced.[16] The government of the EU has engaged with largely the same phenomenon, keeping an eye on and limiting the closing of borders, devising common tracking apps, engaging with Europe-wide travel lists, etc. Much of the work has been technical, undertaken by medical scientists and other experts, with the actual deliberations taking place in committees and agencies at a more technical level. This technical bureaucracy is fed to an important extent by national experts, who in this way partake in supranational decision-making. This phenomenon is one that is replicated globally. Concurrently, the EU government adopted measures in certain fields (such as state aid and public procurement) that temporarily suspended the full operation of applicable EU rules in Member States.[17] For all these measures, national

[12] Although it has been argued that the EU has wider competence in the field of health law and policy than traditionally understood: see K Purnhagen et al., 'More Competences Than You Knew? The Web of Health Competence for European Union Action in Response to the COVID-19 Outbreak' (2020) 11 *European Journal of Risk Regulation* 297.

[13] See, eg A Greene, *Emergency Powers in a Time of Pandemic* (Bristol University Press, 2020); H van Kolfschooten and A de Ruijter, 'COVID-19 and Privacy in the European Union: A Legal Perspective on Contact Tracing' (2020) 41 *Contemporary Security Policy* 478; C Casey, O Doyle, D Kenny and D Lyons, *Ireland's Emergency Powers During the COVID-19 Pandemic* (Irish Human Rights and Equality Commission, 2021); KD Ewing, 'COVID-19: Government by Decree' (2020) 31 *King's Law Journal* 1; DR Knight, 'Stamping Out COVID-19 in New Zealand: Legal Pragmatism and Democratic Legitimacy' [2021] *PL* 241; A Goudge, 'Balancing Legality and Legitimacy in Canada's COVID-19 Response' (2021) 41 *National Journal of Constitutional Law* 153; C Corradetti and Oreste Pollicino, 'The "War" against COVID-19: State of Exception, State of Siege or (Constitutional) Emergency Powers?: The Italian Case in Comparative Perspective' (2021) 22 *German Law Journal* 1060.

[14] A-L Beaussier and Lydie Cabane, 'Strengthening the EU's Response Capacity to Health Emergencies: Insights from EU Crisis Management Mechanisms' (2020) *European Journal of Risk Regulation* 1.

[15] VA Schmidt, 'Theorising Institutional Change and Governance in European Responses to the COVID-19 Pandemic' (2020) 42 *Journal of European Integration* 1177, 1179.

[16] ibid 1183.

[17] A Georgopoulos, 'The EU's Joint Procurement Agreement in Light of COVID-19: Learning the Correct Lessons from the Pandemic and Identifying Actions for Improvement' in S Arrowsmith, LRA Butler, A La Chimia and C Yukins (eds) *Public Procurement Regulation in (a) Crisis?: Global Lessons from the COVID-19 Pandemic* (Hart Publishing, 2021); A Biondi, 'State Aid in the Time of COVID-19'

and supranational, regulatory impact assessments will not have been undertaken, cost–benefit analyses will not have been prepared and public consultation on the whole will not have occurred.[18] Truly public deliberation will not have taken place in the media or elsewhere, given the asymmetry in knowledge and information sources.

The executive power can be seen to be drifting to a greater or lesser extent from the national to the supranational, but at the same time it may drift away from the other branches of government, parliaments and courts, although the contrary can also be observed.[19] Experts within the executive have a well-known knowledge and information-gathering advantage over the legislative and judicial branches. They are what Cass Sunstein refers to as 'the most knowledgeable branch'.[20] Executive actors exist in formal accountability relationships with other actors, in particular parliaments, courts, ombudspersons and auditors. In those relationships, it is key that executive actors provide information on their action or inaction, deliberate in dialogues with the accountability forums and accept that adverse consequences or sanctions may follow in certain circumstances.[21] Accountability forums may, however, drift away from executive actors; the chances of drifting are increased by remote virtual participation of an accountability forum. This may accentuate the isolation or remoteness of the executive power from the possibility of accountability, through secrecy of information sources, secret internal deliberations, a blurred role of scientific expertise and the ensuing difficulty of connection in a real, substantive manner with accountability forums of various kinds. Who, other than public officials, has input into the decision-making by government, national or supranational? In particular, what are the role and powers of medical scientific advisors in these times? Third, regarding the increasing reliance on private parties and data-based decision-making, what role do private actors play in providing data and technologies that underpin government decisions and action both

(*EU Law Live*, 25 March 2020) https://eulawlive.com/op-ed-state-aid-in-the-time-of-covid-19-by-andrea-biondi/; D Utrilla, 'State Aid and COVID-19: Further Extension of the State Aid Temporary Framework' (*EU Law Live*, 12 May 2020) https://eulawlive.com/state-aid-and-covid-19-further-extension-of-the-state-aid-temporary-framework/; D Ferri, 'The Role of EU State Aid Law as a "Risk Management Tool" in the COVID-19 Crisis' (2021) 12 *European Journal of Risk Regulation* 176; R Luja, 'EU Fiscal State Aid Rules and COVID-19: Will One Survive the Other?' (2020) 4 *EC Tax Review* 147.

[18] EL Windholz, 'Governing in a Pandemic, from Parliamentary Soveriegnty to Autocratic Technocracy' (2020) 8 *The Theory and Practice of Legislation* 93, 100.

[19] In the context of COVID-19 and legislative sidelining, see A Weiss, 'Binding the Bound: State Executive Emergency Powers and Democratic Legitimacy in the Pandemic' (2021) 121 *Columbia Law Review* 1853, 1880–83. But note that Ginsburg and Versteeg argue, in their global survey of legal responses to COVID-19, that checks and balances have remained largely intact, and that courts and legislatures have played a significant oversight role during the crisis. See T Ginsburg and M Versteeg, 'Binding the Unbound Executive: Checks and Balances in Times of Pandemic' (2020) Virginia Public Law and Legal Theory Research Paper 2020-52 and (2020) University of Chicago Public Law Working Paper 747, 26–47.

[20] C Sunstein, 'The Most Knowledgeable Branch' (2016) 164 *University of Pennsylvania Law Review* 1607.

[21] See, in general, M Bovens, RE Goodin and T Schillemans (eds), *The Oxford Handbook of Public Accountability* (Oxford University Press, 2014).

nationally and supranationally? The next two sections address these questions. Section 4 highlights the investigative turn made by the European Ombudsman regarding EU executive technocracy during the ongoing crisis and highlights the knock-on effects that may take root more generally. Section 5 concludes with some optimism as to the role that tailwinds of transparency may play even during periods of considerable turbulence.

2.2. Government by Scientific Expertise

A lot of the scholarly discussion has been on the expansion of executive power and the effects on the role of parliaments as an important part of the response to the COVID-19 emergency.[22] Some claim that executive power arrogated legislative power in some instances.[23] The role of scientists in government decision-making has also received some attention in the literature.[24] Within the executive powers of many states globally, power is concentrated in the hands of a small group. In Australia, for example, this is the National Cabinet, with the principal advisory body being the Australian Health Protection Principal Committee (AHPPC). Chaired by Australia's Chief Medical Officer and comprising all State and Territory Chief Health Officers, it is the key decision-making committee for health emergencies.[25] The AHPPC oversees five standing committees and one advisory group. There are similar set-ups in most European states. In Ireland, for example, the National Public Health Emergency Team (NPHET) is a group within the

[22] Greene (n 13); Ginsburg and Versteeg (n 19); E Griglio, 'Parliamentary Oversight under the COVID-19 Emergency: Striving against Executive Dominance' (2020) 8 *The Theory and Practice of Legislation* 49; J Petrov, 'The COVID-19 Emergency in the Age of Executive Aggrandisement: What Role of Legislative and Judicial Checks?' (2020) 8 *The Theory and Practice of Legislation* 71.

[23] A former member of the UK Supreme Court, Lord Sumption, called it, in the UK context, 'government by decree' and described it in hyperbolic terms as 'the most significant interference with personal freedom in the history of our country'. See J Sumption, 'Government by Decree – COVID-19 and the Constitution' (Cambridge Freshfields Annual Law Lecture 2020, 27 October 2020). See also Ewing (n 13); Greene (n 13). In Italy, too, and in other countries it is also literally government by executive fiat. See, eg Corradetti and Pollicino (n 13).

[24] See, eg J Zielonka, 'Who Should be in Charge of Pandemics? Scientists or Politicians?' in G Delanty (ed) *Pandemic, Politics and Society: Critical Perspectives on the COVID-19 Crisis* (De Gruyter, 2021); PL Bylund and MD Packard, 'Separation of Power and Expertise: Evidence of the Tyranny of Experts in Sweden's COVID-19 Responses' (2021) *Southern Economic Journal* 1; A Esmark, 'How Does Crisis Affect the Conflict between Technocracy and Populism? Lessons from the COVID-19 Pandemic' [2021] *Politics* 1; MA Neblo and JL Wallace, 'A Plague on Politics: The COVID Crisis, Expertise and the Future of Legitimation' (2021) 115 *American Political Science Review* 1524; T Besley and A Velasco, 'Politicians Can't Hide behind Scientists Forever – Even in a Pandemic' (*LSE COVID-19 Blog*, 6 May 2020) https://blogs.lse.ac.uk/covid19/2020/05/06/politicians-cant-hide-behind-scientists-forever-even-in-a-pandemic; M Morvillo, 'I Just Can't Get Enough (of Experts): The Numbers of COVID-19 and the Need for a European Approach to Testing' (2020) 11 *European Journal of Risk Regulation* 366.

[25] Australian Government, Department of Health, *Australian Health Protection Principal Committee (AHPPC)* www.health.gov.au/committees-and-groups/australian-health-protection-principal-committee-ahppc.

Department of Health that oversees and provides direction and expert advice across the health service and the wider public service on the national response to the pandemic.[26] Members of the team are from the Department of Health and other health service executives, as well as consultants, epidemiologists, the Coronavirus Expert Advisory Group and the Irish Epidemiological Modelling Advisory Group – all expert medics or medical scientists. In the UK, the corresponding body is the Scientific Advisory Group for Emergencies.[27] In France, the Law of 23 March 2020 also anchors the scientific advice of the government in a newly created Conseil Scientifique COVID-19.[28] In Italy, it is the Comitato tecnico scientifico, set up on 5 February 2020 by a decree from the Chief of Civil Protection. It is composed of experts and representatives of state administrations (25 in total).[29] In many instances, these groups were criticised early on for their secrecy and lack of independence, and some improvements were introduced along the way.[30]

The executive of the EU has engaged with largely the same phenomenon as its Member States: monitoring and limiting the closing of borders, monitoring the level of COVID-19 virus and vaccination rates,[31] devising common tracking apps and engaging with Europe-wide travel lists. Much of the work has been technical, undertaken by medical scientists and other experts, with the actual deliberations taking place in committees and agencies at a more technical level. This technical bureaucracy is fed to an important extent by national experts, who in this way partake in supranational decision-making. This pattern is one that is replicated globally, although the difference is that the EU has a governance structure that is more sophisticated and more hands on in many ways than global expert international organisations (such as the World Health Organization[32]). The European Commission also set up in 2020 an advisory panel on COVID-19 composed of seven members. It announced that, given the urgency, it was not possible to organise a public call for applications, and that the members of the panel would be appointed immediately, drawing on persons identified by the Commission with

[26] C Casey and D Kenny, 'Ireland – COVID-19 Response Raises Rule of Law Concerns' [2021] 3 *PL* 644.

[27] G Scally et al, 'Editorial: The UK's Public Health Response to COVID-19' (2020) 369 *British Medical Journal* 1.

[28] Ministère des Solidarités et de la Santé, 'Olivier Véran installe un conseil scientifique' (11 March 2020) https://solidarites-sante.gouv.fr/actualites/presse/communiques-de-presse/article/olivier-veran-installe-unconseil-scientifique. See further A Gaillet and M Gerhold, 'Etat d'urgence sanitaire: Wie Frankreich den Coronavirus bekämpft' (*Verfassungsblog*, 27 March 2020) https://verfassungsblog.de/etatdurgence-sanitaire/.

[29] Ministero della Salute, *Comitato Tecnico Scientifico*, www.salute.gov.it/portale/nuovocoronavirus/dettaglioContenutiNuovoCoronavirus.jsp?lingua=italiano&d=5432&area=nuovoCoronavirus&menu=vuoto.

[30] See, eg Scally et al (n 27).

[31] Morvillo (n 24).

[32] M Zürn, 'Democratic Governance beyond the Nation-State: The EU and Other International Institutions' (2000) 6 *European Journal of International Relations* 183.

acknowledged expertise.[33] The experts selected are from national institutes from France, Germany, Denmark, Italy, the Netherlands and Belgium.[34] Moreover, the EU Scientific Advice Platform on COVID-19 was created on 13 November 2020 to provide a forum for peer exchange and coordination among scientific advisors to national governments, offering a space for sharing good practices and mutual learning. It complements the President's COVID-19 advisory panel and the work of the European Centre for Disease Prevention and Control (ECDC). It is composed of 27 members, one nominated by each of the EU countries.

The core resource that enables these scientific experts to perform this role is their medical expertise. Their specialised knowledge and expertise bring, in the words of Windholz, 'status, reputation, and the perception of objectivity and independence. This imbues them with authority and credibility in the public domain. It also enables them to participate in public debate asymmetrically with other participants',[35] giving birth to 'the rise of autocratic technocracy'.[36] Medical scientists are the technocrats in the autocratic technocracy.[37] The reason why they can be considered autocratic is that they can be considered to exist in a type of executive bubble with considerable knowledge and information-gathering advantage over accountability forums that could offer some checks (such as parliaments and courts). They are perceived to have pure motives (science), especially when compared to political, business and commercial interests. When this is coupled with complex and highly technical decisions which have to be made on the basis of incomplete and shifting information, their discretion is considerable and potentially without bounds. As Ignatieff pertinently points out:

> the science on offer was never just technical advice. It provided legitimacy for political decisions so momentous, in terms of their impact on freedom, that they could not be justified on the usual probabilistic or utilitarian grounds. Scientists kept silent when 'political' questions were in play, but their very presence provided politicians with the stamp of a higher authority … in a pandemic, a strict separation of the purely scientific and political aspects is impossible.'[38]

In most cases, the medical experts function formally as advisors and not as actual decision makers. Even within the context of scientific advice, choices must be made and discretion is present.[39] As Weiss has put it: 'the decisions made, both

[33] See European Ombudsman, 'Letter to the European Commission concerning the transparency of the EU Response to the COVID-19 Crisis' (29 July 2020) www.ombudsman.europa.eu/en/doc/correspondence/en/130853.

[34] For details of correspondence with the EO, see European Ombudsman, 'The European Commission and Transparency in the Context of the EU Response to the COVID-19 Crisis', Case SI/4/2020/PL, opened 29 July 2020, www.ombudsman.europa.eu/en/case/en/57422.

[35] Windholz (n 18) 106.

[36] ibid 97.

[37] ibid 105.

[38] Michael Ignatieff, 'The Reckoning: Evaluating Democratic Leadership' in Maduro and Kahn (n 4) 89, 98.

[39] Weiss (n 19) 1877.

in this emergency and in future public health emergencies, are judgement calls, as the dearth of knowledge precludes absolute moral or epistemic certainty. These judgment calls are unavoidably entangled with politics and legislative priorities.'[40] Some governments have made a point of overruling specific, far-reaching and public advice by the medical scientists (eg in Ireland).[41] In other states, the expert transitions from advisor to decision maker, and combines the reputation and trustworthiness of their profession with the imprimatur and power of the state.[42] It can be hard for governments to ignore advice from persons they have put forward as experts. This can also be very limiting for public debate and true deliberation. The same principle applies at the European level. But 'expert technical advisers cannot substitute for democratic judgement in determining the public good – and nor should technical experts attempt to do so'.[43]

Medical scientists as experts are involved in a variety of ways at the European level, but two of the most important and most prominent EU advisory organs are the European Centre for Disease Prevention and Control (hereafter ECDC) and the European Medicines Agency (EMA). The ECDC's role has assumed new significance in light of the pandemic, described by one commentator as 'the rising star of the governance system for health threats management in the EU'.[44] Nonetheless, there has been mounting awareness of the limited powers afforded to the ECDC, which has constrained its ability to respond effectively to the pandemic, particularly in the early months of the crisis.[45] The Commission is seeking to strengthen the mandates of both bodies as part of its proposed way forward to a European Health Union.[46] Thus, the EMA will be empowered to monitor and mitigate shortages of critical medicines, as well as enabling stronger crisis response.[47] The ECDC will be given power to deal with crisis preparedness and response. In addition, the eHealth Network (eHN) is significant. It was set up under Directive 2011/24/EU on patients' rights in cross-border healthcare and connects national authorities responsible for eHealth under the auspices of the

[40] ibid 1878.

[41] F O'Brien, 'Tánaiste Says NPHET Recommendation "Not Thought Through"' *RTÉ* (6 October 2020) https://www.rte.ie/news/coronavirus/2020/1005/1169652-covid-19/.

[42] E Baekkeskov and PO Öberg, 'Freezing Deliberation through Public Expert Advice' (2017) 24 *Journal of European Public Policy* 1006, 1007.

[43] BW Head and S Banerjee, 'Policy Expertise and Use of Evidence in a Populist Era' (2020) 55 *Australian Journal of Political Science* 110.

[44] T Deruelle and I Engeli, 'The COVID-19 Crisis and the Rise of the European Centre for Disease Prevention and Control' (2021) 44 *West European Politics* 1376, 1392.

[45] Beaussier and Cabane (n 14). See also A de Ruijter, 'What Do We Actually Mean by a European Health Union?' (2020) 26(3) *Eurohealth* 30. See too, more recently, the initiative by academics with a manifesto for a European Health Union: https://europeanhealthunion.eu/about.

[46] Most recent is the agreement on a new Health Emergency Response Authority as part of a European Health Union (https://ec.europa.eu/commission/presscorner/detail/en).

[47] Commission, 'Building a European Health Union: Re-enforcing the EU's Resilience for Cross-Border Health Threats' (Communication) COM (2020) 724, https://ec.europa.eu/info/sites/info/files/communication-european-health-union-resilience_en.pdf; Commission, 'Building a European Health Union: Stronger Crisis Preparedness and Response for Europe' (Press Release, 11 November 2020) https://ec.europa.eu/commission/presscorner/detail/en/qanda_20_2042.

Commission. Through this voluntary network, EU countries can give direction to eHealth developments in Europe and help shape policy on eHealth interoperability and standardisation (similar to other networks, such as the one around the European Central Bank). Since the start of the COVID-19 crisis, the eHN has worked intensively to achieve interoperability of tracking apps (contact applications) across Member States and to ensure their contribution to public health efforts by national health authorities.

2.3. Government by Shared Data

Database policy-making has been key in managing the pandemic.[48] At the EU level, one of the main purposes of the ECDC has been to collect information from the Member States, and it has done so in a variety of ways, including the so-called European Surveillance System (TESSy). This is a system to which Member States upload data on diseases under surveillance using standardised formats.[49] It also gives national authorities access to TESSy's extranet, where they can find guidelines and instructions. Another salient source is the so-called Early Warning and Response System of the European Union (EWRS). The EWRS is a notification system for the European Commission and the National Focal Points for Threat Detection in the EU/EEA Member States. It is a notification tool for risk managers in Member States and the Commission (DG SANTE), and the ECDC's role is limited to operating and monitoring the system. The ECDC does not actively participate in the posting of messages on threats. The EWRS is a less structured system than TESSy and extracting information from it in an automated manner is more difficult, as it was not designed to receive large amounts of information. Finally, the ECDC has carried out a number of important surveys upon the request of the Commission. As an example of such a survey, the ECDC was asked to compare the different incidence rates of the virus in all Member States. In order to carry out this analysis, it needed to know what the different testing strategies were in the Member States and thus launched a survey to collect this information. It then published it as part of its weekly outputs to allow decision makers to understand the meaning and quality of the data published by Member States.[50]

Another agency which made large use of data for policy-making is the EMA. In early April 2020, the EMA set up a COVID-19 Pandemic Task Force (COVID-ETF) to take quick and coordinated action related to COVID-19 medicines. When vaccines became available, the EMA examined their scientific data

[48] See also ch 8 in this book by Tommaso Fia.

[49] European Ombudsman, *Report on the Meeting of the European Ombudsman's Inquiry Team with the European Centre for Disease Prevention and Control* (Inquiry OI/3/2020/TE, 5 October 2020) www.ombudsman.europa.eu/en/doc/inspection-report/en/134847.

[50] ibid.

to weigh up the positive benefits and risks for different demographic groups. The EMA has undergone a veritable transparency revolution over the course of the past decade, with many of the stages prompted by inquiries of the European Ombudsman (EO)[51] and judgments of the courts, following appeals from interested parties. In this way, the interlocutors of the EMA have widened beyond those pharma companies seeking authorisation or participating in clinical trials to the public much more generally, and the public interest in scientific documentation is now much more widely recognised, also by the EMA itself, than a decade ago. Until the end of 2010, the EMA treated data and documentation submitted in support of market authorisation for medicinal products as carrying a presumption of confidentiality.[52] Subsequently, efforts were made by the EMA to negotiate with pharmaceutical companies for redacted versions of clinical study reports on a particular drug to be made available to the public. After receiving a complaint, the EO initiated an inquiry in 2014 into how the EMA should approach the issue of public disclosure of documentation on the safety of medicinal products.[53] She concluded that the EMA places too much weight on the commercial interests of the medicine developer, rather than the overriding interest of public health. She noted that while there are exceptions to freedom of information, such as privacy and the protection of commercial interests, these are not relevant where there is overarching public interest in making the document publicly available. She found 'that there is always a public interest in the disclosure of documents containing information on the safety and efficacy of medicines'.[54]

The EMA thus adopted new policies aimed at improving transparency within the organisation, prompted by recommendations from the EO.[55] Members of the public can request access to data submitted as part of the authorisation process, and reports are made available online on the EMA website.[56] In 2015, a supplemental

[51] On the role of the European Ombudsman, see M Lee, 'Accountability and Co-production beyond Courts: The Role of the European Ombudsman' in M Weimer and A de Ruijter (eds), *Regulating Risks in the European Union: The Co-production of Expert and Executive Power* (Hart Publishing, 2017) 217.

[52] D Kim, 'Transparency Policies of the European Medicines Agency: Has the Paradigm Shifted?' (2017) 25 *Medical Law Review* 456, 465.

[53] European Ombudsman, *Decision on Own-Initiative Inquiry OI/3/2014/FOR Concerning the Partial Refusal of the European Medicines Agency to Give Public Access to Studies Related to the Approval of a Medicinal Product* (OI/3/2014/FOR, 8 June 2016) www.ombudsman.europa.eu/en/decision/en/68107.

[54] ibid para 32.

[55] EMA, *European Medicines Agency Policy on Access to Documents (Related to Medicinal Products for Human and Veterinary Use* (2010, Policy/0043, EMA/110196/2006). This was overtaken by a reformulated policy in 2018. See EMA, *European Medicines Agency Policy on Access to Documents* (2018, Policy/0043, EMA/729522/2016). The former European Ombudsman had made major recommendations to overhaul transparency procedures at the EMA. See European Ombudsman, *Decision of the European Ombudsman Closing His Inquiry into Complaint 2560/2007/BEH against the European Medicines Agency* (24 November 2010, 2560/2007/BEH) para 80.

[56] R Coombes, 'European Drug Regulator Fears Return to Days of Data Secrecy' (2019) 367 *British Medical Journal*.

policy to allow the publication of clinical data was introduced.[57] Both of these policies draw on Regulation (EC) 1049/2001 (the Transparency Regulation) and Article 15 of the TFEU. Later, in 2017, the EO, on her own initiative, opened another inquiry into the activities of the EMA.[58] Specifically, she sought to examine 'pre-submission activities', the practice whereby developers of medicinal products seek scientific advice from the EMA prior to a formal submission for marketing authorisation for a particular medicinal product. While the EO acknowledged that such communication may be desirable for public health outcomes, she warned that it was 'important to avoid even the perception that the eventual opinions of EMA on medicines were influenced by these earlier interactions'.[59] In her conclusion, she found that the EMA should strive for the greatest possible degree of separation between those providing advice to developers in the initial stages and those later involved in assessing the product for market authorisation.[60]

Finally, the interaction between public and private emerged clearly in the development of contact tracing apps.[61] Digital contact tracing refers to the use of technologies, in particular mobile apps, to track and rapidly identify the contacts of a confirmed case of COVID-19 based on Bluetooth proximity technology.[62] In June 2020, several Member States launched mobile apps to complement manual contact tracing. Although each Member State developed a national application, the process was largely coordinated by EU institutions, such as the European Commission and the European Data Protection Board (EDPB), within the forum of the eHN. In the end, the decision was to interconnect all the national apps to each other with the creation of a gateway system. Through interoperability, EU citizens would be

[57] EMA, *The European Medicines Agency Policy on Publication of Clinical Data for Medicinal Products for Human Use* (2014, Policy/0070, EMA/240810/2013) www.ema.europa.eu/docs/en_GB/document_library/Other/2014/10/WC500174796.pdf.

[58] It is worth noting that the current EO's practice of initiating inquiries has prompted criticism in some quarters. See, eg T Stein, '"A Supervisory Agency of Its Own Making"? The Questionable Political Agenda of the Current European Ombudsman' (*Verfassungsblog*, 1 September 2019) https://verfassungsblog.de/asupervisory-agency-of-its-own-making.

[59] European Ombudsman, *Decision in Strategic Inquiry OI/7/2017/KR on How the European Medicines Agency Engages with Medicine Developers in the Period Leading Up to Applications for Authorisations to Market New Medicines in the EU* (17 July 2019, OI/2017/KR) www.ombudsman.europa.eu/en/decision/en/116683.

[60] ibid para 32. European Ombudsman, *Suggestions for Improvement: Decision in Strategic Inquiry OI/7/2017/KR on How the European Medicines Agency Engages with Medicine Developers in the Period Leading Up to Applications for Authorisations to Market New Medicines in the EU* (17 July 2019). The EMA's response to the inquiry is available at www.ema.europa.eu/en/news/ema-takes-note-european-ombudsmans-decision-pre-submission-activities.

[61] See generally H Nowotny, 'In AI We Trust: How the COVID-19 Pandemic Pushes Us Deeper into Digitalisation' in Delanty (n 24) 107, 115–18; van Kolfschooten and de Ruijter (n 13); L Bradford, M Aboy and K Liddell, 'COVID-19 Contact Tracing Apps: A Stress Test for Privacy, the GDPR, and Data Protection Regimes' (2020) 7 *Journal of Law & Biosciences* 1; Cong Duc Tran and Tin Trung Nguyen, 'Health vs Privacy? The Risk–Risk Tradeoff in Using COVID-19 Contact-Tracing Apps' (2021) 67 *Technology in Society* 1; Y Bengio et al, 'The Need for Privacy with Public Digital Contact Tracing during the COVID-19 Pandemic' (2020) 2 *The Lancet* 342.

[62] In Europe all the apps are based on Bluetooth while worldwide some countries decided to use GPS technology.

able to install only one app, even when crossing borders, and the health authorities would be able to keep track of contacts between individuals from different Member States. As well as this practical aspect, ensuring interoperability could also lead to the standardisation of national apps.

Interoperability significantly shaped the design of the (national) apps. In order to be interoperable, the apps had to be compatible and share the same standards in terms of privacy, data protection, security, effectiveness and voluntary use.[63] Furthermore, the apps also needed to be based on the same epidemiological criteria to define close contacts for high-risk exposure and to calculate the risk and proximity. The fact that in the end most of the apps adopted a decentralised system was largely due to the pressure coming from the EU institutions, as well as decisions made by Google and Apple.[64] France, one of the few states that adopted a centralised approach, is not connected to the gateway because of this design choice.

Design choices and interoperability affect the way data are processed, hence will affect individuals' private life. Although interoperability and software infrastructures are perceived as mere 'technical aspects', they can impact fundamental rights. In other areas, many scholars have underlined how interoperability could erode cornerstone principles of data protection, such as that of purpose limitation.[65] If considered in isolation, an IT system could be compliant with data protection law. But the moment it is interconnected to other IT systems, new legal issues can arise. Interoperability is a technical function that interconnects IT systems, allowing for the exchange and use of information. Consequently, it broadens the list of controllers, the number of subjects accessing the data, the use of data and, finally, the purposes for the data processing. In this sense, EU rule-making on contact tracing, mainly focused on interoperability, was not only a technicality, but a fundamental process for ensuring the protection of privacy rights of users.

The rule-making process involved a variety of actors at different levels. These included public actors, such as the health authorities of the Member States, EU institutions and the European Data Protection Authorities, and private actors, mainly Big Tech companies (Apple and Google) for the development of the application programming interface (API) and Small Tech companies for the development of the apps. The main channel of discussion was the eHealth Network, composed of members from Member States (and Norway as an observer) and the European Commission. This process led to three main outputs: the API,

[63] Commission, 'European Interoperability Gateway for Tracing and Warning Apps' (19 October 2020) https://ec.europa.eu/commission/presscorner/detail/en/fs_20_1943.

[64] See, eg the Parliament Resolution, the Recommendation by the Commission and the statements and guidelines from the EDPB.

[65] See the Blog Forum for the Project 'Un-owned Personal Data' by the Robert Schuman Centre for Advanced Studies, https://migrationpolicycentre.eu/interoperable-informations-systems-in-the-eu-areafreedom-security-justice/.

by Google and Apple; the contact tracing apps; and the European Federation Gateway Service (EFGS). A preliminary analysis of the information available shows a transparency asymmetry. If the outputs of the contact tracing rule-making process are public and easily accessible,[66] the decision-making process that led to those results is not. If, on the one hand, we even have the source codes of the apps, on the other, it is unknown who designed the app in that specific way. In the European Commission's June 2020 Progress Report, two important channels of discussion are mentioned. The first is within the eHN itself: 'since 25 March 2020, the eHealth Network has held more than 30 meetings (including weekly meetings on COVID-19 coordination actions, and subgroup meeting, with the aim to implement the toolbox)'.[67] On the website of the eHN, however, documentation is available for only two meetings in 2020[68] (the 17th meeting of 3 June 2020 and the 18th meeting of 12–13 November 2020), and there is no information on the sub-groups of the network. Second, the Report also refers to a dialogue established with Google and Apple: 'Separate discussions have taken place at a technical level between individual Member States and the Commission with Google and Apple to ensure that the interoperability solution developed by the eHealth Network would be compatible with the APIs'.[69] However, we have no trace of these meetings.

The main hypothesis is that, since the discussion on interoperability has been considered as 'purely technical', devoid of any democratic value, the documents produced in the decision-making process are not available. In the current section, it was underlined how the consequences of interoperability are relevant to the public, as it can impact individuals' rights. Hence, labelling this discussion as merely technical should not be a justification for opacity of the decision-making process, especially when interlocutors such as Google and Apple are involved. This hypothesis needs to be further tested. At this preliminary stage of the research, it can be stated that information is certainly not easily accessible. However, before concluding that there is a lack of transparency, more empirical work needs to be done. The strategies for the future steps of this research include a more in-depth analysis of the Register of the European Commission, using different keywords, an analysis of national health authorities' websites and follow-up requests for access to (specific) documents.

[66] The source code and technical documentation of almost every app and the API are public, as are the Guidelines on interoperability with the technical specifications.

[67] Commission, 'Mobile Applications to Support Contact Tracing in the EU's Fight against COVID-19' (Progress Report, June 2020) https://ec.europa.eu/health/sites/default/files/ehealth/docs/mobileapps_202006progressreport_en.pdf.

[68] See Commission, 'Meetings of eHealth Network', https://ec.europa.eu/health/ehealth/events_en#anchor0.

[69] Commission, 'Mobile Applications' (n 67).

2.4. Tailwinds of Transparency in the EU: Locating Transparency

Important decisions throughout the pandemic have been made in what appear to be a 'black box' of scientists, civil servants and politicians, and calls for more transparency and more scrutiny have been made.[70] Indeed, transparency has been seen as particularly important in public health emergencies in order to achieve better public health outcomes through effective communication, keeping control of the narrative to the public, and maintaining and building trust with citizens. Without trust, compliance breaks down – and public compliance is vital to ensuring that the adopted measures are effective.[71] Yet, in the pandemic, Ignatieff observed a paradox:

> [C]itizens both demanded transparency, i.e. free debate on risks, on modelling, on social distancing, but they also cried out for the opposite – decisive, debate- ending leadership. They wanted reassurance more than they wanted transparency and so the political task – being transparent while also being decisive – was excruciatingly difficult. It is no wonder, therefore, that few political leaders escaped the crisis with their prestige enhanced.[72]

Transparency is in any event considered a prerequisite for public accountability. Without transparency of the data, of the models, of the information, of the process, of the actors and of the decision-making, further institutional accountability becomes very difficult, if not impossible, for any accountability forum. Transparency can be either passive (subsequent to access to document requests/litigation) or active (when the institution reveals the information proactively and of its own accord). The very word 'transparency' connotes visibility and the ability to see through; it implies a subject seeing as well as the object being seen. In the words of Koivisto, 'a beholder and an object form a complex set of affairs'.[73] The beholder may force the object to react to its 'gaze' and in this sense may be controlling.

Transparency is increasingly understood not only as a coherent normative ideal, but also as a means for a more granular description of processes of government and governance.[74] What Pozen has termed 'a sociological turn' recognises

[70] See, eg I Sample, 'Secrecy Has Harmed UK Government's Response to COVID-19 Crisis, Says Top Scientist' *The Guardian* (London, 2 August 2020); R Girard, 'Accountability, Populism and Expertise: The UK Government's Response to COVID-19' [2021] *PL* 707; O Doyle, D Kenny, D Lyons and C Casey for the Irish Human Rights and Equality Commission, *Ireland's Emergency Powers During the COVID-19 Pandemic*, (IHREC 2021).

[71] P O'Malley, J Rainford and A Thompson, 'Transparency during Public Health Emergencies: From Rhetoric to Reality' (2009) 87 *World Health Organization: Bulletin* 614.

[72] Ignatieff (n 38) 100.

[73] I Koivisto, 'The Anatomy of Transparency: the Concept and its Multifarious Implications' (2016) European University Institute Working Paper, Max Weber Programme MWP 2016/09, https://cadmus.eui.eu/bitstream/handle/1814/41166/MWP_2016_09.pdf?sequence=1&isAllowed=y.

[74] DE Pozen, 'Seeing Transparency More Clearly' [2019] *Public Administration Review* 326.

the relational side to transparency (subject seeing and object been seen), and leads quite naturally to a more empirical focus that studies transparency in its complexity as a social phenomenon and the possible effects on the circulation of power within institutions.[75] It is also about joining up the dots as to who is involved in decision-taking, how and on the basis of what information. Using transparency as a tool to track in a sense those who track others (national administrations, private stakeholders and individuals) and to see if information is available online or otherwise is the thrust of the next section, which looks at two key agencies (the ECDC and EMA), as well as the role of the Commission's experts in constructing a Europe-wide app on contact tracing. For the ECDC and the EMA, the EO has played a role in opening up internal processes to the outside and prompting proactive institutional responses that in turn can potentially contribute to broader public accountability of the EU. These are the 'gusts' of transparency that may predate more systemic turbulence and may also fade over time. At the same time, there can be a build-up that combines to form over time a tailwind pushing forwards a transparency agenda and reality.

2.5. Uncovering Secrecy: An Investigative European Ombudsman

2.5.1. The European Medicines Agency

The EO is independent, but at the same time is closely linked to the European Parliament (EP). It is an independent supervisory body of the EP and has a clearly defined mandate, with distinct powers of investigation. Its powers are non-binding on the executive and take the form of 'recommendations'. Twenty-five years after its creation, it can be said to have gone through different 'phases' depending on the holder.[76] One constant is its problem-solving role when access-to-information disputes arise with citizens; another is a more proactive investigatory role through so-called 'own initiative' inquiries, which often attempt to dig deeper into more structural or institutional issues. The current holder distinguishes herself by adopting what has been called a more political and visible role as a 'driver of change'.[77] This certainly comes to the fore in a very proactive approach based on own initiative investigations. At the same time, her approach to individual complaints has also become more actively investigatory. Some have described her as the 'inspector of the executive'.[78]

[75] ibid.

[76] HCH Hofmann, 'The Developing Role of the European Ombudsman' in HCH Hofmann and J Ziller (eds), *Accountability in the EU: The Role of the European Ombudsman* (Edward Elgar, 2017) 1, especially at 3–5 and 12.

[77] E O'Reilly, Address at the European Ombudsman's 20th Anniversary Colloquium (Brussels, 22 June 2015) http://ombudsman.europa.eu/en/speech/en/60312. See also Hofmann (n 76) 4ff.

[78] Hofmann (n 76) 7.

Own initiative investigations may happen in different contexts. Information may be given to the EO by a whistle-blower; or it may arise from other complaint-driven work in an accountability 'loop', where the EO wishes to take a broad approach in the public interest, in particular on themes where complainants are unlikely to be able to launch complaints. There are a number of accountability chains or loops with the EO at the centre, in various capacities. One relevant example is the EMA. The EMA has undergone a veritable transparency revolution over the course of the past decade, with many of the stages prompted largely by inquiries by the EO.

Until the end of 2010, the EMA treated data and documentation submitted in support of market authorisation for medicinal products as carrying a presumption of confidentiality.[79] Subsequently, efforts were made by the EMA to negotiate with pharmaceutical companies that redacted versions of clinical study reports on a particular drug would be made available to the public. After receiving a complaint, the EO initiated an inquiry in 2014 into how the EMA should approach the issue of public disclosure of documentation on the safety of medicinal products.[80] She concluded that the EMA places too much weight on the commercial interests of medicine developers, rather than the overriding interest of public health. She noted that while there are exceptions to freedom of information, such as privacy and the protection of commercial interests, these are not relevant where there is an overarching public interest in making the document publicly available. She found 'that there is always a public interest in the disclosure of documents containing information on the safety and efficacy of medicines'.[81]

Subsequently the EMA adopted new proactive policies aimed at improving transparency within the organisation, prompted by EO recommendations.[82] Members of the public can now request access to data submitted as part of the authorisation process, and reports are made available online on the EMA website.[83] In 2015, a supplemental policy to allow the publication of clinical data was introduced.[84] Both of these policies draw on Regulation 1049/2001 and Article 15 of the TFEU. Later, in 2017, the EO, on her own initiative, opened another inquiry into the activities of the EMA.[85] Specifically, she sought to

[79] Kim (n 52) 462.

[80] European Ombudsman, *Decision on Own-Initiative Inquiry OI/3/214/FOR Concerning the Partial Refusal of the European Medicines Agency to Give Public Access to Studies Related to the Approval of a Medicinal Product* (8 June 2016, Case OI/3/2014/FOR) http://ombudsman.europa.eu/en/decision/en/68107.

[81] ibid para 32.

[82] EMA 2010 (n 55). This was overtaken by a reformulated policy in 2018. See EMA 2018 (n 55). The former European Ombudsman had made major recommendations to overhaul transparency procedures at the EMA. See European Ombudsman, *Decision Closing Inquiry into Complaint 2560/2007/BEH* (n 55) para 80.

[83] Coombes (n 56).

[84] EMA 2014 (n 57).

[85] It is worth noting that the current EO's practice of initiating inquiries has prompted criticism in some quarters. See, eg Stein (n 58).

examine 'pre-submission activities', the practice whereby developers of medicinal products seek scientific advice from the EMA prior to a formal submission for marketing authorisation for a particular medicinal product. While the EO acknowledged that such communication may be desirable for public health outcomes, she warned that it was 'important to avoid even the perception that the eventual opinions of EMA on medicines were influenced by these earlier interactions'.[86] In her conclusion, she found that the EMA should strive for the greatest possible degree of separation between those providing advice in the initial stages to developers and those later involved in assessing the product for market authorisation.[87]

In July 2020, the EO opened yet another inquiry into the role of the EMA – this time in relation to the role of the pandemic task force (COVID-ETF), which had been established by the EMA in response to the COVID-19 pandemic. The role of the COVID-ETF was to assist the European Commission and EU Member States in the development and regulation of medicinal products designed to treat COVID-19. The concern related to the independence of the evaluation of the vaccines and treatments for COVID-19, as members of the COVID-ETF task force included individuals who had the responsibility for draft evaluation reports by the EMA for COVID-19 treatments.[88] Essentially, the EO requested the EMA to confirm that it applies the same principles previously agreed in the EMA's pre-submission activities to the work of the COVID-ETF and at the same time ensures transparency of all COVID-19-related activities, including the possibility of rapidly publishing clinical data for the products in question.[89]

A long-standing concern of the EO in relation to the EMA has been that there should be a separation between those responsible for providing scientific advice to a medicine developer and those involved subsequently in evaluating a marketing authorisation application for the same medicine.[90] The EMA introduced measures to ensure the separation of these two roles. These adapted measures also apply to COVID-19 medicines. The EMA further clarified that these measures apply to the

[86] European Ombudsman, *Decision in Strategic Inquiry OI/7/2017/KR* (n 59).

[87] ibid para 32. European Ombudsman, *Suggestions for Improvement: Decision in Strategic Inquiry OI/7/2017/KR on How the European Medicines Agency Engages with Medicine Developers in the Period Leading Up to Applications for Authorisations to Market New Medicines in the EU* (17 July 2019). See the EMA's response to the inquiry: EMA, 'EMA Takes Note of the European Ombudsman's Decision on Pre-submission Activities' (19 July 2019) http://ema.europa.eu/en/news/ema-takes-note-european-ombudsmans-decision-pre-submission-activities.

[88] European Ombudsman, *Letter to the European Medicines Agency (EMA) Concerning the Transparency and Independence of the Work of the EMA in Supporting the Development and Evaluation of COVID-19 Medicines* (29 July 2020, Case SI/5/2020/DDJ) http://ombudsman.europa.eu/en/correspondence/en/130852.

[89] ibid.

[90] European Ombudsman, *Strategic Inquiry into Pre-submission Activities Organised by the European Medicines Agency* (Case OI/7/2017/KR, opened 17 July 2017) http://ombudsman.europa.eu/en/case/en/49999.

newly established COVID-ETF, with no member in fact exercising a leading or prominent role in the pre-submission phase.[91]

During the pandemic, and pursuant not only to the EO inquiry but also to some other public pressure,[92] the EMA has recently implemented what it itself terms exceptional measures to maximise the transparency of its regulatory activities on treatments and vaccines for COVID-19 that are approved or are under evaluation.[93] The EMA is achieving this by shortening its standard publishing time frames and publishing information it does not normally publish for other medicines. This includes publishing the list of medicines[94] that have received scientific advice or guidance from the COVID-ETF, whereas normally this information would not be published at all. The EMA confirmed to the EO in its inquiry that measures designed to ensure independence in pre-submission activities applied to the development of COVID-19 treatments, and that it was also implementing 'exceptional measures with regard to medicines for COVID-19, speeding up standard publication timelines and providing more information than is usually the case'.[95] It seems that overall the EO strategy of conducting iterative (own initiative) inquiries concluding with detailed and specific recommendations have been very helpful to the EMA and the cause for public access to its documents at various stages of its regulatory process, and it has also attempted to respond proactively.

At the same time, the fact that the paradigm of access to clinical trial data in the EU has 'tilted' towards greater transparency and availability of data has faced significant headwinds. It has been fought against in the courts by successful pharmaceutical companies who frequently challenge the actual scope of data that can be lawfully released by the EMA.[96] The claim is that the documentation consists of commercially confidential data 'owned' by the companies.[97] The courts rejected the argument that a general presumption of confidentiality

[91] EMA, *Mandate, Objectives and Rules of Procedure of the COVID-19 EMA Pandemic Task Force (COVID-ETF)* (31 March 2020, EMA/166423/2020) http://ema.europa.eu/en/documents/other/mandate-objectives-rules-procedure-covid-19-ema-pandemic-task-force-covid-etf_en.pdf.

[92] See, eg an open letter from 15 October 2020 and EMA's answer to that letter: http://ema.europa.eu/documents/other/reply-open-letter-concerning-transparency-evaluation-vaccines-covid-19_en.pdf. The EMA publishes many responses to open letters on its website (http://ema.europa.eu/en/news-events/publications/open-letters).

[93] EMA, 'Transparency: Exceptional Measures for COVID-19 Medicines', www.ema.europa.eu/en/human-regulatory/overview/public-health-threats/coronavirus-disease-covid-19/treatments-vaccines/transparency-exceptional-measures-covid-19-medicines.

[94] EMA, 'Treatment and Vaccines for COVID-19', http://ema.europa.eu/en/humanregulatory/overview/public-health-threats/coronavirus-disease-covid-19/treatments-vaccines-covid-19.

[95] EMA, *Reply to the European Ombudsman's Letter Concerning Transparency and Independence of the Work of the European Medicines Agency in Supporting the Development and Evaluation of COVID-19 Medicines* (30 September 2020, EMA/516771/2020) http://ema.europa.eu/en/documents/other/reply-european-ombudsmans-letter-concerning-transparency-independence-work-european-medicines-agency_en.pdf.

[96] Kim (n 52).

[97] General Court, 5 February 2018, Case T-235/15 *Pari Pharma v EMA* EU:T:2018:65.

applies to such documents, and also found that the applicants had not demonstrated that the documentation in question seriously undermined their commercial interest, for example by containing information relating to business strategies or a new scientific discovery. In later cases,[98] two pharmaceutical companies sought to annul EMA decisions allowing disclosure to third parties of their documentation encompassing toxicology reports and clinical study reports that had been submitted to the EMA in support of applications for medicinal authorisation for human and animal medicinal products. The applicants argued that the data could be accessed by their competitors and ought to be classified as commercially sensitive information. The court found that there was no general presumption of confidentiality in the context of documentation submitted to support a marketing authorisation application.

On appeal, Advocate General Hogan found exactly the opposite and opined that there was a general presumption of confidentiality, given that access to the clinical data submitted with the application would jeopardise the applicant's commercial interests.[99] In the wake of his opinion, the EMA itself issued a press release stating that if the Court of Justice upheld the Advocate General's decision, its transparency policies 'would be impaired and have to be revised'. The EMA stressed that its current policy generates 'trust in the EU regulatory network, broadens the scientific knowledge base, fosters the development of medicines and ultimately benefits public health'.[100] This is an interesting example of an expert agency positioning itself publicly, and while court proceedings are ongoing pleading in favour of its own evolved transparency policies. The Court of Justice subsequently upheld the decision of the General Court, finding that there was no automatic presumption of confidentiality, but rather that any such presumption was an option for an EU body. Any EU institution retained the power to carry out individual assessments of documents to determine whether they came within the scope of the exceptions in Article 4 of Regulation 1049/2001. The EMA had carried out such individual assessments of the reports, which led to a limited amount of redaction.

All in all, the combination of the proactive stance of the EO in a series of inquiries combined with the support by the General Court (and the Court of Justice on appeal) have strengthened the path of the EMA towards much more proactive transparency of its reports, clinical trials, etc than was previously the case due to

[98] Case C-175/18 P *PTC Therapeutics International v EMA*; Case C-178/18 P *MSD Animal Health Innovation and Intervet International v EMA*.

[99] Opinion of Advocate General Hogan, 11 September 2019, Case C-178/18 P *MSD Animal Health Innovation and Intervet International v EMA* EU:C:2019:710, paras 72–80. The concept of a general presumption of confidentiality has been the subject of considerable criticism, with scholars characterising it as 'detrimental to accountability'. See HCH Hofmann and PL Sandberg, 'An Agenda for Transparency in the EU' (*European Law Blog*, 23 October 2019) http://europeanlawblog.eu/2019/10/23/an-agenda-for-transparency-in-the-eu.

[100] EMA, 'EMA Management Board: Highlights of October 2019 Meeting' (4 October 2019) http://ema.europa.eu/en/news/ema-management-board-highlights-october-2019-meeting.

fears of their potential commercially sensitive nature until now.[101] In this way, the EMA has been engaged in a constructive dialogue with two prominent accountability forums – the EO and the courts – and has adapted its practices in a forward looking way in favour of measures promoting more public access where possible. The interlocutors of the EMA have widened beyond those pharma companies seeking authorisation or participating in clinical trials to the public much more generally, and the public interest in scientific documentation is now much more widely recognised, including by the EMA itself, than a decade ago. At the same time, there are still lacunas on the EMA's website, including that, in some parts of its website, it is focused on direct information, and that older reports may be indirectly eliminated by updates of the website (with older PDFs not remaining available).

2.5.2. The European Centre of Disease Control

With regard to the ECDC, a clear concern by the EO has been to attempt to uncover how exactly it gathered and communicated data from (inter)national sources in the early stages of the pandemic. The lack of transparency on the ECDC's information-gathering tools and its cooperation with Member States and international partners was at the root of a specific EO enquiry. An initial inspection of documents shared at her request took place, followed by a meeting (online) with ECDC representatives, which enabled a more precise pinning of the core issue, which is in relation to the publication of the surveys it undertakes and their results and with whom it has been shared. The issue of confidential information was also raised in this context, in particular whether any Member States requested confidential treatment of information shared with the ECDC in the context of the COVID-19 crisis (including in relation to replies sent to surveys). The EO also wanted to know – if confidentiality was indeed explicitly requested – how the ECDC treated these confidentiality requests.[102] This implies also uncovering whether the ECDC, an EU agency, has information security systems in place, what they are modelled on and how they operate in practice. What are the ECDC's internal rules on confidentiality and how are public access requests dealt with by it as an organisation? The fact that the EO's scope of inquiry focused on these key issues and also required the ECDC to explain and provide internal documentation is potentially an extremely valuable way of uncovering how it actually operates in practice and unveiling its rules and practices regarding access to information

[101] S Röttger-Wirtz, 'An Open Door to More Open Access to Agency Documents? The General Court Rulings on the EMA Transparency Policy' (*EU TARN*, 29 March 2018) https://tarn.maastrichtuniversity.nl/an-open-door-to-more-open-access-to-agency-documents-the-general-court-rulings-on-the-ema-transparency-policy.

[102] European Ombudsman, *Letter from the European Ombudsman to the Executive Director of the ECDC on How the ECDC Gathered and Communicated Information during the COVID-19 Crisis* (11 November 2020, OI/3/2020/TE) www.ombudsman.europa.eu/en/doc/correspondence/en/134848.

which is not publicly available and therefore not in a register of documents or able to be requested by concerned individuals or civil society organisations.[103]

On 5 February 2021, the EO released her decision from the inquiry into the gathering and communication of information by the ECDC during the pandemic. Her inspection report, published on 8 September 2021, examined how the ECDC had performed in the pandemic. The fact that the ECDC was dependent on the provision of data by the Member States (who had inconsistent methods of data collection), lacking powers to inspect or gather information at source, meant that there were obvious issues with discrepancies and inaccuracies in the data. In addition, the ECDC had not adequately communicated changes in scientific advice to the public, most notably the agency's abrupt change of position in relation to face masks – endorsing them just a fortnight after stating that there was 'no evidence' that they were useful for preventing infection. A number of suggestions for improvement were made, including that the ECDC should: clearly indicate when it alters its public health advice based on new scientific evidence; regularly publish its surveys, and data gathered from Member States; and improve its language and communication policy.[104] In response, the EMA released a brief statement welcoming the report, and noting the fact that its mandate would be expanded through the creation of a European Health Union. It promised to 'take into account' the EO's recommendations and to develop an action plan on areas such as surveillance, transparency and public communication.[105] Notably, the ECDC's Strategy Report, published at the end of January 2021 (to carry the organisation into 2027), made relatively few concrete commitments to improving public transparency.[106]

2.6. Conclusions

The title of this chapter speaks of 'gusts' of transparency. 'Gusts' implies the occasional and the exceptional in terms of a wind that propels in the direction of flight, at least when it is a tailwind and not a headwind. The fact that this activity takes place in a context of turbulence – the COVID-19 public health emergency – is significant, but at the same time continues pre-existing positive trends and accentuates them. The likelihood is that gains made in terms of prising more openness from a number of executive technocratic 'bubbles' such as the ECDC and the EMA,

[103] Some ECDC documents can be requested, but broad exceptions exist under Reg 1049/01 – see https://www.ecdc.europa.eu/en/about-us/document-request.

[104] European Ombudsman, *Decision in Strategic Inquiry OI/3/2020/TE on How the ECDC Gathered and Communicated Information during the COVID-19 Crisis* (5 Feburary 2021, OI/3/2020/TE) www.ombudsman.europa.eu/en/decision/en/137815.

[105] European Centre for Disease Prevention and Control, 'ECDC Response to European Ombudsman Inquiry' (Press Release, 9 February 2021) www.ecdc.europa.eu/en/news-events/ecdc-response-european-ombudsman-inquiry.

[106] See ECDC, *ECDC Strategy 2021–2027* (29 January 2021) 16, www.ecdc.europa.eu/en/publications-data/ecdc-strategy-2021-2027.

key players now and in the future in the public health arena in Europe, as part of a system of multi-level governance will remain and become normalised. The wider knock-on effect for other EU agencies and committees cannot be predicted with any certainty, but with a European Ombudsman that is 'investigating' more and more actively and in relative depth the process, documentation and data while governance processes are ongoing, it will inevitably have wider repercussions.

Given the broader context, with the future of these two public health agencies under active consideration and debate, it is important to consider the extent to which active transparency of their work should be built into their changing DNA in the interest of broader public accountability. This is the flip side of the transparency coin. Even assuming that public accountability forums such as the EO and the courts are able to expose activities and data – and that the agencies in question proactively and systematically can continue such activity in the future – the question remains what happens to the disclosed information or data? Who follows up in terms of dialogue, deliberation and eventual consequences? Of course, both the courts and the EO can do this to some extent. The EO can, on its own initiative, investigate more systematically and make recommendations – with the weak point being that there is no enforcement mechanism other than the value of publicity and the moral pressure to change and more proactively self-regulate for more openness. It appears from recent practice that this does, in fact, happen and could well have wider knock-on effects in the future. In this way, there is indeed a tailwind of transparency, and one that is not necessarily only temporary and exceptional. With regard to the courts, the rulings are, of course, binding, but they often and inevitably relate to highly specific challenges – although here, too, as has been the case for the EMA, there may be a more general knock-on effect that propels forward in terms of institutional self-regulation and adaptation over time. The roles of both types of public accountability forum, valuable though they may be in this context, are nonetheless inherently limited and non-systemic. The window of opportunity to reflect more systemically on the broader context of public accountability – and the link with transparency – is now given the impetus that pandemic turbulence has given to calls and plans for (far-reaching) institutional change. One lesson from the wider history of emergencies is the embedded nature of certain problems, in particular the way that information is gathered, stored and shared.[107] In 2022, this requires a more radical rethink also in terms of tailored and possibly new oversight mechanisms, adapted this time to the digital context, which is now a defining element of governing by emergency.

[107] For an interesting much earlier analysis, see A Nicoll and M Sprenger, 'Learning Lessons from the 2009 Pandemic: Putting Infections in Their Proper Place' (2011) 26 *European Journal of Epidemiology* 191.

3

The New Providers on the Block: How Big Tech Responded to the COVID-19 'Krisis'

FRANCISCO DE ABREU DUARTE*

3.1. Introduction – COVID-19 'Krisis' or Opportunity for Whom?

COVID-19 is the single biggest crisis the world has faced since World War II. Its scope, its geographical dissemination and the dire need for cooperation have certainly tested globalisation. It is now clear that this pandemic has reshaped political and societal relationships.

On the one hand, COVID-19 has impacted how states relate to one another and international organisations, demanding a new effort of political coordination between governments. States across the globe were suddenly required to reorganise their health structures and take significant steps backwards to the levels of multilateralism achieved thus far. The World Health Organization (WHO) played a fundamental role in facilitating worldwide intergovernmental cooperation and setting health standards. Coordination of restrictions and vaccine mandates replaced globalism and free exchanges as the new normal among states. On the other hand, individuals had to reinvent social interaction, with prolonged confinements imposed in every country. Individuals had to restructure their communication through the mass adoption of new technology to face growing restrictions to their freedom. Technologies such as videoconferencing, social media platforms, gaming platforms and video-sharing platforms enabled individuals to reconnect with loved ones and their businesses, or to enjoy leisure time. This combination of unprecedented global coordination and the individual technological transition is perhaps the most significant legacy of COVID-19.

* PhD Candidate European University Institute; Visiting Student Researcher UC Berkeley Law School; LL.M New York University (NYU); Associate Researcher Lisbon Centre for Research on Public Law. Email: Francisco.deabreu@eui.eu. I would like to thank Luisa Marin for her insights and valuable comments on earlier versions of this chapter. Any errors or omissions rest with me.

Between one and the other stood big digital business. Companies such as Facebook/Meta,[1] Google, Twitter and Apple quickly understood the relevance of the pandemic to the rise of a new technological status quo. They saw the COVID-19 crisis as an opportunity to help governments and citizens transition to greater levels of technological adoption.

In its most ancient form, κρῐσῐς, or krisis, was a term used in Ancient Greece to describe the delicate moment at which a particular ill patient could succumb to disease or overcome it. The term crisis meant then *opportunity to change*. This chapter discusses precisely how COVID-19 can be understood as a 'krisis/opportunity' moment for Big Tech. It argues that some digital companies have successfully predicted that a global epidemic would strike the decisive blow to our dependence on the physical world while simultaneously instigating governments and international organisations to side more and more with Big Tech. By taking the role of providers of traditional public goods, Big Tech used COVID-19 to reinforce their legitimacy in the eyes of their users. Although it is apparent that it was not COVID-19 launching the digital revolution – that has been growing since at least the 1960s in different shapes and forms – this chapter will ultimately argue that it constituted the defining moment for the legitimisation of Big Tech as the *new providers on the block*.

To explore such an idea, this chapter attempts to answer the following question:

> Have some digital companies taken advantage of COVID-19 as an opportunity to reaffirm their role as providers of public goods? If so, what can explain this new 'public provider' role?

To test this hypothesis, this chapter looks at three different traditional public goods: (i) health information; (ii) financial support during a crisis; and (iii) tracing the spread of a virus.

Section 3.2.1 explores how Facebook, Twitter and YouTube have dealt with the coronavirus's health 'infodemic'[2] on social media. COVID-19 was an excellent opportunity for those companies to ensure that they were up to the task of controlling disinformation after several scandals regarding political interference and political misinformation over the years. This section shows how Facebook, Twitter and YouTube have all played a key role in transmitting information about the best health practices, broadcasting WHO information, debunking conspiracy theories and providing constant access to reliable health information. These companies became de facto sources of health information, playing a key 'public' role in informing the general population about the risks and benefits of specific treatments. Because of this, they were entrusted by global communities with an unprecedented legitimacy to manage health information across the globe and to become trustworthy sources of medical advice.

[1] I shall refer interchangeably to Facebook and Meta as the same entity. The examples provided pertain mostly to the application Facebook, although Meta (the parent company) is also analysed.

[2] WHO, 'Munich Security Conference', speech by WHO Director, 15 February 2020, www.who.int/dg/speeches/detail/munich-security-conference.

Section 3.2.2 turns the attention to Big Tech as financial providers during the pandemic. It might initially sound strange to speak of such companies as financial providers.[3] However, the truth is that Facebook and Google have launched new services, which have contributed to reshaping business in a confinement scenario. Facebook's recovery fund targeted small- and medium-sized enterprises and provided global support to the economic tissue of various economies. Likewise, Facebook's novel 'shops' tool allowed small businesses to transform their physical business into digital stores for free, creating a digital infrastructure that could sustain fully operative clothing or toy shops without any need for physical presence. Likewise, Alphabet/Google launched an unprecedented advertisement credit scheme, ensuring that small businesses could transit from physical to digital and advertise their businesses at no immediate cost. These companies became enablers of small businesses, and communities started to turn to them directly for help. The section exemplifies how even more traditionally state-dependent sectors of society, like culture and arts, have now turned to private digital funds for help instead of recurring to states.

Section 3.2.3 looks at the role of Google and Apple in protecting digital rights, even against states. Here, the chapter analyses how Android and iOS have proven very powerful in shaping the characteristics of COVID-19 tracing apps worldwide. Both companies have managed to define the technical qualities of tracing apps worldwide, including those developed by states. By threatening to ban some apps from their app markets, these two companies effectively defined the technical standards adopted. By portraying themselves as privacy defendants, both companies reaffirmed their commitment to protecting their users' privacy against state centralisation.

The chapter finishes with a deeper analysis of what this trend might mean for the future. If Big Tech have become the de facto providers of public goods during COVID times, what does this mean for the public–private divide? How can one explain such a fact? Will online platforms continue to assume greater public roles in the future? Will they eventually replace states in some core functions? To answer these questions, the chapter suggests the twin concepts of privatisation of public power and publicisation of private power as frameworks to understanding the phenomenon.

Ultimately, this chapter argues that Big Tech companies have become the *New Providers on the Block*, establishing themselves as a valid alternative to the welfare state in providing particular public goods. For the sake of clarity, the chapter does not argue that Big Tech are becoming states or are even comparable to the overarching power of a state.[4] Nor that they have become public utilities.

[3] I am not referring to the legal technical term of a financial provider, but rather to financial provider as an entity which provides financial support, either through loans or grants, to individuals or businesses.

[4] Chander, 'Facebookistan' (2012) 90 *North Carolina Law Review* 1807.

This chapter instead concludes that COVID-19 constituted a moment for a new type of equilibrium between public and private power, in which companies retain their private nature but start to engage more and more with public prerogatives.

3.2. Three Dimensions of Digital Power: Health Misinformation; Financial Support; and Tracing Apps

3.2.1. Freedom of Speech and Health Misinformation

Perhaps the most telling side of social media during the pandemic has been its constant struggle to ensure a balance between freedom of speech and good, reliable information. The problem of 'fake news'[5] and its impact is now widely studied,[6] albeit not fully tackled. Social media giants such as Facebook and Twitter and video-sharing platforms such as YouTube have now considered their role to be more than simple neutral places of speech and actively moderate what their communities are saying. Although most of the scandals with misinformation and disinformation have been connected to politics and political interference, COVID-19 has shed light on another dimension of disinformation that can be as damaging as politics.

[5] The term 'fake news' itself is subject to great controversy. An accepted definition in the literature reads as 'factually dubious content that imitates the format of journalism but is produced with no regard for accuracy or fairness': see Lazer et al, 'The Science of Fake News' (2018) 359 *Science* 1094. For this chapter, however, I prefer to adopt the distinction between disinformation and misinformation. With the first I mean an *unintentional spread of false information in order to influence others' opinions*, while with the second I mean *the intentional spread of false information in order to influence public opinion, obscure the truth or gain political or personal advantage.*

[6] The literature here is enormous, but here are some interesting examples. Studying how 'false' and 'disputed' tags have some degree of success in fighting fake news, see Pennycook and Rand, 'The Implied Truth Effect: Attaching Warnings to a Subset of Fake News Stories Increases Perceived Accuracy of Stories Without Warnings' (unpublished manuscript) https://papers.ssrn.com/sol3/papers.cfm?abstract_id=3035384. Going further on the topic with different conclusions are Clayton et al, 'Real Solutions for Fake News? Measuring the Effectiveness of General Warnings and Fact-Check Tags in Reducing Belief in False Stories on Social Media' (2019) 42(2) *Political Behavior*. Suggesting that lay people might also play a key role in fact-checking, see Pennycook and Rand, 'Fighting Misinformation on Social Media Using Crowdsourced Judgments of News Source Quality' (2019) 116 *Proceedings of the National Academy of Sciences* 2521. Also confirming this is the recent study by the NGO Avaaz, 'White Paper: Correcting the Record – Corrections as an Antidote to Disinformation' (April 2020) https://secure.avaaz.org/campaign/en/correct_the_record_study. On whether fake tweets can produce a larger interest in the news (although with a small number of participants), see the interesting experiment of Tamul, Ivory, Hotter and Wolf, 'All the President's Tweets: Effects of Exposure to Trump's "Fake News" Accusations on Perceptions of Journalists, News Stories, and Issue Evaluation' (2020) 23 *Mass Communication and Society* 301. On the impact of certain public figures or media outlets on disinformation, see Sterrett et al, 'Who Shared It?: Deciding What News to Trust on Social Media' (2019) 7 *Digital Journalism* 783.

According to Google,[7] health-related queries can reach 70,000 per minute, totalling more than 1 billion a day, which confirms that we are trusting the Internet increasingly more to answer our health questions regarding symptoms, diseases or simple nutrition.[8] The way we produce information related to health issues on the Internet is already quite telling of how the future will be. Instead of recurring to health authorities or seeking only the expertise of medical doctors, communities have started to seek advice from one another, creating online medical forums[9] of discussion to exchange information about some disease or treatment. This way of obtaining health information relies strongly on communitarian exchanges. The most significant research on this matter has been conducted regarding anti-vaccination movements and how social media might have enhanced their cause. This research has focused mostly on how the Internet influences the spread of anti-vaccination sentiments[10] or how one ultimately takes the decision not to vaccinate a child,[11] or the impact of online debates and forums on the topic.[12] In all of these studies, it has become clear that health disinformation regarding vaccination was primarily motivated by clusters of social media users who would share and retweet non-verified news on how vaccines would cause autism or lead to death. The truth is, then, that we are relying more and more on the Internet and social media platforms to obtain an early diagnosis, to discuss healing methods or simply to get some peace of mind (the classic 'do I have cancer?' query).[13]

COVID-19 represents the tipping point for such a trend. Disinformation and misinformation on the virus spread so quickly that it led WHO Director-General Tedros Adhanom Ghebreyesus to say that 'we're not just fighting an epidemic; we're fighting an infodemic. Fake news spreads faster and more easily than this virus and is just as dangerous.'[14]

[7] 'Dr Google Will See You Now: Search Giant Wants to Cash In on Your Medical Queries' *The Telegraph* (London, 10 March 2019) www.telegraph.co.uk/technology/2019/03/10/google-sifting-one-billion-health-questions-day/.

[8] Jacobs, Amuta and Jeon, 'Health Information Seeking in the Digital Age: An Analysis of Health Information Seeking Behavior among US Adults' (2017) 3(1) *Cogent Social Sciences* 9.

[9] US Supreme Court, *Packingham v North Carolina* 582 US (2017), 8.

[10] Kata, 'Anti-vaccine Activists, Web 2.0, and the Postmodern Paradigm – an Overview of Tactics and Tropes Used Online by the Anti-vaccination Movement' (2012) 30 *Vaccine* 3778.

[11] Betsch and Sachse, 'Dr Jekyll or Mr Hyde? (How) the Internet Influences Vaccination Decisions: Recent Evidence and Tentative Guidelines for Online Vaccine Communication' (2012) 30 *Vaccine* 3723. See also Xu and Guo, 'Using Text Mining to Compare Online Pro- and Anti-vaccine Headlines: Word Usage, Sentiments, and Online Popularity' (2018) 69 *Communication Studies* 103.

[12] Nicholson and Leask, 'Lessons from an Online Debate about Measles–Mumps–Rubella (MMR) Immunization' (2012) 30 *Vaccine* 3806.

[13] An example of health disinformation can be found on the widespread rumour that argued for the healing effects of apricot seeds in the treatment of cancer even though the general medical community had largely advised against its use and had in fact pointed out its potential poisonous effects. See European Food Safety Authority, 'Acute Health Risks Related to the Presence of Cyanogenic Glycosides in Raw Apricot Kernels and Products Derived from Raw Apricot Kernels' (2016) 14(4) *EFSA Journal*, www.efsa.europa.eu/en/efsajournal/pub/4424.

[14] WHO (n 2).

This infodemic[15] spread quickly across social media platforms[16] with disastrous effects,[17] such as the overdosing of certain substances (like chloroquine, a drug normally prescribed to treat malaria), the disruption of medical and grocery supply chains, and the impacts on public health nutrition and psychosocial health among the affected populations.[18] This chapter is not especially interested in the effects that such disinformation might have played on global health – as important as they might be – but rather on *the actors* which enabled such an infodemic to take place.

A study that analysed 225 pieces of misinformation related to COVID-19 has concluded that a majority (76 per cent) of the sample appeared on social media platforms, while only 9 per cent was televised, 8 per cent was published by news outlets and the remaining 7 per cent just appeared on other websites.[19] This means that the most important actors in spreading COVID-19 disinformation were not the traditional media players, such as television, radio or newspapers; they were social media platforms.[20] These platforms became the enablers of information – more than just attention merchants[21] – confirming the trend of communitarian spreads of information. Although it seems overwhelmingly clear that social media platforms play a critical role in tackling health disinformation, their responses have varied substantially. The same study concluded that on Twitter, for example, 59 per cent of posts rated as false remained up, in comparison to 27 per cent on YouTube and 24 per cent on Facebook. This confirms that some platforms have effectively

[15] WHO, 'Understanding the Infodemic and Misinformation in the Fight against COVID-19' (COVID-19 Factsheet No 5, April 2020) https://iris.paho.org/handle/10665.2/52052.

[16] Szmuda, Syed, Singh, Ali, Özdemir and Słoniewski, 'YouTube as a Source of Patient Information for Coronavirus Disease (COVID-19): A Content-Quality and Audience Engagement Analysis' [2020] *Reviews in Medical Virology*, www.ncbi.nlm.nih.gov/pmc/articles/PMC7323134/.

[17] Cuan-Baltazar et al, 'Misinformation on Vaccination: A Quantitative Analysis of YouTube Videos' (2018) 14 *Human Vaccines and Immunotherapies* 1654.

[18] Tasnim, Hossain and Mazumder, 'Impact of Rumors and Misinformation on COVID-19 in Social Media' (2020) 53 *Journal of Preventive Medicine and Public Health* 171.

[19] Brennen, Simon, Howard and Nielsen, 'Types, Sources, and Claims of COVID-19 Misinformation' (University of Oxford Factsheet, April 2020) https://reutersinstitute.politics.ox.ac.uk/sites/default/files/2020-04/Brennen%20-%20COVID%2019%20Misinformation%20FINAL%20%283%29.pdf.

[20] This dependence on platforms as governors of health speech necessarily comes with a price. While traditional media outlets are publicly scrutinised – whether for having public spaces where the state transmits health information, for being state-owned or simply for being subject to different types of regulatory authorities – digital outlets are not subjected to any kind of fact-checking regulatory body apart from their own decision-making. Although they effectively mediate health information exchange, they are not accountable for it. This is explained by a controversial distinction between media outlets as publishers and social media as a place of gathering, exempted from liability for the content they mediate, host or list. The so-called 'good Samaritans' or 'safe-harbour' clauses vary substantially, but they all tend to agree on the fundamental premise of shielding these platforms from liability for content posted by their users. They depart from the idea that the sharing economy as we know it today would effectively be rendered impossible if Facebook, Twitter or Google had to police every single piece of content posted by their users. The principles of exempted liability/safe harbour, the prohibition of general monitoring and the country of origin are responsible for the creation of the content ecosystem which allowed online platforms to exist.

[21] Wu, *The Attention Merchants: The Epic Scramble to Get Inside Our Heads* (Vintage Books, 2016) 308–40.

fought disinformation while others have not[22] and that among industries, there is still considerable divergence on what constitutes health misinformation and on what actions should be taken to tackle the issue.

Part of the reason that can explain the foundational role of online platforms in protecting global health speech for this shift in responsibilities lies in how Europe has construed platform liability.[23] Unlike section 230 of the Decency Communications Act[24] and American exceptionalism, according to the provisions of the E-Commerce Directive,[25] online platforms must ensure that the unlawful content of which they are alerted does not stay up. Hence, it is for them to interpret what is lawful and unlawful content, and then to take down that content if necessary. Ironically, they represent either the first line of defence of free speech or its worst enemy. The state or public authorities will not become involved until far in the future, and only if litigation is started.

[22] Concluding that user interactions with false content have largely declined in Facebook since 2016 but have steadily risen in Twitter, see Allcott, Gentzkow and Yu, 'Trends in the Diffusion of Misinformation on Social Media' [April–June 2019] *Research and Politics* 1.

[23] Models largely differ across jurisdictions, but one can speak of three models or model types. First, there are those models which privilege online intermediaries' freedom and represent them almost exclusively as marketplaces of ideas and never publishers. A good example is found in s ¶230 of the 1996 Decency Communications Act in the USA, which protects online providers from any liability even in case of knowledge of illegal content. In those cases, online intermediaries are always shielded from being accountable for the information they transfer, host or list, in an effort to stimulate an open, uncensored Internet. A second model rejects such open protectiveness and rather mandates the so-called 'safe harbour' clauses. A 'safe-harbour' clause departs from the same reasoning as s 230 – not considering online providers as liable publishers for user-generated content – but adds an extra layer of responsibility. According to provisions such as Art 14 of Directive 2000/31/EC (E-Commerce Directive) in EU law, online providers are only exempt from liability up to the point that they are aware of the wrongdoing – the moment at which they will be liable for refusing to take down such content. This model, which is far from perfect, places the digital intermediaries in a delicate position of assessing what content should or should not be taken down (including complex balancing of fundamental rights). A third and final model, commonly known as notice-and-transmit, provides a different solution. Instead of placing the responsibility immediately on the online provider (eg the social media platform) to take down the content, the platform has the sole obligation to transfer such a complaint to the original user. In these cases, the litigation is shifted to the original 'publishers', ie it is between the copyright owner that is complaining and the one who posted the original content. A good example of this can be found in US law, pursuant to s 512 of the Digital Millenium Copyright Act. In accordance with such provisions, if an online provider receives a notice on some allegedly unlawful content (in this specific case, copyright infringements), it has an obligation to forward it to the original user while automatically taking down the content. The company is only liable if it fails to forward the notice. What might follow is a counter-notice by the user, which is then once again forward to the copyright owner. After 10–14 days without formal litigation being started by the copyright owner, the company is mandated to reinstate the content.

[24] 47 US Code § 230 c) – Protection for private blocking and screening of offensive material – reveals what some have called American exceptionalism. While the majority of jurisdictions in the world have adopted some dimension of notice-and-take-down procedure, the USA has resorted to an almost unlimited shield from liability. Apart from the exceptions regarding copyright (subject to a specific notice-and-action regime under the Millenium Copyright Act) and federal crimes, it has been exceptionally difficult to hold online platforms liable for content moderation. See the landmark case of *Zeran v America Online, Inc* 129 F.3d 327 (4th Cir 1997).

[25] Directive 2000/31/EC of the European Parliament and of the Council of 8 June 2000 on certain legal aspects of information society services, in particular electronic commerce, in the Internal Market ('Directive on electronic commerce') [2000] OJ L178/1.

This has a natural impact on how individuals relate to public power. Traditionally, in an emergency such as a natural catastrophe or a pandemic, citizens would turn to the state for guidance and support, namely, to obtain trustworthy information. Especially after World War II, it became clear that one of the key aspects of a constitutional state would be to provide, not only to abstain from unlawful conduct. This positive duty[26] represented the constitutional shift from a liberal state into the social or welfare state.[27] However, as the digitalisation of society progresses, the state, traditionally slower to react, became more and more distant from individuals. In the absence of physical contact, people turned to one another through digital means, mediated through social media platforms. However, while, in a traditional media scenario, the content would be curated by an editor or a TV or newspaper curator[28] (subject to editorial and professional regulation), social media is based on the immediacy of inter-user contact, providing almost instantaneous answers. In such a scenario, truth or reliability becomes less important than faster results. Specific diagnoses and treatments are shared millions of times, giving them a certain communitarian authenticity. Health disinformation, even more than misinformation, spreads faster than the virus.

This places obvious responsibilities on online platforms. It also gifts them with a refreshed legitimacy. If they act now as providers of reliable health information, people will turn to them more and more in times of need. Understanding such an opportunity, these companies have responded to the call by taking drastic content-curating measures.

For example, in August 2020, at the peak of the COVID-19 pandemic in the USA, both Facebook and Twitter decided to take down one piece of content (published on both platforms) whereby President Trump endorsed a video hinting that children were simply immune to COVID-19.[29] This constituted a landmark moment for Facebook, which had hitherto kept its commitment to not fact-checking politicians following the long-lasting view of its CEO, Mark Zuckerberg, that there should not be any fact-checking of political figures.[30]

Recently, Twitter retook the lead and launched labelling tools for health disinformation, once again taking an interest in the general public welfare (Figure 3.1).

[26] Discussing precisely the role of positive duties by states regarding the delegation of public responsabilities to big tech, see Kuczerawy, 'The Power of Positive Thinking: Intermediary Liability and the Effective Enjoyment of the Right to Freedom of Expression' (2017) 8 *Journal of Intellectual Property, Information Technology and E-Commerce Law*, www.jipitec.eu/issues/jipitec-8-3-2017/4623.

[27] For an account of the evolution of constitutionalism in its different phases, see Grimm, 'The Constitution in the Process of Denationalization' (2005) 12 *Constellations* 447.

[28] Balkin, 'Free Speech is a Triangle' (2018) 118 *Columbia Law Review* 2011, 2040.

[29] www.siliconrepublic.com/companies/facebook-twitter-children-covid19-immune-donald-trump.

[30] 'I just believe strongly that Facebook shouldn't be the arbiter of truth of everything that people say online' … 'Private companies probably shouldn't be, especially these platform companies, shouldn't be in the position of doing that': 'Zuckerberg Says Facebook Won't Be "Arbiters of Truth" after Trump Threat', *The Guardian* (London, May 2020) www.theguardian.com/technology/2020/may/28/zuckerberg-facebook-police-online-speech-trump.

Figure 3.1 Twitter

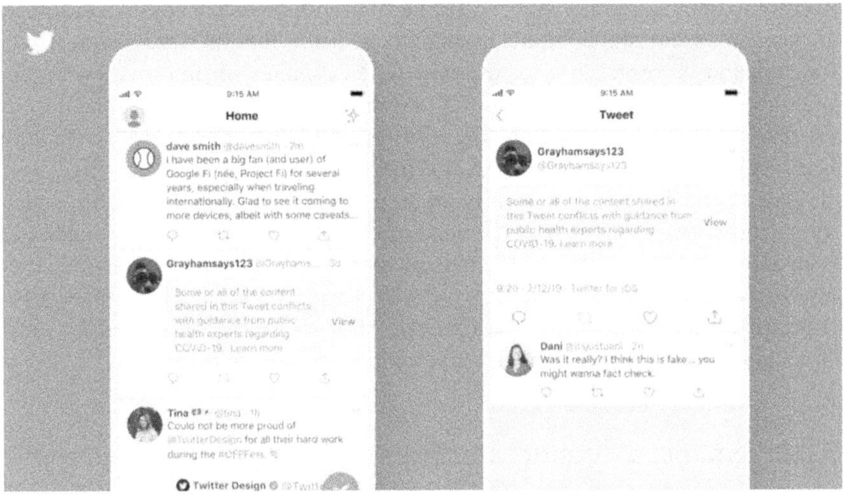

Facebook has also launched several campaigns to ensure that good information would surpass the disinformation campaigns. It allowed its platform to be used by WHO health bots – software designed to answer questions by users via Facebook Messenger – which would reply to health queries with reliable information[31] or redirect users towards reliable sources of information.[32]

Figure 3.2 Facebook Covid-19 Information Centre

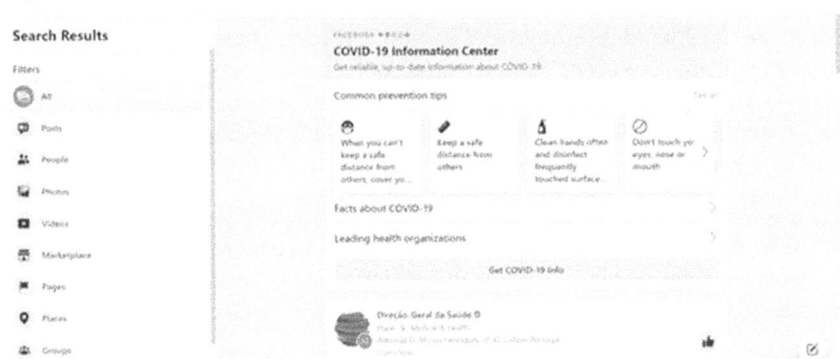

More recently, YouTube decided to adopt even stricter measures relating to content that denied vaccines' efficacy. In an update of its policy guidelines entitled 'Managing Harmful Vaccine Content on YouTube',[33] YouTube took the

[31] www.who.int/news-room/feature-stories/detail/who-launches-a-chatbot-powered-facebook-messenger-to-combat-covid-19-misinformation.

[32] https://www.facebook.com/coronavirus_info/.

[33] 'Managing Harmful Vaccine Content on YouTube' (*Blog.Youtube*) https://blog.youtube/news-and-events/managing-harmful-vaccine-content-youtube/.

bold decision to ban any content which misrepresented vaccines and their effects. According to the company, any content that 'falsely alleges that approved vaccines are dangerous and cause chronic health effects, claims that vaccines do not reduce transmission or contraction of the disease, or contains misinformation on the substances contained in vaccines' will be removed. The company has held to its word, banning Brazilian President Jair Bolsonaro from the platform for a week for his attempt to connect AIDS and COVID-19.[34]

As a conclusion to this first dimension, one point becomes clear. Online platforms and search engines play a crucial role in controlling the dissemination of both information and disinformation/misinformation about COVID-19. They now exercise a role that traditionally we would associate with nation-states rather than private multinationals.[35] Whether this has been willingly delegated by states or is organically created by the digital revolution remains to be proven.

3.2.2. Financial Support and Digital Tools of e-Commerce

A second dimension of how Big Tech have reacted to COVID-19 has to do with financial support to individuals and small businesses in need. Unlike disinformation, a now widely studied facet of the digital world, financial assistance from digital companies is a relatively new dimension worthy of being acknowledged. It represents another classic social/welfare state trait – the ability to provide financial relief directly to populations in need due to catastrophe.

Alphabet/Google[36] is probably at the forefront of such assistance. When COVID-19 hit, the giant search engine/artificial intelligence company decided to advance an ambitious programme of economic recovery meant to help small businesses maintain or reshape their business models and ensure survival under the distress of the pandemic. It issued a new $800+ million commitment to support small- and medium-sized enterprises (SMEs), health organisations, governments and health workers on the frontline of COVID-19.[37] This considerable amount was then divided into working programmes as follows:

- $250 million in advertising grants to help international organisations and governmental agencies (such as the WHO) provide health information about

[34] Reuters, 'Facebook, YouTube Take down Bolsonaro Video over False Vaccine Claim' (*Reuters*, 2021) www.reuters.com/world/americas/facebook-takes-down-bolsonaro-video-over-false-vaccine-claim-2021-10-25/.

[35] Discussing the same idea on intellectual property reforms, see Geiger and Jütte, 'Digital Constitutionalism and Copyright Reform: Securing Access through Fundamental Rights in the Online World' (*The Digital Constitutionalist*) https://digi-con.org/digital-constitutionalism-and-copyright-reform-securing-access-through-fundamental-rights-in-the-online-world/.

[36] For ease of reference I will always address Alphabet, Google's parent and its actual company, merely as Google.

[37] Statement by Sundar Pichai, Google's CEO, 'COVID-19: $800+ Million to Support Small Businesses and Crisis Response', https://blog.google/inside-google/company-announcements/commitment-support-small-businesses-and-crisis-response-covid-19.

COVID-19. Likewise, it committed an additional $20 million in advertising grants to community financial institutions and non-governmental organisations (NGOs);

- $200 million as an investment fund that will support NGOs and financial institutions with direct access to capital;
- an additional $340 million in Google Ads credits available to all SMEs with active accounts over the past year; and
- $20 million in Google Cloud credits for academic institutions and researchers related to COVID-19.

Google's strategy was meant to diversify its support. It interestingly resorted to advertising credit as its primary way to finance SMEs. By promoting small businesses for free, Google allowed small companies to access the single most important digital advertisement market available (Google Ads), contributing to their potential online success as newly formed digital businesses. Part of this advertising credit was also used to finance institutional information from both government and international organisations regarding COVID-19, meaning that effectively Google actually decided which NGO, international organisation, SME or even government was entitled to this grant according to their *own* standards and financial choices.

Facebook has also displayed a creative response to COVID-19. Its financial support took essentially two forms: first, it created novel digital tools, the so-called 'shops' feature, and fund-raising tools for SMEs to ask help from friends and customers; second, it provided direct financial assistance to SMEs in the shape of grants.

On the one hand, Facebook developed new services that directly helped businesses survive the COVID-19 pandemic. Now businesses could create funding campaigns directly on Facebook[38] and ask clients to buy 'gift cards'[39] that would be redeemable in the future when the business would be back on its feet. Facebook does not charge any fee in both situations, although, as now seems clear to everyone, no digital service is ever free in a growing surveillance capitalist model.[40] Perhaps the most exciting roll-out during the pandemic was Facebook Shops.[41] This new tool allows businesses affected by COVID-19 to shift their business models and go fully digital, opening their storefronts with prearranged models on Facebook. Both of these tools have been created with the specific intention of helping small businesses thrive[42] based on a report[43] directed by Facebook itself on the impact of the pandemic on small businesses.

[38] www.facebook.com/fundraisers.

[39] www.facebook.com/business/boost/gift-cards#get-started.

[40] Zuboff, *Surveillance Capitalism* (Profile Books, 2019) 94.

[41] https://about.fb.com/news/2020/05/introducing-facebook-shops/.

[42] Facebook's CEO Mark Zuckerberg states that 'Right now many small businesses are struggling, and with stores closing, more are looking to bring their business online. Our goal is to make shopping seamless and empower anyone from a small business owner to a global brand to use our apps to connect with customers': www.about.fb.com/news/2020/05/introducing-facebook-shops/.

[43] Facebook, 'State of Small Business Report' (May 2020) https://about.fb.com/wp-content/uploads/2020/05/SMBReport.pdf.

More directly, Facebook also decided to grant financial assistance directly under the Facebook Small Businesses Grants Program. This programme provided USD 100 million in cash grants and advertising credits to ensure that SMEs from over 30 countries would be able to withstand the impact of COVID-19.[44]

One question arises out of both cases. Why would any of these companies worry about the recovery of SMEs on a global scale? Why would they pledge considerable amounts of money in helping so many? Two obvious answers come to mind.

The first is to look exclusively at the short-term economic aspect of such a decision. Google and Facebook are multisided markets that produce indirect network effects,[45] working as platforms that connect individual users to advertisers.[46] In all accounts, Facebook and Google need to have SMEs ready to invest in advertisements in order to generate the necessary revenue that makes their platforms 'free' for individual users. COVID-19 could indirectly affect Google and Facebook by reducing the available budget that SMEs have to spend on advertisement. Without SMEs' cash flow, Big Tech would lose on both fronts, either by losing direct customers (SMEs as users) or by indirectly losing advertisement revenues as SMEs could no longer invest.[47] This is the straightforward answer: they supported them because they needed them.

The second, more long-term thinking, is that Big Tech have understood that COVID-19 was the perfect opportunity to invest in the digitalisation of SMEs (and individuals, for that matter). By providing small businesses with these new tools, these platforms are ensuring that the transition from physical to digital business is made on their respective platforms, and their dominion is maintained. Given the high 'costs of change'[48] that come with the use of any technology (especially omni-platforms such as Facebook or search engines such as Google), these companies are effectively securing customers. They are investing in the digital transition of clients more than just securing them over the short term.

There is, however, an inadvertent effect from all those possibilities that transcends the mere economic opportunity. As state aid is classically more bureaucratic and slower to arrive in a crisis, these companies have taken the opportunity to project themselves as the first line of support, providing the immediate financial relief that many businesses and individuals needed during the pandemic. This reaction comes with non-economic consequences. Communities in need would

[44] www.en-gb.facebook.com/business/small-business/grants.

[45] Crémer, Yves-Alexandre de Montjoye and Schweitzer, 'Competition Policy for the Digital Era' (European Commission, 2019) 19–23.

[46] Barwise and Watkins, 'The Evolution of Digital Dominance: How and Why We Got GAFA' in Moore and Tambini (eds) *Digital Dominance* (Oxford University Press, 2018) 26–27.

[47] The numbers seem to prove the strategy right. While in 2019 there was a decline, the following years of pandemic (2020–21) saw a return to growth in advertising revenue for Facebook. In the third quarter of 2021, Facebook's advertising revenue amounted to an astonishing 28.276 billion USD. See www.statista.com/statistics/277963/facebooks-quarterly-global-revenue-by-segment/.

[48] www.observador.pt/2020/04/22/artistas-apelam-ao-facebook-e-a-google-para-que-criem-apoios-ao-setor-em-portugal/.

perceive platforms such as Google or Facebook as providers in times of need, similar to the social welfare state. In fact, they would perceive them as providers who could help them more quickly and better than the state. An excellent example of this is the reaction of some artistic/cultural communities to the pandemic.

In Portugal, for example, the culture sector turned immediately to Facebook and Google for support to ensure the continuation of their activities. In a manifesto subscribed to by over 200 entities,[49] the sector asked Facebook and Google to help Portuguese artists, either by creating a monetary fund to support the sector directly or by granting a monthly allowance (under a sort of Facebook ads credit) to promote their work on their platforms. Artists wanted Facebook to help them restore the audiences that the state had denied them due to health-related measures. They wanted direct financial support from a giant American company – something unusual (or even maybe unheard of) in the context of the Portuguese crisis.

Another example is Ireland. In a joint effort, Facebook Ireland and the Irish Department of Culture made available a grant system, made possible through Facebook's funds, to give financial support to artists. The initiative would allow money to be given directly to these small businesses and individuals to digitally broadcast (through Facebook again) a series of performances.[50]

One can then ask whether this represents something more than some sort of enhanced corporate social responsibility (CSR).[51] Although CSR has been studied from different angles, ranging from pure economics to politics, social integration and even ethics,[52] Big Tech seems to transcend the classic CSR doctrines. They seem to truly conflate the role of private and public power in providing public goods. Scherer, Palazzo and Matten put it clearly when stating:

> Globalisation calls for a fresh view concerning the political role of business in society and its creativity and contribution to social innovations and the public good. These phenomena need to be embedded in a new concept of the business firm as an economic and political actor in market societies and as an actor that contributes to both private and public interests.[53]

Interestingly, these two cases are not only about a private American company that helps specific communities at risk. This is not unheard of, and has been part of the social engagement of many multinationals around the world for many decades

[49] www.gerador.eu/mais-de-100-artistas-e-entidades-nacionais-juntam-se-para-pedir-apoio-ao-facebook-e-google/.

[50] The initiative took the hashtag of #Irelandperforms and can be found at www.cultureireland.ie/news/article/culture-ireland-and-facebook-ireland-announces-details-of-ireland-performs.

[51] Scherer, Palazzo and Matten, 'The Business Firm as a Political Actor: A New Theory of the Firm for a Globalized World' (2014) 53 *Business & Society* 143.

[52] Melé, 'Corporate Social Responsibility Theories' in Crane, McWilliams, Matten, Moon and Siegel (eds), *The Oxford Handbook of Corporate Social Responsibility* (Oxford University Press, 2009) ch 3. On this topic see also the critique of Scherer and Palazzo, 'The New Political Role of Business in a Globalized World: A Review of a New Perspective on CSR and Its Implications for the Firm, Governance and Democracy' (2011) 48 *Journal of Management Studies* 21.

[53] Scherer et al (n 50) 148.

now. What is interesting is how *the same* set of companies are being asked to support *different* communities in *different* locations of the planet. It suggests that artists in Portugal or in Ireland have a similar connection to Google or Facebook and see in them the potential to save the artists from a complicated situation. This relationship seems to be more than purely economic in nature. Communities perceive those companies as transnational providers, ready to help in times of need.

Although some company leaders have served as providers of given local communities,[54] especially with the so-called company-towns[55] in the USA, the scope and transnational character of these companies hints at something more significant. They seem to be facing a transformation of legitimacy, increasingly blurring the borders of public and private.

3.2.3. Digital Tracing Applications and App Markets

A final dimension of this hypothesis is connected to how technology helped trace the virus around the globe.[56] A few months after the pandemic hit, it became clear that global movements of people would constitute a challenge to contain the COVID-19 virus and that it was, therefore, crucial to come up with tracing tools to check who was infected and with whom that person had been in contact. The EU understood the transnational dimension of the virus and alerted that 'No single Member State can succeed alone in combating the COVID-19 crisis', pushing for a common approach (the so-called Toolbox)[57] whereby Member States would agree on a set of standard specifications and governance mechanisms.

Perhaps most importantly, the Commission understood the need for an interoperable interface that would allow different tracing apps to work in different jurisdictions. Such interoperability was finally agreed on in July, with the European Commission enacting an implementing decision[58] that set out a framework to

[54] Balkin, 'Free Speech' (n 28).

[55] The landmark case here remains the US Supreme Court in *Marsh v Alabama* 326 US 501 (1946). The case dealt with a Jehovah's Witness who was being criminally charged for distributing leaflets on the sidewalk of a purely private company town in Alabama. The Supreme Court sided with the Jehovah's Witness, stating that ownership did not always mean absolute dominion and that individuals had to respect the statutory and constitutional rights of those who use their property. Revisiting the case and discussing its applicability to big tech, see Shefa, 'First Amendment 2.0: Revisiting Marsh and the Quasi-public Forum in the Age of Social Media' (2018) 41(1) *University of Hawai'i Law Review* 159.

[56] For a brief analysis of 10 different technologies which are being used to fight the virus, see Kritikos, 'Ten Technologies to Fight Coronavirus' (European Parliamentary Research Service, April 2020).

[57] Commission, 'On a Common Union Toolbox for the Use of Technology and Data to Combat and Exit from the COVID19 Crisis, in Particular Concerning Mobile Applications and the Use of Anonymised Mobility Data', Recommendation No 2020/518, 8 April 2020.

[58] Commission, 'Amending Implementing Decision (EU) 2019/1765 as Regards the Cross-Border Exchange of Data between National Contact Tracing and Warning Mobile Applications with Regard to Combatting the COVID-19 Pandemic', Commission implementing Decision No 2020/1023, 15 July 2020.

facilitate the interoperability of contact tracing and warning apps allowing citizens to cross jurisdictions within the EU using only one app. This 'Federation Gateway Service' would then be approved by consensus on the 2 September 2020, by the eHealth Network,[59] a voluntary network set up under Article 14 of Directive 2011/24/EU.[60]

However, these efforts of harmonisation were countered by a robust nationalistic approach. It quickly became apparent that such a pan-European effort would be challenging to perfect.

The first obstacle was Member States' decision to develop or acquire their own national tracing apps unilaterally. Even before any discussion was held on a potential pan-European app (which was attempted to no avail at one point),[61] states rushed to develop national tracing apps that could detect COVID-19 contacts and alert authorities and citizens of such contacts. This led to an apparent second obstacle: because not all apps were designed the same way, the technology varied substantially from country to country. While most states introduced Bluetooth decentralised tracing technology (a decentralised model where data is stored only on the mobile device and not centralised on any governmental database),[62] others preferred data collection via network services/Bluetooth and storage on a main centralised government database. The French case was particularly worrisome: first, because of its general failure[63] with the French population, with StopCOVID app (the French tracing app) being downloaded a mere 2.3 million times by September 2020;[64] secondly, because of the decision by the French government to maintain a centralised system, which raised several concerns among privacy NGOs and data protection authorities.[65]

[59] eHealth Network, 'European Proximity Tracing An Interoperability Architecture for contact tracing and warning apps' (September 2020) www.ec.europa.eu/health/sites/health/files/ehealth/docs/mobileapps_interop_architecture_en.pdf.

[60] European Parliament and the Council of the European Union, 'On the Application of Patients' Rights in Cross-Border Healthcare', Directive 2011/24/EU, 9 March 2011.

[61] See the so-called Pan-European Privacy-Preserving Proximity Tracing, a flexible software which could have been used by different apps across Europe, www.pepp-pt.org/.

[62] See Godano and Sartor, ch 9 of this book.

[63] A new app is ready to be deployed, the so-called TousAntiCOVID, in an attempt to get to wider part of the French population: www.francetvinfo.fr/replay-radio/le-choix-franceinfo/covid-19-apres-le-flop-de-stopcovid-la-nouvelle-version-de-l-application-de-tracage-tousanticovid-reussira-t-elle-a-decoller_4132957.html.

[64] For an overview of how applications have been working, see www.thelocal.com/20200909/do-any-of-europes-coronavirus-phone-apps-actually-work.

[65] The Commission Nationale Informatique et Libertés (French Data Protection Authority) was also very critical of the application in its initial version, ruling that the StopCOVID app was not in compliance with the GDPR. See CNIL, 'Délibération n° 2020-046 du 24 avril 2020 portant avis sur un projet d'application mobile dénommée "StopCOVID"', Demande d'avis n° 20006919. It then enacted a second opinion where it praised some advancements but maintained the red line regarding the purpose and use of the data gathered. See 'Délibération n° 2020-056 du 25 mai 2020 portant avis sur un projet de décret relatif à l'application mobile dénommée "StopCOVID"', Demande d'avis n° 20008032. A group of French tech specialists also wrote a document raising awareness to the risks of the app, 'Mise en garde contre les applications de traçage', www.attention-stopcovid.fr/. The NGO Privacy International also showed some concerns regarding centralised systems such as the Norwegian or the Colombian: www.privacyinternational.org/examples/apps-and-covid-19.

Once again, under the apparent confusion of the multiplicity of solutions and the emergency of the crisis, Big Tech saw an exciting opportunity to help.

In this field, the two most essential tech players are Google and Apple, two American companies which quickly came forward with their own solutions. The two companies partnered up,[66] in an unprecedented move among tech competitors, to develop a framework application programming interface[67] that could allow for the different applications across Europe to be made available on both the iOS and Android/Google Play app markets. The idea seems truly altruistic and helpful at first glance, as two significant competitors joined forces to provide states with a technical solution they dearly needed at the time. One could maybe naively ask: why would states reject such straightforward help? However, a deeper analysis might shed some light on the power dimension of this move.

In fact, not all states were happy with this advancement by tech companies. By creating a particular common framework, Apple and Google were de facto defining the architectural requisites of all technologies that wish to be interoperable[68] and work in both markets. The French Secretary of State for the Digital Economy, Mr Cedric O, said in a statement: 'I'm not taking a stand against Apple and Google; I'm saying that I don't want to be constrained by the internal policy choices of any company on a matter of public health.'[69]

The problem ends up being one of regulatory control. Like Lessig identified such a long time ago,[70] the most critical regulatory tool in the digital world is the power to design the digital architecture itself. Unlike the 'real world', where such constraints exist by default (being the laws of physics the most evident), the 'digital world' is 100 per cent built, and one can define core rules which simply set the rules of the game.[71] By controlling such architecture in the first place, Apple and Google would be binding national tracing apps to constraints, ranging from privacy standards to software design. For example, Google and Apple actively refused to let their solution accept any kind of centralised database of cases (a solution defended by France and initially by the UK, for example) or let Bluetooth tracing work in the background on mobile phones. Both companies argued it could lead to privacy breaches by the state.[72] Their persuasive power was so great that big powers like

[66] www.apple.com/newsroom/2020/04/apple-and-google-partner-on-covid-19-contact-tracing-technology/.

[67] The technical data can be found at www.covid19.apple.com/contacttracing.

[68] On the impacts of interoperability for EU law, see Brito Bastos and Curtin, 'Interoperable Information Sharing and the Five Novel Frontiers of EU Governance: A Special Issue' (2020) 26(1) *European Public Law* 59.

[69] Politico, 'How Google and Apple Outflanked Governments in the Race to Build Coronavirus Apps' (15 May 2020) www.politico.eu/article/google-apple-coronavirus-app-privacy-uk-france-germany/.

[70] Lessig, *Code and Other Laws of Cyberspace* (Basic Books, 1999). This was upgraded in a new, revised version: Lessig, *Code: Version 2.0* (Basic Books, 2006) 83–120.

[71] On the point of architecture connected to the moderation powers of the so-called 'Game Gods', see Noveck and Balkin (eds), *The State of Play: Law, Games, and Virtual Worlds* (NYU Press, 2006) 3–12 and 86–113.

[72] www.uk.reuters.com/article/us-health-coronavirus-france-tech/france-accuses-apple-of-refusing-help-with-stopcovid-app-idUKKBN22H0LX.

the UK decided to abandon their initial plans to develop a centralised solution and instead opted for Google and Apple's decentralised system.[73] Both platforms were actively tendering for privacy rights, even against nation-states.

Using COVID-19 as an opportunity to increase their legitimacy, Google and Apple reinforced their existing duopoly[74] over the app markets while maintaining the image of de facto enforcers of digital rights. It is therefore no surprise that Apple and Google felt entitled to 'flex their muscles'[75] against sovereign governments during the pandemic. By joining together in a commercial partnership, the two American companies could control virtually the entirety of the app market in which the tracing apps would be deployed. Every tracing app can generally only aim at success if it is downloaded by the majority of the population of a country. Without the Android/Google Play and iOS markets to make them available, the entire effort would simply be jeopardised.

3.3. Understanding the Phenomenon: The Privatisation of Public Power and the Publicisation of Private Power

It is now time to take a step further and answer the initial question:

Have some digital companies, known as Big Tech, taken advantage of COVID-19 to reaffirm their role as public providers? And, if so, what can explain this new 'public'-like role?

[73] www.theguardian.com/world/2020/jun/18/uk-poised-to-abandon-coronavirus-app-in-favour-of-apple-and-google-models.

[74] The fact is that Google and Apple constitute a de facto duopoly in the mobile operating system market, with Android/Google Play and iOS representing together a total of 98% of the market share. In comparison, giants such as Microsoft, which arrived on the mobile applications market later, have a mere 0.03% of market share, demonstrating the difficulties to enter such a closed market. This dominion over the two most relevant app markets has consistently been contested in different ways. In 2019, Spotify issued a formal complaint against Apple with the European Commission, arguing that the app levy (a 30% fee over profits) distorted competition – see open letter by Daniel EK, 'Consumers and Innovators Win on a Level Playing Field' (13 March 2019) www.newsroom.spotify.com/2019-03-13/consumers-and-innovators-win-on-a-level-playing-field/. In June 2020, the European Commission decided to proceed with a formal antitrust/competition law investigation into Apple's conduct, especially taking into consideration the 30% purchase fee and the restrictions that Apple imposed on developers not to inform users of alternative purchasing possibilities outside of the Apple system. At least two other companies have joined Spotify in voicing their concerns with the European Commission (Rakuten, with a complaint related to e-books, and Tile, related to Bluetooth services). See Commission, 'Antitrust: Commission Opens Investigations into Apple's App Store Rules' (Press Release, 16 June 2020) www.ec.europa.eu/commission/presscorner/api/files/document/print/en/ip_20_1073/IP_20_1073_EN.pdf. The procedure also gave rise to a parliamentary question by MEP Carmen Avram (from the S&D group): www.europarl.europa.eu/doceo/document/E-9-2019-002996_EN.html.

[75] Politico, 'How Google and Apple Outflanked Governments in the Race to Build Coronavirus Apps' (15 May 2020) www.politico.eu/article/google-apple-coronavirus-app-privacy-uk-france-germany/. See also how Google and Apple rejected the most recent update of the UK's app on the grounds of privacy: www.theguardian.com/world/2021/apr/12/apple-and-google-block-nhs-covid-app-update-over-privacy-breaches.

It is evident that the only possible answer to the first question is a big yes. COVID-19 constituted an extraordinary moment for many online companies as people necessarily resorted to their services to continue life as usual. From the merely commercial point of view, the pandemic was objectively good for Big Tech.[76]

The second question, however, is more delicate. How can one explain that Big Tech have acquired such a position in such a short amount of time? Two remarkable phenomena can help answer that question.

On the one hand, there seems to have been a tacit delegation or co-optation of public authority to private companies.[77] Way before the pandemic, states had already delegated fundamental challenges to online companies, gifting them with public authority. Challenges such as online disinformation are fought by social media or video-sharing platforms, which are asked by states to control the limits of free speech. They are deciding on the lawfulness or unlawfulness of much digital content online. Privacy standards, such as the right to be forgotten[78] or the architecture of tracing apps, are now enforced and protected by app store owners.[79] Their app markets host the most crucial health tools to track the virus. This delegation of private power has assumed different names, such as 'devolved enforcement',[80] 'intermediarization'[81] or 'privatised enforcement'.[82] They all translate this same idea of transferring classic public responsibilities to private digital companies. They are an integral part of the digital regulatory equilibrium between public and private power.

On the other hand, an almost symmetric movement occurred. Due to this tacit transfer of responsibilities by states, Big Tech needed to adapt to new challenges. These companies adapted to fulfilling public mandates through a process of

[76] Ovide, 'How Big Tech Won the Pandemic' *New York Times* (New York, 30 April 2021) www.nytimes.com/2021/04/30/technology/big-tech-pandemic.html.

[77] Cutler, Haufler and Porter (eds), *Private Authority and International Affairs* (State University of New York, 1999) 389; Mattli and Büthe, 'Setting International Standards: Technological Rationality or Primacy of Power?' (2003) 56 *World Politics* 1, 3.

[78] Hulvey, 'Companies as Courts? Google's Role Deciding Digital Human Rights Outcomes in the Right to Be Forgotten' (Carr Center for Human Rights Policy Harvard Kennedy School, 2022) 14.

[79] Arguing precisely this are Kuczerawy and Ausloos, 'From Notice-and-Takedown to Notice-and-Delist: Implementing Google Spain' (2016) 14 *Colorado Technology Law Journal* 219, 232–35. A good example of it can be found in Google's current reform of the use of third-party cookies for advertisement purposes. A small change such as the one currently proposed (the so-called Privacy Sandbox) could lead to a regulatory earthquake in the online advertisement world. These subtle changes can have a bigger impact that major pieces of regulation – Katsifis, 'How Tech Platforms Act as Private Regulators of Privacy' (*The Platform Law Blog*, 26 October 2020) www.theplatformlaw.blog/2020/10/26/how-tech-platforms-act-as-private-regulators-of-privacy/.

[80] McNamee, 'The Slide from "Self-Regulation" to Corporate Censorship' (European Digital Rights, 2011) Discussion paper 2011/01, 7, https://www.edri.org/files/EDRI_selfreg_final_20110124.pdf.

[81] Farrand, 'Regulatory Capitalism, Decentered Enforcement, and Its Legal Consequences for Digital Expression: The Use of Copyright Law to Restrict Freedom of Speech Online' (2013) 10 *Journal of Information Technology & Politics* 404, 404–22.

[82] Coche, 'Privatised Enforcement and the Right to Freedom of Expression in a World Confronted with Terrorism Propaganda Online' (2018) 7 *Internet Policy Review* 1.

mimesis,[83] mimicking classic state structures. More and more, these companies refer to themselves as 'governments',[84] 'countries'[85] or public squares,[86] while some authors call them 'kingly prerogatives',[87] 'emergent transnational sovereigns'[88] or 'virtual civil society'.[89] They ultimately realise their role for the 'public good[90] by incorporating narratives and internal procedures that resemble public law. They start describing themselves as providers, speaking of public duties towards their users.

Throughout this process, these companies shifted in nature (perhaps inadvertently). They started to resemble more and more governments to their communities, feeling ultimately responsible for their well-being.

These two trends could be graphically described as a downwards *privatisation of public power* (1) and an upwards *publicisation of private power* (2) (Figure 3.2).

Figure 3.3 The relationship between private and public providers

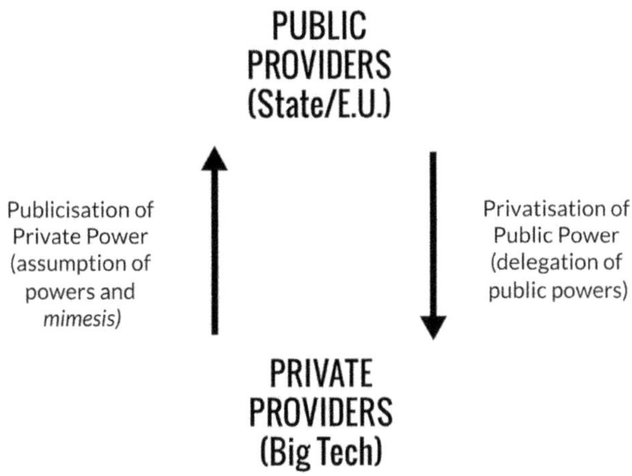

[83] I adapt the concept proposed by Papakonstantinou and De Hert of mimesis. Both authors use it in three different ways: definitional, substantive and institutional. They describe how transplants can occur from some legal regimes to others (eg from the GDPR to the new Digital Services Act). I use mimesis to describe the use of existing definitions, institutions and substantive standards from public law as applied by private companies. Papakonstantinou and De Hert, 'Post GDPR EU Laws and Their GDPR Mimesis. DGA, DSA, DMA and the EU Regulation of AI' (*European Law Blog*, 1 April 2021) www.europeanlawblog.eu/2021/04/01/post-gdpr-eu-laws-and-their-gdpr-mimesis-dga-dsa-dma-and-the-eu-regulation-of-ai/.

[84] Foer, 'Facebook's War on Free Will', *The Guardian* (London, 19 September 2017) www.theguardian.com/technology/2017/sep/19/facebooks-war-on-free-will.

[85] Zittrain, 'A Bill of Rights for the Facebook Nation' *The Chronicle of Higher Education* (20 April 2009).

[86] Rolling Stone, 'Twitter CEO Jack Dorsey: The Rolling Stone Interview', www.rollingstone.com/culture/culture-features/twitter-ceo-jack-dorsey-rolling-stone-interview-782298/.

[87] Borrowing from Senator John Sherman, see Wu, 'The Curse of Bigness: Antitrust in the New Gilded Age' (Columbia Global Reports, 2018) 21.

[88] Cohen, 'Law for the Platform Economy' (2017) 51 *University College Davis Law Review* 199.

[89] Landis, 'Facebook Blocked in Syria: Virtual Civil Society Banned' (*Syria Comment*, 22 November 2007) http://joshualandis.com/blog/?p=489.

[90] Drahos, 'The Regulation of Public Goods' (2004) 7 *Journal of International Economic Law* 323.

This tendency was exacerbated during COVID-19.

Firstly, during COVID-19, states have accepted Big Tech's exercise of public power, whether by controlling free speech, providing financial support to communities in need or developing apps that trace public health concerns. This privatisation of public power did not follow classic privatisation techniques.[91] In the case of COVID-19 and Big Tech, there is simply no express delegation of public power, nor are any regulatory mechanisms instituted. Instead, states acknowledged the role of Big Tech and accepted their growing legitimacy before their communities. In this situation, the state asks the private enterprise to exercise specific judgement calls and to serve as the frontline of defence of fundamental rights.[92] When a social platform is mandated to take down content that constitutes hate speech in 24 or 72 hours, as the German Netzwerkdurchsetzungsgesetz imposes,[93] the state is unilaterally imposing a delegation of public power, mandating the private enterprise to exercise a judgement call on what constitutes admissible speech. When the state accepts that Apple and Google are to define the technological standards that enforce privacy rights, it asks the private enterprise to set and enforce fundamental rights. When the state welcomes the role of Google and Facebook in giving monetary assistance to SMEs, it is tacitly recognising their role as financial providers in times of need. Ultimately, states are privatising: what admissible or inadmissible speech is; what is the best way to control a pandemic; and which standard of privacy should be used in a tracing app.

Secondly, perhaps in response to this delegation of public prerogatives, these companies have internally adapted to perform them. Because of the judgement calls that these companies need to make in relation to speech (what content is reliable health information), financial assistance (who should receive support) or privacy (how should data be processed), there is a growing approximation of their internal structures to public law procedures such as court proceedings or administrative due process. This is what Swati Srivastava describes as 'autogenous private governance':[94]

> unlike privatisation, this private governance does not take a previously public or governmental function and perform it through private actors. Instead, autogenous private governance reflects the opposite of privatisation, where previously private activities assume a public character given its scope of action and stakes for society.[95]

This 'publicisation' of their activities explains why most of these companies have complex governance models which encompass narratives of rights,

[91] Davies, 'Public Law and Privatisation' in Feldman and Elliott (eds), *The Cambridge Companion to Public Law* (Cambridge University Press, 2015) ch 9, 172–93.

[92] Discussing the role of states and the limits of such a cooptation, see Kuczerawy (n 26).

[93] *Gesetz zur Verbesserung der Rechtsdurchsetzung in sozialen Netzwerken*, 'Netzwerkdurchsetzungsgesetz vom 1. September 2017' (BGBl I S 3352), ¶2. For an interesting analysis of this law, see Stjernfelt and Lauritzen, *Your Post Has Been Removed: Tech Giants and Freedom of Speech* (SpringerOpen, 2020) 174–81.

[94] Srivastava, 'Not Just a Social Network: Facebook's Global Scandals and Political Responsibility', paper presented at the American Political Science Association Annual Conference, 2020.

[95] Srivastava, 'Not Just a Social Network: Facebook's Global Scandals and Political Responsibility', paper presented at the American Political Science Association Annual Conference, 2020, 12.

administrative-like procedures or 'supreme courts'.[96] As their businesses grow and their activities become indispensable to their communities, there is a growing need to regulate inter-user interaction. They are then forced to develop what Jack Balkin calls 'private bureaucracies', a part of his larger theory on 'New Speech Regulation'.[97] While Balkin's theory is applied to freedom of speech, its consequences extend to larger realities. His theory departs from the idea that contemporary free speech interaction is no longer a bilateral discourse between citizens and the state but rather a triangle, as represented in Figure 3.3.

Figure 3.4 The speech triangle. From JM Balkin, 'Old-School/New-School Speech Regulation' (2014) 127 *Harvard Law Review* 2296

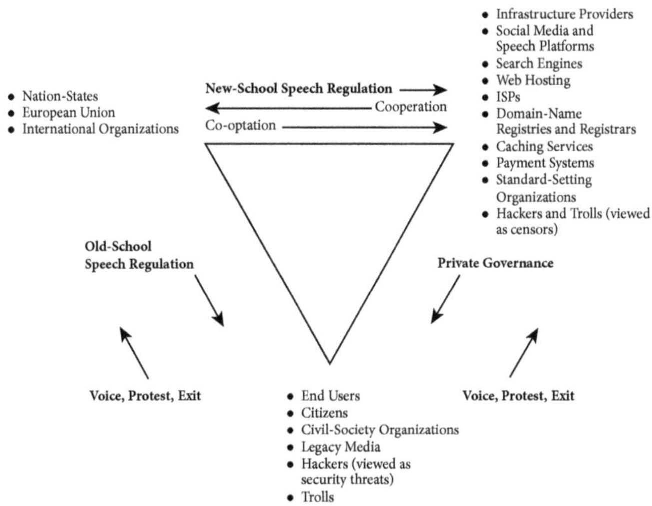

This triangle means the existence of different power centres within the same community, all working in parallel. It confirms the ideas of nodal governance,[98] in which multiple centres of norm creation and enforcement exist simultaneously. It points towards, as Ruggie puts it, a model in which multiple different legitimacies constitute 'a dynamic interplay between two different centres of power, each with its own basis for authority'.[99] The citizen/user interacts simultaneously with both

[96] www.about.fb.com/news/2019/04/input-on-an-oversight-board/. See Doeuk, 'Facebook's "Oversight Board:" Move Fast with Stable Infrastructure and Humility' (2019) 21(1) *North Carolina Journal of Law & Technology* 46. See also Facebook's Oversight Board Charter, www.about.fb.com/news/2019/01/oversight-board/.

[97] Balkin, 'Old-School/New-School Speech Regulation' (2014) 127 *Harvard Law Review* 2296.

[98] Shearing and Wood, 'Nodal Governance, Democracy, and the New "Denizens"' (2003) 30 *Journal of Law and Society* 400, 401–05, especially 403; Holley and Shearing, 'A Nodal Perspective of Governance: Advances in Nodal Governance Thinking' in Drahos (ed), *Regulatory Theory* (ANU Press, 2017) 163, 165.

[99] Ruggie, 'Multinationals as Global Institution: Power, Authority and Relative Autonomy' (2017) 12(3) *Regulation and Governance* 11. Here the author suggests a political science approach by looking at these multinationals in terms of power over their stakeholders and authority even over states (in that complex interplay). Ruggie does not go so far as to claim they possess true state-like powers, as Scherer admits.

centres of power (the state and the digital company) according to the specific problem and the capacity of each to respond to the need. It does not mean that both centres of power exclude each other mutually; rather, they complement each other under new synergies.[100] In fact, under such a triangle, states and online platforms cooperate to moderate speech. The same is apparent to other public goods, such as financial support or privacy standards.

This raises the ultimate question of whether the COVID-19 pandemic might have shed light on an existing trend: *that the division between public and private power is becoming less straightforward than it was before*. The digital revolution has gifted these companies with very specific legitimacies, which are continuously confirmed by their digital communities. Although states remain convinced of their regulatory power at the top of the delegation pyramid, the fact is that they are no longer themselves capable of exercising public power in every situation, given the transnational dimension of crisis. As Davies puts it:

> These policies have altered the government's role, reducing the emphasis on the direct provision of services and encouraging it to focus instead on regulating private firms (in the case of privatisation) and on deciding what services are required, selecting contractors and supervising their activities (in the case of contracting out).[101]

3.4. Concluding Remarks

In conclusion, one should remark on the fundamental changes that COVID-19 has brought about. One cannot ignore Big Tech companies' role in securing rights and tending for their communities during the pandemic. States remain fundamental in the economic recovery that will follow. However, it becomes clear that a post-COVID-19 world will be very different from what we expected. Our conceptions of public and private power will increasingly blur as big companies obtain more legitimacy before their communities. In key sectors such as speech, financial support and the enforcement of digital rights such as privacy, online platforms will be at the forefront in protecting their communities. This will have a foundational impact on how we relate to public and private power.

It appears undeniable that COVID-19 constituted an opportunity for Big Tech to solidify this position as a new centre of power. The future will tell if new technologies like the metaverse will further enhance this trend. For now, finally, as we cross to the other margin of the COVID-19 Rubicon, one must start addressing this institutional evolution and make sense of the impact of Big Tech on the future of the public–private divide.

[100] Knill and Lehmkuhl, 'Private Actors and the State: Internationalization and Changing Patterns of Governance' (2002) 15 *Governance* 42.

[101] Davies (n 91) 188.

4

What Did the COVID-19 Crisis Teach Us about European Solidarity? Incomplete Integration, Conflicts of Sovereignty and the Principle of Solidarity in EU Law

LUISA MARIN*

'this crisis is no one's doing and … it should not be everyone's undoing'

European Parliament, Resolution of 17 April 2020[1]

4.1. The EU Facing 'a Human Tragedy of Potentially Biblical Proportions'[2] with the Usual Legal Toolkit

When the first wave of COVID-19 arrived in Europe, nobody was ready for the pandemic. For its account, the EU was caught in the situation of having to provide answers to such an epochal challenge with an incomplete constitution, or rather a fragmented metabolic constitution,[3] having a limited mandate in policy areas

* Marie Skłodowska-Curie Fellow at the Law Department, European University Institute. I acknowledge funding from the European Union's Horizon 2020 research and innovation programme, Marie Skłodowska-Curie grant agreement No 891762. The views I express here do not represent the funding institution. I wish to thank all the participants of the workshop 'The Day After Covid-19', held in November 2020 at the EUI, as well as Emanuela Pistoia, Giuseppe Morgese, Luigi Daniele and the editors for comments exchanged on a previous draft of this chapter.

[1] European Parliament resolution of 17 April 2020 on EU coordinated action to combat the COVID-19 pandemic and its consequences (2020/2616(RSP)) www.europarl.europa.eu/doceo/document/TA-9-2020-0054_IT.pdf.

[2] M Draghi, 'Draghi: We Face a War against Coronavirus and Must Mobilise Accordingly' *Financial Times* (London, 25 March 2020).

[3] The literature on this issue is vast. *Ex multis*, see F Snyder, 'The Unfinished Constitution of the European Union: Principles, Processes and Culture' in JHH Weiler and M Wind (eds), *European*

such as public health, crisis management and economic union, which are crucial for tackling the pandemic and its consequences.[4] This mandate originates from a complex patchwork of (different types of) competences which are intertwined with the prerogatives of the Member States. In another perspective, it should not be forgotten that protection of public health, public safety and security, and dealing with crisis situations and fiscal and economic policies, represent core state powers, and domestic governments have been and still are very clear in asserting their competences and duties in the crisis situations generated by COVID-19.

It is precisely in this scenario that the outbreak of the pandemic within the European Union, with Italy being the first and worst hit country of the first wave, drove states to act, initially, in an uncoordinated manner, triggering initiatives in many directions, some of them protectionist and selfish.[5] Within the EU, Member States acted as competing sovereign entities, in a context characterised by lack of coordination and loyal cooperation between Member States and also towards European institutions. However, after this first chaotic moment, around mid-March 2020 the Commission intervened with a view to fostering coordination and limiting the effects of the uncoordinated and protectionist approaches of the Member States; in doing so, it managed to set itself up as an actor in the governance of the crisis, rescuing its reputation and reinforcing its legitimacy.

Since March 2020, European institutions, under the leading role of the Commission, have managed to decide on a number of measures: first, on pooling medical equipment and on research on a vaccine to defeat the virus; and secondly, coordinating efforts to allow EU citizens stranded outside the EU to travel back home, and also imposing limited freedom of movement – during lockdowns – for selected categories of persons in the healthcare sector.[6] From the perspective of governance of the economic policy, the EU has taken steps to compensate the economic consequences of the pandemic, with a relaxation of state aid rules and with the suspension of the Stability and Growth Pact, alongside the financial, economic and social aspects of the crisis. Among the first measures adopted was the SURE (Support mitigating Unemployment Risks in Emergency) programme, a €100 billion 'solidarity instrument' to support workers' incomes and business in navigating through the pandemic. Additionally, the Pandemic Emergency Purchase Programme (PEPP) of the European Central Bank (ECB) guaranteed

Constitutionalism beyond the State (Cambridge University Press, 2009) 55–73; from a different perspective, focusing on the means the EU has in terms of budget and administration, see C Fasone and P Lindseth, 'Europe's Fractured Metabolic Constitution: From the Eurozone Crisis to the Coronavirus Response', LUISS Working Paper Series, SOG-WP61/2020.

[4] F Casolari, 'Prime considerazioni sull'azione dell'Unione ai tempi del Coronavirus' (2020) 1 *Eurojus* 95.

[5] AM Pacces and M Weimer, 'From Diversity to Coordination: A European Approach to COVID-19' [2020] *European Journal of Risk Regulation* 283.

[6] G Caggiano, 'COVID-19. Competenze dell'Unione, libertà di circolazione e diritti umani in materia di controlli delle frontiere, misure restrittive della mobilità e protezione internazionale' (2020) I *Post di AISDUE* No 7, 72 (www.aisdue.eu).

liquidity for €750 billion. Alongside funds for research on a vaccine (€140 million), for the EU Civil Protection Mechanism (€125 million) and for the European Centre for Disease Prevention and Control (€3.6 million),[7] the Commission managed to propose and broker a €750 billion long-term recovery plan, called Next Generation EU, which was approved in 2020.[8]

The COVID-19 (corona) crisis is, however, not the first crisis to hit the EU. For more than a decade, the EU has been navigating through a turbulent period: first was the financial crisis, which evolved into a 'euro-crisis' (or eurozone crisis); then came the migration or refugee crisis, in addition to two major existential crises of the EU as a project: Brexit and the rule of law crisis. With the corona crisis, more recently, as with the eurozone and refugee crises, the EU has experienced a governance crisis which has been originated by an external factor. In mainstream narratives, these crises are the result of incomplete integration processes, alongside the recent emergence of competition and contestation between sovereign authorities, which is taking place since the rise of populist parties in a number of Member States.[9] To some extent, both processes (incomplete integration and competing sovereignties) feed and reinforce each other in a vicious circle, which damages the EU and the integration process. However, with the pandemic, the EU has managed to provide a timely answer to this crisis: my aim is to focus on this answer and on its lessons for the future of integration.

Against this background, the main purpose of this chapter is to analyse and assess how the EU has reacted to the pandemic, considering that no Treaty reform has been undertaken and that a pivotal role has been played by the principle of solidarity. Solidarity can assume a special role in the governance of crises. Secondly, it is precisely through the prism of solidarity that I will look at the COVID-19 crisis as a governance crisis and at its meaning for European integration. This chapter will focus on the role played by the principle of solidarity, which is one of the vectors of flexibility of the European legal system, and on how it is used to mitigate the negative effects that competing sovereignties display on the functioning of the EU. Solidarity is invoked as the principle to fix integration fractures, precisely like in the Japanese kintsugi technique, where a gold fluid is used to put together the pieces of broken ceramics; solidarity is supposed to reconcile the EU and its Member States when conflicts emerge in a traumatic manner and, consequently, to boost the legitimacy of the EU, in the sense of capacity to deliver policy reforms and public goods when needed. Solidarity is also meant to supplement the capacity

[7] France Diplomacy, 'European Solidarity in the Face of COVID-19', www.diplomatie.gouv.fr/en/french-foreign-policy/europe/news/article/european-solidarity-in-the-face-of-covid-19.

[8] For an overview, see Commission, 'Q&A: Next Generation EU – Legal Construction'.

[9] On conflicting sovereignties as expression of the political conflict between neo-sovereigntist populist parties and traditional politics, see C Bickerton, '"Parliamentary", "Popular" and "Pooled": Conflicts of Sovereignty in the United Kingdom's Exit from the European Union' (2019) 41 *Journal of European Integration* 887; see also N Brack, R Coman and A Crespy, 'Unpacking Old and New Conflicts of Sovereignty in the European Polity' in N Brack, R Coman and A Crespy (eds), *Understanding Conflicts of Sovereignty in the EU* (Routledge, 2021).

of the EU to deliver to citizens' expectations irrespective of the limited or sectoral (depending on the context considered) competences it has been vested with – an expression of the incompleteness of the integration process, which finds expression in its similarly incomplete constitution.

Having introduced the context of the research and its purpose and aim, the next section will expound on the conceptual framework underpinning it, namely discussing the incomplete integration and the conflicts of sovereignty which have emerged in a predominant manner in the last decade of integration and that are the consequences of the constitutional design of the EU. The chapter will then elaborate on the principle of solidarity as a core principle of European integration, and its function in managing crises, expounding on the challenges underpinning its achievement. In another section, the attention will turn on the solutions designed to fix the economic component of the COVID-19 crisis, focusing on the Next Generation EU to understand some lessons on how solidarity is used to ensure the achievement of a crucial target for the EU, namely recovery of the economies of the Member States,[10] before concluding with some reflections learned on the principle of solidarity as a flexibility vector of the overall open and incomplete system of integration which is the EU.

4.2. The EU and its 'Crises', between Incomplete Integration Processes and Conflicts for Sovereignty

4.2.1. Governance Crises as Side-Effects of Incomplete Integration Processes

This section elaborates on the past 'crises' of the EU as governance crises, to understand the role played by the principle of solidarity in these contexts. It is here argued that a common element of EU crises rests, primarily, in the incompleteness of the European integration processes, which has attributed to the EU legal competences that have created a system of incomplete powers to fulfil its mandate. This situation is the result of a preference – chosen since the Treaty of Maastricht – for limited transfers of sovereignty; this, in turn, creates conflicts of sovereignty, for example on the definition of the contours of these competences, as has happened with the *Gauweiler* and *Weiss* saga with the German Constitutional Court.[11] Within the EU legal system, these crises can be managed and 'composed' thanks to the overall flexibility of the system, though composition presupposes

[10] To this purpose, one could debate whether this target is a public good of the EU or of the Member States.

[11] CJEU, 16 June 2015, Case C-62/14 *Gauweiler v Deutscher Bundestag* ECLI:EU:C:2015:400; CJEU, 11 December 2018, Case C-493/17 *Weiss and Others* ECLI:EU:C:2018:1000.

acceptance of the core values and rules of the EU: in these contexts, the principle of solidarity plays a pivotal role and is supposed to correct the dysfunctionalities of the system, as it has been designed in its legal construction, be it in primary law or in secondary law.

This situation dominated by a crisis narrative can be explained with several reasons,[12] which all relate to the overall construction of the European Union. First of all, in the design of the architecture of European integration, the decision was taken to boost integration in some policy areas, but without extending it to closely related areas. The European Monetary Union (EMU) provides a typical example of it: a political science and economic narrative explains the eurozone crisis as the effect of incomplete integration. This incompleteness also concerns the legal institutional arrangements designed to achieve the integration process, codified into an 'unfinished constitution'[13] or 'fragmented metabolic constitution'.[14] In particular, the latter interpretation explains that the EU is called on to deliver public goods without having the toolkit typical of states, namely budgetary sovereignty and taxation powers. If we look at the policy domains, the EU is getting closer to the exercise of core state powers[15] without having the mandate and toolkit that states normally have, namely the capacity to mobilise resources for fulfilment of these targets, in particular concerning budget and administration. This leads to the third aspect: in several domains which have been marked by a crisis, we must consider that the EU is made up of a complex and multi-level governance system; in these governance crises, a role has been played by Member States.[16]

Unpacking these factors, we start from the incomplete integration rationale. As has been observed by scholars across disciplines, integration processes are often incomplete.[17] For example, in the context of the EMU, the fathers of the euro have built a single currency on an incomplete post-national sovereign idea: monetary union as exclusive competence of the EU, while fiscal and economic policies are firmly left in the hands of the Member States. Rosas and Armati described it as a house built starting with the roof, ie monetary policy without laying the necessary foundations of economic policy.[18] Economic scholars alike have observed that the EMU was fabricated on wrong premises, and that it looked like 'a half-built house', in the words of the American economist Rogoff.[19] He argued it was a 'catastrophic

[12] T Haughton, 'Editorial: Is Crisis the New Normal? The European Union in 2015' (2016) 54 *Journal of Common Market Studies* 5.

[13] Snyder (n 3).

[14] Fasone and Lindseth (n 3).

[15] P Genschel and M Jachtenfuchs (eds), *Beyond the Regulatory Polity* (Oxford University Press, 2014).

[16] T Borzel, 'From EU Governance of Crisis to Crisis of EU Governance: Regulatory Failure, Redistributive Conflict and Eurosceptic Publics' (2016) 54(S1) *Journal of Common Market Studies* 8.

[17] A Hinarejos, *The Euro Area Crisis in Constitutional Perspective* (Oxford University Press, 2015).

[18] 'Building a House by Starting with the Roof? Economic and Monetary Policy' in A Rosas and L Armati, *EU Constitutional Law. An Introduction* (Hart Publishing, 2012).

[19] P Eleftheriadis, 'Solidarity in the Eurozone' (January 2019) Bank of Greece Working Paper No 256.

mistake to put monetary union ahead of fiscal and political union', concluding that a 'monetary union without a fiscal union is an accident waiting to happen'.[20] In similar terms, Bergsten wrote that 'the European crisis is rooted in a failure of institutional design'. In his view, the solution would be to 'rewrite the Eurozone's rule book and complete the half-built euro house'.[21] From an economic perspective, in the USA these problems are addressed through fiscal transfers. In contrast, in EU monetary governance, on the one hand, states have lost control over their monetary toolkit, while the ECB, on the other hand, is constrained by the prohibition on monetary financing laid down in Article 123 TFEU.[22]

The incompleteness of integration, in different perspectives, also applies to the refugee and rule of law crises. Though the legal and policy contexts differ from the EMU in many aspects, it is here suggested that incompleteness of the integration process is a feature that characterises asylum and migration control policies for several reasons: the EU is exercising shared competences and, though it has developed an administrative machinery which is coordinating and supporting national administrations' activities, with the EU agencies Frontex and EASO, which are increasingly gaining weight in the practice, it nevertheless requires full organisational and financial commitment from states, which are controlled and monitored in the way they comply with EU rules. Incompleteness also means a sectoral or piecemeal approach to integration, in the sense that the common external borders did not imply a supranational asylum law policy, but rather a policy coordinating competences and duties of the Member States in asylum. The system set up with the Dublin Regulation is built upon this logic, and its downsides are also affecting the Schengen area: states have reintroduced controls at internal borders, putting the Schengen system under jeopardy. The Dublin system codifies geographical disparities between frontline states and states concerned by secondary movements, and has never been radically reformed.[23] On its side, the guardian of the treaties is not taking active steps to bring legality back into the Schengen area.[24]

[20] K Rogoff, 'Crash Time', quoted by Eleftheriadis, 'Solidarity in the Eurozone' (n 19).

[21] CF Bergsten, 'Why the Euro Will Survive' (2012) 9–10 *Foreign Affairs* 216. Feldstein himself assessed the eurozone in its dynamic dimension, observing that the macroeconomic challenges and risks of the eurozone could only be exacerbated by the fact that the single currency was built upon economies which kept growing in a divergent manner even after the introduction of the euro. This review of assessments by economists on the design of the eurozone is provided by Eleftheriadis, 'Solidarity in the Eurozone' (n 19) 29ff.

[22] A Viterbo, 'The PSPP Judgment of the German Federal Constitutional Court: Throwing Sand in the Wheels of the European Central Bank' (2020) 5 *European Papers* 671.

[23] The Dublin system was first thought of as a mechanism to allocate jurisdiction and therefore responsibilities for dealing with asylum applications, thus compensating for the lifting of controls at the internal borders. Because of their geographical positions, some states are more affected than others by migration.

[24] S Salomon and J Rijpma, 'A Europe without Internal Frontiers: Challenging the Reintroduction of Border Controls in the Schengen Area in the Light of Union Citizenship' (2021) 22 *German Law Journal* 1.

Incomplete integration here means that a high level of fragmentation characterises these policies,[25] as does a poor level of compliance with EU rules by (some) states. The measures of the Commission's New Pact on Migration and Asylum of September 2020 do not represent a radical change in this trend, which is worrisome as to the willingness of the EU to improve its position as a migration actor on the global stage.

This story of incompleteness could be repeated for the rule of law crisis, which concerns Eastern European states, mainly Poland and Hungary, which, after efforts and engagements in the integration path during the pre-accession phase, have turned towards illiberal avenues and are breaching the values of liberal democracies enshrined in Article 2 TEU. In this case, what has been framed as a 'nuclear weapon'[26] – Article 7 TEU – proved not to be so effective because of the required unanimity rule.[27] In this crisis, too, the governance of the EU revealed its fragility and its incompleteness, eventually undermining the whole credibility of the EU as a legal system.

Because of these choices in the constitutional setting of the EU and the context-specific policy design, integration has led to the codification of the structural disparities existing between states and has limited the options previously available to states to mitigate the negative effects of external events. At the same time, the Union is driven to react to crises with innovative policy solutions. It is precisely in this context of incompleteness that vertical conflicts for sovereignty are proliferating.

4.2.2. The Unbearable Lightness of … Incompleteness: Conflicts of Sovereignty as the Result of Incomplete Integration Processes

In this section I will expound on conflicts of sovereignty as the consequence of incomplete integration processes. The thesis argued here is that vertical conflicts of sovereignty are nurtured by incomplete integration processes. The incompleteness of integration can be worked out in multiple different perspectives: it can mean sectoral integration (EMU), fragmented integration deprived by an adequate enforcement at supranational level (asylum and migration) or integration paralysed by unanimity rules, meaning that the decision-making can be held hostage by vetoing minorities (rule of law).

[25] Borzel (n 16).

[26] D Kochenov, 'Busting the Myths Nuclear: A Commentary on Article 7 TEU' (Department of Law, San Domenico di Fiesole, 2017) EUI Working Papers, LAW 2017/10.

[27] K Lane Scheppele and L Pech, 'Is Article 7 Really the EU's "Nuclear Option"?' (*Verfassungsblog*, 6 March 2018).

Dialogical processes concerning core features of the EU legal system and their meaning are not new within the context of European integration.[28] However, depending on the actors, and on the quality of the interactions in each context, we can have a dialogical or a conflictual interaction, which can lead to claims touching upon core sovereignty tenets. Since the early days of European integration, the European Court of Justice and higher domestic courts have contended the boundaries of the transfer of sovereignty initiated with the integration process. At the beginning of European legal integration, the interactions between the Court of Justice of the European Union (CJEU) and higher national courts, including constitutional courts, have been centred around conceptions of supremacy of EU law and its implications on national legal orders. Several courts have engaged in this dialogue, and these interactions have proved to be fruitful for the development and consolidation of a new legal order, which did not federalise Member States and thus left supreme courts with a margin of appreciation in definition of the interactions between themselves and the supreme court of the Union, the Court of Justice.

These interactions have been rationalised in scholarship with the theories of constitutional pluralism, which had the merit to explain and compose dialogical and non-conflictual interactions between courts.[29] On its side, the Court of Justice has never written its doctrine of European sovereignty; instead, it has built a doctrine of supremacy or primacy which presupposed sovereignty of the European legal order,[30] and it has completed it with its doctrine on the autonomy of the EU legal order, expressed in Opinion 2/13.[31] This autonomy 'obsession' is, together with primacy, nothing but the sovereignty doctrine of the Court of Justice.[32]

Opposed to this, and departing from the dialogue narrative, the conflict of sovereignty is a process of competition between actors in sovereignty claims and open contestation between authorities;[33] these processes emerged dramatically after the enlargement of 2004, the Treaty of Lisbon and also as a consequence of the rise of neo-sovereigntist and populist politics, which increasingly contest

[28] B De Witte, 'Direct Effect, Primacy and the Nature of the Legal Order' in P Craig and G de Búrca (eds), *The Evolution of EU Law* (Oxford University Press, 2021) 187.

[29] The literature is vast. For some references, see N MacCormick, 'The Maastricht-Urteil: Sovereignty Now' (1995) 1 *European Law Journal* 259; N Walker, 'The Idea of Constitutional Pluralism' [2002] *MLR* 317; M Poiares Maduro, 'Contrapunctual Law: Europe's Constitutional Pluralism in Action' in N Walker (ed), *Sovereignty in Transition* (Hart Publishing, 2003) 501–38; A Bobić, 'Constitutional Pluralism Is Not Dead: An Analysis of Interactions between Constitutional Courts of Member States and the European Court of Justice' (2017) 18 *German Law Journal* 1395.

[30] G de Búrca, 'Sovereignty and the Supremacy Doctrine of the European Court of Justice' in Walker (n 29) 449–60.

[31] See, *ex multis*, D Halberstam, '"It's the Autonomy, Stupid!" A Modest Defense of Opinion 2/13 on EU Accession to the ECHR, and the Way Forward' (2015) 16 *German Law Journal* 105.

[32] C Eckes, 'EU Autonomy: Jurisdictional Sovereignty by a Different Name?' (2020) 5 *European Papers* 319.

[33] RD Kelemen, P Eeckhout, F Fabbrini, L Pech and R Uitz, 'National Courts Cannot Override CJEU Judgments: A Joint Statement in Defense of the EU Legal Order' (*Verfassungsblog*, 26 May 2020).

the process of European integration and the EU in general. The Treaty of Lisbon provided the toolkit for the emergence of conflicts of sovereignty and processes of contestation between the supranational and national constituencies of the Union: Article 50 TEU and Article 4(2) TEU are cases in point.[34] It is not by chance that Hungary and Poland have become big sponsors of constitutional identity and constitutional pluralism, though the meanings they give to these concepts are foreign to European constitutionalism.[35]

Against this background of 'old and new sovereignisms' that are gaining ground on the political and legal stage of the EU,[36] it is argued here that the policy domains considered have become the object of conflicts of sovereignty. The element defining a conflict of sovereignty is the challenge towards the source of authority. One prime example is given by the *Weiss* judgment of the German Federal Constitutional Court (Bundesverfassungsgericht, BVerfG) on the Public Sector Purchase Programme (PSPP) of 5 May 2020,[37] but also the conduct of countries such as Hungary in the context of its migration control policies enacted in the aftermath of the refugee crisis represents a (politically driven) legal conflict of sovereignty.

The *Weiss* judgment of the BVerfG is a judgment of a court that is aware of creating a conflict of sovereignty, because it had declared as ultra vires and not applicable in Germany the judgment of the CJEU in *Weiss* and also the decisions adopted by the European Central Bank on the PSPP. The BVerfG used its own domestic interpretation of the principle of proportionality to question the legitimacy of the reasoning of the CJEU.[38] Secondly, the BVerfG refrained from interrogating the European Court a second time, but questioned the interpretation of the CJEU on EU law and stated that some parts of the CJEU's judgment in *Weiss* were ultra vires:[39] thus, it has approached the CJEU in a hostile way, in

[34] About Art 50 TEU, see D Dixon, 'Article 50 and Member State Sovereignty' (2018) 19 *German Law Journal* 901. About Art 4(2) TEU, see M Dobbs, 'Sovereignty, Article 4(2) TEU and the Respect of National Identities: Swinging the Balance in Favour of the Member States?' (2014) 33 *Yearbook of European Law* 298.

[35] As observed, there is a growing political dimension in these conflicts. See N Brack, R Coman and A Crespy, 'Unpacking Old and New Conflicts of Sovereignty in the European Polity' (2019) 41 *Journal of European Integration* 817, 818.

[36] See G Halmai, 'Abuse of Constitutional Identity. The Hungarian Constitutional Court on Interpretation of Article E) (2) of the Fundamental Law' (2018) 43 *Review of Central and East European Law* 36; RD Kelemen and L Pech, 'Why Autocrats Love Constitutional Identity and Constitutional Pluralism? Lessons from Hungary and Poland' (September 2018) Reconnect Working Paper No 2.

[37] BVerfG, Judgment of the Second Senate of 5 May 2020 – 2 BvR 859/15, paras 1–237.

[38] This would not amount to a breach of one of the contrapunctual law principles formulated by Poiares Maduro (n 29).

[39] Section 119 states as follows: 'In its Judgment of 11 December 2018, the CJEU held that the Decision of the ECB Governing Council on the PSPP and its subsequent amendments were still within the ambit of the ECB's competences (see aa below). This view manifestly fails to give consideration to the importance and scope of the principle of proportionality (Art 5(1) second sentence and Art 5(4) TEU), which also applies to the division of competences, and is no longer tenable from a methodological perspective given that it completely disregards the actual effects of the PSPP (see bb below).

a clear denial of the CJEU's competence to interpret EU law. The uncooperative model chosen by the BVerfG makes this judgment a conflict of sovereignty. The reaction of the Court of Justice, with the most assertive press release of the story of European integration, witnesses this conflict touching upon the primacy of EU law. Recently, the Commission has initiated an infringement procedure, an approach that has been advocated in scholarship.[40] Therefore, by choosing to refrain from activating a second preliminary reference to the CJEU, the BVerfG has chosen a conflictual approach, in a clear denial of the CJEU's role as *primus inter pares*, ie as the first European law court.[41] With the judgment on the PSPP, the German Federal Constitutional Court chose an uncooperative model, and a contentious attitude towards the European higher court, unlike what has happened in the Italian *Taricco* saga, for example.[42]

In the context of new sovereigntists, instead, the challenges to the EU and its sovereignty are caused by illiberal governments, with Poland and Hungary heading the group. Populist governments challenge the core elements of the EU legal system (liberal constitutionalism, rule of law, primacy) on many occasions and aspects, be it Poland, with political control of the judiciary, or Hungary, with capture of its higher court and its approach to migration and asylum, to mention just some of the issues at stake. These states engaged in a conflictual and confrontational attitude with EU institutions, fuelling political conflicts which have been translated into legal battles.[43] In doing this, they became big sponsors of the notion of 'constitutional identity', used like a mantra to cover illiberal and unconstitutional measures, and of 'constitutional pluralism', which is deprived of its actual meaning if it lies in the hands of illiberal democracies. Domestic higher courts in these countries are now captured.[44] It is in these contexts that we observe conflicts of sovereignty, whose main explanation is to be found in a deliberate choice, by governments and (some) courts, for illiberalism and a contextual betrayal of the values of constitutionalism, both national and European.

Therefore, the Judgment of the CJEU of 11 December 2018 manifestly exceeds the mandate conferred upon it in Art 19(1) second sentence TEU, resulting in a structurally significant shift in the order of competences to the detriment of the Member States. To this extent, the CJEU Judgment itself constitutes an ultra vires act and thus has no binding effect [in Germany] (see cc below).'

[40] European Commission, June infringements package: key decisions, 9 June 2021, https://ec.europa.eu/commission/presscorner/detail/en/inf_21_2743; F Fabbrini, 'Suing the BVerfG' (*Verfassungsblog*, 13 May 2020); Kelemen et al (n 33).

[41] F Strumia, 'When Managed Recognition Turns into Outright Denial' (*Verfassungsblog*, 18 May 2020).

[42] CJEU, 8 September 2015, Case C-105/14 *Ivo Taricco and others* ECLI:EU:C:2015:555; the judgment caused the reaction of the Italian Constitutional Court (ICC), with Order No 24 of 2017; later on, the CJEU returned to its case law with CJEU, 5 December 2017, Case C-42/17 *MAS e MB* ECLI:EU:C:2017:936; the saga has been closed by the ICC with judgment No 115 of 2018.

[43] I Goldner Lang, 'No Solidarity without Loyalty: Why Do Member States Violate EU Migration and Asylum Law and What Can Be Done?' (2020) 2 *European Journal of Migration and Law* 39.

[44] G Halmai, 'Dismantling Constitutional Review in Hungary' (*Rivista di diritti comparati*, 15 February 2019).

For example, in Hungary, the conflict of sovereignty which emerged in the context of the arrival of asylum seekers has been deliberately fuelled by the government, which refused to be among the beneficiaries of the relocation decisions.[45] For a long time now, the government has challenged the EU's competences – for example, with the migrant quota referendum of 2016[46] – and has not properly implemented instruments of asylum law.[47] In the Hungarian case, the refugee crisis intersects with the rule of law crisis: as well as being a by-product of incomplete integration, in the sense of a system where ultimately states are left to deal with the consequences of migration based on geographical criteria, this crisis is also a choice enabled by the incompleteness of the enforcement system of EU law, which structurally relies on Member States' bureaucracies to be implemented. Additionally, the Article 7 TEU procedure requires unanimity, with the exclusion from the vote of the Member State concerned. More recently, Poland has added an episode to the conflict of sovereignty saga with judgment K 3/21 of the Polish Constitutional Tribunal of 7 October 2021,[48] in which Poland refuses *tout court* the primacy of EU law, offering another direct challenge to EU law and a blatant conflict of sovereignty.

If this section shows that conflicts of sovereignty are increasing, concern different types of actors and are based on a multitude of rationales, it must be acknowledged that the preference expressed since the Treaty of Maastricht for limited transfers of competences to the EU, in a context of limited administrative and substantive integration, has shown some limitations: indeed, incomplete integration processes bring with them conflicts of sovereignty on the definition of the boundaries of the transfer of sovereignty, or on the implications of asymmetric integration process on a state's competences. Additionally, if incomplete integration does not replace the provision of domestic common goods with supranational ones, it might create disequilibria that could and should be fixed with the flexibility of the system, which is one of the functions performed by the principle of solidarity. The next section will elaborate on the principle of solidarity within the legal system of the EU.

[45] L Marin, 'Governing Asylum with (or without) Solidarity? The Difficult Path of Relocation Schemes, Between Enforcement and Contestation' (2019) No 1 *Freedom, Security & Justice: European Legal Studies* 55.

[46] T Gessler, 'The 2016 Referendum in Hungary' [2017] *East European Quarterly* 85.

[47] See, eg the case law of the Court of Justice on the failures of the Hungarian reception centres. See L Marin, 'La Corte di Giustizia riporta le "zone di transito" ungheresi dentro il perimetro del diritto (Europeo) e dei diritti (fondamentali)' in A Bufalini, G Del Turco, FL Gatta, M Savino, FV Virzì and D Vitiello (eds), *Annuario ADiM 2020: raccolta di scritti di diritto dell'immigrazione* (Editoriale scientifica, 2021) 696–705.

[48] The judgment is published in Poland's Official Gazette of 12 October 2021. See H Hofmann, 'Sealed, Stamped and Delivered. The Publication of the Polish Constitutional Court's Judgment on EU Law Primacy as Notification of Intent to Withdraw under Art 50 TEU?' (*Verfassungsblog*, 13 October 2021).

4.3. 'One, No One and One Hundred Thousand':[49] Is There a Core Meaning for the Principle of Solidarity in EU Law?

4.3.1. What Solidarity for the EU?

The principle of solidarity is having a crucial but complex life in the context of the EU. It is a general principle of the EU, to be found in core Treaty provisions, as well as in the case law of the Court of Justice, and it is invoked by political actors and policymakers during crises. Yet its precise legal meaning as a general principle of EU law is not fully clear; this affects its justiciability. At the same time, in the last few years we have been able to observe difficulties in translating this legal principle into solidarity-driven policies and legal instruments. Though it is acknowledged that solidarity policies and practices can be contingent upon context-related factors,[50] it is here suggested that the COVID-19 crisis can be considered a learning point for European governance and can teach us something new as to the nature of the principle of solidarity within the EU.

The principle of solidarity permeates the founding provisions of EU law, since it is enshrined in the Treaties and in the Charter of Fundamental Rights, as one of the overarching themes inspiring the rights of the Charter. Together with fairness, (mutual) trust and loyal cooperation, it is a core principle and rule governing the European legal system, not only as a legal principle, but also as a social value of the European construction and integration.[51]

In the Treaties, solidarity finds its place among the founding values of the EU (Article 2 TEU), as a value common to the Member States and permeating European societies.[52] Solidarity is also a core tenet of market integration, one of the founding values of the internal market (Article 3 TEU) and a guiding principle of the relations of the EU with the wider world (Article 3(5) TEU). In all these instances, alongside a core meaning, the principle has different implications, be it intergenerational solidarity, solidarity of the EU towards the international community (Article 21 TEU) or solidarity between Member States (Article 24(2) TEU), but also in the peculiar meaning of solidarity from the Member States towards the EU (Article 24(3) TEU). The principle of solidarity also permeates other policies of the EU, notably asylum and migration (Articles 67 and 80 TFEU),

[49] The reference is to L Pirandello's novel about Vitangelo Moscarda, who decides to break up his life to distance himself from all the perceptions others have about him.

[50] P Genschel and M. Jachtenfuchs, 'Postfunctionalism Reversed: Solidarity and Rebordering during the COVID-19 Pandemic' (2021) 28 *Journal of European Public Policy* 350.

[51] S Morano-Foadi, 'Solidarity and Responsibility: Advancing Humanitarian Responses to EU Migratory Pressures' (2017) 19 *European Journal of Migration and Law* 223, 227.

[52] G Morgese, 'Solidarietà di fatto … e di diritto? L'Unione europea allo specchio della crisi pandemica' [2020] *Eurojus* special issue 'L'emergenza sanitaria COVID-19 e il diritto dell'Unione europea. La crisi, la cura, le prospettive' 77.

but also economic policy (Article 122 TFEU), without forgetting, of course, the solidarity clause in the case of a terrorist attack or a natural or man-made disaster (Article 222 TFEU).

Solidarity has different meanings across policies, and presupposes multiple situations and relations involving both state and institutional actors (at all levels), and individuals and human beings more generally. Within the EU, at this historical moment, there are two crucial questions: one concerns the emergence of a vertical dimension of solidarity, ie solidarity from the Union to the Member States in crisis situations; the second one, which is an effect of the first one, is the complex affirmation of a redistributive effect of wealth between Member States across national constituencies, since the EU does not have autonomous taxation powers.

In the international context, the most classical situation is solidarity between states, or negative solidarity, which is the more embryonal meaning of solidarity, and it applies to the extent that it is legally appropriate in the context of existing intergovernmental contracts.[53] In this context, the fiscal consequences of solidarity are considered more important than the social ones. In this line of reasoning, negative solidarity has few chances to increase political and social integration; on the contrary, it can result in desolidarisation and disintegration. Within a supranational integration context such as the European one, solidarity is emancipating itself from this international framing, but it has not yet developed as a general principle of EU law, having a thick legal meaning across policies. In the context of the internal market, with the case law on European citizenship, we have witnessed the challenges of the emergence of a transnational dimension of solidarity having a social content,[54] and this can be seen even more in the context of migration and asylum. The apex of complexity is reached when the addressees of solidarity are citizens of third states.[55] All in all, solidarity as a legal principle of the EU displays effects on multiple types of relations, and if the most classical paradigm is the one operating between Member States, the most complex ones entail forms of redistributive effects, which are not adequately dealt with within the current institutional structures and procedural mechanisms of the EU.[56] An interesting alternative might be to frame solidarity as a corrective flexibility provision of the

[53] P Trein, 'Federal Dynamics, Solidarity, and European Union Crisis Politics' (2020) 29 *Journal of European Public Policy* 980. According to Trein, negative and positive solidarity can be defined as follows: 'In short, negative solidarity entails that governments consider solidarity only appropriate in the strict sense of existing intergovernmental contracts and that fiscal consequences should have priority over social consequences. Positive solidarity means that actors regard solidarity morally appropriate, even if it goes beyond existing intergovernmental contracts, and give priority of social consequences over fiscal consequences.'

[54] A Sangiovanni, 'Solidarity in the EU' (2013) 33 *OJLS* 213; S Giubboni, 'La solidarietà come scudo. Il tramonto della cittadinanza sociale transnazionale nella crisi europea' (2018) 38 *Quaderni costituzionali* 591.

[55] *cf* Art 67 TFEU enshrining the principle of fairness towards TCNs.

[56] P Eleftheriadis, 'Corrective Justice among States' (2020) 2 *Jus Cogens* 7. See also Sangiovanni (n 54).

EU legal system, a clause which should at least entail a corrective dimension of the disparities and asymmetries consolidated by incomplete integration processes.

The following section will expound on the core meaning of solidarity as a crisis management tool.

4.3.2. The Challenges of Transnational Solidarity as a Crisis Management Tool: Lessons from the Eurozone and Refugee Crises

As explained above, with the EMU a single currency has been built, but fiscal and economic policies have been left in the hands of the Member States. In short, the EU has been entrusted by states with limited instruments to govern the economic aspects connected with this currency, and vice versa: states have lost control of their monetary policies, and were bound, until COVID-19,[57] by the rules of the Stability and Growth Pact. This combination made it a non-optimal currency area, since this decoupling between monetary and economic policies can create uneven distributive effects within it.[58] The constraints of the Stability and Growth Pact have long hindered countercyclical fiscal policies in the countries where they were needed most.

This was observed in all its consequences during the financial crisis of 2008, which further amplified the internal imbalances between Member States' 'debtors' and 'creditors'. The so-called 'debtor countries' could not adopt counter-recessive policies because of the limits on public debt; not having a monetary policy to use, they felt 'their hands were tied'. This had multiple negative effects, since it contributed to the nurturing of anti-Europe movements in many countries, while, at another level, it contributed to creating poverty and social tensions in some countries, such as Greece.

In this context, solidarity has played an important role, and it was invoked after the crisis had demonstrated the pitfalls in the design of the single currency. Solidarity has been invoked to create mechanisms to compensate for the consequences of the 'fundamental disequilibrium' that emerged within the single currency zone. After the crisis, and when it became evident that the monetary union had exacerbated the differences existing before the integration project, 'creditor' states became aware of the necessity to assist the most badly affected states, such as Greece, Ireland, Portugal, Spain and Cyprus, via emergency loans.

[57] The Pact provides for a general escape clause that was activated at the outbreak of the pandemic. See the Statement of EU Ministers of Finance on the Stability and Growth Pact in Light of the COVID-19 Crisis of 23 March 2020.

[58] K Rogoff has stated that the problem at the heart of the euro crisis is that 'the Eurozone is a half-built house' and that it was a 'catastrophic mistake to put the monetary union ahead of fiscal and political union': K Rogoff, 'Crash Time', quoted by Eleftheriadis, 'Solidarity in the Eurozone' (n 19) 29–30.

These corrective justice instruments were sought outside the Treaty framework, with the European Stability Mechanism (ESM), enabled by a modification of Article 136 TFEU. The ESM was operating on the basis of stringent conditionality, an expression of the crisis which originated the measures. Notwithstanding the constraints imposed by the Treaties – prohibition of transfer union – the Member States agreed to activate a solidarity mechanism strongly framed by conditionality, because of context-specific aspects, such as distrust towards Greece.

Incomplete integration, on the one side, can create conflicts of sovereignty; on the other side, it creates externalities that should be addressed with solidarity inspired at least by a paradigm of correction of disparities and asymmetries created or consolidated by EU law.

The second example considered comes from the refugee crisis, which has witnessed the experimentation of emergency-driven solidarity in reply to the surge in irregular migration fluxes. Here, in contrast to the EMU, solidarity is strongly embedded in the Treaties (Articles 67, 78 and 80 TFEU) as a guiding principle, together with fair sharing of responsibility, especially as an expression of interstate solidarity and responsibility. It has an external aspect as well, in the sense that in the relations towards third country nationals it expresses one of the founding values of the EU, which also finds applications in the external dimension of EU policies, as stated in Article 3(5) and Article 21 TEU.[59] However, while the Treaties posit solidarity as a systemic value underlying the foundations of the EU, its actual realisation has been more complex.[60]

The translation of the principle of solidarity into policies and practices of solidarity has been a tortuous exercise in the last few years.[61] The 2015 refugee crisis revealed itself as a European governance crisis, in the sense that it showed the weakness of EU policies on migration, borders and asylum, based on a codification of existing asymmetries. By keeping in place many diverse national reception and asylum systems, largely working according to different rules and standards, the EU has done nothing but consolidate existing geographical asymmetries between states. The creation of a common external border, based on the juxtaposition of many national parcels of borders, has wrongly given the illusion that, by consolidating the external dimension of border controls, the internal dimension of integration could have been safeguarded. Yet, Schengen is 'in check' because of the unresolved dilemmas of the asylum system.

In 2015, the Council adopted two decisions establishing a temporary and mandatory system of relocations of asylum applicants to the benefit of Greece

[59] Morano-Foadi (n 51); V Moreno Lax, 'Solidarity's Reach: Meaning, Dimensions and Implications for EU (External) Asylum Policy' (2017) 24 *Maastricht Journal of European and Comparative Law* 756.

[60] L Marin, 'Waiting (and Paying) for Godot: Analyzing the Systemic Consequences of the Solidarity Crisis in EU Asylum Law' (2020) No 1 *European Journal of Migration and Law* 60.

[61] Morano-Foadi (n 51); E Tsourdi, 'Solidarity at Work? The Prevalence of Emergency-Driven Solidarity in the Administrative Governance of the Common European Asylum System' (2017) 24 *Maastricht Journal of European and Comparative Law* 667.

and Italy, which were the countries most concerned by migration fluxes, together with Hungary.[62] This latter country should originally have been among the beneficiaries of the measures, but it opposed this, preferring to be among the countries compelled to take a quota of migrants to be relocated. It probably did so in order to have the grounds to engage in a political sovereignty conflict with the EU. Overall, the system of relocations did not work: irrespective of the opposition of the Visegrad states, which led to litigation before the Court of Justice,[63] few relocations have been arranged, even among countries that supported the system.[64] This is due to the difficulties of getting administrations of different countries to communicate and cooperate.

Why does the governance crisis of the asylum system look so complex? Political scientists argue that states have few incentives to change the status quo, since most of them can enjoy the advantages given by the codification of original asymmetries.[65] Thus, in this context, solidarity has the function of correcting structural inequalities, codified in the first entry criterion, which is still one of the core principles of the European asylum system.[66] Solidarity therefore has a corrective dimension here too, in the sense that it aims to compensate for the consequences of structural asymmetries which consolidate the inequalities of the system. However, since the consequences of a fully fledged competence of the EU on asylum would affect domestic welfare systems, states are reluctant to cede sovereignty on what they see as core state powers. The COVID-19 crisis has also reverberated on the governance of asylum, with domestic lockdowns and 'closed port' practices complicating disembarkation and reception of asylum seekers and migrants while assuring quarantine for the same.[67] To sum up, neither before

[62] Council Decisions (EU) 2015/1523 of 14 September 2015 and 2015/1601 of 22 September 2015, establishing provisional measures in the area of international protection for the benefit of Italy and Greece [2015] OJ L248/80.

[63] CJEU (GC), Judgment of 6 September 2017, Joined Cases C-643/15 and C-647/15 *Slovak Republic, Hungary v Council of the European Union* ECLI:EU:C:2017:631.

[64] For an assessment, see E Guild, C Costello and V Moreno Lax, 'Implementation of the 2015 Council Decisions Establishing Provisional Measures in the Area of International Protection for the Benefit of Italy and of Greece' (EP Studies, 2017).

[65] N Zaun, 'States as Gatekeepers in EU Asylum Politics: Explaining the Non-adoption of a Refugee Quota System' (2018) 56 *Journal of Common Market Studies* 44; S Lavenex, 'Failing Forward towards Which Europe? Organized Hypocrisy in the Common European Asylum System' (2018) 56 *Journal of Common Market Studies* 1195.

[66] Despite attempts to reform and adjust the situation already with the Juncker Commission, by focusing on the legislation (for example, the Dublin Regulation and the 2016 reform proposal) and with relocations, many issues linked with the imbalances created by the systems originally in place and by secondary movements remained unsolved. The new Pact on Migration and Asylum recently proposed by the von der Leyen Commission in September 2020 again had to face challenges concerning the realisation of forms of solidarity within the EU asylum system.

[67] L Marin, 'The COVID-19 Crisis and the Closure of External Borders: Another Stress-Test for the Challenging Construction of Solidarity Within the EU?' (2020) 5 *European Forum/European Papers*; F Munari, 'Il decreto interministeriale per gestire l'emergenza COVID-19 nell'ambito degli obblighi dell'Italia ai sensi della convenzione SAR: l'insostenibile 'intermittenza' del luogo sicuro per i migranti diretti verso l'Italia' (*Quaderni di SIDIblog*, 16 April 2020); S Nicolosi, 'Non-refoulement During a Health Emergency' (*EJIL Talk*, 14 May 2020).

nor during the COVID-19 crisis did solidarity in asylum materialise beyond the emergency dimension,[68] and its implementation has been rather unsuccessful for various reasons.[69]

To conclude, solidarity entails a complex set of relations, vertically and horizontally. As to the state–individual relationship, a crucial challenge is that the beneficiaries of solidarity are third country nationals and not citizens of other Member States. On the horizontal side, the issue is that horizontal cooperation is motivated by a corrective justice rationale, which is, however, not adequately supported by the EU in organisation and financial terms. Hence, states are interested in limiting the external monitoring of their domestic systems.

4.4. Post-pandemic Solidarity: Towards a New Meaning of Solidarity within the EU?

4.4.1. Old-Fashioned Solidarity and its Limits

Former ECB president Mario Draghi has defined the coronavirus pandemic as a 'human tragedy of potentially biblical proportions',[70] and highlighted its economic consequences, namely an increase in public spending and the need to cancel private debts. Economists agreed quite readily that an external factor – a pandemic caused by a virus – has caused a massive symmetrical economic shock, the consequences of which, however, will be asymmetrical, both economically and socially.[71]

The type of crisis, its magnitude and its long-term effects were immediately clear, beyond the exact quantification of the 'damage' caused by the corona pandemic. It is precisely because of the unprecedented nature of this challenge that some leading scholars immediately pointed to the necessity of finding solutions by thinking outside the box, thus intervening in a debate that was already showing a high level of polarisation.[72] This perspective was put on the table after politicians had taken the first steps towards tackling the corona crisis with the same toolkit that had been used for the sovereign debt crisis, which hinged on the ESM.[73] The ESM has been controversial because it was based on a 'strict conditionality' and it

[68] Tsourdi, 'Solidarity at Work? (n 61); see also E Tsourdi, 'COVID-19, Asylum in the EU, and the Great Expectations of Solidarity' (*Kaldor Centre for International Refugee Law blogpost*, 28 April 2020).

[69] Guild et al (n 64).

[70] Draghi (n 2).

[71] See also Commission, 'Summer 2020 Economic Forecast: Overview. A Deeper Recession with Wider Divergences' (7 July 2020).

[72] C Closa, G Papaconstantinou and M Poiares Maduro, 'EU and COVID-19: Time to Think Outside the Box' (*Euractiv*, 21 April 2020).

[73] For a full account of the evolution of the political debate, see Genschel and Jachtenfuchs, 'Postfunctionalism Reversed' (n 50).

was constituted of loans; additionally, it has been associated with economic policies based on austerity and focused on the reduction of public debt. This recipe has caused severe economic consequences in several states, and additional tragic social consequences in Greece,[74] as recognised even by the troika;[75] furthermore, this approach has been seen as unfit for the crisis caused by the COVID pandemic.[76]

The European answer to counter the economic crisis caused by the corona crisis took shape with an initial emergency package and a long-term response, developed over a longer time frame.

As mentioned in section 4.1 above, the first emergency package consisted of the Pandemic Crisis Support (PCS) of the ESM, of up to €240 billion, and SURE,[77] of €100 billion, to be funded from loans raised by the Commission against the EU budget, with Member States' guarantees as collateral. In particular, the PCS, decided by the Eurogroup on 9 April 2020 and finalised and made operational with a decision of the ESM Board of Governors on 15 May 2020, was based on the existing Enhanced Conditions Credit Line – a precautionary credit line that grants access to credit up to a maximum of 2 per cent of the respective Member State's GDP. The measure follows the provisions of the ESM Treaty, and the funds are to be made available within two weeks after the request by a state. The credit will be available until the COVID-19 crisis is over and in any case until the end of 2022. So far, no state has requested to activate this line of support.

Another consequence of the economic crisis caused by the pandemic has been the necessity to activate instruments to protect the labour markets, with measures such as wage support funds or other solidarity measures for self-employed people. SURE aimed to mitigate the risks of unemployment and constitutes a loan programme to support Member States. The €100 billion are first borrowed by the EU on the financial markets, and the EU retains the primary responsibility to repay its loans in case of default by a state on repayment of its own loans to the EU. However, the Member States are invited to contribute to the instrument by voluntarily counter-guaranteeing the EU's risk. The SURE Regulation required that €25 billion had to be guaranteed by states in order to make SURE available, without requiring upfront financial contributions by states. The instrument became operational in September 2020, and 19 states have already received support, with a

[74] UN High Commissioner for Human Rights, Greece: '"Troika Bailout Conditions Are Undermining Human Rights," Warns UN Expert on Debt and Human Rights' (Press Release, 1 May 2013); E Doxiadis and A Placas (eds), *Living Under Austerity: Greek Society in Crisis* (Berghahn Books, 2018).

[75] L Papadimas and R Maltezou, 'For Hard-hit Greeks, IMF Mea Culpa Comes Too Late' (*Reuters.com*, 6 June 2013).

[76] See D Gros, 'EU Solidarity in Exceptional Times: Corona Transfers Instead of Coronabonds' (*VoxEU*, 5 April 2020); D Furceri, P Loungani, JD Ostry and P Pizzuto, 'Fiscal Austerity Intensifies the Increase in Inequality after Pandemics' (*VoxEU*, 3 June 2021).

[77] Council Regulation (EU) 2020/672 of 19 May 2020 on the establishment of a European instrument for temporary support to mitigate unemployment risks in an emergency (SURE) following the COVID-19 outbreak [2020] OJ L159/1.

total amount of €91.8 billion disbursed (as of March 2022).[78] In practice, SURE has given states access to low-interest loans; it is based on the EU budget, and the EU borrows the funds on the financial markets, guaranteeing it with the emission of bonds. The reputation of the EU protects states in a position of need, and therefore SURE constitutes an expression of solidarity (its legal basis is Article 122 TFEU) which entails mutualisation of risks between states.[79]

This process of mutualisation of risks has become central to the core instrument designed by the EU to counter the COVID-19 crisis, which is the Next Generation EU (NGEU) initiative. This instrument represents a change of paradigm that has been strongly invoked by some states, such as Italy, which were persuaded that the previous toolkit – ie the ESM, based on strong conditionality – was insufficient to address the economic crisis caused by the pandemic.

4.4.2. The 'Boosted' Solidarity of Next Generation EU: The Hamiltonian Moment of European Integration?

The long-term recovery fund has materialised with the NGEU initiative, which has been defined as the 'Hamiltonian moment' of the European Union.[80] In reality, it is a temporary instrument meant to boost recovery and to create a long-term resilience, in harmony with the European Green Deal and with the digital agenda, and adopted in an effort towards systemic solidarity to react to the heavy economic legacy of the pandemic.[81] Additionally, the NGEU represents the long-awaited alternative to the contentious corona-bonds, strongly supported by some states and steadfastly opposed by others. Beyond the political dimension, the legal road for corona-bonds might have been a tortuous one: being a form of debt mutualisation, corona-bonds might require a Treaty reform; additionally, in some cases, constitutional constraints at domestic level might have further hindered the process.[82]

Instead, with the NGEU, states have agreed on a recovery plan, which represents a change of paradigm for its size, composition and design. With a total size of €750 billion, the NGEU represents the most significant financial effort undertaken

[78] European Commission, official information page on the SURE instrument, https://ec.europa.eu/info/business-economy-euro/economic-and-fiscal-policy-coordination/financial-assistance-eu/funding-mechanisms-and-facilities/sure_en.

[79] S Giubboni, 'Crisi pandemica e solidarietà europea' (2021) 41(1) *Quaderni costituzionali* 218.

[80] German Finance Minister O Scholtz referred to A Hamilton, who, in 1790, together with Madison and Jefferson, persuaded the American states to agree to a new national capital in return for the federal government taking over their war debts.

[81] Commission, 'Recovery Plan for Europe', https://ec.europa.eu/info/strategy/recovery-plan-europe_en.

[82] In addition to the well-known position of the German BVerfG, see also the Finnish case described by P Päivi Leino-Sandberg, 'Solidarity and Constitutional Constraints in Times of Crisis' (*Verfassungsblog*, 8 April 2020).

by the EU so far, considering that the yearly amount of the total EU expenditure for 2020 was €155.4 billion, for example.[83] Its final composition combines €390 billion in grants or subsidies with loans of €360 billion.[84] The initial proposal of the Commission was for €500 billion for the grant component and €250 billion for the loans, but this was met with criticism from the 'frugal countries' (Austria, the Netherlands, Denmark and Sweden, often joined by Finland). The final distribution is still momentous in symbolic terms, because the subsidy component remains larger than the loans. Within the NGEU, the Recovery and Resilience Facility (RRF) amounts to €672.5 billion, and is the most innovative and significant (post-corona) funding scheme the EU has adopted so far. As already happened before, this funding is an expression of conditionality, in the sense that the Member State must submit a plan of economic reform (the National Recovery and Resilience Plan) to the Commission, and this must be approved by the Council. These plans must be in line with the recommendations of the European Semester.

Considering the constitutional constraints imposed by the Treaties, most notably the no bail out clause of Article 125 TFEU, which prohibits the EU from 'saving states', on the one side, and the principle of the budgetary balance enshrined in Article 310 TFEU, which states that the EU cannot take out loans,[85] on the other, the NGEU has been grounded on a creative legal solution. The idea has been to link the NGEU initiative to the European budget by massively expanding it, and by financing the NGEU through the long-term issuance of debt on the financial markets by the Commission on behalf of the EU. The debt would be repaid through the EU budget between 2028 and 2058, so over a potentially long time period. To some extent, the road to the NGEU was paved by the German Constitutional Court with the *Weiss* judgment of May 2020. Even without considering the size of the investments needed after the COVID-19 crisis, after that judgment, it became clear in several arenas, both European and national, that political institutions had to face their responsibilities and that the technical and monetary solutions – namely, the Outright Monetary Transactions (OMT) programme and other instruments, such as the PSPP, which could be considered as the blueprint for the PEPP, provided

[83] Council of the EU, 'EU Budget for 2020: Council Endorses Deal with Parliament' (Press Release, 25 November 2019), at https://www.consilium.europa.eu/en/press/press-releases/2019/11/25/eu-budget-for-2020-council-endorses-deal-with-parliament/. It is nevertheless worth observing that several EU states have topped the EU funding with internal recovery instruments. For Germany, the Konjunkturpaket, known as the Wumms Recovery Plan, amounts to 130 billion euros, which is the 3.8% of the German GDP. Source: Innovation and R&D in COVID-19 Recovery Plans: The Case of France, Germany and Italy, at https://www.ofce.sciences-po.fr/blog/innovation-and-rd-in-covid-19-recovery-plans-the-case-of-france-germany-and-italy/.

[84] Commission, 'EU's Next Long-Term Budget & NextGenerationEU: Key Facts and Figures' (November 2020) https://ec.europa.eu/info/sites/default/files/about_the_european_commission/eu_budget/mff_factsheet_agreement_en_web_20.11.pdf.

[85] GL Tosato, 'The Union's Budget Balance Pursuant to Art. 310 TFEU: What Is the Impact on European Anti-coronavirus Measures?' (17 April 2020) Luiss SEP Policy Brief 21/2020. On the legal dimension of EU public finance law, see also B De Witte, 'The European Union's COVID-19 Recovery Plan: The Legal Engineering of an Economic Policy Shift' (2021) 58 *CML Rev* 635, 659ff.

earlier on by the ECB under the presidency of Mario Draghi – could have led to constitutional challenges, especially in some states, like Germany.[86] So, without a Treaty reform, the European Commission has tabled proposals for two regulations, the European Union Recovery Instrument Regulation[87] and the Recovery and Resilience Facility (RRF) Regulation,[88] and the Own Resources Decision (ORD),[89] which empowers the Commission to borrow funds on the financial markets and provides for the overall volume of the EU's liabilities and the essential conditions for the repayment. The ORD included an agreement on an exceptional and temporary increase of the EU's own resources ceiling by 0.6 per cent of the GNI of all the Member States, which is reserved upfront to pay back the NGEU debt. The function of the Recovery Instrument Regulation is to allocate the proceeds of the borrowing on the markets to different control measures and programmes it indicates, and for this reason has been defined as the 'control room' of the overall system,[90] whereas the RRF Regulation governs the functioning of this brand new funding scheme, inspired by solidarity in recovery after the crisis, but also by a long-term EU vision of resilience, which finds expression in the connection of the RRF with the existing plans of the Commission for digital and sustainable economic transitions. In other words, the European budget has been used as a shortcut for all the constitutional constraints that were in the process of being put in place and that, in some cases, were also framed as sovereignty conflicts.[91] Once again, in Germany there has been a constitutional challenge, this time by the extreme right party Alternative for Germany on the German ratification by Parliament of the ORD decision. Though a first interim decision of the BVerfG prohibited the Chair of the Bundestag from approving the ORD, two weeks later the court rejected the injunction on promulgation of the domestic act ratifying the European decision, thus giving its green light to ratification of the ORD.[92]

To sum up, we can conclude that the NGEU does not represent a federal treasury since it is guaranteed by the European budget, and it does not create a permanent system of mutualisation of outstanding debt. Furthermore, in order to

[86] F Costamagna, 'Il Next Generation EU e la costruzione di una politica economica europea: quale ruolo per democrazia e solidarietà?' (2021) III *I Post di AISDUE*.

[87] Council Regulation (EU) 2020/2094 of 14 December 2020 establishing a European Union Recovery Instrument to support the recovery in the aftermath of the COVID-19 crisis [2020] OJ L433I/23.

[88] Regulation (EU) 2021/241 of the European Parliament and of the Council of 12 February 2021 establishing the Recovery and Resilience Facility [2021] OJ L57/17.

[89] Council Decision (EU, Euratom) 2020/2053 of 14 December 2020 on the system of own resources of the European Union and repealing Decision 2014/335/EU, Euratom [2020] OJ L424/1.

[90] A de Gregorio Merino, 'The Recovery Plan: Solidarity and the Living Constitution' (*EULAWLive*, 6 May 2021) 4.

[91] On these aspects, see De Witte, 'The European Union's COVID-19 Recovery Plan (n 85); de Gregorio Merino (n 90). For example, the German Constitutional Court has rejected a challenge on the RRF.

[92] BVerfG, Order of 15 April 2021, 2 BvR 547/21. See also the press release of the Court: 'Unsuccessful Application for Preliminary Injunction against Promulgation of the Domestic Act Ratifying the EU Own Resources Decision ('EU Recovery Package')', Press Release No 29/2021 (21 April 2021).

represent a truly Hamiltonian moment it should also be matched by autonomous taxation competence of the EU; instead, the Own Resources Decision of the EU budget is actually composed of transfers or contributions from the Member States. In other words, the EU's own resources are in reality transferred resources.[93] For these reasons, the NGEU is not linked to the emergence of a fiscal capacity of the EU, nor to the creation of a European taxation power or to Eurobonds, long discussed in the aftermath of the euro-crisis, but unacceptable for some countries. Nevertheless, with the NGEU, solidarity is manifested in the liability dimension of the funding instruments.[94] The borrowing on the capital markets is guaranteed by the EU budget. Therefore, the COVID-19 recovery fund makes a clear step in the direction of politically supported interstate and systemic solidarity in the sense of debt and risk mutualisation.

4.5. Conclusions: What Did the COVID-19 Crisis Teach Us about the European Principle of Solidarity?

Being a common value of European society, solidarity was recognised as a founding value of the European Union in Article 2 TEU, together with pluralism, non-discrimination, tolerance, justice and equality between women and men, which are all framed as values common to European society. Its meaning as a legal principle and as an expression of a value is also recognised in several provisions in the Treaties, though its content and definition are far from being delineated precisely in their normative details and contours. However, despite some vagueness in its normative identity, amply recognised in the literature,[95] solidarity has a polymorphic dimension as a legal principle because the same Treaties codify different meanings of the principle of solidarity. This implies a variety of relational dimensions as well, be it solidarity of the Union with the Member States or among the Member States, or even solidarity between generations, just to give some examples of how the Treaties codify solidarity. Considering the context of European integration, it is here argued that solidarity has a systemic meaning, in the sense that it also concerns the citizens of the Member States as beneficiaries of solidarity in its transnational dimension,[96] and, in the contexts of asylum and migration, protection seekers and third country nationals more generally.[97]

[93] See also De Witte, 'The European Union's COVID-19 Recovery Plan' (n 85) 660; D Rinoldi, 'BILANCIO UE/La battaglia Parlamento-Consiglio in arrivo a settembre' (*Il Sussidiario*, 27 July 2020).

[94] As argued by T van den Brink and M Gargantini, 'Models of Solidarity in the EMU. The Impact of COVID-19 after Weiss' (2021) 17(3) *Utrecht Law Review* 80.

[95] See Morgese (n 52); E Küçük, 'Solidarity in EU Law: An Elusive Political Statement or a Legal Principle with Substance?' in A Biondi, E Dagilytė and E Küçük (eds), *Solidarity in EU Law: Legal Principle in the Making* (Edward Elgar Publishing, 2018).

[96] On this aspect, see Sangiovanni (n 54); Giubboni, 'La solidarietà come scudo' (n 54).

[97] Moreno Lax, 'Solidarity's Reach' (n 59).

In other words, proper consideration of the scope of integration suggests that solidarity has reached a transnational dimension, which is, however, far from being unproblematic. The case law of the Court of Justice reflects this variety, offering a kaleidoscopic panorama of visions and interpretations; for example, the same court is also not univocal in its propensity to rely in its reasoning on solidarity as a constitutional principle, at least giving it an operational meaning across the different Treaty pillars.[98]

However, in spite of this complexity, which goes beyond the scope of this work, I advance some interim conclusions on solidarity as a legal principle of EU law, elaborating on some common threads that can be found in the normative fabric of solidarity across the different policy domains and in the case law of the Court of Justice.

A first, preliminary observation one must, however, address is the – hopefully – exceptional nature of the COVID-19 crisis. Because of its magnitude and size, and because it is a crisis shared and spread across all the Member States, the EU has managed to give a response that, though linked with responsibility and conditionality, is nevertheless stating the capacity of the EU to react as an effective governance system, to a great extent protecting the public goods it has created, such as the euro and freedoms of movement.[99] Within this framework the principle of solidarity still plays a pivotal role.

I argue that the fact that solidarity does not have a univocal normative identity does not mean one cannot draw conclusions on some of the core features of solidarity as a core legal principle of the EU. First, it is a legal principle which has a programmatic nature, and needs to be translated into legislative instruments, where the legislator has a high degree of discretion on how to enact solidarity in the specific contexts considered. Secondly, it is closely connected with a principle of responsibility. Responsibility is often a counterpart of solidarity, and it concerns at least two dimensions: one from the beneficiary of solidarity towards the actors that give their solidarity, and that often place conditions on that solidarity: hence the conditionality a state must accept, as respect for parameters, reforms and values such as the rule of law. The other one runs in the opposite direction, from the actors that give solidarity towards the addressees, and here responsibility concerns the sharing of a common trajectory as well as the sharing of the fate of

[98] For example, in the context of relocation decisions, the CJEU has been reluctant to frame solidarity as the foundation of the system differently from what has been done by the Advocate General. Cf CJEU (n 63); Opinion of Advocate General Bot, delivered on 26 July 2017, Cases C 643/15 and C 647/15 *Slovak Republic, Hungary v Council of the European Union* ECLI:EU:C:2017:618. In contrast, in the domain of energy, the Court has recently judged that the principle of energy solidarity plays a fundamental role. See also CJEU, Case C-848/19 P *Germany v Poland* ECLI:EU:C:2021:598.

[99] As observed by several authors, such as Morgese (n 52); Genschel and Jachtenfuchs, 'Postfunctionalism Reversed' (n 50). In a different perspective, it should be observed that EU has managed to learn from its mistakes, perhaps also thanks to the painful Greek experience with the euro-crisis.

fellow states, as a consequence of the integration path taken together. It is precisely at this juncture that solidarity shows its very core, meaning its nature of a flexibility 'clause' in a governance system based on incomplete and open contracting,[100] as it is the system enacted with the Treaties which has provided for political and technical institutions. Furthermore, it has also been argued that the EU Treaties have set up situations of incomplete integration, as provided for in the contexts examined here.

However, irrespective of this 'agreed incompleteness', integration produces interdependences and also externalities. When these appear in all their effects, the principles of loyalty, together with solidarity and responsibility, require intervention to correct the negative effects created by integration. This corrective dimension of solidarity is a crucial aspect of its identity as a legal principle of EU law and it is inspired by principles of corrective justice.[101] The corrective justice dimension has been stressed as crucial in the context of the eurozone, because EMU has consolidated pre-existing asymmetries,[102] but the same narrative also applies in asylum and migration management. Integration with Schengen and the Dublin system has produced consolidation of pre-existing asymmetries, to the disadvantage of the most exposed countries, ie the frontline states. It is therefore of paramount importance that solidarity, which is a legal principle of the EU and which has a connotation of corrective justice, can be effective and address the unbalances already existing, and can also be consolidated by the policies adopted within the framework of EU law. This corrective justice dimension has been addressed properly in the case of the Next Generation EU, because of the provision for grants as well as loans, and also because of the link with EU guaranteed obligations, thus avoiding a massive increase in the public debt of states, which are in a less strong financial situation when they have been hit by the pandemic. This corrective justice dimension is therefore a crucial aspect of the principle of solidarity in EU law, and the COVID-19 pandemic has taught us that the higher the values of the goods at stake, the higher the interest in finding a political content to solidarity. The interdependence created with integration reveals a good component of self-interest in the choice for solidarity.

However, we could make some additional reflections in the perspective of relations between public authorities and individuals underlying the principle of solidarity. In particular, when EU law addresses authentic transnational relations having redistribution effects among citizens of different Member States, the political and legal salience of solidarity is higher.[103] This happens with similar dynamics in migration and asylum, from a twofold perspective. The first perspective is that of solidarity of a Member State towards an asylum seeker, ie a third country national.

[100] A Stone Sweet, 'The Court of Justice' in Craig and de Búrca (n 28).
[101] Eleftheriadis, 'Solidarity in the Eurozone' (n 19).
[102] ibid.
[103] See Küçük (n 95); Sangiovanni (n 54).

The second concerns the relation between the EU and Member States at this juncture of accepting the EU's competence in an area where the EU is getting close to becoming a core state power, like that of deciding who has access to a Member States' territory and welfare system. This case helps us to understand a crucial challenge in the development of the principle of solidarity in the EU, namely its redistributive effects and also its capacity to touch upon core states' values, in the sense of redefining the community of beneficiaries of a state measure.

The EU is in a critical phase of its life, and solidarity is confirming this picture. The EU is evolving from negative solidarity towards a more organic form of solidarity which can have redistributive effects across and within its communities, but this evolution is complex and full of politicisation. The governance of the EU, which in some areas is hindered by forms of inter-governmentalism and paralysed by veto powers,[104] contributes by fuelling these challenges.[105] What the corona crisis has taught us is that Member States are ready to engage in solidarity when the prize at stake is high and shared between states, albeit to different extents; in other words, when the challenge is common to several Member States, solidarity can be expressed as a positive form of solidarity and its heritage can also be high for European integration. The dimension of self-interest is also there, but it can be reconciled with altruism. This factor has contributed to defusing the political conflict about self-interest, with the exception of the persistent divergent visions of the 'frugal' states; consequently, this has contributed to limiting the conflict in this context, and to avoiding it turning into a sovereignty conflict, as has been experienced before.

[104] The declaration by Mark Rutte entering a European Council meeting with a book on Chopin epitomises this veto power. See 'Dutch Leader, Prepared for EU Summit Impasse, Brings Book to Read' (*Reuters*, 20 February 2020).

[105] See B De Witte, 'Constitutional Design of the European Union: Getting Rid of the Unanimity Rule, video recording of 'Conversations for the Future of Europe 2020', European University Institute.

5

Tracing Transparency: Public Governance of Algorithms and the Experience of Contact Tracing Apps

FRANCESCA PALMIOTTO ETTORRE*

5.1. Introduction

Contact tracing was considered one of the most effective tools to address the health emergency before the vaccination programme started. Initially carried out by human professionals, manual contact tracing covers the identification and tracking of people that have potentially been in contact with an infected person. The contacts are then asked to self-isolate and take a test if they develop symptoms. When entering the so-called 'Phase 2' of the COVID-19 crisis, many EU countries decided to enhance this tool through technology by developing contact tracing apps (CT apps). At the time of writing, most EU Member States have launched applications for proximity tracing.[1]

The use of these apps has also raised several concerns. Governments have used mobile phones to track contacts and movements and verify compliance with COVID-19 rules worldwide,[2] leading to the 'normalisation of surveillance'.[3] The amount of data collected by this means represents a powerful tool and, as such, is prone to misuse. During and after the pandemic, governments could use a sensitive database created by contact tracing for purposes unrelated to the management of the COVID-19 crisis, such as for policing or migration control. In the light of these risks, the use of digital contact tracing has attracted unprecedented political, academic and media attention. While opinions regarding which

* PhD researcher at European University Institute. I would like to thank Tommaso Fia for the revisions on the first draft of this chapter.

[1] More precisely, apps are live in 22 EU Member States. Last update 14 October 2021. For an updated list of apps in EU Member State, see http://archive.today/Y617G.

[2] 'The Rise of AI Surveillance' (*POLITICO*, 26 May 2021) www.politico.eu/article/the-rise-of-ai-surveillance-coronavirus-data-collection-tracking-facial-recognition-monitoring/.

[3] F Chiusi in ibid.

is the best technological solution to adopt differed vastly (centralised v decentralised system),[4] everybody agreed on the importance of one specific requirement of these apps: their transparency. As far as digital contact tracing is concerned, transparency has the ambition to increase trust by the users, enhance accountability, improve the security of the system and safeguard against abuses.

Scholars have often advocated transparency as a panacea solution against the adverse effects of algorithmic opacity.[5] Nevertheless, it also has shortcomings, as highlighted in a second strand of research.[6] At the moment, the definition of algorithmic transparency and what this concept entails has not reached a uniform consensus. This chapter uses the European experience of digital contact tracing to test the concept of algorithmic transparency *empirically*. More specifically, the chapter will investigate two main intertwined aspects. The first relates to the translation of transparency from theory into practice; the second regards the effectiveness of this approach. The main research questions are: how was transparency translated into practice? Has transparency lived up to the expectations?

This study answers these questions with a specific analysis tool: the Transparency Scorecard. After a brief introduction on digital contact tracing, section 5.2 will illustrate the concept of transparency as interpreted in the literature, as a legal requirement and in the specific context of CT apps. This section will underline why transparency has been considered crucial for CT apps' success and the alleged benefits of this approach. The next part of the chapter will focus on the Transparency Scorecard, a table that will guide the scoring of each national CT app. Confronting analogies and dissimilarities between the apps will be useful for answering the research questions of this work. Discussion and results follow.

This chapter finally argues that the experience of digital contact tracing has shown that transparency is not a myth and that its implementation can bring considerable benefits to users. This consideration holds not only for digital contact

[4] See generally the project DP-3T available at http://archive.today/i005g.

[5] See, eg DK Citron, 'Technological Due Process' (2008) 85 *Washington University Law Review* 66; A Datta, S Sen and Y Zick, 'Algorithmic Transparency via Quantitative Input Influence: Theory and Experiments with Learning Systems' in 2016 IEEE Symposium on Security and Privacy (SP) 598; A Koene et al, 'A Governance Framework for Algorithmic Accountability and Transparency' (Panel for the Future of Science and Technology (STOA) at the European Parliamentary Research Service, 2019); A Rauber, R Trasarti and F Giannotti, 'Transparency in Algorithmic Decision Making' (*ERCIM News*, 2019) 116; J Walmsley, 'Artificial Intelligence and the Value of Transparency' [2020] *AI & Society*; J Zerilli et al, 'Transparency in Algorithmic and Human Decision-Making: Is There a Double Standard?' (2019) 32 *Philosophy & Technology* 661.

[6] See, eg M Ananny and K Crawford, 'Seeing without Knowing: Limitations of the Transparency Ideal and Its Application to Algorithmic Accountability' (2018) 20 *New Media & Society* 973; PB de Laat, 'Algorithmic Decision-Making Based on Machine Learning from Big Data: Can Transparency Restore Accountability?' [2017] *Philosophy & Technology*; N Diakopoulos, 'Algorithmic Accountability Reporting: On the Investigation of Black Boxes' (Tow Center for Digital Journalism, Columbia University, 2014); JA Kroll et al, 'Accountable Algorithms' (2016) 165 *University of Pennsylvania Law Review* 633; M Perel and N Elkin-Koren, 'Black Box Tinkering: Beyond Disclosure in Algorithmic Enforcement' (2017) 69 *Florida Law Review* 181.

tracing, but for many other technologies used for different public purposes. This study aims to show that in a comparable legal situation, ie when software is used for public interests and may impact individual rights, transparency can be used as a model for the governance of technologies used for public purposes.

5.2. The Role of Transparency in Contact Tracing Apps

5.2.1. Contact Tracing Apps: Benefits and Concerns

COVID-19 spreads through human interactions. Consequently, identifying all the contacts of an individual who tested positive in the shortest time possible is crucial for effectively limiting the propagation of the disease and interrupting the transmission chain. Contact tracing implies that 'public health authorities rapidly identify all contacts of a confirmed COVID-19 patient, ask them to self-isolate, and rapidly test and isolate them if they develop symptoms'.[7] When carried out by humans, this activity is labour-intensive and requires significant time and resources.[8] Furthermore, it also largely relies on the individual's memory, thus lacking reliability.[9] Manual contact tracing alone can be infeasible given the high proportion of transmission from asymptomatic individuals.[10]

Digital tools, if used in parallel with manual contact tracing,[11] can give substantial support in this fundamental activity, identifying with precision both the known and unknown contacts of a confirmed COVID-19 case.[12] The use of technologies, such as smartphones, promises to speed up the tracing process through automation, leading to increased accuracy and a substantial saving of resources. Furthermore, it represents a suitable solution for facing the challenges of freedom of movement in the Schengen Area, whereby manual contact tracing is not feasible. In addition, anonymised and aggregated data derived from such applications, combined with information on disease incidence, could be used to assess the effectiveness of community and physical distancing measures and to understand transmission dynamics.

[7] Commission, Recommendation 2020/518/EU of 8 April 2020, 15.

[8] See generally C Dumbrava, 'Lifting Coronavirus Restrictions, the Role of Therapeutics, Testing and Contact-Tracing Apps (EPRS PE 652.016, July 2020).

[9] R Ranisch et al, 'Digital Contact Tracing and Exposure Notification: Ethical Guidance for Trustworthy Pandemic Management' [2020] *Ethics and Information* 2.

[10] L Ferretti et al, 'Quantifying SARS-CoV-2 Transmission Suggests Epidemic Control with Digital Contact Tracing' (2020) 368 *Science* 1.

[11] The use of manual contact tracing is in fact still recommended in particular for those, such as elderly or disabled persons, who are more vulnerable to the virus but are less likely to have a smartphone. See eHealth Network, 'Common EU Toolbox for Member States (Mobile Applications to Support Contact Tracing in the EU's Fight against COVID-19)' (15 April) 7.

[12] ibid 7.

After the first lockdown in Europe, digital contact tracing was considered a crucial complementary tool for containment during de-escalation scenarios and easing restrictive measures.[13] In particular, the study by Ferretti et al suggested that the use of CT apps 'would be sufficient to stop the epidemic if used by enough people, in particular when combined with other measures such as physical distancing'.[14] At the dawn of the second infection wave in Europe in late 2020, health authorities warned that the number of cases was escalating so quickly that they could not track the contacts anymore. In both scenarios, digital contact tracing could have played a significant role in fighting the pandemic, although it was revealed to be unsuccessful.[15]

The functioning of a CT app is simple. Each device is associated with a code that does not contain personal information,[16] called a temporary contact number (TCN). As people move around, their smartphones exchange the TCN with other smartphones they encounter via Bluetooth. In this way, a network of contacts between devices is created and stored locally in the device. The phone regularly checks if the user has contacted an infected person. When a close contact is detected, the app will send an alert. If a user tests positive, they can confirm the infection with the app. There is a crucial difference in how the TCN is created depending on the system chosen.[17]

In a centralised model, the trusted authority defines the TCN; when a person is positive, their phone shares the entire list of contacts with the TCN of the past 14 days. The central authority will then create a risk score and send notifications. This system is also called 'contact tracing in the stricter sense'.[18] By contrast, in a decentralised model, the TCN generation is defined by the operating system (iOS or Android) and stored locally on the phone; when someone tests positive, the phone will look for a match of TCNs stored locally and send the alerts.[19] The contact will receive a notification on the phone (exposure notification system). The Apple–Google application programming interface (API) initiative is based on this second variant. At the moment, most EU countries have adopted a decentralised approach, with the notable exception of France, which opted for a centralised model in both versions of the app.[20]

Both choices have raised several concerns in terms of individual rights standards. As underlined by the European Commission, CT apps can impact a wide range of human rights, such as human dignity, respect for private and family life, protection of personal data, non-discrimination, freedom of movement, and

[13] Commission, Recommendation 2020/518/EU, para 14; Ranisch et al (n 9) 1.

[14] Ferretti et al (n 10) 1.

[15] See ch 6 in this book by M Catanzariti.

[16] A numerical code such as 095638883 and not FrancescaPalmiotto1993.

[17] N Oliver, 'Renew Europe Webinar on COVID-19 Contact Tracing Applications' (24 April 2020) https://www.reneweuropegroup.eu/news/2020-04-24/covid19-apps-tracing-the-virus-should-not-mean-tracking-citizens.

[18] Ranisch et al (n 9) 2.

[19] Oliver (n 17).

[20] See the official website of TousAntiCOVID, http://archive.today/zchca.

conduct of a business, assembly and association.[21] These concerns have also been reiterated by civil society organisations, academics, privacy advocates and institutions, triggering a lively debate on the best solution to adopt.[22]

The fear of a state of perpetual surveillance is undoubtedly among the most pressing risks deriving from the employment of technology during emergencies. To give a concrete example, as the demonstrations after the death of George Floyd were escalating in Minnesota, contact tracing apps have been used for profiling and tracking protestors.[23]

In the time frame between March and June 2020, a plethora of guidelines, recommendations and scientific works have been produced to address these legal and ethical issues, setting requirements for trustworthy CT apps. While opinions regarding what best technological solution to adopt differed vastly, everybody agreed on the importance of one specific requirement of these apps: their transparency.

In one of the earliest declarations made by the European Data Protection Supervisor, he stated: 'Legality, *transparency* and proportionality are essential for me' (emphasis added).[24] A Joint Statement signed by several prominent scholars stated that 'any considered solution must be *fully transparent*' (emphasis added).[25] Also, the European Parliament demanded full transparency of the functioning of the apps.[26] Considered a *condicio sine qua non*, transparency paved the way for a responsible and privacy-preserving pan-European approach to CT apps.

5.2.2. Transparency and Data Protection: The General Data Protection Regulation

Transparency generally refers to the idea that if something is visible, it can be controlled.[27] The main goal is to enable people to oversee a process, and it is often

[21] Commission, Communication 2020/C 124 I/01 of 17 April 2020.

[22] Joint Statement on Contact Tracing (19 April 2020) www.esat.kuleuven.be/cosic/sites/contact-tracing-joint-statement/; 'Coronavirus Pandemic in the EU Fundamental Rights Implications: With a Focus on Contact Tracing Apps' [21 March 2020] No 4 *Fundamental Rights Agency Bulletin* 45; Irish Council for Civil Liberties and Digital Rights Ireland; in France, a group of NGOs asked the Parliament to reject the adoption of an app.

[23] A Meek, 'Minnesota Is Now Using Contact Tracing to Track Protestors, as Demonstrations Escalate' (*BGR*, 31 May 2020) https://bgr.com/2020/05/30/minnesota-protest-contact-tracing-used-to-track-demonstrators/. However, the police denied the statement later: S Morrison, 'Minnesota Law Enforcement Isn't "Contact Tracing" Protesters, Despite an Official's Comment' (*Vox*, 1 June 2020) www.vox.com/recode/2020/6/1/21277393/minnesota-protesters-contact-tracing-COVID-19.

[24] W Wiewiórowski, 'EU Digital Solidarity: A Call for a Pan-European Approach against the Pandemic' (6 April 2020) https://edps.europa.eu/data-protection/our-work/publications/speeches-articles/eu-digital-solidarity-call-pan-european_en.

[25] Joint Statement (n 22).

[26] European Parliament, Resolution 2020/2616(RSP) of 17 April 2020.

[27] See generally Ananny and Crawford (n 6); I Koivisto, 'Thinking Inside the Box: The Promise and Boundaries of Transparency in Automated Decision-Making' (European University Institute, 2020) Working Paper.

associated with the notions of accountability and trust.[28] With the rise of automated systems and artificial intelligence, a strong strand of research advocates for transparency as instrumental in understanding how algorithms work and as a tool for enhancing accountability.[29] Algorithmic transparency refers to 'the possibility to have a complete view on a system, i.e. all aspects are visible and can be scrutinised for analysis'.[30] More recently, in Europe, the notion of transparency has also been celebrated as a fundamental pillar of algorithmic governance in several reports,[31] policy recommendations and guidelines.[32]

At the same time, transparency has also acquired a specific legal dimension in data protection and privacy law. Its origins can be traced back to the 31st International Conference of Data Protection and Privacy Commissioners held in Madrid in 2009,[33] but only in 2018 did the General Data Protection Regulation (GDPR) translate this concept into a binding legal requirement of data processing. To celebrate transparency as a core value of data protection, Article 5(1)(a) GDPR states that personal data must be processed 'lawfully, fairly and in a transparent manner in relation to the data subject'. More specifically, transparency in the GDPR is information duties for data controllers (Articles 13, 14, 15, 22 and 34 GDPR) and specific modalities for communicating such information (Article 12, Recitals 39 and 58 GDPR).

5.2.3. Beyond the GDPR: The Benefits of Transparency of CT Apps

In the context of CT apps, references to transparency as a requirement for them can be found in almost every document, guideline[34] or scientific article produced

[28] eg M Hosseini et al, 'Four Reference Models for Transparency Requirements in Information Systems' (2018) 23 *Requirements Engineering* 251.

[29] See, eg DK Citron and F Pasquale, 'The Scored Society: Due Process for Automated Predictions Essay' (2014) 89 *Washington Law Review* 1.

[30] R Hamon et al, 'Robustness and Explainability of Artificial Intelligence: From Technical to Policy Solutions' (European Commission, 2020) 11.

[31] See, eg Rauber et al (n 5); 'Statement on Algorithmic Transparency and Accountability' (ACM Europe Policy Committee, 2017); A Rieke, M Bogen and D Robinson, 'Public Scrutiny of Automated Decisions' (Upturn and Omidyar Network, 2018); Koene et al (n 5).

[32] eg High-Level Expert Group on Artificial Intelligence, 'Ethics Guidelines for Trustworthy AI' (European Commission, 2019); European Commission for the Efficiency of Justice, 'European Ethical Charter on the Use of Artificial Intelligence in Judicial Systems and Their Environment'.

[33] See generally H Felzmann et al, 'Transparency You Can Trust: Transparency Requirements for Artificial Intelligence between Legal Norms and Contextual Concerns' (2019) 6 *Big Data & Society*.

[34] Joint Statement (n 22); Commission Recommendations 2020/518/EU; eHealth Network, 'Common EU Toolbox for Member States' (n 11); European Parliament Resolution 2020/2616(RSP) of 17 April 2020; Communication from the Commission 2020/C 124 I/01; Joint Statement on Digital Contact Tracing by Alessandra Pierucci, Chair of the Committee of Convention 108 and Jean-Philippe Walter, Data Protection Commissioner of the Council of Europe (28 April 2020); European Data Protection Board, 'Guidelines 04/2020 on the Use of Location Data and Contact Tracing Tools in the Context of the COVID-19 Outbreak' (21 April 2020) 11.

on the topic.[35] Undoubtedly, data controllers of the app's data must comply with the provisions on information duties in the GDPR. The element of novelty relies on the fact that transparency has acquired a much broader dimension in the debate surrounding CT apps than the one it has in the GDPR. Transparency is not only information duties and modalities of communication for fair data processing, but also a magnet for several wider benefits.

First and foremost, transparency aims to enhance public trust and social acceptance of CT apps.[36] This promise strictly reconnects to the equation sight = control, which is at the very core of the concept of transparency. In this sense, one cannot trust something obscure and not visible – only something completely verifiable.[37] In the words of the European Parliament, through transparency, people can 'see whether the application functions as the authorities are claiming'[38] and consequently trust it. Building trust by users is considered a necessary condition for uptake by individuals in the use of CT apps.[39] According to a well-known study by a team at Oxford University, for a CT app to be effective it should be downloaded by 60 per cent of the population.[40] It is thus clear why citizens' trust in the proper functioning of CT apps is crucial to determine the success and effectiveness of digital contact tracing strategies.

Secondly, transparency allows for public oversight and, consequently, easier detection of errors and bugs,[41] and verification of their compliance with data

[35] See, eg MM Mello and CJ Wang, 'Ethics and Governance for Digital Disease Surveillance' (2020) 368 *Science* 954; R Vinuesa et al, 'A Socio-Technical Framework for Digital Contact Tracing' [2020] arXiv:2005.08370; F Luciano, 'Mind the App: Considerations on the Ethical Risks of COVID-19 Apps' (2020) 33 *Philosophy & Technology* 167; A Lodders and JM Paterson, 'Scrutinising COVIDSafe: Frameworks for Evaluating Digital Contact Tracing Technologies' (2020) 45 *Alternative Law Journal* 153; J Morley et al, 'Ethical Guidelines for SARS-CoV-2 Digital Tracking and Tracing Systems' [2020] https://papers.ssrn.com/sol3/papers.cfm?abstract_id=3582550.

[36] Commission Recommendations 2020/518/EU §30: 'Transparency … will be paramount to ensuring public trust'; Fundamental Rights Agency, 'Efforts to Make the Apps Source Code Public Should Continue to Enhance Transparency and Confidence in Using Such Tools' (Press Release); European Data Protection Board (EDPB), 'Guidelines 04/2020 on the Use of Location Data and Contact Tracing Tools in the Context of the COVID-19 Outbreak' (21 April 2020) 11; WHO Interim Guidance, 'Establishing Integrated Nationwide Contact Tracing Systems' (6 July 2020) 7. In the literature, see RA Fahey and A Hino, 'COVID-19, Digital Privacy, and the Social Limits on Data-Focused Public Health Responses' [2020] *International Journal of Information Management* 4. On the website of the German app Corona-Warn it reads: 'Only through transparency can we earn the trust of the end-users and increase app adoption.'

[37] *cf* A Wnuk, T Oleksy and D Maison, 'The Acceptance of COVID-19 Tracking Technologies: The Role of Perceived Threat, Lack of Control, and Ideological Beliefs' (2020) 15 *PLOS ONE* e0238973, where they examine whether the acceptance of technologies that pose a potential threat to privacy and civil rights depends on the situational sense of personal control in a time of pandemic and perceived personal threat.

[38] European Parliament Resolution 2020/2616 (RSP), para 52.

[39] eHealth Network, 'Common EU Toolbox for Member States' (n 11) 21.

[40] 'Digital Contact Tracing Can Slow or Even Stop Coronavirus Transmission and Ease Us out of Lockdown' www.research.ox.ac.uk/article/2020-04-16-digital-contact-tracing-can-slow-or-even-stop-coronavirus-transmission-and-ease-us-out-of-lockdown.

[41] EDPB Guidelines 04/2020, 14.

protection law.[42] In this sense, transparency protects users from abuses, safeguards their privacy and minimises the risk of errors.[43] In addition, transparency is instrumental in challenging their results and obtaining remedies, as proving mistakes can be difficult where a decision involves an algorithm whose logic may not be transparent.[44]

Specifically, as an engineering concept, a software system is transparent 'when it makes the information it deals with transparent, along with its internal functioning process, which is called information transparency and process transparency respectively, and when all its functionalities are disclosed to its users'.[45] In this sense, transparency entails that the source code, specifics and technical documentation are publicly available. From a legal perspective, open source implies

> licensing IPRs, possibly free of charge, for use by third-parties in commercial applications for a specific purpose, such as using, modifying or sharing the source code, blueprint or design, typically on the condition that any improvements that are developed are made available on the same terms.[46]

In addition, the open source approach requires the software to be developed in a collaborative public manner. This latter aspect has been particularly underlined in the project team of the Corona Warn App, the CT app used in Germany, where the public participation in the development of the software has been considered key in increasing 'security and data privacy protection by detecting issues early and helping to solve them'.[47] The website displays an iconic motto: *No security through obscurity*.[48]

To conclude, transparency in the context of digital contact tracing is twinned with a series of positive results, such as enhancing public oversight and trust, allowing for public scrutiny, thus reducing the risk of errors; respecting data protection law; and protecting users from abuses and increasing their security.

5.2.4. Research Objective and Scope

The idea that transparency can be, inter alia, a valid safeguard for digital applications is not new. Nevertheless, disagreements persist even on the very meaning of algorithmic transparency. The proposed definitions range from narrow interpretations – merely referring to the disclosure of the source code – to broader

[42] ibid 8.
[43] Mello and Wang (n 35) 952.
[44] ibid 951.
[45] Hosseini (n 28) 253.
[46] World Trade Organization (WTO), 'Information Note on the Trips Agreement and COVID-19' (15 October 2020) 5.
[47] Website of 'Corona Warn App' www.coronawarn.app/en/.
[48] ibid.

concepts encompassing notions of knowledge, availability, accessibility and understandability of relevant information on the system's functioning.[49]

The main objective of this work is to test the concept of transparency empirically. The underlying idea is that the European digital contact tracing experience offers a unique opportunity for such an assessment for three reasons. First, it provides an appropriate number of cases for in-depth analysis: 23 CT apps. Although a single European app was initially proposed, in the end, almost every Member State decided to adopt a national CT app.

Second, the apps are very similar, albeit not identical. All the apps have been adopted taking into account the recommendations provided by the EU institutions under the unifying framework of the GDPR. Furthermore, the heated debate that preceded their launch paved the way for setting common standards.

Third, there is wide consensus over the need for transparency for the first time. This might then set a precedent for advocating transparency in other public interest sectors. Therefore, the COVID-19 emergency has become a laboratory for testing transparency as a tool for governing technologies.

More specifically, this work investigates two aspects of transparency. The first relates to the translation of transparency from theory to practice. As seen above in the previous paragraph, transparency has multiple dimensions and connotations. It is a theoretical concept that promises to provide accountability and trust – a legal requirement enshrined in the GDPR – and an engineering concept. *How have these dimensions been reunited with the development of CT apps?* The second aspect concerns the effectiveness of this approach *in concreto*. As mentioned earlier, transparency has been associated with a list of several benefits. *Has transparency kept its promises?*

This chapter will investigate these research questions through the 'Transparency Scorecard', a table composed of four criteria on which each national app will be evaluated and numerically scored. Before continuing, some clarifications in terms of scope are needed. The intent of the Scorecard is not only to assess the normative compliance of the app with the requirements of the GDPR; rather, it is a tool for guiding the analysis. Consequently, the scores attributed to each app do not reflect their quality or lawfulness, but only their level of transparency. Furthermore, this work will not include considerations on the privacy policies. Lastly, the Scorecard will be applied only to CT apps, not symptom checker apps or apps with information functionalities.

5.3. Scoring Transparency in Contact Tracing App

5.3.1. Methods

The Transparency Scorecard (Table 5.1) has been built following three steps: (i) analysis of relevant materials; (ii) creation of the criteria and sub-criteria; and

[49] eg P Hayes, I van de Poel and M Steen, 'Algorithms and Values in Justice and Security' [2020] *AI & Society*.

(iii) the scoring. First and foremost, I focused on the debate on digital contact tracing prior to the launch of the apps to frame why, by whom and what type of transparency has been demanded. The source of information ranged from hard and soft law, ethical guidelines and scientific papers to newspapers articles. More specifically, the analysis focused on several documents published by different EU Institutions – such as, inter alia, the Guidelines of the European Data Protection Board, the eHealth Network and the European Commission, resolutions by the European Parliament and reports by the Fundamental Rights Agency – relevant provisions of the GDPR, specific laws adopted by the Member States on contact tracing, contractual clauses with the software companies and academic papers, as well as newspapers articles. The main outcome of this section consists of an inventory of the specific transparency requirements.

In the second step, this inventory has been modelled into a set of criteria and sub-criteria for assessing each app's overall level of transparency. A complete list with the logic underlying each criterion is provided in the next section. Finally, I have scored each national app launched at the time of writing.[50] The scoring is based on information available on the official website of the app, government and/or Minister of Health of the country. A preliminary step was a labour-intensive listing of the apps available. Although some inventories are available, they are not constantly updated.

Furthermore, when information was not available or sufficiently clear, I have always requested information. When not available in English, I have used the software DeepL for translation. This work builds on the theoretical framework on transparency, and it is strongly inspired by the research approach adopted by the RAND Corporation in its report[51] and on the work of Vinuesa et al.[52]

As mentioned previously, the Scorecard only applies to CT apps launched and/or in use in EU countries. This choice is justified by the fact that the GDPR has undoubtedly played a role as a unifying legal framework among Member States in developing the apps. The GDPR contains all the principles that, if respected, can provide adequate protection of individuals against abuses of these apps. The European Commission and the European Data Protection Board (EDPB) worked together to ensure that principles such as purpose limitation and privacy-by-design could be enforced and respected at the national level. In particular, the

[50] Ada Lovelace Institute, 'COVID-19 Digital Contact Tracing Tracker' www.adalovelaceinstitute.org/our-work/identities-liberties/COVID-19-digital-contact-tracing-tracker/; *MIT Technology Review*, 'COVID Tracing Tracker' www.technologyreview.com/tag/COVID-tracing-tracker/.

[51] B Boudreaux et al, 'Strengthening Privacy Protections in COVID-19 Mobile Phone-Enhanced Surveillance Programs' www.rand.org/content/dam/rand/pubs/research_briefs/RBA300/RBA365-1/RAND_RBA365-1.pdf.

[52] Vinuesa et al (n 35).

EU Commission's Guidance aims to limit the intrusiveness of the app functionalities to ensure compliance with the EU personal data protection and privacy legislation.

Furthermore, being a Regulation, the GDPR is directly applicable to all Member States. This aspect is even more critical since the EU common approach has been constructed via instruments of soft law that are not legally binding. The homogeneity of cases and legal frameworks allows me to draw consistent conclusions for the EU context.

5.3.2. Criteria

The 'Transparency Scorecard' is based on four main criteria: (i) availability of the source code; (ii) availability of technical documentation; (iii) quality of information on the programme; and (iv) audits and external review. For each criterion, the app can receive a score ranging from 0 to 2, depending on whether it fully satisfies (2), partly satisfies (1) or does not satisfy (0) the requirements.

The first criterion is the availability of the *source code*. The source code is 'the version of the software as it is originally written by a human in plain text'.[53] The disclosure of the source code is considered the most basic form of algorithmic transparency and, among all the criteria, has gained the widest consensus.[54] Reference to the source code can be found in almost every document produced on the topic. The eHealth Network recommended app developers to 'Openly publish the source code for the apps, as a way to maximise re-use, interoperability, auditability and security'.[55] Also, Communication 2020/C 124 I/01 from the European Commission suggested publishing the source code and making it available for review.[56] Likewise, the Guidelines by the EDPB stress the relevance of the source code's availability to allow for the broadest possible scrutiny.[57] This latter aspect has also been underlined in the literature by Vineusa et al, who recommend the use of open-source software with the possibility of contributing to participatory and multidisciplinary development. Even the largest association of hackers in Europe, Chaos Computer Club, has endorsed the free availability of the

[53] The Linux Information Project, 'Definition of Source Code' http://www.linfo.org/source_code.html.

[54] Commission Recommendation 2020/518/EU; eHealth Network, 'Common EU Toolbox for Member States' (n 11); Communication from the Commission 2020/C 124 I/01; EDPB Guidelines 04/2020, Council of Europe Joint Statement.

[55] eHealth Network, 'Common EU Toolbox for Member States' (n 11).

[56] Communication from the Commission 2020/C 124 I/01 §3.8.

[57] EDPB Guidelines 04/2020 §37.

source code and infrastructure without access restrictions to allow audits by all interested parties.[58]

The second criterion relates to the *availability of technical documentation.* Software is not only source code, but also the documentation on the design, ideas and policies behind it. According to the Joint Statement on Contact Tracing of 19 April 2020, a fundamental principle is transparency in the sense that also 'the protocols and their implementations, including any sub-components provided by companies, must be available for public analysis'.[59]

The third criterion assesses the *quality of information on the functioning of the programme.* Especially when the audience is not specialised, the mere availability of information may not be sufficient. According to Recital 58 GDPR and Article 12 GDPR, the information given to data subjects shall be concise, intelligible, easily accessible and easy to understand, and provided in clear and plain language. Additionally, where appropriate, visualisation should be used. Furthermore, according to the statement of the EDPB, 'data subjects should receive transparent information on the processing activities … The information provided should be easily accessible and provided in clear and plain language'.[60] The main focus of this criterion is to evaluate the usefulness of the information provided to the audience, in terms of 'providing them with decision-making capabilities through the disclosed information',[61] adopting the view of an average individual without specialised skills in computer science.

In all of the criteria mentioned above, I refer to the availability of the information online, mainly from the apps' official websites. In fact, according to Recital 58 of the GDPR on the principle of transparency, information 'could be provided in electronic form, for example, when addressed to the public, through a website'. Moreover, if the recipient of the information is the user of the contact tracing app, it is presumed that they have easy access to the Internet.

The fourth and final criterion refers *to audits and external reviews.* Among others, in the Common EU Toolbox, the eHealth Network particularly underlined the importance of security testing and independent review, setting a requirement for national authorities to 'ensure that the security of the app and the backend is reviewed and tested by independent experts before deployment and after each change … It is important that security researchers, experts, citizens and organisations, can report errors'.[62] Also, the EDPB Guidelines explicitly mention the auditability of the algorithms and the need for regular reviews by independent experts.

[58] Chaos Computer Club, '10 Requirements for the Evaluation of Contact Tracing Apps' (6 April 2020) www.ccc.de/en/updates/2020/contact-tracing-requirements 2020.

[59] Joint Statement (n 22) 2.

[60] EDPB Guidelines 04/2020.

[61] Hosseini (28) 252.

[62] eHealth Network.

Table 5.1 The Transparency Scorecard

<table>
<tr><td colspan="3">[Country]
[App name]</td></tr>
<tr><td colspan="3">**1. Availability of the source code**</td></tr>
<tr><td>Fully satisfied (2)</td><td>Partly satisfied (1)</td><td>Not satisfied (0)</td></tr>
<tr><td colspan="3">• Fully satisfied: the software is open source; the source code is accessible online; there is the possibility to contribute to the development of the app;
• Partly satisfied: the source code is open but not accessible online and/or not possible to contribute;
• Not satisfied or unclear: the source code is proprietary, or it is unclear</td></tr>
<tr><td colspan="3">**2. Availability of technical documentation**</td></tr>
<tr><td>Fully satisfied (2)</td><td>Partly satisfied (1)</td><td>Not satisfied (0)</td></tr>
<tr><td colspan="3">• Fully satisfied: the technical documentation is publicly available; it is constantly updated, it is easy to access online (from the website of the app);
• Partly satisfied: when one of the above conditions is missing;
• Not satisfied: when more than one condition is not fulfilled</td></tr>
<tr><td colspan="3">**3. Quality of information on the functioning of the program**</td></tr>
<tr><td>Fully satisfied (2)</td><td>Partly satisfied (1)</td><td>Not satisfied (0)</td></tr>
<tr><td colspan="3">• Fully satisfied: the functioning of the program is sufficiently explained in a clear and concise way; information is available also in English, information is provided not only in written form but also through images, audio or video support
• Partly satisfied: one of the above conditions is missing
• Not satisfied: more than one condition is not fulfilled</td></tr>
<tr><td colspan="3">**4. Audits and external reviews**</td></tr>
<tr><td>Fully satisfied (2)</td><td>Partly satisfied (1)</td><td>Not satisfied (0)</td></tr>
<tr><td colspan="3">• Fully satisfied: audits or reviews are possible and have been carried out before the launch of the app
• Partly satisfied: audits are possible, but they have not been carried out before the app launch
• Not satisfied: audits are not possible, or there is insufficient information available to check this criterion</td></tr>
<tr><td colspan="3">**TOT.**</td></tr>
</table>

5.3.3. The Transparency Scorecard

In this section, a summary of the overall score of the apps is presented. The Transparency Scorecard for each app can be found in Annex 1.

Table 5.2 European CT apps scored (last update 4 October 2021)

	Country	**App**	**Score**	**Launch and Downloads*** *Data from Liberties
1	Austria	StoppCorona	5/8	Launch in Mar. 20 Downloads 16% Feb. 21
2	Belgium	CoronaAlert	8/8	Launch in Sep. 20 Downloads 20% Jan. 2
3	Bulgaria	ViruSafe	4/8	Launch Apr 20 Downloads 0.8% Feb 21 Based on location data
4	Croatia	Stop Covid-19	On hold	Launch Jul 20 Downloads 2% Feb 21 Information was very hard to find
5	Cyprus	CovTracer	2/8	Launch Apr 20 Downloads 9& Feb 21 Based on location data; source code is not available
6	Czech Republic	eRouska	7/8	Launch Apr 20 Downloads 14% Feb 21 Exciting features of the website: specific section on "Audit and code" and a live chat
7	Denmark	Smitte|Stop	2/8	Launch Jun 20 Downloads 38% Feb 21 The source code is not available for security reasons
8	Estonia	HOIA	8/8	Launch Aug 20 Downloads 20% Feb 21
9	Finland	Koronavilkku	7/8	Launch Aug 20 Downloads 45% Feb 21

(continued)

Table 5.2 ***(Continued)***

	Country	**App**	**Score**	**Launch and Downloads*** *Data from Liberties
10	France I	StopCovid	7/8	Launch Jun 20 The source code is mainly public; only a tiny part is not available due to security reasons Public contributions as the key point of the project
11	France II	TousAntiCovid	5/8	Re-launch of StopCovid in late October 20 Downloads 20% Mar 21
12	Germany	Corona Warn App	8/8	Launch Jun 20 Downloads 33% Strong emphasis on the open source approach to increase trust and security of the app
13	Hungary	VirusRadar	1/8	Launch May 20 Downloads 0.8% Sep 20 Private developer company which donated the App to the Government
14	Ireland	Covid Tracker	6/8	Launch Jun 20 Downloads 49%
15	Italy	Immuni	8/8	Launch Jun 20 Downloads 17% Apr 21 Public procurement for choosing the App
16	Latvia	Apturi Covid	6/8	Launch NA Downloads NA
17	Malta	CovidAlert	On hold	Launch Sept 20 Downloads 19% Feb 21
18	Netherlands	CoronaMelder	7/8	Launch Oct 20 Downloads 26%
19	Poland	ProteGO Safe	7/8	Launch Jun 20 Downloads 4%

(continued)

Table 5.2 ***(Continued)***

	Country	App	Score	Launch and Downloads* *Data from Liberties
20	Portugal	StayAwayCovid	7/8	Launch Sept 20 Downloads 25% Late publication of the source code
21	Slovakia	ZonstanZdravy	1/8	Launch NA Downloads NA
22	Slovenia	OstaniZdrav	On hold	Launch Aug 20 Downloads 19% Feb 21
23	Spain	RadarCovid	6/8	Launch Aug 20 Downloads 16% Apr 21

5.3.4. Discussion and Results

In terms of results, one can easily infer from Figure 5.1 that the scores are quite diverse, although most apps reached the sufficiency bar (4.8/8). Probably the most surprising result is that under Criterion 3, on the quality of information, many apps scored 0 points. This is particularly problematic as this criterion is the only one that translates a binding legal requirement (see section 5.3.2 above). On the other hand, the criterion that most apps fulfil is full disclosure of the source code.

Figure 5.1 Scores per criterion

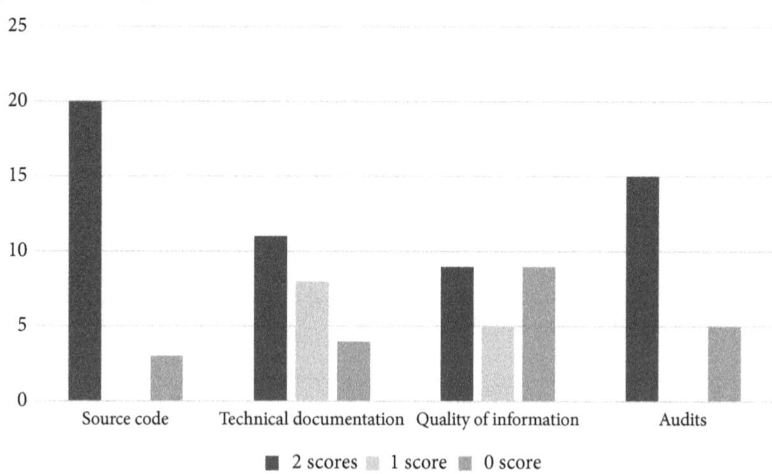

From these results, I will try to answer the research questions guiding this work.

RQ[1]: What Does Transparency Mean in the Context of CT Apps?

The first answer is that transparency is undoubtedly more than the information duties enshrined in the GDPR. The criterion where almost every app scored the maximum was the availability of the source code. In contrast, the third criterion, specifically on the quality of information communication, received several low scores (nine apps scored 0 and five apps scored 1). One can then conclude that the engineering translation of transparency is the disclosure of the software's source code and its technical documentation. This aligns with the core meaning of transparency, connected to the equation sight/control. After information requests, many answers that I received stated: 'also, the source code is open so you can directly look at it yourself'.

One can conceptualise two forms of transparency in this context: 'design transparency', through the publication of the source code and the technical documentation, and 'information transparency', pursuant to the provisions in the GDPR on the quality of information given to data subjects. Finally, audits on the software are allowed through disclosure to specific subjects of design transparency. This provides for validations or certifications of the software from third parties.

RQ[2]: Has Transparency Kept Its Promises?

The First Promise: Enhancing Uptake in the Population

Some countries have celebrated the success of their apps, such as Switzerland[63] and the UK, claiming that digital CT helped reduce cases by 20 per cent.[64] Others had to admit their failure,[65] compared to the initial expectations, especially in the USA.[66] As a necessary foreword, it is crucial to keep the concept of uptake separate

[63] 'SwissCOVID the Most Downloaded App in Switzerland Last Year' (*SWI swissinfo.ch*) www.swissinfo.ch/eng/sci-tech/swissCOVID-the-most-downloaded-app-in-switzerland-last-year/46733358.

[64] J Drake, 'How "Digital Contact Tracing" Reduced COVID-19 Cases in the UK by 20%' (*Forbes*) www.forbes.com/sites/johndrake/2021/05/21/how-digital-contact-tracing-reduced-COVID-19-cases-in-the-uk-by-20/. See also the study from the Alan Turing Center, 'NHS COVID-19 App Alerts 1.7 Million Contacts to Stop Spread of COVID-19' (*GOV.UK*) www.gov.uk/government/news/nhs-COVID-19-app-alerts-17-million-contacts-to-stop-spread-of-COVID-19.

[65] In Poland: 'Polish Contact Tracing App Not Worth the Investment, Data Suggest' (*AlgorithmWatch*) https://algorithmwatch.org/en/tracers/polish-contact-tracing-app-not-worth-the-investment-data-suggest/; in the Netherlands: D Klinkenberg, K Leung and J Wallinga, 'CoronaMelder – Modelstudie Naar Effectiviteit. Digitaal Contactonderzoek in de Bestrijding van COVID-19' (RIVM Rijksinstituut voor Volksgezondheid en Milieu, 2021) https://rivm.openrepository.com/handle/10029/624996.

[66] 'Contact Tracing Applications Did Not Turn Out to Be as Successful During the Pandemic as They Were Expected to Be' www.digitalinformationworld.com/2021/06/contact-tracing-applications-did-not.html.

from that of effectiveness.[67] The Irish app, for instance, had a high number of downloads, but research showed that the app was not effective in reducing cases, as only a few users were sharing their positive tests on the app.[68] Likewise, in Finland, while holding the record for downloads in Europe, experts claimed that the app produced few benefits due to the low number of active users.[69] This analysis focuses on the number of downloads rather than on assessing the efficacy of the apps in fighting the pandemic.

Initially, an Oxford University study[70] set a mainstream narrative according to which CT apps would have been effectively useful only if downloaded by 60 per cent of the population.[71] The actual numbers of downloads of all apps are significantly lower than that threshold. Data gathered by Liberties in the Knowledge Hub on COVID-19 in the EU[72] shows that the highest downloads as percentages of population are 45 per cent in Finland, 38 per cent in Denmark, 36 per cent in England and Wales, 49 per cent in Ireland and 32.5 per cent in Germany. At the other end of the spectrum, countries with the lowest download levels include Bulgaria (0.8 per cent), Croatia (2 per cent), Hungary (0.8 per cent), Poland (4 per cent) and Cyprus (9 per cent). In the middle, countries like Italy (17 per cent), France (20 per cent), Netherlands (26 per cent) and Spain (15.5 per cent) performed much lower than expected.

There might be several reasons for this lack of success. However, this chapter is focusing on the relationship between transparency and uptake. By confronting the scores of percentage downloads, it is difficult to find a clear pattern. If we take countries with higher downloads, such as Finland, Denmark and Ireland, their transparency scores are quite different, at 7/8, 2/8 and 6/8 respectively. Denmark, in particular, scored low on the Transparency Scorecard as they decided to keep the source code secret for security reasons.

[67] G Grekousis and Y Liu, 'Digital Contact Tracing, Community Uptake, and Proximity Awareness Technology to Fight COVID-19: A Systematic Review' (2021) 71 *Sustainable Cities and Society* 102995; 'Digital Contact Tracing Apps: Do They Actually Work? A Review of Early Evidence' (*Algorithm Watch*) https://algorithmwatch.org/en/analysis-digital-contact-tracing-apps-2021/. For research on the estimated effect of the apps in reducing the pandemic, see T Murata and K Yamashita, 'Estimating the Effect of COVID-19 Contact Tracing Application Using Agent-Based Simulation', 2021 5th IEEE International Conference on Cybernetics (CYBCONF) (2021).

[68] S Burns, 'Concerns Raised about COVID-19 Tracker App's "Limited Benefits"' (*Irish Times*) www.irishtimes.com/news/health/concerns-raised-about-COVID-19-tracker-app-s-limited-benefits-1.4531027.

[69] 'Finland's Exposure Notification App Has Limited Use, Experts Claim' (*Algorithm Watch*) https://algorithmwatch.org/en/tracers/finlands-exposure-notification-app-has-limited-use-experts-claim/.

[70] 'Digital Contact Tracing Can Slow or Even Stop Coronavirus Transmission and Ease Us out of Lockdown' www.research.ox.ac.uk/article/2020-04-16-digital-contact-tracing-can-slow-or-even-stop-coronavirus-transmission-and-ease-us-out-of-lockdown.

[71] Later, however, other research showed that CTAs could have been effective even with a lower number of downloads. See C Wymant et al, 'The Epidemiological Impact of the NHS COVID-19 App' (2021) 594 *Nature* 408.

[72] 'COVID-19 Digital Contact Tracing Tracker' www.adalovelaceinstitute.org/project/covid-19-digital-contact-tracing-tracker/.

On the other hand, countries with low download rates, including Poland, Bulgaria, Cyprus and Hungary, also had the most divergent transparency scores, at 7/8, 4/8, 2/8 and 1/8 respectively. While transparency may allow for higher uptakes, this research shows that it is not possible to draw a causal link between transparency and effective uptake as expected.

The Second Promise: Reducing the Risk of Errors and Increasing Security

Design transparency allowed for thorough scrutiny of the apps compared to proprietary apps. The publication of the source code and technical documentation allowed anyone with sufficient coding skills to submit comments on the software's design, spotting bugs and errors that could have impacted the security and the correct functioning of the apps. Many examples show that design transparency was crucial to ensure early and effective identification of errors.

In June 2020, a study conducted by Guardsquare considered 17 Android mobile CT apps from different countries, including Europe, the USA and Asia. They found that most CT apps did not employ sufficient security protections, making the apps easy targets for hackers.[73] The study used static and dynamic analysis,[74] which means that the researchers went through each app's code to find any possible defect and then executed the code to analyse the output.[75] In other words, design transparency allowed tests to be performed on the app, which would have otherwise required specific authorisation from the software developer if the source code was proprietary.

A second large-scale study conducted, by Hatamian et al, analysed 28 apps launched in 2020.[76] In this research, they also conducted static and dynamic testing, along with security analysis of each app's program code to detect possible vulnerabilities. The study concluded that 'developers of these apps need to take more cautionary steps to ensure code quality and address security and privacy vulnerabilities'.[77]

In the UK, in May 2020, researchers spotted security flaws during the pilot phase of the CT app using a static analysis of the released source code for the UK's app and an evaluation of high-level design documents.[78]

[73] 'REPORT: Most Government-Sanctioned COVID-19 Tracing Apps Risk Exposing Users' Data and Privacy' www.guardsquare.com/blog/report-proliferation-COVID-19-contact-tracing-apps-exposes-significant-security-risks.

[74] ibid.

[75] On the difference between these techniques for software testing, see 'Static & Dynamic Analysis in Software Testing' (Testing Brain, 14 July 2011) www.testingbrain.com/whitebox/static-dynamic-analysis.html.

[76] M Hatamian et al, 'A Privacy and Security Analysis of Early-Deployed COVID-19 Contact Tracing Android Apps' (2021) 26 *Empirical Software Engineering* 36.

[77] ibid.

[78] C Culnane, 'Security Analysis of the NHS COVID-19 App' (*State of IT*) https://stateofit.com/UKContactTracing/.

Publishing the source code allows for wider scrutiny of the software's functioning. Moreover, spotting errors is facilitated by the early publication of the source code. The case of Spain is exemplary. Initially, the source code was not public. For subsequent versions, however, the Spanish authorities decided to fully follow the open source philosophy as it allows for the identification of bugs before users install that version.[79]

Another successful example of the open source philosophy is the German app. Corona-Warning-App was considered the most prominent open-source project ever implemented in Germany by the government.[80] In an interview, the software developer (SAP) stated that 'More than 109,000 visitors viewed the code and approximately 7,250 community and project members participated'.[81] In fact, during the app development, bug hunters at GitHub Security Lab helped identify crucial security vulnerabilities in the software. The team then worked with SAP to fix the issues.[82] The lead of the group stated that 'building these applications on open source not only offers transparency to users about what data is being collected, but it also allows others to help spot security holes, which in turn builds critical public trust'.[83]

The majority of the EU CT apps analysed had adopted this approach, developing the systems on GitHub, with the notable exception of the Google and Apple exposure notification framework (GAEN). The API, which is at the basis of the technical architecture of all the decentralised apps, was initially not public. Later, Apple and Google decided to make the source code and technical documentation available.[84] Subsequently, different experts extensively reviewed their framework (GAEN). For instance, a student in cybersecurity in Portugal detected a bug while researching for his master thesis. The bug has been recognised by Google, who gave the student and his professor an honourable mention from the company.[85] A more controversial event involved the privacy analysis firm AppCensus.[86] According to the study, Google's implementation of GAEN logs crucial information to the system log, which can be read and used for privacy attacks.[87] This error was first communicated to Google, filing a report to Google's bug bounty

[79] https://radarCOVID.gob.es/faq-liberacion-codigo-fuente.

[80] 'German COVID-19 Contact-Tracing Vulnerability Allowed RCE' https://threatpost.com/german-COVID-19-contact-tracing-vulnerability-rce/161419/.

[81] ibid.

[82] ibid.

[83] ibid.

[84] https://developer.apple.com/exposure-notification/ https://github.com/google/exposure-notifications-server.

[85] 'Portugal: Cybersecurity Student Detects Bug in Exposure Notification Apps' (*AlgorithmWatch*) https://algorithmwatch.org/en/tracers/portugal-cybersecurity-student-detects-bug-in-exposure-notification-apps/.

[86] J Reardon, 'Why Google Should Stop Logging Contact-Tracing Data – The AppCensus Blog' https://blog.appcensus.io/2021/04/27/why-google-should-stop-logging-contact-tracing-data/.

[87] ibid.

program. However, Google did not consider the flaw severe enough, according to their standards, to justify a correction of the system.[88]

The Third Promise: Preserving Data Protection

During the first wave of COVID-19, worrisome episodes involving CT apps used outside Europe echoed in the news. In Minnesota, during the Black Lives Matter movement's protests, a police commissioner said in a press conference that law enforcement was using 'contact tracing' on arrested protesters.[89] The app Citizen, used in Los Angeles, which launched a contact-tracing feature and a citywide COVID surveillance programme, exposed users' health data on the Internet.[90] In addition, a massive data breach hit the CT app used in Pennsylvania,[91] the data collected by the CT app in Australia was used for policing[92] and a severe data breach occurred in Indonesia.[93]

European institutions, privacy advocates, scholars and media were fully aware of these potential risks in employing CT apps. In the Netherlands, a data leak affected the app Corona Check, which is not the Dutch CT app, but the system used for proving that an individual is vaccinated, has tested negative or has recovered from COVID-19. Consequently,[94] the CT app was halted over similar fears in April 2021.[95] With this notable exception, to date, there have been no severe accidents of data leaks regarding CT apps in Europe (last updated November 2021). Has transparency played a role in preserving data protection?

Design transparency alone does not guarantee that the system complies with privacy rules. A system can be proprietary and yet be privacy-preserving, or it can be transparent but in violation of privacy rules. The difference relies on the fact

[88] 'Google Promised Its Contact Tracing App Was Completely Private – But It Wasn't – The Markup' https://themarkup.org/privacy/2021/04/27/google-promised-its-contact-tracing-app-was-completely-private-but-it-wasnt.

[89] According to Minnesota public health authorities, the officer was referring to the normal process of law enforcement investigations. He did not mean that the police were using data from COVID-19 contact tracing efforts or tools to assist in those investigations. Morrison (n 23).

[90] 'Crime App Citizen Exposed Users' COVID Data' www.vice.com/en/article/qj8kwq/citizen-safe pass-privacy-COVID-data-exposed.

[91] 'After Contact Tracing Data Breach, Pa. Sidesteps Scrutiny on Proposed $34M Contract' (*WHYY*) https://whyy.org/articles/after-contact-tracing-data-breach-pa-sidesteps-scrutiny-on-proposed-34m-contract/.

[92] '"Massive Breach of Public Trust": Police Access Data from SafeWA Contact Tracing App' (*7NEWS*, 15 June 2021) https://7news.com.au/news/western-australia-police/wa-police-accessed-contact-tracing-data-c-3118713.

[93] 'Around 1 Million People Potentially Affected by Suspected Breach in Indonesia's COVID-19 App: Report' (*Healthcare IT News*, 2 September 2021) www.healthcareitnews.com/news/asia/around-1-million-people-potentially-affected-suspected-breach-indonesias-COVID-19-app.

[94] 'Major Data Leak Affects Dutch COVID-19 Testing System and App' (*AlgorithmWatch*) https://algorithmwatch.org/en/tracers/major-data-leak-affects-dutch-COVID-19-testing-system-and-app/.

[95] 'Dutch Government Pauses Coronavirus App over Data Leak Fears' (*AP NEWS*, 29 April 2021) https://apnews.com/article/europe-data-privacy-coronavirus-technology-health-9d26edd107a 146d32fd29b157ed53515.

that, through design transparency, a third party can check what the system actually does.

Design transparency undoubtedly aids in preserving privacy the moment it allows for easier identification of errors through the open source code community. The research mentioned above on the German app shows how bugs and errors enshrined in code can severely affect individuals' privacy. Additionally, technological design choices can impact data protection greatly. For CT apps, the choice of the technical model was more important than transparency. For instance, a centralised system would have posed significant risks for privacy insofar as it would have led to the creation of an extensive database of individuals' contacts in the hands of health authorities. Design transparency is relevant because it guarantees that the software implements the model they claim to implement.

The possibility of scrutinising the app through the source code and technical documentation allows checking which technical choices have been implemented and whether they are appropriate for privacy and security. In the case of AppCensus and Google, the company did not find a bug but rather criticised the choice of Google in logging tracing data. This technical feature, in the words of Reardon, poses risks 'even for Apple users and Android users who do not have any app that uploads their system logs, though there are greater risks for Android users who do have their logs uploaded by these third-party apps'.[96] Consequently, those who have one user's logs can learn much information on that person, even their identity, health status and location trails.[97]

5.4. Conclusions and Lessons for the Future

CT apps will not just be a memory of the past in a post-pandemic world. An Erudite analysis shows that the global market of CT apps will grow to $1218.9 million by 2027.[98] Technological solutions based on the Internet of Things have facilitated a network to share real-time data, track contacts and enforce social distancing. These instruments will continue to grow in the future and be crucial for safeguarding public health. The experience of CT apps in Europe should be considered successful in regard to the benefits brought by transparency. Two main lessons can be learnt.

5.4.1. Lesson 1: Transparency Empowers the Public

A remarkable aspect of CT apps is that the public debate occurred before their deployment and not after serious flaws were detected, as has often happened

[96] Reardon (n 86).
[97] ibid.
[98] 'Outlook of Global Contact Tracing App Market: Research Report' (*OpenPR*, 23 June 2021) www.openpr.com/news/2311382/outlook-of-global-contact-tracing-app-market-research-report.

in the past.[99] The public discussion, which involved researchers and academics from different disciplines, found a broad echo in the media, thus strengthening their concerns, gaining the attention of politicians and raising the awareness of citizens. The high level of attention paid to the apps ensured design transparency from the very first phase of the software development.

The first lesson this experience has taught us is that transparency empowers: it empowers governments in their relationship with private software providers, the community of experts taking on the role of watchdogs of the apps, and the public at large through the possibility to be informed, debate and eventually act. Through transparency, CT apps were spotlighted, increasing public control over these technologies.

First, governments had the power and will to impose contractual agreements with software providers, requiring the app to be open source and developed publicly.[100] In Italy, for instance, the software developer was chosen through public procurement, increasing transparency even in the selection process. Moreover, the Italian government has decided to specifically regulate systems of digital contact tracing with decree-law No 28 of 30 April 2020. Article 6 imposes the public ownership of the app and its release under an open licence. Similarly, in France, decree No 650 of 29 May 2020 provides that the source code of StopCOVID will be made public and accessible online. An interesting clue for future research is to put the success of the open source philosophy in relation to the intellectual property rights that usually have been a barrier to disclosure. In the case of CT apps, it is clear that companies have been rewarded with a different economic incentive than the profit that derives from the trade secret of the application.

Second, the open source community, privacy advocates and institutions could play the role of watchdogs thanks to transparency. Recalling the AppCensus validation study, the US Department of Homeland Security appointed the start-up to test the GAEN.[101] After finding the bug, the researchers reached out to Google – which, however, did not consider it a serious flaw. Subsequently, AppCensus had a long debate about the ethics of making this public and finally decided to do so, hoping that it would lead to a fix, accountability and improved privacy protections for consumers.[102] Thanks to their tests and publication, a class action was filed in

[99] T Zerdick, 'What Does COVID-19 Reveal about Our Privacy Engineering Capabilities?' (EDPS, 4 January 2021) https://edps.europa.eu/press-publications/press-news/blog/what-does-COVID-19-reveal-about-our-privacy-engineering_en.

[100] This statement holds true insofar as small tech companies are concerned. In the relationship with big tech providers, such as Google and Apple, governments did not have the same power, as emerges in ch 3 of this book by De Abreu Duarte and ch 10 by Petit.

[101] 'News Release: S&T Awards to Develop Security and Privacy Testing of COVID-19 Contact Tracing Apps' (Department of Homeland Security, 8 February 2021) www.dhs.gov/science-and-technology/news/2021/02/08/news-release-st-awards-develop-security-and-privacy-testing-COVID-19-contract-tracing-apps.

[102] Reardon (n 86).

the US District Court of California.[103] Users contend Google violated the state's Confidentiality of Medical Information Act and constitutional privacy rights.[104]

5.4.2. Lesson 2: Getting Transparency Right

Transparency is a relational concept that assumes different forms and dimensions depending on the audience (transparency to whom?), the purpose (why transparency?) and the object (transparency of what?). This chapter has taken into account the end user as audience and the inner workings of the software as its object. It has then shown how the fundamental purposes of this type of transparency is to reduce errors, increase the app's security, and empower the public to control and oversee these technologies.

Trust is not just about the transparency of the app itself. It is broader than that. For instance, a report by *MIT Technology Review*, analysing the failure to downloads the apps in the USA, identified the lack of trust in the government and big tech companies as the leading cause of failure, next to the 'downward spiral of mistrust' created by the low usage. This study showed that the apps' failure must be found elsewhere and not blamed on transparency.[105]

On the other hand, a study on the German app demonstrated that monetary incentives effectively promote the adoption of such apps.[106] Likewise, the scholar Luciano Floridi proposed a lottery mechanism as an exogenous incentive to enhance uptake.[107] It might not be a coincidence that the countries with higher downloads are northern EU countries, where traditionally people have more trust in the public sector. In fact, from the statistics of the OECD, the states that have higher trust in governments are Germany, Sweden, Denmark, Luxembourg, the Netherlands, Finland, Norway and Switzerland, where the apps were more widely downloaded. At the same time, Poland, Italy, Spain, France, Hungary and the USA scored significantly lower.[108] Another critical element is citizens' trust in Google and Apple, since most of the EU CT apps were based on their GAEN. According

[103] 'Android Users Sue Google over Alleged Security Flaw Exposing COVID-19 Contact-Tracing Data' (*The Recorder*) www.law.com/therecorder/2021/04/28/android-users-sue-google-over-alleged-security-flaw-exposing-COVID-19-contact-tracing-data/.

[104] ibid.

[105] 'We Investigated Whether Digital Contact Tracing Actually Worked in the US' (*MIT Technology Review*) www.technologyreview.com/2021/06/16/1026255/us-digital-contact-tracing-exposure-notification-analysis/. See also 'Contact Tracing Applications Did Not Turn Out' (n 66).

[106] V Fast and D Schnurr, 'Incentivising the Adoption of COVID-19 Contact-Tracing Apps: A Randomised Controlled Online Experiment on the German Corona-Warn-App' in *Proceedings of the 2021 on Computers and People Research Conference* (Association for Computing Machinery, 2021) https://doi.org/10.1145/3458026.3462158.

[107] Luciano (n 35).

[108] 'General Government – Trust in Government – OECD Data' http://data.oecd.org/gga/trust-in-government.htm.

to the report by *MIT Technology Review*, mistrust of American citizens in big tech companies heavily influenced the low uptake.[109]

Furthermore, the role of communication campaigns is crucial. As shown in the research by Rodríguez et al, 'After a substantial communication campaign, we estimate that at least 33% of the population adopted the technology and further showed relatively high adherence and compliance as well as a quick turnaround time'.[110]

Design transparency alone surely does not enhance trust when the public is the target. The benefits of design transparency need to be explained to increase trust. A layperson may have difficulties understanding what an open source app is and why it is essential for their privacy and security. As an individual, I would be reassured that experts are reviewing or have already tested the app and are under public oversight. Unfortunately, on many apps' websites, very few highlight that they are open source or explain its relevance. In many cases, I only found out that the source code was public by searching for the project on GitHub. Nevertheless, transparency can play a role if inserted in a media campaign that emphasises the value and benefits of this approach.

An explanation tells me how the software works so that anybody can understand, but design transparency proves that it works in the way the designers claim it works. In other words, transparency can only promise trustworthiness to the public if its value is explained.

Information transparency also has a crucial role for end users. Providing effective education and information on how to use the tool, the expected risks, its purpose, and how and why data are being collected can help citizens understand and trust the app – even though, paradoxically, all the apps scored low in that criterion. In a study on the German app, the authors argue that knowledge about the app significantly reduces privacy concerns. Users have far lower privacy concerns than non-users, but they also know more about the app.[111]

5.5. Final Remarks

To conclude, this chapter aimed to use the experience of CT apps to test empirically how transparency has been translated into practice and if it was beneficial. It has proven that transparency is not a myth and that its implementation can bring

[109] 'We Investigated Whether Digital Contact Tracing Actually Worked in the US' (n 105). See also 'Contact Tracing Applications Did Not Turn Out' (n 66).

[110] P Rodríguez et al, 'A Population-Based Controlled Experiment Assessing the Epidemiological Impact of Digital Contact Tracing' (2021) 12 *Nature Communications* 587.

[111] S Pape, D Harborth and JL Kröger, 'Privacy Concerns Go Hand in Hand with Lack of Knowledge: The Case of the German Corona-Warn-App' in A Jøsang, L Futcher and J Hagen (eds), *ICT Systems Security and Privacy Protection* (Springer International Publishing, 2021).

considerable benefits to users. This consideration holds not only for digital contact tracing, but for many other technologies used for different public purposes. As an example, technologies used in criminal justice raise similar legal concerns to CT apps. In both cases, the software serves for public purposes (protection of public health v criminal law enforcement), there is the involvement of public authorities (health authorities v law enforcement authorities) and the impact on individual rights can be extremely severe (right to health v freedom of movement). Even though these two situations are comparable, the level of transparency and the intensity of political attention are not.

I would like to conclude by hoping that future legislative proposals, such as the recent one by the European Commission on the AI Act,[112] will take into account the enormous benefits brought by this experience and extend design transparency requirements to technologies employed in other fields of public law.

[112] Commission, Proposal for a Regulation of the European Parliament and of the Council Laying Down Harmonised Rules on Artificial Intelligence (Artificial Intelligence Act) and Amending Certain Union Legislative Acts, COM (2021) 206 final.

6

Data under Threat for the 'Health' of Nations

MARIAVITTORIA CATANZARITI*

6.1. Introduction

Paraphrasing Adam Smith on the rise of the wealth of nations,[1] the last two years have dramatically mirrored the global wealth in public health. The stream of goods and services that normally measures the level of well-being in terms of productivity and profit of states has been replaced by the hope that data tracing could have saved nations' health against the 'ugly' virus. Waiting for the start of vaccination campaigns and not foreseeing the Western aftermath of anti-vaccine protests or the proliferation of virus variants,[2] one of the common approaches at the frontline of the crisis management and recovery was envisaged by fostering the free flow of information to monitor the risk exposure. This approach was based on the parallel assumption that free competition may lead to the best economic results, and the free circulation of information may produce more knowledge to oppose the spread of the virus.[3] Until the advent of vaccines in many parts of the globe, this was revealed to be only a theoretical framework that, translated into practice, was very disappointing.[4] The reasons are many and different – the strong idea of personal freedom weirdly combined with the unreliability of technologies[5] – but the main

* Research Associate, European University Institute and Adjunct Professor, LUISS University.

[1] A Smith, *An Inquiry into the Nature and Causes of The Wealth of Nations* (Methuen, 1904).

[2] See P Krugman, 'No, Vaccine Mandates Aren't an Attack on Freedom' *New York Times* (New York, 1 November 2021) www.nytimes.com/2021/11/01/opinion/vaccine-mandates-biden-republicans.html.

[3] For an overview on the Smithian theory of knowledge, see PJ Buckley, 'Adam Smith's Theory of Knowledge and International Business Theory and Practice' (2014) 45 *Journal of International Business Studies* 102; see also YN Harari, 'Lessons from a Year of COVID' *Financial Times* (London, 26 February 2021) www.ft.com/content/f1b30f2c-84aa-4595-84f2-7816796d6841.

[4] E Poillot, G Lenzini, G Resta and V Zeno-Zencovich, *Data Protection in the Context of COVID-19, A Short (Hi)story of Tracing Applications* (Roma tr-e press, 2021) 148.

[5] R Ranish et al, 'Digital Contact Tracing and Exposure Notification: Ethical Guidance for Trustworthy Pandemic Management' (2021) 23 *Ethics and Information Technologies* 285.

lesson has been that data-driven solutions are not enough if they are the only ones supporting exit strategies.[6] They need to be integrated within a human plan that does not completely depend on forms of delegation towards technology or specialised expertise but is strongly rooted in the civic virtues that profoundly question the individualistic drift of society.[7] If we try to understand the societal context of the use of technology to combat the outbreak, then we could also understand the reasons why the project of app tracing has generally failed in democratic societies so far.[8] Technology is commonly perceived as a means to achieving a certain goal and not as an instrument that nuances our capacity to follow ethical rules and principles of common sense.[9]

Unfortunately, the whole world has already experienced several waves of the pandemic and is continually trying to escape the next one around the corner, though the trade-offs are still significant. Data tracing has not proved to be an efficient means to prevent the spread of COVID from any perspective. There has been an intense debate on the operational solutions offered by digital contact tracing apps to counter the spread of the COVID-19 pandemic and to avoid protracted social distancing measures. However, considering the radical change experienced by law and society, data tracing has marked a threshold: the more rigorous the data protection, the less data is available to public health authorities. A surveillance society will certainly create the most efficient app tracing system. But are we sure that privacy, and more generally personal liberty, is the counter of health, or is such polarisation not somehow misleading? What went wrong?

This chapter is based on a sociolegal approach that transversely examines the main legal and regulatory challenges presented by app tracing from the perspective of citizens, data subjects and public health. In particular, in respect of citizens' safety and security, the aim of app tracing is to achieve the social need of identifying hotspots without identifying individuals; for data subjects, app tracing should ensure data anonymity, differentiated consent and a limited time of data storage, besides the exclusion of the use of any form of geolocation of the individual; finally, from the perspective of public health, the most important challenge is to ease the pressure on the overworked medical system through an automated system of notifications, disclosure, registration, isolation and treatment that is compliant with a human rights framework.

[6] E Massé, O Reich and Symon, 'One Year under COVID-19 Contact Tracing Apps: What Has Europe Learned?' www.accessnow.org/cms/assets/uploads/2021/10/COVID-19-contact-tracing-apps-europe-digital-rights.pdf.

[7] P Kift, 'Not Tracking: The Antipolitics of Contact-Tracing Applications' (2021) 33(2 (94)) *Public Culture* 137.

[8] D Sui and S-L Shaw, 'Outlook and Next Steps: Understanding Human Dynamics in a Post-pandemic World – Beyond Mapping COVID-19 in Space and Time' in S-L Shaw and D Su (eds), *Mapping COVID-19 in Space and Time Understanding the Spatial and Temporal Dynamics of a Global Pandemic* (Springer, 2021) 347–58.

[9] G Owen Schaefer and A Ballantine, 'Ethics of Digital Contact Tracing Wearables', *Journal of Medical Ethics* https://jme.bmj.com/content/early/2021/05/13/medethics-2020-106958.

6.2. A Variable Geometry of Tracing

The expectations for digital contact tracing were high during the first wave. One unconsciously had the feeling that using data tracing to combat the spread of the pandemic could have provided full monitoring of all individual trails. Identifying and managing the contacts of a COVID-19 case aims at providing an early diagnosis in order to interrupt the onward transmission of the contagion.[10]

Now, one is at least aware that digital tools, namely app tracing, should be considered – as the World Health Organization predicted[11] – as complementary solutions to manual tracing conducted 'by qualified public health personnel, who can sort out whether close contacts for usually more than fifteen minutes are likely to result in virus transmission or not'.[12] In fact, the basic requirement for integrating the use of app tracing into an efficient system of monitoring and healthcare should be an ordinary functioning of territorial medicine. Without an immediate follow-up to the alert by health authorities, app tracing is quite useless. Given this premise, all the debate on privacy is redundant. In fact, the downside of privacy-friendliness has been a quite low degree of effectiveness in the fight against COVID-19. The triangulation between the intrinsic means of emergency, the most relevant constitutional interests to protect and the variable geometry of data protection at least in Europe – which is not configured in any primary or secondary law as a property right in the individual sphere but as controllership[13] – has also not resulted in a sole model of app tracing. There are many variants, which differ in the type of technological architecture adopted, in the type of data – geolocation data or proximity data – collected, in the extent of data processing, in the use of data and finally in the voluntary or mandatory nature of adhesion to the system itself.[14] The first option was the less invasive solution consisting in the acquisition, by telecommunication companies and/or Internet service providers and social networks, of anonymous data related to the location of users in order to track mobility trends

[10] ECDC, 'Contact Tracing in the European Union: Public Health Management of Persons, Including Healthcare Workers, Who Have Had Contact with COVID-19 Cases – Fourth Update' (October 2021) www.ecdc.europa.eu/sites/default/files/documents/TGU-20211019-1878.pdf.

[11] WHO, 'Digital Tools for COVID-19 Contact Tracing. Annex: Contact Tracing in the Context of COVID-19' (2 June 2020) https://apps.who.int/iris/bitstream/handle/10665/332265/WHO-2019-nCoV-Contact_Tracing-Tools_Annex-2020.1-eng.pdf?sequence=1&isAllowed=y; WHO, 'Digital Tools for COVID-19 Contact Tracing. Interim Guidance (1 February 2021) https://apps.who.int/iris/handle/10665/339128.

[12] EDPB, Guidelines 04/2020 on the use of location data and contact tracing tools in the context of the COVID-19 outbreak, adopted on 21 April 2020, § 36, https://edpb.europa.eu/sites/default/files/files/file1/edpb_guidelines_20200420_contact_tracing_COVID_with_annex_en.pdfhttps://edpb.europa.eu/sites/default/files/files/file1/edpb_guidelines_20200420_contact_tracing_COVID_with_annex_en.pdf.

[13] See JQ Whitman, 'The Two Western Cultures of Privacy: Dignity Versus Liberty' (2004) 113 *Yale Law Journal* 1151; S Rodotà, *Tecnologie e diritti*, 2nd edn (Il Mulino, 2021) 43–96; KN Peifer and PM Schwartz, 'Transatlantic Data Privacy Law' (2017) 106 *Georgetown Law Journal* 115.

[14] JP Kahn and J Hopkins (eds), *Digital Contact Tracing for Pandemic Response. Ethics and Governance Guidance* (John Hopkins University Press, 2020).

and analyse the epidemiological evolution through the mapping of the devices of persons who tested positive, and not users' movements. The second model put forward was mainly for repressive purposes, in order to check compliance with contagion containment measures through geolocation data processing. However, this appears to be in tension with the principle of proportionality that inspires data protection law. The third option was based on the idea of making available to citizens an application that allows, through Bluetooth Low Energy technology, the recording and maintenance in encrypted form on single devices (ie the terminal equipment of the users) of anonymous traces of the close contacts of a person who has tested positive (within a certain spatial distance and for a certain period of time) in the epidemiologically relevant period.[15]

On the basis of these possibilities, two alternative types were available: (i) an application that could automatically send an anonymous alert signal to close contacts of a positive-tested subject, who would be invited to contact the health-care personnel for appropriate assessments (decentralised solutions); or (ii) the health authorities, by directly accessing the data stored on a centralised platform and using a decryption key, could identify the contacts at risk and reach them quickly to take the necessary measures (centralised solutions).[16] According to § 5 of European Data Protection Supervisor (EDPS) Guidelines 4/2020, these alternatives usually correspond either to the use of a contact tracing app that notifies individuals of the fact that they have been in the proximity of someone who eventually tests positive in order to limit the contagion as early as possible, or to the use of geolocation data to assess the effectiveness of confinement measures. An alert can be notified based on a time-stamped possible exposure without any identifying data in both cases.[17]

The different rationales are based on the fact that proximity data detects the presence of other devices through identifiers that are stored in a 'contact history', while location data keeps a record of location trails of a person who has tested positive.[18] The European approach – based on a common exit strategy for Member States in assessing the efficiency of digital solutions to address the outbreak[19] – was for a proximity data-driven model based on Bluetooth technology instead of geolocation data based on a global positioning system (GPS) because the assessment of proximity between devices offers better privacy safeguards. However, even this

[15] M Zastrow, 'Coronavirus contact-tracing apps: can they slow the spread of COVID-19?' (2020) *Nature* 10.1038/d41586-020-01514-2.

[16] This debate is duly described by Godano and Sartor in ch 9 of this book.

[17] To better explore the different models, see J González-Cabañas, Á Cuevas, R Cuevas and M Maier, 'Digital Contact Tracing: Large-Scale Geolocation Data as an Alternative to Bluetooth-Based Apps Failure' (2021) 10 *Electronics* 1093.

[18] Poillot et al (n 4) 6.

[19] This strategy includes an EU toolbox for the use of mobile applications for contact tracing and warning as well as a Commission Recommendation on a common Union toolbox for the use of technology and data to combat and exit from the COVID-19 crisis and a Guidance to ensure full data protection standards of apps fighting the pandemic, https://ec.europa.eu/commission/presscorner/detail/en/ip_20_670.

model presents limits: in none of the cases is one sure if the users are wearing masks or are separated from each other by a wall; GPS consumes more battery power, while Bluetooth has been shown to be not very accurate, especially outdoors and for longer distances, and may create many false positives. The European approach opted for a model that allows health authorities to notify risky contacts without the need to identify them. This approach risked insufficient coverage, the lack of enforcement (voluntary basis) and the production of a high number of false negatives: if the uptake is insufficient, then information is unreliable, and the subject who downloads the app is negatively affected. Essential workers, who frequently interact with many people, are more likely to be notified of exposure, but they are also more likely to wear personal protective equipment. Proximity tracing tracks the distance between smartphones and not the distance between human users; proximity tracking applications are therefore likely to generate under-inclusive exposure notifications: users who fail to keep their smartphones on their person when interacting with others are likely to be under-notified, unlike persons who always keep their devices on their person or receive notification despite not being exposed to risky contacts in reality.[20]

A maximal approach regarding access permission was typified by the South Korean government's centralised and triangulated matching of actively and passively collected data with scanned quick responses codes;[21] a minimal approach was initially tailored on the Decentralised Privacy-Preserving Proximity Tracing[22] and finally on the Apple/Google Exposure Notification, and a diverse range of middle-ground approaches aimed to augment manual contact tracing with the collection of digital data that could be shared with public health authorities.

In Italy, with Immuni, the Italian government has adopted an exposure notification solution.[23] Although it has not delivered the expected results, recently the downloads have increased along with the fourth wave. It was developed by the Special Commissioner for the COVID-19 Emergency (Presidency of the Council of Ministers), in collaboration with the Ministry of Health and the Ministry for Technological Innovation and Digitalisation. This app exemplifies a decentralised model managed by public infrastructures. It in fact only uses public infrastructures located within the national borders. It is exclusively managed by the public company Sogei SpA. The source code was developed for the Presidency of the

[20] V Shubina, A Ometov, A Basiri and E Lohan, 'Effectiveness Modelling of Digital Contact-Tracing Solutions for Tackling the COVID-19 Pandemic' (2021) 74 *Journal of Navigation* 853.

[21] MS Kim, 'Seoul's Radical Experiment in Digital Contact Tracing', www.newyorker.com/news/news-desk/seouls-radical-experiment-in-digital-contact-tracing.

[22] The first version of the European app, the Pan-European Privacy-Preserving Proximity Tracking (PEPP-PT), was centralised and based on the ROBust and privacy-presERving proximityTracing.

[23] The legal basis for the exposure notification system in Italy is Decree No 28/2020 of 28 April. It provides that the controller is the Ministry of Health and that proximity data can be processed only for the purpose of the exposure notification's risk, whereas aggregated and anonymous data can be processed also for purposes of public health, statistics or scientific research.

Council of Ministers by Bending Spoons SpA, and it is released under a GNU Affero General Public License version 3. It features an exposure notification system that leverages Bluetooth Low Energy and drives an iOS and Android smartphone app. It collects data in a purely anonymous form, does not identify individuals and does not use geolocation data.[24] It is interoperable with other European digital contact tracing apps.

The legal options of digital contact tracing face an inherent tension between data interoperability and the effective control and management of data flows, for at least three reasons: (i) to be efficient in a world where lockdown measures have progressively relaxed, apps should be interoperable across countries; (ii) if the technical architecture is based upon a non-centralised model under which data is stored on individual devices, there might be an issue in terms of data storage outside of the EU, eg data transfers if the app is developed by private actors established in the USA, like Google and Apple; and (iii) decentralised data tracing encourages the narrative of a model in which nobody can appropriate data or use it, whether private actors, health authorities or individuals, with the consequence that the data cannot be used to effectively limit contagion.

According to European Data Protection Board (EDPB) Guidance 4/2020 on the use of location data and contact tracing tools in the context of the COVID-19 outbreak, as well as Commission Recommendation (EU) 2020/518, the main data-driven options to combat the pandemic are the following: the collection of aggregate data on communication flows in an anonymous form; geolocation and selective tracking of the movements of individual users; and proximity tracking through specific applications made operational through mobile telephony services. Decentralised models are more likely to pursue the objectives laid down by data protection law: the purpose limitation principle; open management; the temporal limitation of data storage; anonymization; the minimisation of risks; the lawfulness, fairness and transparency of the processing; data minimisation; accuracy; integrity and confidentiality; and accountability.

The effectiveness of anonymisation relies on avoiding the potential risk of re-identification that is abstractly possible if an individual is isolated in a larger group based on the data (singling out); if two records concerning the same individual are linked together (linkability); and if unknown information about an individual is inferred on a probability basis (inference).[25] The EDPB guidelines indicated the following as the relevant requirements of tracing apps: (i) the legal basis for the processing is the necessity for the performance of a task in the public interest pursuant to a national legal provision defining the conditions and limits of interference with the personal sphere, according to Article 6(1)(e) and Article 9(2)(i)

[24] To quote some examples of Bluetooth Low Energy with a decentralised architecture, in Germany the app was Corona-Warn-App, in Britain and Wales NHS COVID-19, and CoronAlert in Belgium. In France, it was the initial StopCOVID and the consequent TousAntiCOVID.

[25] EDPB, Guidelines 04/2020 (n 12) § 16, https://edpb.europa.eu/sites/edpb/files/files/file1/edpb_guidelines_20200420_contact_tracing_COVID_with_annex_en.pd.

of the General Data Protection Regulation (GDPR), but can also consent for data processing as an additional legal basis to the performance of a task carried out in the public interest (§§ 29 and 32 GDPR); (ii) the categories of data and purposes for which the personal data may be disclosed should be identified in advance (§ 31); (iii) the data retention period should be non-disproportionate (§ 35); and (iv) the application's source code should be made publicly available for the widest possible scrutiny (§ 37).[26]

In short, the legal basis of digital contact tracing apps is Article 9(2)(i) GDPR, which means that processing of personal health data in the specific case of tracing apps can be performed

> for reasons of public interest in the area of public health, such as protecting against serious cross-border threats to health or ensuring high standards of quality and safety of healthcare and of medicinal products or medical devices, on the basis of Union or Member State law which provides for suitable and specific measures to safeguard the rights and freedoms of the data subject, in particular, professional secrecy.

Once the legal basis of processing for reasons of public interest is met, there is no additional need for individual consent, which can be added as an extra control but cannot replace the legal basis.[27]

Public interest can thus be considered the common thread linking together the rationales of all the digital operations revolving around the pandemic. It offers a reading of the relationship between control and information from three perspectives: from the viewpoint of data processing, when the reasons of public interest trigger the processing of special categories of personal data in the areas of public health without the consent of the data subject; with regard to data access, limiting barriers to data access for reasons of public interest – as observed by Tommaso Fia in chapter eight of this volume – acts as the counter to data processing for public interest: as far as data is lawfully processed for reasons of public interest, it shall be lawfully accessed for the same reasons; and finally, from the perspective of technological transparency, as maintained by Francesca Palmiotto in chapter five, the use of software for public interest should enhance the public control over the use of technologies.

6.3. The Reverse Side of Technological Neutrality

The principle of technological neutrality dictates that specific technological solutions cannot be imposed on citizens.[28] This means that the protection of health

[26] ibid.

[27] Poillot et al (n 4) 23–24.

[28] The GDPR contains this principle in Recital 15. In order to prevent creating a serious risk of circumvention, the protection of natural persons should be technologically neutral and should not depend on the techniques used. The protection of natural persons should apply to the processing of personal data by automated means, as well as to manual processing, if the personal data are contained

should be technologically neutral and cannot depend on the techniques that are used. The voluntariness of the adhesion to digital contact tracing programs means that individuals who download the app or not cannot suffer any detrimental effects as a consequence of their free choice.[29] For example, the Chinese app Alipay Health Code, although not formally mandatory, in fact affects the possibility to gain access to certain places, goods and services because people who do not download and use it are not allowed to freely participate in social life.[30] Policymakers cannot pick technological winners. In addition, as also expressed by EDPS, 'individuals who decide not to or cannot use such applications should not suffer from any disadvantage at all'.[31] This principle has resulted in the choice for a decentralised model in most European countries, except for France, the Czech Republic, Denmark, Lithuania and Slovakia, based on the assumption that a state's interference through data processing by health authorities, although conducted on a voluntary basis, would have imposed a monitoring model not compatible with data protection safeguards.[32] In reality, this option has been imposed by Apple and Google, given the dominance of their mobile phone operating systems and their app store services. As correctly pointed out by Tamar Sharon:

> Effectively, Apple and Google did not just contribute their technical expertise to the pandemic response, but also determined – in some instances over and above sovereign states – which path to take, setting down the conditions for which apps could exist and how governments could use them.[33]

This has implied that, although the final option has met basic requirements of individual protection, it has pushed the market towards a solution that favours the major service providers. They have been in the position to mandate a technological option to states because they have been the most efficient at providing that option.

The reverse side of the decentralised model is that the apps can, in fact, only be supported by updated and new generation devices, and not by obsolete ones. This factor has obviously increased the digital divide, but has also increased the reluctance to adhere to app tracing programs without incentives. A person who downloads the app may potentially find herself in a situation where she can be more disadvantaged with respect to a person who did not download the app if she

or are intended to be contained in a filing system. Files or sets of files, as well as their cover pages, which are not structured according to specific criteria should not fall within the scope of this Regulation.

[29] Commission, 'Guidance on Apps Supporting the Fight against COVID-19 Pandemic in Relation to Data Protection' (Communication) (2020/C 124 I/01).

[30] ATY Chen and WW Thio, 'Exploring the Drivers and Barriers to Uptake for Digital Contact Tracing' (2021) 4 *Social Sciences and Humanities* 3.

[31] EDPB, Guidelines 04/2020 (n 12) § 24.

[32] See Commission, 'Guidance on Apps Supporting the Fight (n 29); C Troncoso et al, 'White Paper on Decentralized Privacy-Preserving Proximity Tracing' (2020) https://github.com/DP-3T/documents/blob/master/DP3T%2520White%2520Paper.pdf.

[33] T Sharon, 'Blind-Sided by Privacy? Digital Contact Tracing, the Apple/Google API and Big Tech's Newfound Role as Global Health Policymakers' (2020) *Ethics and Information Technology*, https://link.springer.com/article/10.1007/s10676-020-09547-x.

behaves well and contacts the health authorities. On the other hand, the lack of any sanctions or monitoring mechanisms for non-respectful behaviours, ie non-compliancy with social distancing measures, limits the general application of the apps' functioning towards all individuals. If it is true that a protective choice for the decentralised system apparently favours liberty, the underlying logic is individualistic and not altruistic: data sharing on a voluntary basis, in fact, means bearing the weight of being exposed to liberty restrictions in case one tests positive or receives an alert because one has been in contact with virus carriers. Making data available for the common good through a form of data altruism does not create any incentive from a utilitarian perspective if not based on the idea of enhancing trust in data sharing to pursue a common interest. She who downloads the app does not feel much safer, but is nevertheless subject to the major ethical concern of informing her doctor or not. Additionally, the imposition of mandatory isolation measures is then adopted against those who have voluntarily fulfilled a civic duty.

From the perspective of civil liability, it is not clear to what extent receiving an alert from the system and ignoring it could have legal consequences. Interesting legal questions may arise in case of civil disputes seeking compensation for damages deriving from contagion. The main thorny issue that arises is whether, in the absence of compulsory use of the tracking app, a hypothesis of individual liability for damages to health caused to third parties can arise.

As making downloading the app an obligation has been considered inadvisable by the EDPS and by the European Commission, the effectiveness of app tracing programs has obviously been watered down in Europe because the non-mandatory character of digital contact tracing has created a hybrid solution, one that is somehow technologically cumbersome yet strategically inefficient, in other words, based on the goodwill of people.[34] The lack of resources to follow up the digital tracing and the dependence of the effectiveness of the system on the number of app downloads have been two additional obstacles to the success of such a solution. A model that in no way incentivises data sharing or lays down user-friendly conditions to communicate with the health authorities subsequent to an alert appears inefficient. The number of subjects willing to use the app, combined with timely diagnostic tests of subjects tracked as being at risk, has an impact on its efficiency because the information is only reliable if the uptake is high.

A hypothesis that could have perhaps better guaranteed the mapping of the infection is the division of the data into clusters of relevance rather than the generalised use of apps. However, from the perspective of the non-discrimination principle, this would be an example of data management in which the opening of an interoperable space for data sharing would be guaranteed by the enclosure of physical spaces: internal inclusion by external exclusion.

[34] L Symko, J Lucas Chang, P Maggie Jiang, R Calo, F Roesner and P Tadayoshi Kohno, 'COVID-19 Contact Tracing and Privacy: A Longitudinal Study of Public Opinion' (4 December 2020) https://arxiv.org/pdf/2012.01553.pdf.

6.4. A Path Towards Interoperability

In addition to national solutions, Europe has provided a data interoperability gateway. The interoperability gateway enables decentralised national apps of Member States to interact with each other when a person travels to another country. As laid down by the EDPB statement on interoperability, it aims to supplement the national app systems, not substitute them. Apps for combating COVID-19 in many countries, such as Italy and France, are under a regime of public ownership, which is released under an open licence. Conversely, an extensive notion of health data interoperability should mean not only that, according to the eHealth Network guidelines, apps should be interoperable regardless of jurisdictions and national borders, but that data should be at the disposal of private actors, individuals and health authorities on a solidarity basis and also simultaneously. On 13 May 2020, the eHealth Network described interoperability in the context of contact tracing applications as

> being able to exchange the minimum information necessary so that individual app users, wherever they are located in the EU, are alerted if they have been in proximity, within a relevant period, with another user who has notified the app that he/she has tested positive for COVID-19.[35]

There may be different levels of interoperability. Foundational interoperability establishes the interconnectivity requirements needed for apps to securely communicate data to and receive data from one another. Structural interoperability defines the format, syntax and organisation of data exchange, including the level for interpretation. Semantic interoperability provides for common underlying models and codification of the data, including the use of data as representative elements with standardised definitions from publicly available value sets and coding vocabularies, providing shared understanding and meanings to the user. Organisational interoperability includes governance, policy, social, legal and organisational considerations to facilitate the secure and timely communication and use of data both within and between different actors. These components enable shared consent, trust and integrated end-user processes. The interoperability of digital contact tracing apps works provided that national health authorities can track the entire history of individual diseases, which depends on the common application programming interface (API) provided by Google and Apple being used across countries.

The eHealth Network proposed Interoperability Guidelines for approved contact tracing mobile applications in the EU,[36] aiming to develop a single app independently of the Member States where users are located. This is based on

[35] EDPB, Statement on the data protection impact of the interoperability of contact tracing apps, adopted on 16 June 2020.

[36] https://ec.europa.eu/health/sites/default/files/ehealth/docs/contacttracing_mobileapps_guidelines_en.pdf.

the different steps that compose the overall process, such as epidemiological heuristics,[37] proximity detection, infection confirmation, exposure risk calculation, exposure alert and follow-up, exposure risk calculation, exposure alert and follow-up of cross-border transmission chains.

However, the purpose of digital contact tracing apps could also be to make public sector data available for reuse in situations where such data is subject to the rights of others; to share data among businesses and public actors, against remuneration in any form; to allow personal data to be used with the help of a 'personal data-sharing intermediary', designed to help individuals exercise their rights under the GDPR; and to enhance health data use on altruistic grounds.[38] Reuse of data in the context of app tracing is currently only available for research, historical and statistics purposes,[39] but a decentralised model that is favourable from the perspective of privacy creates a privileged position for Apple and Google as interlocutors for research data exchanges. One model for managing app tracing could be the altruistic use of data for research based on a legal concept of interoperability that enables specific entities to access data and use them for tailored purposes; another option might be a sort of expropriation for public purposes which promotes the social function of the property in terms of the largest possible access to users for public purposes (tailored on the model of Article 42 of the Italian Constitution).[40]

This, in practice, means putting into place a logic of exclusion, because Google and Apple, the two main providers that own app stores, may not grant the download of centralised apps. They are, of course, not entitled to any property right over personal data, but by providing the API, they open up their application's data and functionalities to health authorities under certain conditions. The most relevant requirement is that the API is configured in such a way as to exclude that the matching between the alerts happens on the central server of health authorities and is made instead on local devices.

This means that, quite paradoxically, in order to protect personal data, private actors may *behave as* data owners excluding from their app stores alternative forms to decentralised models.[41] From this point of view, an interesting study explores the multifaceted concept of ownership in relation to different labels:[42] collection,

[37] It means the measurements determined by the national health authorities for identifying a epidemiologically relevant contact personc and the level of a contact person's risk of exposure.

[38] I Specht et al, 'The Case for Altruism in Institutional Diagnostic Testing', www.medrxiv.org/content/10.1101/2021.03.16.21253669v1.full.pdf.

[39] J Hansen et al, *Assessment of the EU Member States' Rules on Health Data in the Light of GDPR* (Publications Office of the European Union, 2021) 57–81, https://ec.europa.eu/health/sites/default/files/ehealth/docs/ms_rules_health-data_en.pdf.

[40] On the constitutional evolution of the idea of property and its relativisation, see S Rodotà, *Il terribile diritto* (Il Mulino, 1981) 273, 374, 387.

[41] F Lucivero, N Hallowell, S Johnson, B. Prainsack, G Samuel and T Sharon, 'COVID-19 and Contact Tracing Apps: Ethical Challenges for a Social Experiment on a Global Scale' (2020) 17 *Journal of Bioethical Enquiry* 835, www.ncbi.nlm.nih.gov/pmc/articles/PMC7445718/.

[42] For a very informative empirical study, see L Bennett Moses, 'Who Owns Information? Law Enforcement Information Sharing as a Case Study in Conceptual Confusion' (2020) 43 *University of New South Wales Law Journal* 615.

which refers to the fact that an entity obtained or received information; obligation, which denotes responsibility; availability, which denotes accessibility to the entity; physicality, which involves an analogy with a hand's grasp or is associated with something the entity physically controls; influence, covering the term control; and custody, which, through analogy with child custody, suggests influence and obligation. This much depends on different conceptualisations of ownership: whether ownership is considered as the allocation of power or as the control over information flows, or if we rely more on the allocation of responsibilities for information. From the first perspective, the owner would be entitled to exclude others from the disposal, whereas from the latter, owners can be multiple and therefore responsible in different respects for information sharing.[43] It is clear that the idea of ownership of personal data is radically different for a public lawyer than for a private one: whereas the first is more inclined to consider it in terms of control of information, the second denies the existence of ownership without a legal basis, which includes limited ways of disposal as well as the right to exclude others. In fact, regarding apps and ultimately the property of digital infrastructures, it becomes more intuitive and concrete to reason in terms of data ownership, not in the sense of appropriation of individual data in a strict sense, which is in principle excluded by data protection safeguards, but in terms of power to grant access to digital services because of the capacity to process data in a more efficient manner. Providing technical means that enable the government to process data gives owners of platforms a leading position in their role as relevant interlocutors of public entities, leading to the multifaceted phenomenon of data platformisation well described by Fia in this volume.

Nonetheless, are we sure that the big debate on privacy is something useful? Privacy protection is exactly the same argument used by Google to deny data access to public authorities.[44]

Generally speaking, the relationship between the effectiveness to combat the pandemic on the one hand and data protection safeguards on the other seems to be overestimated if we look at the real impact that the design of digital contact tracing apps may have on individuals: the downloading on a voluntary basis, the voluntary reporting of positive tests as well as of responses to alerts, the apparent lack of any central traceability, the storage on end users' devices, and the absence of hints as to the identity of positive-tested persons.

Nevertheless, it is worth reflecting on some of the side issues, as digital tracking represents an example of algorithmic rationality, albeit one that has been revealed to not be self-sufficient, at least to this point. The algorithmic rationality of tracking apps could be achieved through an interoperable data model between health authorities and platforms that is not referable to any particular jurisdiction.

[43] ibid, 624.

[44] Sharon (n 33); V Zeno Zencovich, 'I limiti delle discussioni sulle "app" di tracciamento anti-COVID e il futuro della medicina digitale' (*Media Laws*, 26 May 2020) www.medialaws.eu/i-limiti-delle-discussioni-sulle-app-di-tracciamento-anti-COVID-e-il-futuro-della-medicina-digitale/.

This naturally clashes with the legal limits set by the various systems. Some authors, especially in the seminal debates, argued that, in order to safeguard the principle of voluntary use of the app in a fruitful way, a centralised data management model by public health authorities, not dependent on the initiative of individuals or on the management of alerts by Google and Apple, would tend to safeguard the principle of individual responsibility while respecting individual rights and freedoms.[45]

Hiding the complexity of fighting the pandemic under the veil of privacy shows the weakness of regulators in identifying mechanisms of delegation. Certainly, delegation cannot be solely based on data-driven solutions when the liberty of individuals needs to be preserved. Data-driven solutions can provide the most efficient solutions only when they cut the costs of transactions deriving from the protection of rights.

6.5. Lesson Learned from Exposure Notification Apps

Comparing the functioning of apps across Europe, those with integrated but non-consequential functionalities – such as swab tests, and vaccine bookings and certificates – have proven to work better. This is probably due to the way in which the usage of each app is perceived individually. It is considered to be a digital service rather than a way for subjects to self-monitor or restrain themselves. The ultimate goal of downloading an app should generally be to receive a digital service for which one is willing to offer her own data. It is hard to generally be happy to use an app in order to voluntarily receive a sanction. Obviously, this has to do with socio-ethical and civic precepts, such as that of *neminem laedere* (general duty of care), which implies the risk of being sanctioned only for those who voluntarily adhere to the digital tracing programme.

We then face an ethical obligation that generates a legal obligation for individuals who have been tested positive, as well as extra ethical obligations for individuals who receive alerts. This scenario is, of course, not an incentive nor convincing in a context where democratic principles protect both the minority and the majority, and it is the right of anyone to dissent and express conscientious objection at least in ethical matters. However, in the absence of definite ethical precepts – for example, what were the actual conditions of risk under which the contact has occurred? – it is hard to expect individuals to follow them happily. As the app did not register whether a person wore a mask or not, why should a person trust the app any more than her own self-assessment of her compliance with distancing measures? Only to be aware of how many virus carriers there are around? The

[45] C Colapietro and A Iannuzzi, 'App di *contact tracing* e trattamento dei dati con algoritmi: la falsa alternativa fra tutela del diritto alla salute e protezione dei dati personali' [2020] *dirittifondamentali.it* 773, 792.

app's assessment cannot be accurate enough because sometimes people leave their devices at home or switch off the app.

Is the downloading of notification exposure apps ultimately an ethical or a natural obligation?[46] The idea of following a path with no way back may work where there is a strong sense of responsibility within a given community and one can effectively feel ashamed and blameworthy for not having done one thing rather than something else.[47] Here we face a slippery slope where non-binding duties that one can respect can be automatically converted into legal obligations by the use of technology, such as revealing one's health status as relevant to the law, namely for reasons of public interest.[48] In fact, the infringement of quarantine measures is generally punished with civil and sometimes criminal sanctions. Conversely, if one opts for an ethical obligation, the real issue is the awareness that there is no possibility of enforcement other than through social control and reproof. Nonetheless, what seems to be wrong is a detrimental effect on, and unequal treatment towards, persons who voluntarily decide to abide by an ethical duty, as would happen when they receive an alert and must face a curtailment of their liberty (self-isolation) whereas persons who ignore that ethical duty do not.

This discourse can be broadened if we compare different kinds of prevention measures, such as the duty to wear masks, the conduct of self-isolation in case of suspected contacts or the adhesion to vaccination campaigns. All these actions can, of course, be considered ethical obligations, irrespective of whether a sanction is foreseen or not. It is a matter of respect for the community in which one lives, as opposed to behaving like a lonely individual nomad. The disenchanting take is that if ethical obligations cannot be made to converge with desirable legal precepts, then resorting to the provision of legal obligations (such as the case of advocating for compulsory vaccinations) is the *extrema ratio* that a political community can

[46] On the idea of natural obligation as applied to the context of digital contact app tracing, it seems useful to quote two definitions used by EG LaFleur Jr, 'Natural Obligations' (1951) 12 *Louisiana Law Review* 79: 'Why do natural obligations exist? Pothier stated, "The only effect of the obligation merely natural, is that when the debtor has voluntarily paid, the payment is valid and cannot be recalled; because he had just cause to pay, that is to say, to discharge his conscience. Therefore it cannot be said that it was done without cause." Toullier expressed much the same idea. Marcadé had this to say, "We say then that the natural obligation is one which the legislature, after denying to it ordinary efficacy because of the general presumption of nonexistence or of invalidity, later sanctions because of a voluntary performance, a voluntary novation or some other act which reveals the real validity of the debt, proving to the legislature that its presumption was erroneous for this particular case."'

[47] B Zhao, 'Reputation as Social Control in Present China: Use, Misuse, Abuse, and Bankruptcy' (2016) 10 *Asian Journal of Comparative Law* 359.

[48] Some authors argue in favour of a legal obligation to use contact tracing apps, building on Art 15 of the e-Privacy Directive, which allows Member States to restrict the scope of e-privacy rights, granted to users of information society services – in this case, apps – under certain conditions for reasons of, inter alia, national security, defence and public security. See N Nolen, S Balling and P Stockebrandt, 'In Favour of a Legal Obligation to Use Contact Tracing Apps. Health Protection and Less Interference with Fundamental Rights Outweigh Data Protection Concerns' [2021] *Centrum für Europäische Politik* 2, www.cep.eu/fileadmin/user_upload/cep.eu/Studien/cepInput_Contact_Tracing_Apps/cepInput_In_Favour_of_a_Legal_Obligation_to_Use_Contact_Tracing_Apps.pdf.

use to combat the crisis. The contrary is sometimes also valid, in the sense that ethical obligations that are not transformed into legal ones testify to the inability for the law itself to be enforced, so there is then only a systemic choice for non-enforceable duties. This big shortcoming indicates how complex the relationship between law and ethics is.[49] It then becomes clearer that the choice between ethical and legal obligations is often based on the incapacity for the law to comply with ethics, as well as on the incapacity for ethics to stand without the law. If we were *agathói* (virtuous persons), we probably would not need the law.

To conclude, without a mechanism for case-by-case assessment of the matching between devices sought by the app – through manual verification, for example – failures and errors of digital app tracing that are born as 'inaccurate by definition' are inevitable. The issue then is not only the fundamental relevance of a prompt follow-up of alert notifications by health authorities, but also the checking of matchings made by apps, ie whether a matching corresponds to risk exposure and if it needs deeper assessment. In the end, the project of app tracing presents more relevant challenges than the concerns about data protection around which all its legal design has been developed. The focus on data protection safeguards, although necessary, has downplayed other substantial objectives that inspired its development.

[49] HLA Hart, 'On Legal and Moral Obligation' (1974) 73 *Michigan Law Review* 443.

7

'Brave New (Normal) World': Can the COVID-19 Emergency Serve as an Excuse to Increase the Surveillance State with Facial Recognition Technology?

NATALIA MENÉNDEZ GONZÁLEZ*

7.1. Introduction

COVID-19 is an infectious disease caused by one of the most recently identified coronaviruses.[1] The outbreak of this virus and disease began in Wuhan, China, in December 2019.[2] Research data show that COVID-19 is mainly spread from symptomatic persons to those in close contact via respiratory droplets, by direct interaction with infectious individuals or by association with polluted items and surfaces.[3]

There are several vaccines already approved by the competent authorities, and vaccination campaigns have been in place since December 2020.[4] However, this has not prevented other measures from being put in place to stop the spread of the disease and to prevent people getting sick. Such measures include social

* PhD researcher at European University Institute and CAIDP research fellow.

[1] World Health Organization (WHO), 'Coronavirus Disease (COVID-19)' (12 October 2020) www.who.int/emergencies/diseases/novel-coronavirus-2019/question-and-answers-hub/q-a-detail/q-a-coronaviruses.

[2] Matt Reynolds and Sabrina Weiss, 'How Coronavirus Started and What Happens Next, Explained' (*Wired*, 27 May 2020) www.wired.co.uk/article/china-coronavirus.

[3] WHO, *Report of the WHO-China Joint Mission on Coronavirus Disease 2019 (COVID-19)* (2020) 16–24.

[4] 'World Vaccination Tracker' *New York Times* (New York) www.nytimes.com/interactive/2020/science/coronavirus-vaccine-tracker.html.

distancing,[5] self-quarantine,[6] lockdown[7] and the use of face masks.[8] However, these measures have not been scrupulously respected by all individuals.[9] Therefore, a need to deploy mechanisms to track their effectiveness has arisen. One of the tools to have been deployed is facial recognition technology (FRT). FRT has been put forward as a future alternative to current contact-based identification systems, and as a means to ease overcrowding and accelerate processing time when necessary.

Despite these advantages, the adoption of FRT in response to the pandemic has faced some pushbacks.[10] During the pandemic, the European Commission presented the proposal of an AI Act that banned the use of 'real-time' remote biometric identification systems (such as FRT), although with some exceptions.[11] Further, the European Data Protection Board and the European Data Protection Supervisor adopted a joint opinion in June 2021 demanding a blanket prohibition on the use of artificial intelligence (AI) for automatic recognition of human traits in publicly accessible areas, such as recognition of faces.[12]

This chapter will unveil whether these concerns are reasonable or not. Is the technical advantage provided by FRT against COVID-19 enough to justify its massive deployment? Is FRT a real threat to the right to privacy, as many voices claim? To sum up, can the COVID-19 health emergency justify the implementation or enhancement of the surveillance state as far as FRT is concerned? In China, it has been said that 'Intrusive surveillance is already the new normal'.[13]

[5] WHO, 'Advice for the Public: Coronavirus Disease (COVID-19)' www.who.int/emergencies/diseases/novel-coronavirus-2019/advice-for-public; Centers for Disease Control and Prevention, 'How to Protect Yourself and Others' www.cdc.gov/coronavirus/2019-ncov/prevent-getting-sick/social-distancing.html; John Hopkins Medicine, 'Coronavirus, Social and Physical Distancing and Self-Quarantine' www.hopkinsmedicine.org/health/conditions-and-diseases/coronavirus/coronavirus-social-distancing-and-self-quarantine.

[6] WHO, 'Considerations for Quarantine of Individuals in the Context of Containment for Coronavirus Disease (COVID-19): Interim Guidance' (WHO/2019-nCov/IHR_Quarantine/2020.1).

[7] A Sandford, 'Coronavirus Lockdowns: How and When Do European Countries Plan to Ease Restrictions?' (*Euronews*) www.euronews.com/2020/03/19/coronavirus-which-countries-are-under-lockdown-and-who-s-next; J Kaplan, L Frias and M McFall-Johnsen, 'Our Ongoing List of How Countries Are Reopening, and Which Ones Remain under Lockdown' (Business insider, 23 September 2020) www.businessinsider.com/countries-on-lockdown-coronavirus-italy-2020-3?IR=T.

[8] WHO, 'Advice on the Use of Masks in the Context of COVID-19. Interim Guidance' (2019) 6, https://apps.who.int/iris/handle/10665/332293.

[9] K Abnett, 'Belgian Prince Fined for Breaching Quarantine Rules in Spain' (*Reuters*, 10 June 2022) www.reuters.com/article/us-health-coronavirus-belgium-spain/belgian-prince-fined-for-breaching-quarantine-rules-in-spain-idUSKBN23H2Z8.

[10] European Digital Rights, 'Ban Biometric Mass Surveillance. A Set of Fundamental Rights Demands for the European Commission and EU Member States' (2020).

[11] Art 5(1)(d) of the Proposal for a Regulation of the European Parliament and of the Council Laying Down Harmonised Rules on Artificial Intelligence (Artificial Intelligence Act) and Amending Certain Union Legislative Acts.

[12] EDPB-EDPS, Joint Opinion 5/2021 on the proposal for a Regulation of the European Parliament and the Council laying down harmonised rules on artificial intelligence (Artificial Intelligence Act).

[13] L Kuo, '"The New Normal": China's Excessive Coronavirus Public Monitoring Could Be Here to Stay' *The Guardian* (London, 9 March 2020) www.theguardian.com/world/2020/mar/09/the-new-normal-chinas-excessive-coronavirus-public-monitoring-could-be-here-to-stay.

The question then would be 'what, if any, is a level of surveillance that the population refuses to tolerate?'[14]

The chapter proceeds in four parts. Section 7.2 focuses on the use of FRT during the COVID-19 health emergency. Section 7.3 unveils the possible deployment scenario for FRT after the COVID-19 pandemic. Section 7.4 develops the idea of the surveillance state and the role FRT may play in its establishment. Finally, conclusions of the research are offered.

7.2. Facial Recognition Technology: A Weapon for the 'New Normal World'

7.2.1. A Brief Overview of Facial Recognition Technology

FRT produces a 'template'[15] of the face image of the subject and compares it with photos of pre-existing facial portraits to identify or validate an individual's identity.[16] Such images can be found in several places, from driver licence files to social media pages. FRT is a subfield in pattern recognition research and technology.[17]

FRT's origins are closely tied to the law enforcement sector. It dates from the 1960s,[18] but it was not until the 2000s that the technology started to prove useful and dependable. Its first adopters were banks, event managers, forensic investigators and law enforcement agencies, which saw their attempts fail, mainly due to the lack of further development of a technology that was not yet ready. These failed attempts resulted in frustration and bad press regarding FRT.[19]

After that, FRT first drew the attention of the public due to media reaction to a test implementation carried out in January 2001 at the Super Bowl in Tampa, Florida, where fixed cameras took pictures of the spectators in an attempt to compare them with a database of criminal suspects.[20] Finally, in 2010, Facebook

[14] ibid.

[15] On the definition of 'template', see Article 29 Working Party, *Opinion 3/2012 on Developments in Biometric Technologies* (00720/12/EN, WP193, Brussels, 27 April 2012). A29WP was an advisory body independent from the European Commission on data protection issues. It was replaced with the European Data Protection Board by the GDPR, but its opinions are of relevance at this point.

[16] K Hamann and R Smith, 'Facial Recognition Technology: Where Will It Take Us?' *Criminal Justice Magazine* (30 May 2019) www.americanbar.org/groups/criminal_justice/publications/criminal-justice-magazine/2019/spring/facial-recognition-technology/.

[17] L Introna and H Nissenbaum, 'Facial Recognition Technology a Survey of Policy and Implementation Issues', Lancaster University Management School Working Paper 2010/030.

[18] KA Gates, *Our Biometric Future* (New York University Press, 2011).

[19] J Dempsey, *Introduction to Private Security*, 2nd edn (Cengage Learning, 2011).

[20] MJ Thomas, 'Combining Facial Recognition, Automatic License Plate Readers and Closed Circuit Television to Create an Interstate Identification System for Wanted Subjects' (thesis, Naval Postgraduate School Monterey United States, 2015).

created an image identity auto-tagging system based on facial recognition,[21] placing FRT into the mainstream. Progressively, FRT systems started to be empowered by AI, and the scientific community has pointed out that, despite being two different realms, 'it is important to note that most any contemporary, powerful, FRT has certainly been developed using some aspect of AI'.[22]

According to a 2018 report about FRT from the National Institute of Standards and Technology,[23] huge gains in precision were made in the period between 2013 and 2018.[24] The tests performed showed that only 0.2 per cent of searches, in a database of 26.6 million pictures, failed to match the right image, in contrast with a 4 per cent failure rate in the year 2014. Apart from that, a report published in June 2019[25] gauges that by 2024, the worldwide facial recognition market would produce $7 billion of income, upheld by a compound yearly development rate (CAGR) of 16 per cent over the period 2019–24. This timeline illustrates the rapid maturation of FRT in a relatively short amount of time.

FRT can be classified according to its purpose into three different categories: verification, identification or categorisation.[26] Verification and identification both refer to matching distinctive characteristics of individuals to acknowledge their identity. Categorisation entails determining whether an individual belongs to a given group based on their biometric features.

Verification refers to 'one-to-one matching'.[27] It compares and contrasts two 'biometric templates' under the assumption that they belong to the same individual to determine if it is indeed the same individual.[28] For instance, systems employed in border checks at airports perform this function.[29] These systems were used during the COVID-19 pandemic to track quarantine and lockdown compliance.

Identification is a comparison of a person's face template with other templates stored in a database to determine whether the picture is deposited there. FRT returns a score for each comparison of the probability of the two images

[21] Facebook, 'What Is the Face Recognition Setting on Facebook and How Does It Work?' www.facebook.com/help/122175507864081.

[22] M Mann and M Smith, 'Automated Facial Recognition Technology: Recent Developments and Approaches to Oversight' [2017] *University of New South Wales Law Journal* 40.

[23] The standardisation institution which operates within the USA.

[24] PJ Grother, NL Mei and HK Kayee, 'Ongoing Face Recognition Vendor Test (FRVT) Part 2: Identification' (NIST Interagency/Internal Report (NISTIR)-8238, 2018).

[25] Market and Markets, 'Facial Recognition Market by Component (Software Tools (2D Recognition, 3D Recognition, and Facial Analytics and Services), Application Area (Emotion Recognition, Access Control, and Law Enforcement), Vertical, and Region – Global Forecast to 2024' (2019).

[26] From a scientific point of view, recognition only covers identification and verification. See the ISO/IEC 2387-37 definition of 'biometric recognition' under term 37-01-03 on the harmonised biometric vocabulary. However, as stated in A29WP's Opinion 02/2012, face recognition also covers categorisation.

[27] Fundamental Rights Agency, *Facial Recognition Technology: Fundamental Rights Considerations in the Context of Law Enforcement* (2019).

[28] EJ Kindt, *Privacy and Data Protection Issues of Biometric Applications* (Springer, 2013).

[29] These systems are considered to 'protect public safety and promote better services for the public without raising these types of concerns' (referring to surveillance) in B Smith and CA Browne, *Tools and Weapons: The Promise and the Peril of the Digital Age* (Penguin, 2021).

corresponding to the same individual. These systems were used, for instance, to track compliance with quarantine.

Categorisation can be used for profiling purposes.[30] It implies that the technology is not being used to identify individuals and match them, but rather certain features of those individuals. This function is employed within thermal scanners that incorporate FRT or to track the use of face masks.

As mentioned above, FRT's birth entailed stimulating prospects for the law enforcement sector. This point of view is not far from the current applications of FRT within the context of the COVID-19 health emergency. Thus, the next section of the chapter will deal with the use of FRT during the pandemic.

7.2.2. The Use of FRT During the COVID-19 Health Emergency: The War of the Virus

FRT's competitive advantage lies within the fact that 'Biometric surveillance powered by artificial intelligence is categorically different than any surveillance we have seen before. It enables real-time location tracking … of an entire population at a previously impossible scale.'[31] Further, its potential ubiquitous and non-intrusive nature makes it the perfect technology to use in a scenario where social distance is the rule. This section will analyse the diverse uses and functions that FRT performed during the pandemic.

7.2.2.1. Thermal FRT Scanners

High temperature (or fever) is one of the most common symptoms of the coronavirus SARS-CoV-2.[32] Consequently, the union between FRT and temperature detection systems has been one of the most successful combinations during the COVID-19 pandemic.[33] The subjects only have to place themselves in front of a measuring totem at a certain distance and the system will automatically measure their temperature in real time.[34] Then, the values are sent to the control workers

[30] Fundamental Rights Agency, *Preventing Unlawful Profiling Today and in the Future: A Guide* (Publications Office of the European Union, December 2018).

[31] E Greer, 'Don't Regulate Facial Recognition. Ban It' (*BuzzFeed News*, 18 July 2019) www.buzzfeednews.com/article/evangreer/dont-regulate-facial-recognition-ban-it.

[32] LL Maragakis, 'Coronavirus Symptoms: Frequently Asked Questions' (*Johns Hopkins Medicine*, 8 December 2021) www.hopkinsmedicine.org/health/conditions-and-diseases/coronavirus/coronavirus-symptoms-frequently-asked-questions.

[33] M Van Natta et al, 'The Rise and Regulation of Thermal Facial Recognition Technology during the COVID-19 Pandemic' [2020] *Journal of Law and the Biosciences* 7.

[34] These systems 'can not only reduce the risk of cross-infection but also improve traffic efficiency by more than 10 times, which will save time and reduce congestion': H Samsel, 'Why Facial Recognition Systems Could Rise in Popularity during Coronavirus Pandemic' (*Security Today*, 20 March 2020) https://securitytoday.com/articles/2020/03/20/why-facial-recognition-systems-could-rise-in-popularity-during-coronavirus-pandemic.aspx.

through a computer notification. In this way, the temperature measurement will be automatically associated with the subject in question, and any suspected affected person will be appropriately tested for the coronavirus SARS-CoV-2. These systems might require an identification requisite before the temperature detection step, such as scanning an entrance ticket or a boarding pass (the use of such technology has been proposed to track attendees to big events, eg concerts, sports competitions and trade fairs, but also workers' attendance). Another crucial application field of this technology is at border checks, especially in airports. Such systems are already used in Italy to screen people at airports, railway stations, schools, retail malls and on public transit.[35]

Further, thermal cameras equipped with FRT are being used in crowded environments, where the risk of exposure is thought to be higher, as the concerns regarding the protests after George's Floyd death pointed out.[36] The cameras are being used to monitor the crowd and identify people with high body temperature.

However, the use of FRT thermal cameras in a private company was ruled unlawful and contrary to Canada's Act Respecting the Protection of Personal Information in the Private Sector by the Quebec Commission on Access to Information (CAI). The CAI concluded that collecting biometric data as part of a temperature-screening system did not fulfil the proportionality requirements mandatory for collecting sensitive personal information. Thus, the corporation was obliged to erase its employees' temperature information, as well as the biometric templates it had saved.[37] Although European Data Protection Authorities (DPAs) have issued some opinions regarding temperature measurements within the context of the pandemic,[38] the use of FRT for such a purpose has not been analysed by courts and authorities up to this point.

7.2.2.2. Enforcing Quarantine, Lockdown and Use of Face Masks

FRT has also been provided to track unmasked people where mandatory[39] or quarantine/lockdown violators. Probably, the two countries that have bet most vigorously on this technology are Russia and China. Russia has been using FRT and a 170,000 – camera system to detect whether people violated quarantine

[35] C Burt, 'Fever Detection and Facial Recognition Systems Launched to Help Prevent Virus Spread' (*Biometric update*, 25 March 2020) www.biometricupdate.com/202003/fever-detection-and-facial-recognition-systems-launched-to-help-prevent-virus-spread.

[36] 'Watch Again: WHO Tells George Floyd Protesters to Wear Face Masks' (*Euronews*, 8 June 2020) www.euronews.com/2020/06/08/watch-live-who-gives-latest-update-on-COVID-19; A Harmon and Rick Rojas, 'A Delicate Balance: Weighing Protest against the Risks of the Coronavirus' *New York Times* (New York, 7 June 2020) www.nytimes.com/2020/06/07/us/Protest-coronavirus-george-floyd.html.

[37] C Burt, 'Data Protection Authority Blocks Facial Recognition from Thermal Cameras in Quebec' (*Biometric update*, 1 November 2021) www.biometricupdate.com/202111/data-protection-authority-blocks-facial-recognition-from-thermal-cameras-in-quebec.

[38] Agencia Española de Protección de Datos, 'Comunicado de la AEPD en relación con la toma de temperatura por parte de comercios, centros de trabajo y otros establecimientos' (30 April 2020) www.aepd.es/es/prensa-y-comunicacion/notas-de-prensa/comunicado-aepd-temperatura-establecimientos.

[39] https://www.aljazeera.com/news/2020/04/countries-wearing-face-masks-compulsory-200423094510867.html.

and self-isolation.[40] The FRT system is the result of a five-year project to deploy FRT all over the country, mainly for law enforcement purposes. To this end, most of the FRT devices were in the subway system. However, the rising of the pandemic has modified the purpose of the system, which has moved from testing to mass-scale implementation. According to Moscow Police Chief Oleg Baranov, 200 quarantine-breakers had already been identified by FRT by 25 March 2020.

Similarly to Russia, FRT was widespread in China long before the COVID-19 outbreak. Likewise, the Chinese government has strongly bet on this technology to act as a firewall against the virus, along with a wide range of surveillance technologies and so-called 'immunity passports'.[41] For instance, Chinese search giant Baidu has developed a system that uses infrared and FRT to scan and photograph more than 200 people per minute at the Qinghe railway station in Beijing.

Alongside these international examples, European countries have also used these technologies. In a more 'handy' fashion, the Polish government has implemented the free Home Quarantine app, created by a private company for iPhone and Android,[42] which allows police to check whether people are violating the quarantine and, therefore, can be fined.[43] The app was optional at the first stage, but became mandatory on 1 April 2020. It has been installed on about 230,000 devices. As soon as the user activates the app by entering the phone number and a code sent via SMS, they send a reference photo. From time to time, the app delivers a random request to send a new photo in 20 minutes. The system checks both the person (using facial recognition algorithms) and the location, replicating a visit from a police officer. People who are not in quarantine cannot register, because the application is connected to a database of phone numbers belonging to those who indeed are.

The Polish government declared that the data would be stored for six years and may be available to 'police, state governors, the Centre for Information Technology, National Centre for Healthcare Information Systems and the subcontractor'.[44] We do not know at this point whether this six-year period obeys epidemiological

[40] A Marrow, 'Russia's Lockdown Surveillance Measures Need Regulating, Rights Groups Say' (*Reuters*, 23 April 2020) www.reuters.com/article/us-health-coronavirus-russia-facial-reco/russias-lockdown-surveillance-measures-need-regulating-rights-groups-say-idUSKCN2253CM; A Troianovski, 'Not Just a Crisis: Coronavirus Is a Test for Putin's Security State' *New York Times* (New York, 19 March 2020) www.nytimes.com/2020/03/19/world/europe/coronavirus-russia-putin.html. The purchasing contract by the Russian government to supply the equipment to the system (https://zakupki.gov.ru/223/purchase/public/purchase/info/common-info.html?regNumber=31908446382) shows that the city of Moscow ordered 258 servers and 16 of the latest graphic processing units. The Russian newspaper *Kommersant* has estimated that the total planned storage capacity of the system is 9 petabytes. As a comparison, 1.5 petabytes equal 60 billion photos collected by Facebook.

[41] Kuo (n 13).

[42] https://play.google.com/store/apps/details?id=pl.nask.droid.kwarantannadomowa&hl=en.

[43] The app is aimed at residents on the mandatory 14-day quarantine. Upon their arrival, the Border Force takes their temperature, photocopies their passport, writes down their address and asked them to install 'Home Quarantine' for 14 days.

[44] K Uibu, 'Poland Is Making Its Citizens Use a "Selfie" App during the Coronavirus Crisis' (*ABC News*, 24 April 2020) www.abc.net.au/news/2020-04-25/coronavirus-poland-tracking-quarantine-selfie-app/12173884.

criteria or is an arbitrary decision. Furthermore, Poland's DPA claimed it had not been consulted on the app.[45]

7.2.2.3. Online Education

FRT has become an interesting option to track attendance to online classes, to monitor whether students are paying attention or not[46] and, finally, to verify students' identity at online tests to prevent cheating. In this respect, the Spanish DPA issued a report on the use of FRT in conducting online tests.[47] The report mainly focuses on the proportionality of the measure, and it establishes the need for prior and informed consent by the student. This is a very sensitive area since most of the 'affected' people are of minor age.

7.2.2.4. Other Uses

FRT is also closely tied to immunity passports in the context of the COVID-19 pandemic.[48] Immunity passports might use FRT to tie the identity of a subject to its digital identity and prevent theft and/or forgery.[49]

To sum up, FRT has developed an intensive role during the COVID-19 health emergency. Firstly, it might replace paper identification, effectively reducing contact transmission. Secondly, infrared thermography can achieve non-contact measurement, avoiding human interaction and reducing the heavy workload of manual temperature measurement. Thirdly, different FRT-driven solutions have helped police identify quarantine/lockdown violators and non-mask wearing. Lastly, FRT might play a role in a more online-oriented education model.

7.2.3. When Worlds Collide: Facial Recognition Technology's Challenges

7.2.3.1. Accuracy

Another of the preventive measures against COVID-19, face masks, might entail an obstacle for FRT as they mainly cover most of the face. FRT companies have

[45] A Koper and D Busvine, 'In Europe, Tech Battle against Coronavirus Clashes with Privacy Culture' (*Reuters*, 26 March 2020) www.reuters.com/article/us-health-coronavirus-europe-tech-poland/in-europe-tech-battle-against-coronavirus-clashes-with-privacy-culture-idUSKBN21D1CC.

[46] K Anderson et al, 'AI among Us: Agency in a World of Cameras and Recognition Systems' [2020] 2019(1) *Ethnographic Praxis in Industry Conference Proceedings* 38.

[47] Agencia Española de Protección de Datos, 'Informe Jurídico N/Ref: 0036/2020' (2020).

[48] D Gruener, 'Immunity Certificates: If We Must Have Them, We Must Do It Right', Edmond J Safra Center for Ethics COVID-19 White Paper 12.

[49] Onfido, 'The Role of Digital Identity in Immunity Passports', written evidence submitted to the UK Parliament (C190014, 2020).

been working against this drawback almost from the beginning of the health emergency and there are currently two different solutions in development concerning this circumstance. On the one hand, several companies are working on FRT systems that can identify people with facial masks. Chinese firms are the most advanced ones at this moment and some of them have already claimed to achieve positive results.[50] However, some voices expose concerns about the loss of accuracy that this 'twist' can entail for the FRT.[51] In this respect, the National Institute of Standards and Technology of the USA (the highest organ to test the accuracy of worldwide FRT) has declared that it has started to perform new tests on the effect that facial masks may entail for FRT's accuracy.[52] On the other hand, some companies have started to develop face 'transparent' masks that enable FRT systems to work properly.[53] Another consequence of this change of game is the fact that the number of picture searches of people wearing masks in social networks has exponentially increased in the quest for input data for the new FRT systems.[54]

7.2.3.2. Privacy

The use of digital surveillance by governments to respond to the COVID-19 outbreak might lead to broader systematised adoption of digital monitoring in the future. Further, the opacity of FRT systems[55] and their potential to become a tool for mass surveillance[56] is even worse within the pandemic since the unpredictable character of the crisis enhanced a more immediate and less carefully assessed deployment of such technologies.[57]

[50] M Pollard, 'Even Mask-Wearers Can Be ID'd, China Facial Recognition Firm Says' (*Reuters*, 9 March 2020) www.reuters.com/article/us-health-coronavirus-facial-recognition/even-mask-wearers-can-be-idd-china-facial-recognition-firm-says-idUSKBN20W0WL; P Jakhar, 'Coronavirus: China's Tech Fights Back' (BBC News, 3 March 2020) www.bbc.com/news/technology-51717164. The UK company Facewatch said it was working on an algorithm that enables identification based on a person's 'eye region between cheekbones and eyebrows' only (https://www.facewatch.co.uk/2020/05/11/facewatch-launches-facemask-recognition-upgrade/).

[51] T Simonite, 'How Well Can Algorithms Recognize Your Masked Face?' (*Wired*, 5 January 2020) www.wired.com/story/algorithms-recognize-masked-face/; M Murphy, 'Widespread Face Mask Use Could Make Facial Recognition Less Accurate' *The Telegraph* (London, 15 June 2020) www.telegraph.co.uk/technology/2020/06/04/widespread-face-mask-use-could-make-facial-recognition-less/.

[52] ML Ngan, PJ Grother and KK Hanaoka, 'Ongoing Face Recognition Vendor Test (FRVT) Part 6A: Face Recognition Accuracy with Masks Using Pre-COVID-19 Algorithms' (NIST, 2020).

[53] Probably the most important company working on this research line is Huami, a start-up in charge of Xiaomi's Mi Bands: R Liao, 'Fitbit's Chinese Rival Amazfit Mulls a Transparent, Self-Disinfecting Mask' (*Techcrunch*, 18 May 2020) https://techcrunch.com/2020/05/17/fitbits-rival-amazfit-transparent-reusable-mask/.

[54] A Ng, 'Your Face Mask Selfies Could Be Training the Next Facial Recognition Tool' (*Cnet Tech*, 19 May 2020) www.cnet.com/news/your-face-mask-selfies-could-be-training-the-next-facial-recognition-tool/.

[55] EJ Kindt, 'Transparency and Accountability Mechanisms for Facial Recognition' (The German Marshall Fund of the United States, 2021).

[56] T Guimãraes Moraes, E Costa Almeida and JR Laranjeira de Pereira, 'Smile, You Are Being Identified! Risks and Measures for the Use of Facial Recognition in (Semi-)public Spaces' (2021) 1 *AI Ethics* 159.

[57] Yuval Noah Harari, 'The World after Coronavirus' *Financial Times* (London, 20 March 2020) www.ft.com/content/19d90308-6858-11ea-a3c9-1fe6fedcca75.

7.3. The Use of FRT in a Post-pandemic World

7.3.1. From Pandemic to Panopticon

Given the current use of the technology, will the COVID-19 health emergency encourage the adoption of an ever-broader application of FRT? In this case, the technology, given that it minimises face-to-face encounters, might become the norm for scenarios of large numbers of people, not only at airports and border crossings, but also, as mentioned above, in attendance at sports competitions, commuting systems, mass events and even in grocery stores (with the development of 'cashless technology').[58] In this respect, other biometric identification systems that rely on contact, such as fingerprinting, might be phased out, although this will probably be a slow process, given the considerable level of deployment of fingerprint systems at the moment.

This massive deployment will come with huge costs, as

> [w]hen technologies are introduced incrementally and policies are adopted in small units to deal with a few isolated issues, there is less opportunity to stimulate a social debate about whether we are moving in a direction in which we want to go.[59]

In this respect, it must not be forgotten that 'Legislatures will be indifferent or reluctant to act until there is some sort of social outcry or the impact on society is too great to ignore'.[60] Further, the very presence of FRT, which is often covert, is harmful to civil rights since individuals might behave differently if they believe that they are being watched.[61]

In a case such as the COVID-19 health emergency, the virus could be a catalyst for increased surveillance, in a similar fashion to how big events such as the 2008 Olympics held in Beijing or the Shanghai Expo in 2010 were. Following these occurrences, mass monitoring techniques became more permanent.[62]

[58] A Marrow, '"Pay with a glance": Russia's Sberbank Rolling Out Face-Recognition Payments' (*Reuters*, 22 April 2021) www.reuters.com/article/russia-technology-sberbank-face-idUSL8N2MF4BF; 'The First Grocery Store Featuring Payment by Facial Recognition Is Here' (*Caixabank Communications*, 14 November 2019) www.caixabank.com/comunicacion/noticia/the-first-grocery-store-featuring-payment-by-facial-recognition-is-here_en.html?id=42023#; P León, 'Los autobuses de Madrid prueban el reconocimiento facial' (*El País*, 3 October 2019) https://elpais.com/ccaa/2019/10/03/madrid/1570115313_902888.html.

[59] LB Andrews, 'A Conceptual Framework for Genetic Policy: Comparing the Medical, Public Health, and Fundamental Rights Models' (2001) 79 *Washington University Law Quarterly* 221.

[60] NS Kim, *Consentability: Consent and Its Limits* (Cambridge University Press, 2019).

[61] NM Richards, 'The Dangers of Surveillance' (2013) 126 *Harvard Law Review* 1934.

[62] N Yende, 'The Price to Pay to Be Safe in China' (*Linkedin*, 9 March 2020) www.linkedin.com/pulse/price-pay-safe-china-nitin-yende-md/?trk=pulse-article_more-articles_related-content-card.

It is highly unlikely that such economic and technological effort is not going to be limited to the pandemic scenario and, once deployed, the technology will not be easily withdrawn, incurring a case of the sunk cost fallacy.[63]

> The sunk cost fallacy is the tendency for humans to continue down a particular course once they have made significant investment in it. Spending all the resources required for getting the infrastructure built and stoking expectations that the infrastructure is required for social progress would therefore make it hard to change course and accept the reality that previous resources could have been better spent.[64]

For instance, the Singapore contact tracing app has faced backlash because it has been demonstrated that data extracted from the app was used for criminal investigations.[65] Moreover, this tendency to meet the sunk cost fallacy could 'become systematized, super-charged, and turnkey'.[66] And as more mental states, private feelings and behavioural forecasts are encoded from facial records, individuals can lose more and more control of their identities. They might be defined as belonging to communities that they do not associate with or do not want others to know they belong to. Plus, bad actors would have the potential to build even more general security issues by hacking and scraping. All these circumstances are the result of a 'datafication' of human beings in general and their faces in particular.[67] A 'surveillant assemblage' reflects how the body is disassembled and reassembled in diverse contexts via a series of data flows. The result is a decorporealised body, a pure virtuality data double.[68] When the face of a person stops being one of many parts that form a human's identity but is a series of traits to be processed by algorithms with the purpose of extracting more data, the turn towards a surveillance society seems unavoidable.

There was a similar scenario post-9/11, when counterterrorism measures moved from arbitrary, covert and sometimes illegal detention and interrogation to general mass surveillance. On the same lines, the impact on privacy rights will be felt in the immediate aftermath of the COVID-19 health emergency. Similarly, Yuval Noah Harari has warned against 'a dramatic transition from "over the skin" to "under the skin" surveillance', which is unlikely to disappear after the end of the health emergency.[69]

[63] M Guariglia, 'Face Surveillance Is Not the Solution to the COVID-19 Crisis' (*Electronic Frontier Foundation*, 19 March 2021) www.eff.org/deeplinks/2020/03/face-surveillance-not-solution-COVID-19-crisis.

[64] W Hartzog and E Selinger, 'The Inconsentability of Facial Surveillance' (2019) 66 *Loyola Law Review* 101.

[65] K Han, 'Broken Promises: How Singapore Lost Trust on Contact Tracing App' (*MIT Technology Review*, 11 January 2021) www.technologyreview.com/2021/01/11/1016004/singapore-tracetogether-contact-tracing-police/.

[66] Hartzog and Selinger (n 64) 111.

[67] Hartzog and Selinger (n 64) 111.

ew York University Press, 2017).

[68] KD Haggerty and RV Ericson, 'The Surveillant Assemblage' (2003) 51 *Br J Sociol* 605.

[69] Harari (n 57).

Therefore, one must ask: does the deployment of this intensive surveillance scenario lead to a surveillance state?

7.3.2. The Surveillance State:[70] Is 2020 the New 1984?

Social theorist David Lyon is one of the strongest supporters of the view that categorises most current societies as 'observation' ones, characterised by ubiquitous forms of social classification and management. He also states that surveillance is an ethical issue that should be taken seriously from both a moral and a political point of view.[71] A traditional political question in the surveillance studies is whether the security obsession will, like George Orwell's dystopian vision in 1984, lead to the spread of new surveillance techniques pushing for the deployment of 'oppressive totalitarian societies'. Sociologist James Rule, in his introductory research on five British and American mass-tracking systems in the late 1960s and early 1970s, investigated how close each system was to the 'total surveillance society' pictured in the Orwellian masterpiece. He concluded that they share 'many of the sociological qualities … though of course they are much less powerful, and they do not necessarily pursue the same malevolent purposes'.[72]

Rule's study was conducted during the crossover to computerization, offering an invaluable picture of the historical moment and identifying many of the deficiencies of mass surveillance systems (concerning size, centralisation degree, speed of information flow, customer contact, accuracy, etc). Later studies have analysed the impact of computerisation on surveillance practices, including work by David Burnham on the rise of the 'state of the computer'. Much of this literature implies that the uniqueness of these new computer-based surveillance methods is due to the degree to which computers have allowed surveillance systems to come together to form greater 'information infrastructures' or 'surveillance assemblage'.[73] Networked systems enable data to flow from one location to another, back and forth between the state and the private sector, allowing increasingly complex and efficient forms of control. These authors argue that capitalist societies may not accurately reflect the Orwellian vision, but computerisation does allow substantial advances in institutionalised forms of surveillance.

Despite everything explained above, for FRT, it is generally accepted that this technology has already been deployed under varying settings and/or rapidly. These assumptions are not only in the industry and press discourse, but in the surveillance literature. Even those who admit that the technology is not widely used claim

[70] See in a similar line the concept of 'EU security industrial complex' in C Jones, *Market Forces: The Development of the EU Security-Industrial Complex* (TNI and Statewatch, 2017).

[71] D Lyon, *Surveillance Society: Monitoring Everyday Life* (McGraw-Hill Education (UK), 2001).

[72] JB Rule, *Private Lives and Public Surveillance: Social Control in the Computer Age* (Schocken Books, 1974).

[73] Lyon (n 71).

that it is inevitable in the not-too-distant future.[74] However, while experimental systems are already deployed in a variety of situations, the widespread use of these technologies has not been predetermined. The question of whether FRT can achieve what its supporters are aiming for remains open. On the other hand, the advancement and deployment of the technology are sometimes slowed down by the historical picture. In 2020, in the context of the Black Lives Matter movement after the death of George Floyd, three big tech companies decided to stop selling FRT to the police until proper legal safeguards were put in place.[75] Furthermore, as mentioned in the introduction of this chapter, the calls for a ban on the use of FRT are acting as a deterrent at this respect. For instance, in October 2021, MEPs endorsed a resolution (with 377 votes in favour, 248 votes against and 62 abstentions) asking for a permanent ban on automatic facial recognition in public areas and expressing their concern on the use of biometric data to identify persons remotely.[76]

The problem with such assumptions is that the process is more technologically complex than it seems. Understanding the experimental state of technology is as important as the prevailing myth of indispensability that plays an essential role in broader efforts to institutionalise this form of surveillance and in the wider attempt to lead to specific future goals. Making influential predictions about increasingly pervasive and intrusive monitoring techniques promotes public approval and suppresses alternative methods. Validations about the rapid development and convergence of tracking systems support William Bogard's 'imaginary of surveillant control',[77] a hyper-real vision of impeccably functioning and totalising surveillance that is more real than reality itself. In short, people believe in the power and sophistication of monitoring systems, and this belief has significant implications for social organisation and behaviour.[78]

For lawyers, it remains crucial to understand what surveillance is and what it does to keep the principle of reality intact, rather than what the surveillant imaginary thinks is important. There is an actual need to theoretically address the convergence of surveillance systems, but it is also necessary to understand

[74] M Gavet, 'Facial Recognition Technology Is Inevitable – It's Time We Make It Human Centered' (*Fast company*, 7 January 2020) www.fastcompany.com/90522885/facial-recognition-technology-is-inevitable-its-time-we-make-it-human-centered.

[75] 'IBM CEO's Letter to Congress on Racial Justice Reform' (*THINKPolicy Blog*, 8 June 2020) www.ibm.com/blogs/policy/facial-recognition-susset-racial-justice-reforms/; Amazon Staff, 'We Are Implementing a One-Year Moratorium on Police Use of Rekognition' (*About Amazon*, 10 June 2020) https://blog.aboutamazon.com/policy/we-are-implementing-a-one-year-moratorium-on-police-use-of-rekognition; J Greene, 'Microsoft Won't Sell Police Its Facial-Recognition Technology, Following Similar Moves by Amazon and IBM' *Washington Post* (Washington, DC, 11 June 2020) www.washingtonpost.com/technology/2020/06/11/microsoft-facial-recognition/.

[76] European Parliament, Resolution of 6 October 2021 on artificial intelligence in criminal law and its use by the police and judicial authorities in criminal matters (2020/2016(INI)).

[77] W Bogard, *The Simulation of Surveillance: Hypercontrol in Telematic Societies* (Cambridge University Press USA, 1996).

[78] ibid.

precisely how these technologies are developed, how they converged and whose interests they serve. Why are some types of technologies being developed to begin with? What policies and procedures are being introduced to enable system integration? When and why does convergence fail, and what are the consequences of these errors? When are the efforts to converge new technologies and systems effective, and how is that effectiveness determined?

Because public health emergencies may lead to social fragmentation, increasing public health capacity and limiting privacy, the regulators need to consider, as mentioned above, the ethics of their crisis-management policies. In this respect, it might be stated that mass surveillance is often introduced as a solution in an emergency, and, like the passage of the Patriot Act after 9/11, people might respond to emergencies by surrendering freedoms. On the same lines, Scheinin has argued that there are important lessons to be learned from the counterterrorism field, but these are not even close to what many would expect.[79] However, at this point, a clarification must be made that the COVID-19 health emergency case cannot be the same, as antiterrorism entails protecting the people 'from others' whereas in this case the protection is 'from themselves' (and also from others).

The use of biometric surveillance systems generates a dynamic in which the powerful watch over the powerless.[80] This leads to fundamental rights issues, such as the structural inability to get genuinely informed, free and explicit consent to public biometric processing, which makes the observed person even more subordinate (in a similar way to what happens when the students of a school agree to be subject to FRT under the eyes of the School Board). On the other hand, continuous mass surveillance (either intentional or unintentional) might entail the opposite effect, where a false sense that being monitored all the time is acceptable and contributes to societies filled with distrust, misuse and suspicion. Such a scenario could be a perfect attractor for the 'nothing to hide' argument.[81] Some people might share this philosophy of stoicism against 'Big Brother' watching in favour of what is best for the common good.

As the literature has suggested specifically for FRT, 'Building an infrastructure to facilitate surveillance will also provide more vectors for abuse and careless errors'.[82] According to these authors, the more surveillance presence, the more space for both intentional and unintentional mistakes in its performance.

This is intensified by the fact that input data – in this case, the data used to train FRT systems – might be biased and show and encode distortions and the

[79] Online conference 'High-Level Virtual Convening on UN Counter-terrorism & Human Rights', 11 June 2020.

[80] European Digital Rights (n 10); Hartzog and Selinger (n 64).

[81] The argument claims that 'When asked about government surveillance and data mining, many people respond by declaring: "I've got nothing to hide." According to the nothing to hide argument, there is no threat to privacy unless the government uncovers unlawful activity, in which case a person has no legitimate justification to claim that it remains private.' See DJ Solove, 'I've Got Nothing to Hide and Other Misunderstandings of Privacy' (2007) 44 *San Diego Law Review* 745.

[82] Hartzog and Selinger (n 64).

structural discrimination of the society from which they derive. Surveillance and profiling technologies are sorting techniques: they aim to evaluate and categorise risk, and to treat people differently as a result.

The Council of Europe defines mass surveillance as 'non-compliant' monitoring of non-specific individuals,[83] and the EU Fundamental Rights Agency states that such surveillance is initially without prior suspicion. This monitoring often takes place without the 'surveillance subjects' realising what is happening or agreeing to it, as well as with a lack of a real and free choice to participate or refuse.

7.3.3. Avoiding the Surveillance State: Recommendations

In EU law, measures affecting data protection that were taken for 'public safety' should be reviewed in the light of the prerequisite of necessity of Article 9(2)(g) of the General Data Protection Regulation (GDPR) to ensure that the 'substantial public interest' clause is not exploited as a void to justify the use of illegal biometric processing methods. Also, Article 23 GDPR allows the restriction of rights by Member States' law 'when such a restriction respects the essence of the fundamental rights and freedoms and is a necessary and proportionate measure in a democratic society'. Effectiveness is a key element in this context to justify the necessity of an FRT deployment. Unfortunately, there are no figures about the effectiveness of FRT in preventing certain behaviour, apart from a tiny reference by the Russian government.[84]

Therefore, continuing on the ethics of crisis-management policies, it must be taken into account that in the face of the pandemic, the public may be willing to accept the dangers associated with giving biometric data for healthcare purposes, but individuals should not be so quick to give up such data. When scanned by face recognition systems, they must be informed of how their data is being utilised.[85] Moreover, young people born in this 'surveillance society' are used to being 'swamped' by consent forms, paying increasingly less attention to these questions.

When used by public authorities, FRT must go through different integrated stages of guaranteeing without challenging large-scale surveillance. Firstly, human rights law requires that actions that violate fundamental rights must be limited to what is strictly necessary and proportionate to the purpose achieved following Article 52.1 of the Charter. Secondly, the legislative framework governing technology processing (currently insufficient) must meet legality requirements. This means that the rules governing the deployment of biometric

[83] Council of Europe, 'Mass Surveillance' (July 2018).

[84] 'Police say Moscow's 178,000 facial recognition cameras had caught 200 people breaking coronavirus lockdown restrictions by mid-March.' See Marrow, 'Russia's Lockdown' (n 40).

[85] 'Should Facial Recognition Be Used to Identify Individuals with Coronavirus?' (*Security Magazine*, 20 March 2020) www.securitymagazine.com/articles/91953-can-facial-recognition-identify-individuals-with-coronavirus.

technologies must comply with strict conditions, such as foreseeability and the quality of the law. Consequently, any authorisation and implementation of biometric processing should be explicitly prescribed by law and limited to cases strictly necessary to achieve a legally justifiable purpose. The law should be accessible to the public and individuals, and should be clear and consistent enough to anticipate its application and intervention. Among other things, during the deployment of biometric processing, the law will have to provide clear rules regarding storage, retention, access and destruction of personal data. Thirdly, the use of FRT must be accompanied by precautions to prevent the abuse of intrusive force. This will include preliminary Data Protection Impact Assessments, as well as preliminary consultations with relevant supervisory authorities so that individuals: are properly informed about the processing of their biometric data; are allowed to exercise their rights, especially regarding rectification, access and removal; and have the opportunity to challenge processing operations by filing complaints to courts, regulatory authorities and independent judicial or administrative ones to safeguard their rights, including to legal remedy. Fourth, authorities are required to guarantee the safety and integrity of processed personal data.

The European Court of Human Rights, in the case of *S and Marper v the United Kingdom*,[86] ruled that 'blanket and indiscriminate' withholding of biometric data interferes with the right to privacy as it does not meet the requirements of the European Convention on Human Rights and is not considered to be 'necessary in a democratic society'. The Court said the action was 'likely to generate in the minds of the persons concerned the feeling that their private lives are the subject of constant surveillance'.[87] It also 'adversely affects the essence' (the 'untouchable core') of rights to dignity, freedom of expression and association. Consequently, measures that enable continuous, real-time monitoring, including the processing of sensitive, special categories of data such as facial images, violate the essence of fundamental rights and therefore they no longer comply with EU law. On the same lines, the European Commission has stated that the bigger the repercussion on rights, the more safeguards needed.

Similarly, the European Data Protection Supervisor has clarified that the commodification and objectification of people's faces, especially by algorithms and for the benefit of state surveillance, to be used in a large-scale scheme (all of which are intrinsic elements of FRT), contravenes dignity.[88]

All these problems are increasingly complicated by the expanding role of private actors in law enforcement data processing, for instance, due to outsourcing

[86] *S and Marper v the United Kingdom*, 4 December 2008.

[87] ibid para 37.

[88] W Wiewiórowski, 'Facial Recognition: A Solution in Search of a Problem?' (*European Data Protection Supervisor Blog*, 28 October 2019) https://edps.europa.eu/press-publications/press-news/blog/facial-recognition-solution-search-problem_en.

or the provision of complex technologies in which law enforcement officials might not have enough technical expertise.[89] This issue is tackled within the EU proposal for an AI Act, since the increasing complexity of AI requires experts to advise on the design, deployment and assessment of AI-empowered technologies such as FRT.

The proposal establishes a series of safeguards that apply to high-risk AI systems (including FRT). However, it needs to be seen how those safeguards will apply when the deployment of such systems is justified for reasons of public interest, such as the protection of health (Recital 1 of the proposed AI Act). For instance, by exemption from Article 43, any market surveillance authority may authorise the placement on the market or use of specified high-risk AI systems within the territory of a Member State for exceptional reasons of public security or the protection of people's lives and health (Article 47). Further, when high-risk AI technology is developed and used, the proposal imposes 'some restrictions on the freedom to conduct business (Article 16) and the freedom of art and science (Article 13) to ensure compliance with overriding reasons of public interest such as health and the protection of other fundamental rights'.[90] Nevertheless, the proposal contemplates some guarantees in cases of deployment of high-risk AI systems in cases of public health crisis. For instance, Article 54 envisages that personal data legitimately gathered for other reasons may be handled in the AI regulatory sandbox to create and test 'certain innovative AI systems in the sandbox under the following conditions: … for safeguarding substantial public interest in … the following area …: ii) public health and safety, including disease prevention, control, and treatment'.

Therefore, it is important to understand the legal implications and potential consequences of a potential human rights violation, for instance, privacy and data protection. Before using the services, individuals must understand how their data will be used, where they will be stored and who will have access to them. Only in this way will their privacy be protected. The data controllers have to perform responsible data collection, storage and management, and restrict their use to the purpose for which they were originally taken. If not, at the other end of the spectrum, the same data might be used to track a person's activities and habits.

[89] This circumstance has been noticed by different stakeholders at the Office of the High Commissioner United Nations Human Rights's Conference 'Online expert seminar with the purpose of identifying how artificial intelligence, including profiling, automated decision-making and machine-learning technologies may, without proper safeguards, affect the enjoyment of the right to privacy' (27 and 28 May 2020).

[90] Commission, 'Explanatory Memorandum on the Proposal for a Regulation of the European Parliament and of the Council Laying Down Harmonised Rules on Artificial Intelligence (Artificial Intelligence Act) and Amending Certain Union Legislative Acts' COM (2021) 206 final 2021/0106 (COD), s 3.5.

7.4. The Testaments: Conclusion

The COVID-19 health crisis has been a powerful catalyst for FRT. Either as a contactless alternative for identification or registration systems or as a surveillance/law enforcement tool for avoiding quarantine or lockdown violations, the initial estimations for its deployment have been considerably enhanced by the COVID-19 pandemic. However, FRT's pervasive character and potential to harm privacy make this technology a weapon in the arms of the surveillance state. Consequently, it is unclear whether legislation will be enough to ensure the consistent and balanced use of FRT as these technologies become widespread.

Furthermore, public health experts argue that another similar pandemic is possible and even likely in the future. To achieve effective use of FRT to reduce the risk of another pandemic, a regulatory framework that promotes such use, as well as the protection of people's privacy and fundamental rights, is necessary. Once the crisis is solved and life is back to normal, it may be worthwhile for the different stakeholders involved (representatives of the technology field, privacy advocates and legal agents) to work together to create a regulatory framework that protects privacy and fundamental rights by encouraging the use of FRT to reduce the likelihood of similar public health emergencies in the future with proper privacy and data protection safeguards in place. The EU proposal for an AI Act might be the first cornerstone in this respect. However, since it is still a regulatory proposal and we need to see its final formulation and implementation, only time will tell.

8

Data Governance to Tackle COVID-19: Some Lessons to be Learnt from the Pandemic

TOMMASO FIA*

8.1. Technology, COVID-19, Data Governance and the Law

December 2019 will be remembered as the month in which the world we had known for a while went away. We have heard the story on many occasions now. At that time, a novel coronavirus broke out in Wuhan (China) and rapidly spread out across the world, resulting in a pandemic in the subsequent months.[1] The magnitude of the global health tragedy caused a surge in demand for health-related goods that could be the difference between life and death. Countries across the world battened down the hatches and hastily produced on a large scale masks, swabs, medical ventilators and drugs, while expanding the number of ICU beds in hospitals. Medical researchers throughout the globe, meanwhile, have been hurrying since the very beginning to find a vaccine.[2] Social scientists, for their part, have viewed the global health crisis from different perspectives. Some economists, for instance, have investigated the active role of the governments in handling the repercussions of the virus spread.[3] COVID-19 has posed political and legal

* PhD Researcher, Department of Law, European University Institute (Florence). I would like to thank Peter Drahos, Natalia Menéndez and Francesca Palmiotto for their helpful comments to the earlier paper drafts. Any errors or omissions rest entirely with me.

[1] S Boseley, 'WHO Declares Coronavirus Pandemic' *The Guardian* (London, 11 March 2020) www.theguardian.com/world/2020/mar/11/who-declares-coronavirus-pandemic.

[2] N Kommenda and F Hulley-Jones, 'COVID Vaccine Tracker: When Will We Have a Coronavirus Vaccine?' *The Guardian* (London, 14 August 2020) www.theguardian.com/world/ng-interactive/2020/aug/14/COVID-vaccine-tracker-when-will-we-have-a-coronavirus-vaccine.

[3] Mariana Mazzucato, 'The COVID-19 crisis is a chance to do capitalism differently' *The Guardian* (London, 18 March 2020) www.theguardian.com/commentisfree/2020/mar/18/the-COVID-19-crisis-is-a-chance-to-do-capitalism-differently.

challenges of different natures, stemming from questions on authority, legitimacy, coercion, power and cooperation.[4] Numerous jurists have questioned the role of national and supranational institutions in addressing the pandemic, scrutinising the use of exceptional powers and their impact on (public) law and 'rule of law'.[5] Others have focused on the interplay between law and technology in the COVID-19 crisis.[6] People have indeed resorted to digital devices to resume their working and leisure activities, attend classes and reach out to their loved ones on the back of the coronavirus lockdown. Organisations' occupations have moved online as well. The law has therefore grappled with historic challenges bringing about a cultural shift in how we conduct our lives.

The chemistry between law and technology has fascinated numerous scholars. Law and technology normally interact when norms affect the development of technology, and when 'society decides that technology produces undesirable results and employs legal rules to contain or modify those results'.[7] Storytelling about the social consequences of technology can thus be optimistic or pessimistic, and can be extended to the current pandemic.[8] There exist pessimistic stories of surveillance enabled by high-tech tools, such as facial-recognition systems, smartphone trackers and ubiquitous sensors.[9] Meanwhile, one may tell stories of how digital products allow people to remain safe working from home, or how smart devices can detect and mitigate the impact of COVID-19.[10]

This contribution will tell an optimistic story that has to do with cooperation between entities to fight the virus spread. It is an invisible form of cooperation which concerns immaterial assets. Since the outbreak of the global health tragedy, researchers, digital companies and non-research public bodies have collected and processed non-personal data and information of different types (together 'COVID-19 data').[11] Such practices have taken place on a large scale, and have

[4] U Pagallo, 'Sovereigns, Viruses, and the Law: The Normative Challenges of Pandemics in Today's Information Societies' (2020) 37 *Law in Context* 1.

[5] See ch 3 in this book by F De Abreu Duarte. See also A von Bogdandy and P Villarreal, 'International Law on Pandemic Response: A First Stocktaking in Light of the Coronavirus Crisis' (2020) https://ssrn.com/abstract=3561650.

[6] Again, see other chapters of this book exploring the intersections between the use of technology to tackle COVID-19 and the law.

[7] DJ Gifford, 'Law and Technology: Interactions and Relationships' (2007) 8 *Minnesota Journal of Law Science & Technlogy* 571, 572.

[8] The storytelling metaphor is drawn by P Drahos, 'Information Feudalism in the Information Society' (1995) 11 *The Information Society* 209, 209–10.

[9] YN Harari, 'The World after Coronavirus' *Financial Times* (London, 20 March 2020) www.ft.com/content/19d90308-6858-11ea-a3c9-1fe6fedcca75; M Ienca and E Vayena, 'On the Responsible Use of Digital Data to Tackle the COVID-19 Pandemic' (2020) 26 *Nature Medicine* 463, 463–64. See also Harari's updated view: YN Harari, 'Lessons from a Year of COVID' *Financial Times* (London, 26 February 2021) www.ft.com/content/f1b30f2c-84aa-4595-84f2-7816796d6841.

[10] DSW Ting et al, 'Digital Technology and COVID-19' (2020) 26 *Nature Medicine* 459, 459.

[11] Throughout the chapter, 'data' means any digital representation (in the form of binary codes) which amounts to a lack of uniformity in the real world, whereas 'information' indicates data having a particular meaning (semantic content). Thus, information is a more appropriate label to single out scientific statements and findings. For a thorough analysis, see L Floridi, *Information: A Very Short Introduction* (Oxford University Press 2010). As for the chapter's scope, see below.

proven crucial to addressing the COVID-19 emergency. In short, they serve a public interest purpose. To assess how central data processing operations have been in the global crisis and in conducting a consistent analysis, it is important to pose some questions that can orient the lines of reasoning. First, we should interrogate *what* data has been collected, processed and exchanged, and *who* has drawn on these datasets. Second, we need to investigate *how* the actors in question govern data, understanding whether they keep it for themselves or share it with others.

8.1.1. What and Who

Humankind has always achieved scientific progress through data analysis. Based on what data can 'tell' and how accurate scientific modelling is, scientists can elaborate insights into a given topic and propose scientific statements and theories.[12] As Karl Popper maintained, the latter hold true until they are proved false by novel experimentation. Qualitatively 'good' and quantitatively 'big' digital data and powerful analytical tools are key to opening today's scientific research opportunities, making them 'potentially boundless'.[13] This holds true for global health tragedies such as the COVID-19 pandemic. To make sense of the complex networked research environments, we ought to look into the producers of data and the nature of the data they have produced. Fundamentally, COVID-19 data includes two types of digital resources. The first category encompasses a large variety of research and scientific data (eg data input vital to find a vaccine or drugs), but also statistical data, anonymised data and research inputs.[14] Actors collecting them in the first place are researchers in the fields of natural and social sciences, operating in academia or commercial contexts ('scientific and research data', SRD). A second type includes data of various content, such as geographical, aggregated data and economic indicators, whose analysis shows the evolution of the pandemic. Private actors, such as digital conglomerates and non-research public bodies (national and supranational authorities, agencies), routinely hoard this data in the first place as a by-product of their activities. When this data forms datasets, it can prove useful for public interest purposes (including research purposes) since it can furnish insights into the evolution of the pandemic. I will

[12] See more specifically H Hosni and A Vulpiani, 'Forecasting in Light of Big Data' (2018) 31 *Philosophy and Technology* 557.

[13] JH Reichman and RL Okediji, 'When Copyright Law and Science Collide: Empowering Digitally Integrated Research Methods on a Global Scale' (2012) 96 *Minnesota Law Review* 1362, 1365. On 'big data' and its impact on society, see generally the classic V Mayer-Schönberger and K Cukier, *Big Data: A Revolution That Will Transform How We Live, Work, and Think* (Houghton Mifflin Harcourt, 2013).

[14] Research resources are usually distinguished between 'research data', which is considered the input of research activities, and 'research publications', which are the finalised output protected by copyright. For present purposes, SRD will encompass both categories. Moreover, scientific data created by corporate research entities fall within the SRD category.

label it 'privately and publicly collected data' (PPCD). Overall, there are multiple sources of both data categories, and therefore to list them all is quite onerous (Tables 8.1 and 8.2).[15]

Table 8.1 COVID-19 data processing and its features

<table>
<tr><th>Data Category (What?)</th><th>Data Producer (Who?)</th><th>Data Governance Approach (How?)</th><th colspan="2">Data Processing Practices (Examples)</th><th>Kinds of Data (Examples)</th></tr>
<tr><td rowspan="2">Scientific & Research Data (SRD)</td><td rowspan="2">Researchers (in academic and commercial contexts)</td><td>Proprietorial science</td><td rowspan="2">Data collection and reuse to obtain scientific insights into the COVID-19 pandemic</td><td rowspan="4">'Data platformisation'</td><td rowspan="2">Vaccine data
Clinical trial data
(Bio-)medical data
Statistical data
…</td></tr>
<tr><td>Open science</td></tr>
<tr><td rowspan="2">Privately & Publicly Collected Data (PPCD)</td><td rowspan="2">Private actors (eg digital companies)
Non-research public bodies</td><td>'Data ownership'</td><td rowspan="2">Aggregation and anonymisation of personal data to elaborate statistics</td><td rowspan="2">Statistical data
Geographical information
(Real-time) economic indicators
…</td></tr>
<tr><td>Open data approaches</td></tr>
</table>

'COVID-19 data' is non-personal data and information processed for the public interest purpose of obtaining insights into the COVID-19 pandemic.

Table 8.2 The variables of COVID-19 data governance and chapter sections

	Access barriers	Open data approaches
Scientific & Research Data (SRD)	Section 8.2.1	Section 8.3.1
Privately & Publicly Collected Data (PPCD)	Section 8.2.2	Section 8.3.2

[15] See the thorough list of (open-access) data sources of the US National Institutes of Health Office of Data Science Strategy, 'Open-Access Data and Computational Resources to Address COVID-19' (National Institutes of Health) http://datascience.nih.gov/COVID-19-open-access-resources#computational.

8.1.2. How: Ownership versus Access

Actors have embarked on COVID-19 data processing practices at various levels. We can single out two main trends in data governance, both of which apply to PPCD and SRD. On the one hand, there exists a data governance approach resting on access barriers restricting access to data and having proprietary features. Conversely, an alternative governance mode adopts an 'open data approach', which is based on extensive data availability across different sectors and environments (Tables 8.1 and 8.2).

8.1.3. Chapter Structure

This chapter describes the two opposite data governance approaches that have emerged during the COVID-19 pandemic, its main focus being the large-scale processing practices of non-personal data for public interest purposes.[16] Drawing on this analysis, it shows the restrictions of access barriers and the advantages of open data approaches in critical times, and explores the implications for policymaking. The remainder of the chapter comes in three sections. Section 8.2 investigates the data governance model that is based on a set of access barriers to COVID-19 data. Access barriers affect the availability of data on a large scale and can impact the general progress of the study of the pandemic. They are analysed in relation to SRD (section 8.2.1) and PPCD (section 8.2.2). Section 8.3 deals with the emergence of open data approaches to address the pandemic. Specifically, it concentrates on how different actors have built data governance based on access (sections 8.3.1 and 8.3.2). Section 8.4 concludes by presenting some legal policy recommendations, mostly dealing with the shortcomings of intellectual property laws in global tragedies such as the COVID-19 crisis. It advances the lessons that legislators and policymakers should learn from the access-enabling initiatives that mitigate access barriers to COVID-19 data and

[16] For present purposes, 'non-personal data' is all data that falls outside the scope of the definition of 'personal data' under the EU data protection legislation, ie Regulation (EU) 2016/679 of the European Parliament and of the Council of 27 April 2016 on the protection of natural persons with regard to the processing of personal data and on the free movement of such data, and repealing Directive 95/46/EC (General Data Protection Regulation) [2016] OJ L119/1, art 4(1): 'any information relating to an identified or identifiable natural person ("data subject"); an identifiable natural person is one who can be identified, directly or indirectly, in particular by reference to an identifier such as a name, an identification number, location data, an online identifier or to one or more factors specific to the physical, physiological, genetic, mental, economic, cultural or social identity of that natural person'. Data protection obligations apply only to personal data and form a legal barrier to its access. This aspect would clearly require a more challenging balancing of interests and rights which falls outside this contribution.

thus encourage scientific progress. This may well help to tackle future global health crises.

8.2. Access Barriers to COVID-19 Data

The COVID-19 crisis has prompted the collection, storage and reuse of large-scale data in digital format to tackle the pandemic in multiple ways and contexts. This has not meant, however, that the data has always been available on a large scale. On the contrary, its unavailability has to do with the fact that data and information are subject to an 'intellectual land-grab', resting on the dual capacity to bolster access to information in some cases while restricting such access in others.[17] As Hess and Ostrom put it:

> These technologies have generated greater access to important information about history, science, art, literature, and current events, while at the same time enabling profit-oriented firms to extract value from resources previously held in common and to establish property rights.[18]

Data in digital format, unlike knowledge, is perfectly excludable, and can be stored and used for the sole purpose of the collecting entity.[19] Data holders, by storing large-scale datasets, can restrict competition in the markets ('winner-takes-it-all' effect)[20] and erect barriers to knowledge. In this sense, data is more akin to a tangible private good than an immaterial public good. It does not avoid mechanisms of appropriation. Fostering its access means affecting the relation between data itself and those controlling it.[21] One may think of how industries defend data exclusivity by means of technological protection measures (TPMs), such as encryption, and how this makes data open to appropriation.[22]

Having considered the nature of digital resources, I will now delve into the proprietorial features of both categories of COVID-19 data, which follow from a set of access barriers.

[17] See generally C Hess and E Ostrom, 'Ideas, Artifacts and Facilities: Information As a Common-Pool Resource' (2003) 66 *Law and Contemporary Problems* 111; C Hess and E Ostrom, 'Introduction: An Overview of the Knowledge Commons' in C Hess and E Ostrom (eds), *Understanding Knowledge as a Commons* (MIT Press, 2007).

[18] Hess and Ostrom, 'Ideas, Artifacts and Facilities' (n 17) 112.

[19] Y-S Hu, 'The Impact of Increasing Returns on Knowledge and Big Data: From Adam Smith and Allyn Young to the Age of Machine Learning and Digital Platforms' (2020) 36 *Prometheus* 10, 25.

[20] R Caso, 'La Scienza Non Sarà Più La Stessa. Più Condivisione, Cooperazione e Solidarietà Dopo Il COVID-19?' (2020) 1 *BioLaw Journal* 617 www.biodiritto.org/content/download/3822/45433/version/1/file/40+Caso.pdf; M Ricolfi, 'Il Futuro Della Proprietà Intellettuale Nella Società Algoritmica' [2019] *Giurisprudenza Italiana* 10.

[21] F Brancaccio, 'Appropriation, Common Property, the Inappropriable: Notes on the Law of the Common in Platform Capitalism' (2019) 118 *South Atlantic Quarterly* 857, 863–64.

[22] See below ss 8.2.1 and 8.2.2.

8.2.1. Proprietorial Science and Access Barriers to Scientific and Research Data: How Access Barriers Strengthen the Crisis of Science in Times of Health Tragedies

Three typologies of access barriers concern SRD: legal, behavioural and technological barriers.[23] Legal barriers are anchored in intellectual property rights (IPRs) restricting access to scientific knowledge. Behavioural barriers mostly refer to researchers' behavioural motives not to disclose data to others. Technological barriers concern technology-related obstacles preventing IT systems and devices from communicating data to one another. All types of barriers to SRD access, as I will show before honing in on each barrier typology, relate to the crisis of science manifesting capitalism's processes of commodification[24] and the dominant protectionist narrative around intellectual property rights IPRs.

The crisis of science reflects a phenomenon that economic scholars usually refer to as the undersupply of global public goods. Science has a major role in the growth of capital because of the phenomenon of capitalism's processes of commodification.[25] The commodification of resources, Marx argues, lies at the heart of capitalist accumulation. To state it briefly, something which is uncontaminated by commerce is commodified if it is assigned an economic value ('exchange value') and enters commercial relationships in everyday usage. Newly commodified assets are the raw material for individual capitalists to prevail over others and survive in a system of competition.[26] Being integrated into this process, novel commodities form 'capitalist innovation', greasing the wheel of a relentless expansion of capital.[27]

Marx's analysis serves as a heuristic for grasping how science ties in with the tragedy of commodification and, more generally, capitalism's historical evolution. Science, along with property and ownership, is one of the two institutions forming capitalist innovation.[28] Since the nineteenth century, science applications have transformed into the key component for making (industrial) machines capable of 'harnessing natural forces'.[29] The bigger the power for exploiting natural phenomena, the greater the prospects for survival and predominance in competitive markets.

From there it is a short step to erecting legal barriers to access to knowledge and information. Capitalists' advantage of fencing science in for their own

[23] The notion of 'access barrier to data' is drawn by DL Rubinfeld and MS Gal, 'Access Barriers to Big Data' (2017) 59 *Arizona Law Review* 339.

[24] P Drahos, 'Responsive Science' (2020) 16 *Annual Review of Law and Social Science* 327, 328–33.

[25] ibid 330.

[26] ibid 331; Caso (n 20) 619–22.

[27] Drahos, 'Responsive Science' (n 24) 331.

[28] ibid.

[29] ibid, citing K Marx, *Capital: A Critique of Political Economy. Volume One*, 2nd edn (Ben Fowkes tr, Penguin, 1990) 508.

purposes finds legitimacy in IPRs, such as patents and copyright, and – even more fundamentally today – quasi-IP rights, such as trade secrets.[30] Property and quasi-property rights in abstract objects confer legal monopolies, which in turn give distinctive forms of power to their holders.[31] As a result,

> as property rights push ever deeper into science's world of knowledge intangibles, scientists find rewards dangling before them, such as the start-up holding intellectual property that can be sold to the larger capitalist firm for a huge profit.[32]

Over the years, IPRs have gone through a far-reaching process of overprotection and overextension (better known as IP protectionism),[33] impacting on scientific progress. This has especially been the case for copyright and patent provisions. As Caso and Guarda point out, recent developments in free trade agreement negotiations show there are no plans to break with the past. In fact, new regulatory instruments still foster a 'protection of IPRs [that] goes beyond the level that is economically and socially justifiable … promoting the creation of technological and knowledge monopolies'.[34] Being designed this way, the IP apparatus stifles the role that science can play in global emergencies. The rigid lines of overprotection of IPRs, however, blur when the biggest capitalists' interests and privileges need maintenance. One may recall the 'double standard' approach of a well-known pharmaceutical company in South Africa during the 1990s, and in the USA in the early 2000s. Briefly, the pharma conglomerate did not pledge (or open up access to) their patents throughout the HIV/AIDS pandemic in South Africa, whereas it supported the American government during the 2001 anthrax attacks by 'show[ing] generosity in disregarding its patents and willingness to cooperate with the American administration'.[35] Therefore, IP protection ultimately depends on its 'actual use', stemming from the de facto hegemony exercised by a handful of powerful actors.[36] As a confirmation of these opposing trends, during the COVID-19 crisis several pharmaceutical companies strengthened their IPRs to maximise their revenues,

[30] The nature of trade secrets is controversial. To use a private law terminology, European jurists are more inclined to deem them a form of 'possession' (T Aplin, 'Right to Property and Trade Secrets' in Christophe Geiger (ed), *Research Handbook on Human Rights and Intellectual Property* (Edward Elgar 2015); Ricolfi, 'Il Futuro della Proprietà Intellettuale' (n 20)), whereas some US scholarship seconds a proprietarian view (MA Lemley, 'The Surprising Virtues of Treating Trade Secrets as IP Rights' (2008) 61 *Stanford Law Review* 311).

[31] P Drahos, *A Philosophy of Intellectual Property*, 2nd edn (ANU eText, 2016) 171ff.

[32] Drahos, 'Responsive Science' (n 24) 331.

[33] See, amongst others, JH Reichman and PF Uhlir, 'A Contractually Reconstructed Research Commons for Scientific Data in a Highly Protectionist Intellectual Property Environment' (2003) 66 *Law & Contemporary Problems* 315.

[34] R Caso and P Guarda, 'Copyright Overprotection Versus Open Science: The Role of Free Trade Agreements' in L Corbin and M Perry (eds), *Free Trade Agreements: Hegemony or Harmony* (Springer, 2019) 46.

[35] U Mattei and L Nader, *Plunder: When the Rule of Law Is Illegal* (Blackwell Publishing, 2008) 85.

[36] ibid 83ff.

whereas others have nominally not enforced their COVID-19-related patents against other manufacturers.[37]

Legal barriers to data access, as well as behavioural and technological barriers, are a striking manifestation of the overarching commodification phenomenon. Data is the basic unit of knowledge, and its governance approach affects its use. The governance of SRD is rooted in a proprietary gridlock.[38] The IP subject areas in question include copyright (as to research publications), database rights and trade secrets (with regard to data inputs, pre-publication data, and (un)structured datasets). In particular, any written non-factual representation of an idea (also in digital format) is protected by copyright. In the EU, *sui generis* database protection protects databanks that have been organised and curated. Trade secrecy applies to SRD, which (i) is secret in the sense that it is not generally known among or readily accessible to persons within the circles that normally deal with the kind of information in question; (ii) has commercial value because it is secret; and (iii) has been subject to reasonable, under the circumstances, steps taken by the person lawfully in control of the information to keep it secret.[39]

The capitalist aspiration to competition has even influenced researchers' attitudes and behaviours in carrying out research activities. Behavioural barriers to data access relate to researchers' practices in carrying out research. Scientists often rely on informal exchanges of data amongst them, which form a dynamic 'underground economy' and 'play an important role in such processes as the brokering of collaborations'.[40] They are, however, often reluctant to share their findings with the rest of the scientific community if they do not receive reputational reward. In fact, social and scientific scholars generally want to obtain suitable credit for their activities.[41] Moreover, they will often only share data if they have incentives to do so[42] (for example, if they need to strengthen existing relationships and connections). On the contrary, researchers will refrain from disclosing data if they are concerned about losing a competitive advantage when prompting collaborations with others (the so-called 'competition effect'). This is especially the case for early-stage researchers that need to pile publications up to qualify for academic positions.[43] Furthermore, researchers shy away from disclosing data if they have to

[37] G Santavicca, 'Intellectual Property Resilience in the Era of COVID-19' (*Media Laws*, 21 April 2020) www.medialaws.eu/intellectual-property-resilience-in-the-era-of-COVID-19/; M Boldrin, D Levine and F Toxvaerd, 'Should Patents on COVID-19 Vaccines Be Waived?' (*Economics Observatory*).

[38] S Hilgartner and SI Brandt-Rauf, 'Data Access, Ownership, and Control: Toward Empirical Studies of Access Practices' (1994) 15 *Science Communication* 355, 366.

[39] MW Carroll, 'Sharing Research Data and Intellectual Property Law: A Primer' (2015) 13 *PLoS Biology* 1, 2–3.

[40] Hilgartner and Brandt-Rauf (n 38) 357.

[41] Reichman and Okediji (n 13) 1368–69. See also V Gewin, 'Six Tips for Data Sharing in the Age of the Coronavirus' *Nature* (19 May 2020) www.nature.com/articles/d41586-020-01516-0.

[42] K Seokbeom and M Kazuyuki, 'Incentive or Disincentive for Disclosure of Research Data? A Large-Scale Empirical Analysis and Implications for Open Science Policy' (2020) RIETI Discussion Paper Series 20-E-058 2, www.rieti.go.jp/jp/publications/dp/20e058.pdf. Data-sharing practices mostly differ across disciplines. The most open model on data is in physics.

[43] ibid.

bear expenses or economic losses ('publish or perish' logic).[44] Researchers operating in commercial contexts are subject to business policies that normally label SRD as confidential and exclusive.

Embedding proprietary rules into a technological architecture makes technological barriers an self-enforcement system giving private actors considerable leeway to curtail access to information goods.[45] Finally, technological barriers to access SRD include obstacles to making data interpretable, reusable and transferable to other systems. 'Interpretability' means having sufficient expertise to evaluate data integrity and to understand the meaning of the data on the back of the records showing the data production, processing and sources.[46] 'Reusability' indicates the ability to reproduce data,[47] including the ability to retrieve data 'over time, via consistent pointers'.[48] 'Transferability' means the possibility of transmitting data to other systems. Research data is not usually in transferable formats.[49] A striking illustration of the technological barriers concerns the early phases of the COVID-19 pandemic. In April 2020, the massive amount of biomedical data generated an overload of some standard publication systems, restricting data access opportunities.[50] Furthermore, considerable technological barriers result from the fencing practices of the commercial publishers to which researchers regularly transfer the exclusive rights in their publication. Publishers implement TPMs, which are tools enabling the safeguard of creative works in the digital environments (eg watermarks, encryption etc.). TPMs 'cannot be penetrated or pried open even for purposes of scientific research without violating global norms rooted in an array of multilateral, regional, and bilateral treaties, as well as in a host of national legislative and regulatory instruments'.[51]

Overall, access barriers to SRD end up setting access barriers to knowledge which is crucial for tackling the COVID-19 crisis.[52] The IP framework, being 'dominated by [IP] makers' rights and fram[ing] the rights of the public(s) as exceptions to protection or permitted acts',[53] is mostly opposed to the need of

[44] ibid.

[45] For example, on the effects of 'digital rights management' (DRM) systems on information, see A Ottolia and D Wielsch, 'Mapping the Information Environment: Legal Aspects of Modularization and Digitalization' (2004) 6 *Yale Journal of Law & Technology* 174, 238–48.

[46] CL Borgman, 'The Conundrum of Sharing Research Data' (2012) 63 *Journal of the American Society for Information Science and Technology* 1059, 1072.

[47] ibid.

[48] S Kowalczyk and K Shankar, 'Data Sharing in the Sciences' (2011) 45 *Annual Review of Information Science and Technology* 247, 248.

[49] Borgman (n 46) 1060.

[50] J Homolak, I Kodvanj and D Virag, 'Preliminary Analysis of COVID-19 Academic Information Patterns: A Call for Open Science in the Times of Closed Borders' (2020) 124 Scientometrics 2687 https://link.springer.com/article/10.1007/s11192-020-03587-2> accessed 23 September 2020.

[51] Reichman and Okediji (n 13) 1369.

[52] K Walsh et al, 'Intellectual Property Rights and Access in Crisis' (2021) 52 *IIC International Review of Intellectual Property and Competition Law* 379, 384–86.

[53] ibid 385.

scientific researchers in the current data-intensive scientific environment.[54] As further investigated in section 8.3, numerous pleas have thus been made at a global level to make intellectual property available free of charge to fight the COVID-19 pandemic.[55]

8.2.2. Ownership of Privately and Publicly Collected Data: Features and Shortcomings

As signalled in the introduction to this chapter, numerous private actors and non-research public bodies carry out data processing practices on a large scale. They engage in hoarding and storing data to various degrees and for different purposes. Much data is personal and is (or can be) anonymised to produce information having direct implications for manifold activities. Large-scale datasets which private companies and public sector bodies generate can be reused for public interest reasons, such as obtaining insights into the COVID-19 pandemic and addressing urgent societal harms.

Digital companies and non-research public bodies, however, can legitimately refuse to make data available[56] since the governance approach of PPCD, as much as the one governing SRD, is mainly proprietarian. Data appropriation, exclusion of others and restriction of access by third parties are its pivotal features.[57] An effective way of investigating 'data ownership'[58] is to look into where it derives from. Its distinctive characteristic lies in a set of access barriers impacting on the links of the data value chain, ie collection, storage, analysis and (re)use.[59] We can single out three types of barrier: technological, behavioural and legal. Despite the traits of each type, access barriers are closely intertwined. Each of them mutually reinforces the others.

[54] Reichman and Okediji (n 13); MJ Madison, 'Data Governance and the Emerging University' in JH Rooksby (ed), *Research Handbook on Intellectual Property and Technology Transfer* (Edward Elgar Publishing, 2020) 367–73.

[55] See the Open COVID Pledge, http://openCOVIDpledge.org.

[56] P Andanda, 'Towards a Paradigm Shift in Governing Data Access and Related Intellectual Property Rights in Big Data and Health-Related Research' (2019) 50 *IIC International Review of Intellectual Property and Competition Law* 1052, 1073.

[57] T Fia, 'An Alternative to Data Ownership: Managing Access to Non-personal Data through the Commons' (2021) 21 *Global Jurist* 181.

[58] On the 'data ownership' debate, see generally J Drexl, 'The (Lack of) Coherence of Data Ownership with the Intellectual Property System' in N Bruun et al (eds), *Transition and Coherence in Intellectual Property Law: Essays in Honour of Annette Kur* (Cambridge University Press, 2021). 'Data ownership' is quite an unclear term, as it conjures up institutions of private law having specific legal features: see, amongst others, the classic AM Honoré, 'Ownership' in AG Guest (ed), *Oxford Essays in Jurisprudence* (Oxford University Press, 1961). It is therefore more correct to refer more generically to trends of data appropriation. In the following, I will nevertheless use 'data ownership' as a synonym for 'data appropriation' and other similar expressions since it has gained traction as the major accepted form, especially within the IP literature.

[59] Rubinfeld and Gal (n 23) 349ff.

Technological barriers can be considered in three veins. First, they occur when an actor can deploy more efficient technologies than others. In this case, they result in several economic phenomena which are typically studied in microeconomics (eg economies of scale, economies of speed, multisided markets and positive network externalities).[60] A second type arises from utilising TPMs, as has been mentioned above. Even where mass unstructured datasets fall short of copyright protection,[61] the TPMs used to protect them do not enjoy actual legal protection,[62] but amount to self-enforced restrictions of data access.[63]

Behavioural barriers mostly occur where there are contractual limitations to some data processing practices.[64] Such exclusionary behaviours are mostly indicative of unequal bargaining power between the contractual parties.[65] Other barriers of this kind stem from the factual and arbitrary behaviours preventing data from being accessible, eg one entity's choice not to release data upon another's request. As for public bodies, a lack of transparency and accountability ensues in these cases, since they cannot account for decision-making impacting on people's lives.

Legal barriers to access stem from the allocation of intellectual property rights or, with regard to publicly collected data, even state secrets. Most legal scholars agree that only trade secrecy fits massive unstructured sets of non-personal data.[66] Secret holders are protected if they take reasonable steps to keep information secret.[67] Legal protection depends on (the extent of) factual secrecy of the data or information. Holders of large-scale datasets keep them secret by implementing

[60] See ibid.

[61] TJ Farkas, 'Data Created by the Internet of Things: The New Gold without Ownership?' (2017) 23 *Revista La Propiedad Inmaterial* 5, 8–9.

[62] TPMs are legally recognised if targeted to prevent copyright-infringing behaviours (Directive 2001/29/EC on the harmonization of certain aspects of copyright and copyright related rights in the information society of 22 May 2001 [2001] OJ L167/10, art 6). See H Ullrich, 'Technology Protection and Competition Policy for the Information Economy. From Property Rights for Competition to Competition without Proper Rights?' (Max Planck Institute for Innovation and Competition, 2019) Research Paper No 19-12, 20–21.

[63] See similarly Ullrich (n 62) 27; F Mezzanotte, 'Access to Data: The Role of Consent and the Licensing Scheme' in S Lohsse, R Schulze and D Staudenmayer (eds), *Trading Data in the Digital Economy: Legal Concepts and Tools. Münster Colloquia on EU Law and the Digital Economy III* (Nomos, 2017) 168.

[64] See, more specifically, N Tusikov, 'Precarious Ownership of the Internet of Things in the Age of Data' in B Haggart, K Henne and N Tusikov (eds), *Information, Technology and Control in a Changing World: Understanding Power Structures in the 21st Century* (Palgrave Macmillan, 2019) 127; M Ricolfi, 'IoT and The Ages of Antitrust' (2017) 1 *Concorrenza e Mercato* 215, 223–24; M Grünberger, 'Data Access Rules: The Role of Contractual Unfairness Control of (Consumer) Contracts' in German Federal Ministry of Justice and Consumer Protection Max Planck Institute for Innovation and Competition (eds), *Data Access, Consumer Interests and Public Welfare* (Nomos, 2021) 255ff.

[65] J Drexl et al, 'Position Statement of the Max Planck Institute for Innovation and Competition of 26 April 2017 on the European Commission's "Public Consultation on Building the European Data Economy"' (Max Planck Institute for Innovation and Competition, 2017) Research Paper No 17-08, 10.

[66] H Zech, 'Data as a Tradeable Commodity' in A De Franceschi (ed), *European Contract Law and the Digital Single Market: The Implications of the Digital Revolution* (Intersentia, 2016) 62–65; Ricolfi (n 64); Ricolfi (n 20).

[67] Trade Secrets Directive, Art 2(1)(c).

organisational measures (eg access authorisations to offices), contractual arrangements (non-disclosure agreements) and technical measures (eg data encryption).[68] On the other hand, public authorities can rely on state secrecy to restrict data access as a result of the process of 'securitisation' of public policies such as defence, law enforcement, public health, climate change and finance.[69]

By relying on data ownership, both the private sector and public bodies have restricted access to PPCD during the COVID-19 pandemic, especially in its early phase (mid- and late 2020). On the one hand, private sector companies can simply prevent access to large-scale datasets even if they may prove useful for reuse for research or other public interest purposes.[70] This has been the case in Italy. In October 2020, Andrea Crisanti, an Italian parasitologist, claimed that researchers need to rely on data collected by digital platforms (eg Facebook) and search engines to navigate the coronavirus tragedy, threatening to bring a criminal lawsuit against them to open up data access.[71] Amongst other purposes, Facebook's (anonymised) data is of use in tracking the spread of COVID-19 and predicting outbreaks of the virus. Meanwhile, in some cases, public bodies refused to open up data access to researchers. Researchers generally report a lack of globally available datasets of COVID-19 information and 'comprehensive information beyond typical registry resolution'.[72] Moreover, the exercise of (state) secrecy prevents scientists and statisticians from identifying countries that are coping with the pandemic in more effective ways than others.[73] Illustrative of the problem is, again, the approach of the Italian government in 2020. In June 2020, the Accademia dei Lincei, one of the most important Italian public science organisations, urged the national government to make epidemiological data publicly available to researchers and academics.[74] National and local health authorities,

[68] A Wiebe and Nico Schur, 'Protection of Trade Secrets in a Data-Driven, Networked Environment – Is the Update Already Out-Dated?' (2019) 14 *Journal of Intellectual Property Law and Practice* 814, 818–21.

[69] In particular, governments increasingly consider public health issues as a potential security threat to which secrecy of information should be expanded. See B Rittberger and KH Goetz, 'Secrecy in Europe' (2018) 41 *West European Politics* 825, 827.

[70] J Ausloos, P Leerssen and P ten Thije, 'Operationalizing Research Access in Platform Governance What to Learn from Other Industries?' (Algorithm Watch, 2020) 17, https://algorithmwatch.org/wp-content/uploads/2020/06/GoverningPlatforms_IViR_study_June2020-AlgorithmWatch-2020-06-24.pdf. See Commission, 'A European Strategy for Data' (Communication) COM (2020) 66 final, 6, pointing out that 'Several of the issues concern the availability of data for the public good' and specifying that data for the public good is data 'created by society and *can serve to combat emergencies*, such as floods and wildfires, *to ensure that people can live longer and healthier lives*' (emphasis added).

[71] P Pagliaro, 'Dati attendibili sono il primo vaccino' *9Colonne* (Rome, 19 October 2020) www.9colonne.it/278994/dati-attendibili-br-sono-il-primo-vaccino#.X47ZNS8QPMI.

[72] CV Cosgriff, DK Ebner and LA Celi, 'Data Sharing in the Era of COVID-19' (2020) 2 *The Lancet Digital Health* e224, e224, www.thelancet.com/journals/landig/article/PIIS2589-7500(20)30082-0/fulltext.

[73] HM Baniamin, M Rahman and MT Hasan, 'The COVID-19 Pandemic: Why Are Some Countries Coping More Successfully than Others?' (2020) 42 *Asia Pacific Journal of Public Administration* 153, 153.

[74] Accademia Nazionale dei Lincei, 'Dati pubblici, governo delle epidemie e democrazia' (2020) Report of the Commissione COVID-19, www.lincei.it/sites/default/files/documenti/Commissioni/ANL_Comm_COVID-19_dati_pubblici_1giugno2020.pdf.

however, refrained from sharing it.[75] In November 2020, the Hume Foundation, an Italian institution doing statistical research, made a plea to the government to create a publicly accessible database of epidemiological data collected by health authorities, and to make other publicly collected data available.[76] Similarly, on 10 November 2020, the non-profit organisation Ondata launched a petition to the Italian government. It specifically asked to 'make available, open and interoperable (machine readable) and disaggregated, all the data communicated by the Regions to the Government since the beginning of the epidemic' and to 'establish a national COVID-19 data centre which imposes standards and formats, coordinates and integrates new collection systems, and identifies critical issues in the existing ones'.[77] In 2021, issues of the same sort reappeared when tackling the subsequent pandemic waves. In October 2021, even though the Accademia dei Lincei has been provided with access to epidemiological data, only a few institutions could access this information held by the Accademia, leaving out independent researchers and non-recipient entities.[78] In December 2021, a major Italian newspaper complained about the fact that the Italian Ministry of Education would not release data about infections in schools.[79] Analogous issues have concerned other countries throughout the various pandemic waves. For instance, on 5 November 2020, the UK Office for Statistics Regulation requested that the UK government publish the sources of data which is 'used publicly', or the data itself 'alongside any press briefing and associated slides to allow people to understand their strengths and limitations'.[80] Moreover, they asked the government to make underlying data available 'where key decisions are justified by reference to statistics or management information' to foster transparency of decisions.[81] On the other side of the Atlantic, state and local officials in California and other US states denied researchers access to in-depth

[75] See A Capocci, 'Gli scienziati scrivono al governo: "Misure drastiche subito" o il virus andrà fuori controllo' *Il Manifesto* (Rome, 23 October 2020) http://ilmanifesto.it/gli-scienziati-scrivono-al-governo-misure-drastiche-subito-o-il-virus-andra-fuori-controllo, mentioning that Italian scientists and researchers asked health authorities to release data on the pandemic; L Ricolfi, 'Altro che modello italiano sulla pandemia. Intervista a Luca Ricolfi' (Fondazione David Hume, 3 September 2020) www.fondazionehume.it/politica/altro-che-modello-italiano-sulla-pandemia-intervista-a-luca-ricolfi, claiming that most data held by public authorities is classified and cannot be accessed to elaborate statistical models on the pandemic.

[76] Fondazione David Hume, 'Un appello e un decalogo per salvare l'Italia' (2020) 5, www.fondazionehume.it/wp-content/uploads/2020/10/Operazione-verità_4.pdf.

[77] Ondata, '#datiBeneComune' (2020) https://datibenecomune.it/?fbclid=IwAR3IgC5bdgVxHINIeVqynTlMRNmcpeXBk5dbxtmN1ph2xDVsJrT9hqGV8FM.

[78] A Twitter user carrying out independent research activities brought up this issue: https://twitter.com/SignorErnesto/status/1446106574800388101?s=20.

[79] D Fiori, 'Gli italiani a caccia dei tamponi, tra il Natale e i casi nelle scuole: l'incidenza tra gli under 20 è la più alta, ma il ministero non diffonde i dati' *Il Fatto Quotidiano* (Rome, 21 December 2021) www.ilfattoquotidiano.it/2021/12/21/gli-italiani-a-caccia-dei-tamponi-tra-il-natale-e-i-casi-nelle-scuole-lincidenza-tra-gli-under-20-e-la-piu-alta-ma-il-ministero-non-diffonde-i-dati/6433439/.

[80] Office for Statistics Regulation, 'OSR Statement Regarding Transparency of Data Related to COVID-19' (5 November 2020) https://osr.statisticsauthority.gov.uk/news/osr-statement-regarding-transparency-of-data-related-to-COVID-19/.

[81] ibid.

data on the pandemic, adducing multiple reasons, such as workload constraints and privacy reasons.[82]

8.3. Data Access to Tackle the Pandemic and End the Proprietorial Gridlock

Left alone, proprietary governance approaches could dramatically curtail the diffusion of knowledge about how to tackle COVID-19. There have, however, been a number of opposing forces that have fostered access to SRD and PPCD. On the one hand, numerous initiatives bolstering access to SRD characterise scientific production. By relying on open data approaches, researchers form the basis for 'Open Science'.[83] PPCD is the other side of the coin. The need to address the pandemic has caused private conglomerations and non-research public bodies to open up data access in the public interest. In some cases, corporate actors and public institutions have come up with efficient means of organising data sources ('data platformisation'). These data sources encompass both SRD and PPCD.

8.3.1. Access to Scientific and Research Data and COVID-19

Data access initiatives to tackle the COVID-19 crisis have emerged since the first phase of the pandemic. As analysed in section 8.2, during global tragedies such as pandemics, the withholding of COVID-19 data slows scientific progress. This aspect has been clear for some time now and has prompted the scientific community to come up with open data approaches. For example, the lack of data sharing impacted on the management of the 2013–16 Ebola disease outbreak in Western Africa.[84] Instructive cases such as this one have persuaded the scientific community to find alternatives. In fact, during the World Health Organization (WHO) consultation in September 2015, multiple stakeholders agreed that opening up data access must become the 'global norm' in public health tragedies[85] and ought to be viewed as a 'moral obligation'.[86]

Yet, making data and information available for the purposes of scientific research is not an entirely novel idea. It revolves around the notion of 'Open Science'. Based on Robert K Merton's institutional norms of 'priority' and 'communism',

[82] C Piller, 'Data Secrecy May Cripple US Attempts to Slow Pandemic' (2020) 369 *Science* 356.
[83] See section 8.3.2 below.
[84] V Moorthy et al, 'Data Sharing for Novel Coronavirus (COVID-19)' (2020) 98 *Bulletin of the World Health Organization* 150, 150.
[85] K Modjarrad et al, 'Developing Global Norms for Sharing Data and Results during Public Health Emergencies' (2016) 13 *PLoS Medicine* 1.
[86] Gewin (n 41).

Open Science balances the claims of the scholar who is the first to discover a natural phenomenon with the interests of the scientific community and the general public in accessing the knowledge.[87] For present purposes, Open Science means that SRD should, as a rule, be freely available.[88] 'Free' implies both senses of 'no charge' and 'with no restrictions in reuse'.[89] In this sense, Open Science espouses an open, indiscriminate and free approach to data access.

Put that way, the conceptual framework of Open Science may be at odds with proprietorial science and especially the nature of IPRs. There exist, however, mechanisms to drive down the 'highly protectionist' IP standards[90] and make them fit for purpose. Copyright is an instructive subject area in this respect. Copyright protection encompasses both economic rights (right to gain economic advantages from the creative work) and moral rights (right of attribution or paternity). Open science implies that the first set of rights and prerogatives in a work are to be (contractually) transferred to the public, whereas the merits of the work are still attributed to the author and recognised as such.[91] This is certainly one of the current trends in scientific research. Since the early 2000s, academic researchers and scientists have been more inclined to match and pool data collected in databases and waive IPRs in them.[92] This has facilitated the emergence of contractual schemes aimed at opening up scientific data, including Creative Commons (CC) licences.[93] Furthermore, the Open Knowledge Foundation has developed open licences for databases and data which are not copyrightable, ie the Open Data Commons Open Database License, the Open Data Commons Attribution License and the Open Data Commons Public Domain Dedication and Licence.[94]

[87] Caso and Guarda, 'Copyright Overprotection Versus Open Science' 39, citing RK Merton, 'Priorities in Scientific Discovery: A Chapter in the Sociology of Science' (1957) 22 *American Sociological Review* 635.

[88] B Fecher and S Friesike, 'Open Science: One Term, Five Schools of Thought' in S Bartling and S Friesike (eds), *Opening Science: The Evolving Guide on How the Internet is Changing Research, Collaboration and Scholarly Publishing* (Springer, 2014) 25–32.

[89] Caso and Guarda (n 34) 37. In this respect, the Internet has certainly been a fundamental turning point in making digital communications easier and freer.

[90] Reichman and Uhlir (n 33).

[91] JF Córdoba-Marentes, 'Towards a Fair Intellectual Property Framework for Open Science: A Comparative Law Approach' in DJ Gervais (ed), *Fairness, Morality and Ordre Public in Intellectual Property* (Edward Elgar Publishing, 2020) 271; Caso and Guarda (n 34) 38.

[92] SM Maurer, 'New Institutions for Doing Science: From Databases to Open Source Biology' (2003) Paper presented at the European Policy for Intellectual Property Conference on Copyright and database protection, patents and research tools, and other challenges to the intellectual property system, 3–6, http://www.merit.unimaas.nl/epip/papers/maurer_paper.pdf. Researchers working for companies (eg multinationals, start-ups) are subject to corporate policies on data sharing, which are normally more restrictive in this sense (see s 8.2.1).

[93] M Maggiolino and ML Montagnani, 'Standardized Terms and Conditions for Open Patenting' (2013) 14 *Minnesota Journal of Law, Science and Technology* 785; Caso and Guarda (n 34) 38. The most used typologies of CC model clauses include CC Attribution (CC BY) and CC Attribution-Share-Alike (BY-SA): see Creative Commons, 'About the Licenses' (Creative Commons) http://creativecommons.org/licenses.

[94] See Open Knowledge Foundation, 'Licenses' (Open Data Commons: Legal Tool for Open Data) http://opendatacommons.org/licenses.

The COVID-19 crisis has prompted numerous research institutions to adopt open data approaches. Two main trends can be singled out in this respect. First, there are research organisations that are committed to opening up access to SRD by relying on opening large cooperative datasets.[95] The latter concern, inter alia, genetic features of the virus and statistics on the worldwide evolution trend of the pandemic. Genome information has been hoarded through data lakes[96] such as Genbank,[97] Nextstrain[98] and Gisaid.[99] As for statistical information, the Complexity Science Hub, an Austrian organisation operating in 'the research of complex systems, system analysis and big data science',[100] has released a large database on the non-pharmaceutical interventions taken by national governments through a CC, BY-SA.[101] Second, access to scientific publications and research papers has been fostered on the back of public pleas. Research institutions, public funders and governments have advocated a shift in the default ownership-like governance approach with regard to SRD owned by large-sized commercial publishers.[102] For example, on 27 October 2020, the heads of UNESCO, WHO and CERN appealed for a 'global push towards "open science"', embracing solidarity as a 'model for the future' to tackle global challenges.[103] As a result, scientific publishers have temporarily released contributions that might prove useful in the common struggle against COVID-19.[104] Researchers, for their part, are more inclined to release their outputs in preprints, which are mostly shared with the rest of the scientific community through online platforms (eg SSRN). Releasing preprints accelerates the diffusion of scientific findings[105] and allows researchers to shy away from some opaque and slow systems of peer review.[106]

Ultimately, open science initiatives have played a crucial role in the pandemic world by mitigating the proprietary characteristics of access barriers to SRD.[107]

[95] Caso (n 20) 619.

[96] ibid 620.

[97] GenBank, www.ncbi.nlm.nih.gov/genbank.

[98] Nextstrain, http://nextstrain.org.

[99] Gisaid, http://www.gisaid.org.

[100] Wikimedia Foundation, 'Complexity Science Hub Vienna' (Wikipedia) http://en.wikipedia.org/wiki/Complexity_Science_Hub_Vienna.

[101] Complexity Science Hub, COVID-19 Control Strategies List (GitHub) http://github.com/amel-github/COVID19-interventionmeasures.

[102] VWJ van Gerven Oei, 'Viral Open Access in Times of a Global Pandemic' (Punctum Books, 19 March 2020) https://punctumbooks.pubpub.org/pub/viral-open-access-global-pandemic-covid-19-corona/release/3; K Finley, 'Global Officials Call for Free Access to COVID-19 Research' (*Wired*, 13 March 2020) www.wired.com/story/global-officials-call-free-access-covid-19-research/. Both sources are cited by Caso (n 20) 619–20.

[103] 'UN Agency Chiefs Appeal for "Open Science" beyond COVID-19, Citing Dangers of Secrecy and Denial' (27 October 2020) www.ungeneva.org/en/news-media/news/2020/10/un-agency-chiefs-appeal-open-science-beyond-COVID-19-citing-dangers-secrecy.

[104] Caso (n 20) 619.

[105] MA Johansson et al, 'Preprints: An Underutilized Mechanism to Accelerate Outbreak Science' (2018) 15 *PLoS Medicine* 1.

[106] Caso (n 20) 620.

[107] See s 8.2.1 above.

There is nevertheless the other side of the coin (ie access to PPCD), which deserves further attention now.

8.3.2. Access to Privately and Publicly Collected Data for the Public Interest: Open Data Approaches and Data Platformisation

Private enterprises and public bodies are involved at various levels in providing data that is useful for carrying out research activities. Public (non-research) entities traditionally embark on producing data used in scientific environments and education, and funding academic and not-for-profit institutions.[108] Companies, for their part, generate data that is essential to academic research as a by-product of their research and development activities.[109] Such data production is especially the case of (large) actors deploying data-driven technologies.[110] On the other hand, businesses usually provide access to databases which 'are of value to science, even if they no longer possess significant direct commercial value to the firm',[111] or even release scientific material to promote their products.[112]

The COVID-19 crisis has confirmed these trends and has underscored at least two tendencies that counterbalance data ownership. First, the global dimension of the pandemic has prompted companies to endorse pledges such as the Open COVID Pledge to make intellectual property accessible free of charge.[113] This concerns not only access to datasets, but also patents on pharmaceutical products, vaccinations and other medical devices.[114] The most recent standard Open COVID Licence (OCL-PC v1.1) provides a 'non-exclusive, royalty-free, worldwide, fully paid-up licence (without the right to sublicense) … solely for the purpose of diagnosing, preventing, containing, and treating COVID-19'.[115] The OCL is effective (retroactively) as of December 2019 and 'lasts until one year after the World Health Organization declares the COVID-19 Pandemic to have ended, but in any event not beyond January 1, 2023, unless otherwise extended by the Pledgor'.[116] All copyright and related rights in the Open COVID Licence are waived by means of a CC0 licence.[117]

[108] Reichman and Uhlir (n 33) 325–51.
[109] ibid 352.
[110] See generally Mayer-Schönberger and Cukier (n 13).
[111] Reichman and Uhlir (n 33) 352.
[112] ibid.
[113] See Open COVID Pledge, http://openCOVIDpledge.org.
[114] Caso (n 20) 619.
[115] OCL-PC v1.1, https://openCOVIDpledge.org/v1-1-ocl-pc/.
[116] ibid.
[117] ibid. On Creative Commons licences, see s 8.3.1 above.

Second, both private sector and public entities have engaged in matching and organising data (both SRD and PPCD) and data sources, stocking them onto platforms which everyone can freely access. This reflects the phenomenon of the 'platformisation' of data resources. Notably, access to pooled data is provided free of charge through licences which adopt an open data approach. Concrete examples concerning both the private and the public sectors demonstrate this trend. On the one hand, major tech businesses have opened up access to statistical and geographical data, which turns out to be crucial for predicting the evolution of the COVID-19 pandemic. For instance, Facebook has added 'tools and initiatives that can help organisations respond to the COVID-19 pandemic' to Data for Good, a data-sharing platform whose aim is to tackle global humanitarian issues.[118] Pooled data includes publicly available datasets, maps, data visualisations and dashboards, and so forth. All material is released under a CC BY licence or otherwise falls in the public domain.[119] Similarly, Alphabet (Google) has created a COVID-19 Open Data databank 'which combines numerous publicly available COVID-19 and related datasets at a fine geographic level',[120] and has released the code used to create it as an open source.[121] Meanwhile, Amazon has curated a data lake which includes up-to-date and curated datasets regarding the spread and featured of the coronavirus and COVID-19.[122] A second set of examples regards (non-research) public and international law bodies, which have fostered the use of data-sharing platforms to promote the availability of data sources. On 20 April 2020, the EU Commission launched the COVID-19 Data Platform to acquire and share research data (eg viral sequences, gene and protein data).[123] Similarly, the National Institutes of Health, the agency of the US government 'responsible for biomedical and public health research',[124] has listed numerous open-access data and computational resources to address COVID-19.[125] By the same token, the WHO has built a repository for its COVID-19 Technology Access Pool (C-TAP) initiative, aiming to foster voluntary sharing of intellectual property, knowledge and data amongst developers of COVID-19 therapies and manufacturers.[126]

[118] Facebook Data for Good, 'Our Work on COVID-19' (Facebook) https://dataforgood.fb.com/docs/COVID19.

[119] Facebook, 'Humanitarian Data Exchange', http://data.humdata.org/organization/facebook?sort=metadata_modified+desc.

[120] Alphabet, 'COVID-19 Public Datasets: Our Continued Commitment to Open, Accessible Data' (Google) http://cloud.google.com/blog/products/data-analytics/publicly-available-COVID-19-data-for-analytics.

[121] ibid.

[122] Amazon Web Services, 'AWS S3 Explorer COVID19-lake', http://dj2taa9i652rf.cloudfront.net.

[123] COVID-19 Data Portal, www.COVID19dataportal.org.

[124] Wikimedia Foundation, 'National Institutes of Health' (Wikipedia) https://en.wikipedia.org/wiki/National_Institutes_of_Health.

[125] US National Institutes of Health Office of Data Science Strategy (n 12).

[126] World Health Organization, 'Operationalising the COVID-19 Technology Access Pool (C-TAP): A Concept Paper', https://cdn.who.int/media/docs/default-source/essential-medicines/intellectual-property/who-COVID-19-tech-access-tool-c-tap.pdf?sfvrsn=1695cf9_36&download=true.

8.4. A Mixed Conclusion. The Law for Data Access and Cooperation

The COVID-19 pandemic has struck the world and changed it forever. All countries have been taken aback by the global spread of the virus. However, historic crises, as Pagallo drives home, mean big decisions and 'force us to think hard'.[127] How we rebuild our societies will depend to a great extent on the decisions that are made today. Data governance for the public interest is a crucial issue reflecting only one side of the fascinating chemistry between the law and technology.

This chapter has investigated how researchers, private actors and public bodies have governed access to COVID-19 data. There are two data governance approaches. The first one relies on legal, behavioural and technological barriers affecting access to SRD and PPCD. In respect of SRD, access barriers originate from the overarching phenomenon of capitalism's tragedy of commodification. The second mechanism of data governance revolves around adopting open data approaches. Researchers and research institutions have resorted to open science solutions, implementing contractual measures which foster data sharing and reuse (eg Creative Commons and Open Data Commons licences). Similarly, both businesses and non-research public bodies have committed to bolster access by bringing together different sources and making data accessible (data platformisation).

At this stage, taking stock of things in light of the opposing governance approaches presented across this chapter proves difficult. It is challenging to draw a single conclusion, given the current situation of data flows and exchanges. It is rather a mixed conclusion, consisting of proprietorial tendencies and more promising access-enabling solutions. We have seen that barriers to data access are not desirable when it comes to dealing with critical times. On multiple occasions, research institutes, researchers, intergovernmental institutions and governments have underscored how important cooperation and data availability are to addressing the COVID-19 pandemic. Sharing opportunities mostly depend on commitments and actions of the IP owners and pledgors, though. This might disappoint the expectations of the cheerleaders for voluntary data sharing. The Open COVID Pledge and the C-TAP are illustrative in this respect. Large-size leading businesses, such as Facebook, Amazon, Intel, IBM and Microsoft, have adopted the Open COVID Pledge. In contrast, pharmaceutical conglomerations have not signed on.[128] Given the complicated framework, we can draw up several proposals which can mitigate the shortcomings of the ownership-oriented governance approach and foster data access.

First, we need decentralisation of the commons[129] in the form of data collected by IP/data holders (private or public). As scrutinised above, open data approaches

[127] Pagallo (n 4) 10.
[128] Walsh et al (n 52) 391.
[129] JL Contreras and JH Reichman, 'Sharing by Design: Data and Decentralized Commons' (2015) 350 *Science* 1312.

rely on voluntary (contractual) actions of researchers, research institutions, private organisations and public bodies. However, obligations to provide access to SRD and PPCD on public-interest grounds are still missing.[130] In this sense, the proposal of the EU Commission to foster data availability for the public good, that is, inter alia,

> data [which] is created by society and *can serve to combat emergencies*, such as floods and wildfires, *to ensure that people can live longer and healthier lives*, to improve public services, and to tackle environmental degradation and climate change, and, where necessary and proportionate, to ensure more efficient fight against crime[,][131]

is a promising departure point for creating a right to data access for the purposes of public interest (eg research, education, societal needs).[132] Several fundamental rights can serve as a foundational basis for a right of data access, such as the rights to culture and science,[133] and the freedom of information (in a broad sense).[134] Getting down to the nitty-gritty of shaping such a right to data access is more complicated, though. Numerous authors tend to consider sector-specific data access rights as more viable than a general right of access to non-personal data held by private companies.[135] Establishing data access rights may mean adopting a mandatory access approach instead of a voluntary-based forms of data sharing. In this sense, several scholars have claimed that compulsory licences are a viable way to provide access to datasets.[136] However, current rules on compulsory licensing of patents are also stringent and onerous, as access seekers can only apply for a compulsory licence three years after the patent has been issued.[137] Extending the same rules to establish compulsory licences of SRD and PPCD could stymie the innovation related to some vital categories of data, such as time-sensitive real-time data on the pandemic's developments. Novel rules should consider how data is different from inventions subject to patent law in the way in which it is crucial for scientific progress and innovation. Mandatory access points may be limited to

[130] There exist, however, several domestic exceptions, such as the French Law for a Digital Republic (Loi No 2016-1321 du 7 octobre 2016 pour une République numérique), allowing the public sector to access certain (private sector) data of general interest.

[131] Commission, COM (2020) 66 final, 6–7 (emphasis added).

[132] Fia (n 57).

[133] C Geiger, 'Reconceptualizing the Constitutional Dimension of Intellectual Property – An Update' (Center for International Intellectual Property Studies, 2019) Research Paper No 2019-11, 17–21, http://papers.ssrn.com/sol3/papers.cfm?abstract_id=3496779.

[134] ibid 21–24; J Drexl, 'Legal Challenges of the Changing Role of Personal and Non-personal Data in the Data Economy' in A De Franceschi and R Schulze (eds), *Digital Revolution: Data Protection, Smart Products, Blockchain Technology and Bitcoins Challenges for Law in Practice* (Beck/Nomos, 2019) 29–31.

[135] Drexl et al (n 65) 11–16; W Kerber, 'Rights on Data: The EU Communication "Building a European Data Economy" from an Economic Perspective' in Lohsse et al (n 63) 129–30.

[136] RH Weber, 'Improvement of Data Economy Through Compulsory Licenses?' in Lohsse et al (n 63); Mezzanotte (n 63). With regard to compulsory licensing in the COVID-19 crisis, see F Tietze et al, 'Crisis-Critical Intellectual Property: Findings From the COVID-19 Pandemic' *IEEE Transactions on Engineering Management* (forthcoming) 1.

[137] Walsh et al (n 52) 403.

specific temporal circumstances requiring urgent opening up of data access, such as the declaration of a state of emergency in a given country. Drawing from these premises, the proposed Data Act of the European Commission[138] sets out to make data available to public sector bodies in exceptional circumstances. Article 14(1) of the proposal reads: 'Upon request, a data holder shall make data available to a public sector body or to a Union institution, agency or body demonstrating an exceptional need to use the data requested.' Article 15 further sets the limits of the 'exceptional need to use data': this occurs where, amongst other items, 'the data requested is necessary to respond to a public emergency' and 'the data request is limited in time and scope and necessary to prevent a public emergency or to assist the recovery from a public emergency'.[139] The public sector recipient of the data is entitled to (re-)share data with individuals or organisations 'in view of carrying out scientific research or analytics compatible with the purpose for which the data was requested, or to national statistical institutes and Eurostat for the compilation of official statistics'.[140] The proposed Data Act, moreover, specifies that '[t]he existence of a public emergency is determined according to the respective procedures in the Member States or of relevant international organisations'. This may include, for instance, the declaration of a state of emergency.

A second force for opening up data access lies in rejigging the overly exclusive aspects of intellectual property laws. Bolstering data access means restricting the prerogatives and rights of IP holders and, ultimately, limiting intellectual property rights on public interest grounds in light of other fundamental rights and humanitarian values. This is especially the case of research material and information which falls under copyright protection (eg publications). A burgeoning body of literature has explored the relationship between science, human rights and intellectual property.[141] In this sense, Article 27 of the Universal Declaration of Human Rights (UDHR, 1948) and, more specifically, Article 15 of the International Covenant on Economic, Social and Cultural Rights (ICESCR, 1966) put this interaction on a sound footing.[142] In particular, Article 15(1)(b) ICESCR, setting out the right of everyone to 'enjoy the benefits of scientific progress and its applications', might be a promising foundational backdrop. Yet, a human rights perspective has its Achilles' heel in its lack of effectiveness or hermeneutical support as to tearing access barriers to science down.[143] An interpretation of Article 27 UDHR which values access to knowledge is at odds with the WTO-driven IP regime which has

[138] Commission, 'Proposal for a Regulation of the European Parliament and of the Council on harmonised rules on fair access to and use of data (Data Act)' (Communication) COM (2022) 68 final.

[139] ibid Art 15(a)(b).

[140] ibid Art 21(1).

[141] Drahos, 'Responsive Science' (n 24) 336ff; C Geiger, 'The Social Function of Intellectual Property Rights, or How Ethics Can Influence the Shape and Use of IP Law' in GB Dinwoodie (ed), *Methods and Perspectives in Intellectual Property* (Edward Elgar Publishing, 2013).

[142] Drahos, 'Responsive Science' (n 24) 336.

[143] ibid 337.

been instituted within the last 25 years.[144] Similarly, international treaties such as the ICESCR are differently ratified, implemented and enforced at the national level, depending on precarious political decisions to a large extent.[145] A more promising but less investigated way to restrict IP maximalism values the theory of social function of (intellectual) property.[146] By recognising the existence of a public interest-driven restriction of IP, a right to data access may concern the subject matter that is excluded from the scope of application of IP laws. To enact the social function, public institutions can count on factual elements to pinpoint a public interest issue grounding an IP restriction. For example, as the OCL-PC v1.1 demonstrates, legislators can refer to temporal limitations (eg one year after the WHO declares the end of the COVID-19 pandemic). In a similar sense, the proposed Data Governance Act[147] establishes the conditions for reuse of public-sector data that is subject to third-party rights.

Thirdly, national and transnational authorities should restrict (state) secrecy over publicly collected data that proves essential for research and scientific purposes. Setting limitations to secrecy would also enhance transparency and make institutions more accountable, since researchers and scientists could develop independent analysis to orient the decision-making of public institutions.

A final way of lowering access barriers (especially behavioural ones) is by promoting cooperation amongst all actors that are involved in scientific production. This would mean, ultimately, placing science in the service of humankind, rather than of profit.

[144] L Shaver, 'The Right to Science and Culture' (2010) 1 *Wisconsin Law Review* 121, 179–80.

[145] ibid 177–79.

[146] Geiger (n 138); C Sganga, *Propertizing European Copyright: History, Challenges and Opportunities* (Edward Elgar Publishing, 2018) 191–232.

[147] Commission, 'Proposal for a Regulation of the European Parliament and of the Council on European data governance (Data Governance Act)' (Communication) COM (2020) 767 final, Arts 3–8.

9

Contact Tracing and Techno-surveillance Clusters in Asia and Europe

FRANCESCO GODANO* AND GALILEO SARTOR†

9.1. Introduction: The Pandemic and Technologies

The outbreak of the SARS-CoV-2 (COVID-19) pandemic has pushed technological development forward fast. With the virus hindering ordinary physical connections in social life, much attention has been put into designing technological solutions both to ensure continuity in economic, social and political life and to face the pandemic in a more effective way.

A vast array of digital health technologies have been brought forward by governments, companies and scientific institutions, with several purposes and different actors involved, both private and public, within complex socio-technical strategic frameworks. Artificial intelligence and data analytics, blockchain, robotics, 3D printing and other technologies are rapidly being directed in various ways towards the fight against COVID and used in several domains, such as telehealth, epidemiology, bioengineering and public health policies.[1]

In this contribution we analyse some of the so-called 'COVID apps', mobile phone applications used to collect and manage individuals' data within public health systems. In particular, we focus on contact tracing, ie the process of tracking at-risk physical contacts between infected people, in order to reduce the transmission of the virus. We identify its features and its role in the pandemic; we also point out the often-unclear differences of this technology with a larger set of tools which have a similar public health aim but different technical features, functionalities and governance objectives.

* Research fellow, European University Institute, Florence, Italy. Email: francesco.godano@eui.eu.
† Research fellow, University of Turin, Turin, Italy. Email: galileo.sartor@unito.it.

[1] M Kritikos, *Ten Technologies to Fight Coronavirus: In-Depth Analysis* (European Parliament, 2020); DSW Ting et al, 'Digital Technology and COVID-19' (2020) 26 *Nature Medicine* 459.

COVID apps fall within the category of the so-called 'mobile health' or 'mHealth' tools (ie mobile device functionalities used to support medicine and public health)[2] to contain the spreading of the disease. Such tools attracted much interest in the first phase of the pandemic (March–June 2020), especially in the form of smartphone implementations.[3] Many countries have adopted these apps within their counter-pandemic strategies: their different features and limitations have been classified in several databases available online.[4]

In Europe, the second wave of the pandemic (from autumn 2020 on) showed the limits of these technologies to contain the spread of the virus, particularly in view of the slow take-up by the population. Consequently, their role has been marginalised, with attention moving on to the vaccination process. We shall try to examine the path of this 'ephemeral' deployment, the persisting vitality of these technologies and the possible new functionalities they could acquire. Moreover, the analysis of the different features and objectives and the relations between these anti-COVID tools will offer an insight into the more general role of technology in (public health driven) social regulation and policymaking.

9.2. Contact Tracing and Other Social Monitoring Technologies

During the first months of the pandemic, the debate and efforts related to COVID apps centred (at least in Europe) around contact tracing. Contact tracing is a well-established method to 'identify potentially newly infected persons who may have come into contact with existing cases, in order to reduce further onward transmission'.[5] It consists in determining if any persons have been in close contact with an infected person and must therefore be considered at-risk and subject to preventive medical testing and movement restriction (quarantine).

Contact tracing is traditionally a 'manual' operation: when dealing with infected persons, public health authorities gather information about their earlier movements and contacts, and follow up persons who have been exposed.[6] With the COVID emergency, technological means for 'automatic' contact tracing have

[2] S Adibi, *Mobile Health: A Technology Road Map*, vol 5 (Springer, 2015).

[3] K Servick, 'Can Phone Apps Slow the Spread of the Coronavirus?' (2020) 368 *Science* 1296.

[4] See the annex to M Ciucci and F Gouardères, 'National COVID-19 Contact Tracing Apps' (Policy Department for Economic, Scientific and Quality of Life Policies Directorate-General for Internal Policies, 2020) www.europarl.europa.eu/RegData/etudes/BRIE/2020/652711/IPOL_BRI(2020)652711_EN.pdf. See also https://mhealth-hub.org/mhealth-solutions-against-COVID-19; 'A Flood of Coronavirus Apps Are Tracking Us. Now It's Time to Keep Track of Them' (*MIT Technology Review*) www.technologyreview.com/2020/05/07/1000961/launching-mittr-COVID-tracing-tracker/.

[5] European Center for Disease Prevention and Control, 'Contact Tracing for COVID-19: Current Evidence, Options for Scale-up and an Assessment of Resources Needed' 2, www.ecdc.europa.eu/en/publications-data/contact-tracing-COVID-19-evidence-scale-up-assessment-resources.

[6] D Klinkenberg, C Fraser and H Heesterbeek, 'The Effectiveness of Contact Tracing in Emerging Epidemics' (2006) 1 *PloS One* 12.

been put in place, namely in the form of mobile phone applications linked to public health systems.

In its strict sense, therefore, contact tracing is a tool that identifies 'at-risk physical proximity' between individuals. However, the concept has often been used in the last months in a more general and slightly ambiguous way, to describe a larger set of 'track-keeping' instruments deployed by governments and private actors to monitor and regulate people's behaviour – and therefore the spreading of the virus. Such tools are (or can be) closely intertwined with proximity detection, working within an integral regulatory strategy.

Following commonly used classifications,[7] we can identify five main uses of technology against COVID. The first one is contact tracing in the strict sense described above. In the following subsections, we will briefly describe the other four.

9.2.1. Symptom Checking

Symptom checkers are tools which collect and analyse users' symptoms and offer a possible diagnosis.[8] They can be associated with general information chatbots which offer insights into various aspects of the pandemic trend, and the data collected from them can be used for large-scale epidemiological analysis. Symptom checking is a digital health tool which existed before COVID, and was then implemented in specific pandemic management devices, whose effectiveness is still under consideration in the scientific literature.[9] An example of a COVID-specific symptom checker is Germany's Corona Health app.[10]

9.2.2. Quarantine Compliance

Quarantine compliance tools have been deployed to help enforce individual restriction measures.[11] When a citizen tests COVID positive or is otherwise subject to quarantine (eg returning from abroad), these apps monitor compliance with these requirements. These apps may show a high level of pervasiveness, often being tied to facial recognition and location technologies, and displaying opaque relations with law enforcement agencies. Poland's Home Quarantine app, for

[7] U Gasser et al, 'Digital Tools against COVID-19: Taxonomy, Ethical Challenges, and Navigation Aid' (2020) 2 *The Lancet Digital Health* 425; Ciucci and Gouardères (n 4).

[8] AC Berry, 'Online Symptom Checker Applications: Syndromic Surveillance for International Health' (2018) 18 *Ochsner Journal* 298.

[9] N Munsch et al, 'Diagnostic Accuracy of Web-Based COVID-19 Symptom Checkers: Comparison Study' (2020) 22 *Journal of Medical Internet Research* 21299.

[10] https://www.corona-health.net/en/.

[11] Z Liu et al, 'Mobile Application-Based Behaviour Change Techniques to Encourage Quarantine Compliance during the COVID-19 Pandemic' [2020] 197 *Public Health* 6.

instance, was created to support quarantine obligations issued to people returning from abroad.[12] It periodically requests geolocalised selfies and is allegedly creating shadow profiles that are sent to the police.[13]

9.2.3. Mobility/Flow Modelling

Among the public health technologies against COVID can be counted mobility and flow modelling tools, which analyse large-scale movements of people on the basis of large quantities of data and offer insights for 'demographic-governance' strategies and epidemiological studies. While these technologies are not specifically linked to a mobile application, they mostly employ data collected by apps and other devices. A significant example is Google's Mobility Reports. These reports are made public to

> provide insights into what has changed in response to policies aimed at combating COVID-19. The reports chart movement trends over time by geography, across different categories of places such as retail and recreation, groceries and pharmacies, parks, transit stations, workplaces, and residential areas.[14]

9.2.4. Combined Tools for Individual Movement Restriction

Certain tools – particularly in Asian countries – reveal a more comprehensive purpose of public health surveillance. This is achieved through a combination of the tools described above, resulting in a single system benefiting from different data sets and acting at multiple levels, integrating public health actions strategically. The main example of this approach is China's Health Code system, which will be described in section 9.5.1.

After describing what contact tracing is, we shall highlight its relations with these other instruments as they have been deployed around the globe, and in Europe in particular. To understand their role in the pandemic management, and the challenges they raise, it is important to understand their technological features as well as their social and political purposes.

[12] J Pinkas et al, 'Public Health Interventions to Mitigate Early Spread of SARS-CoV-2 in Poland' (2020) 26 *Medical Science Monitor* 924730-1.

[13] https://www.abc.net.au/news/2020-04-25/coronavirus-poland-tracking-quarantine-selfie-app/12173884.

[14] https://www.google.com/COVID19/mobility/.

9.3. Contact Tracing Systems

In this section, we analyse the technological features of contact tracing, focusing on data transmission mechanisms, different architectural models and implementations.

Most digital contact tracing systems are based on Bluetooth Low Energy (BLE), a development in Bluetooth technology used in low-power devices, like Internet of Things gadgets. As specified in the glossary at the end of this chapter, Bluetooth is a technology used for medium- to short-range data transmission between multiple devices.

In a contact tracing system based on BLE, two devices (phones) can exchange the data necessary for the risk evaluation of contact with a COVID-positive person.

Let us consider Bob and Alice, two persons walking on the street with their contact tracing systems active. The devices both send and receive data (identifiers) continuously. If Bob and Alice get close enough, their phones will exchange this data. If Bob then tests positive for COVID, he will notify the system. Finally, if the contact between Bob an Alice is deemed to be at risk by the system (for duration and distance), her device will show a notification, prompting her to get tested for COVID-19.

Sometimes, GPS tracking is considered as an alternative means to BLE for the purpose of contact tracing, and the two technologies are often listed together in describing contact tracing.[15] However, as we shall see in section 9.4, GPS does not actually identify proximity between devices: the confusion can probably be linked to the different approaches between the 'Asian' and 'European' models of contact tracing.

9.3.1. Centralised versus Decentralised Solutions

There are two main models of contact tracing architectures: a centralised and a decentralised one, differing in the role of a central data server. The internal workings of the two models are presented in the following sections, focusing on data creation and transmission between devices.

The protocols described are Decentralised Privacy-Preserving Proximity Tracing (DP-3T), used in the decentralised model, and Pan-European Privacy-Preserving Proximity Tracing (PEPP-PT), used in the centralised model. These are far from the only systems available, but they are the more common, and have available documentation. These two systems (developed initially through research studies) have been the technical basis for different implementations.

[15] See, eg Ciucci and Gouardères (n 4) 6–10.

9.3.1.1. Data Transmission in DP-3T

DP-3T is a decentralised open protocol that uses BLE to transmit proximity data between participating devices.[16]

The main characteristics of the DP-3T architecture are:

- the only data transmitted between devices is a temporary identifier and the strength of the signal; and
- there is a central server that only keeps the IDs of people identified as COVID positive.

If Bob is close to Alice for a certain duration of time, Alice's phone will register the Bob's ID of (transmitted periodically) and Bob's phone will register Alice's ID. If Bob is detected to be positive to COVID-19, he will upload his ID for the past 14 days (the period of possible infection) to a central server. Periodically, the phones of Bob and Alice will download from the central server the list of IDs belonging to COVID-positive users. Alice's phone will see that one or more of the IDs are present both on the server and on her phone. She has no way of knowing who the IDs belong to. Alice is notified of the possible at-risk contact and is prompted to get a swab. If she is positive, she will also upload her ID.

To ensure anonymity, the protocol is designed to make use of an ephemeral data seed that is randomly generated every day (SK_t, where t is the current day).

This seed is calculated as a cryptographic hash function (such as SHA-256):

$$SK_t = H\,(SK_{t-1})$$

The first key, SK_0, is calculated via a digital signature encryption algorithm (Ed25519) calculated via an elliptic curve Diffie–Hellman key scheme. During the day, the smartphone will generate the ID that will be transmitted from this initial seed. The ephemeral ID (EphID from now on) is updated randomly every 10–15 minutes, according to the BLE rotation that devices normally do to ensure anonymisation. Each ID is valid only for an epoch (ie a certain time duration). From the SK_t daily key, the devices compute an EphID:

$$S_E phID(BK) = PRG(PRF(SK_t, BK))$$

where *BK* is a random string and *PRG* and *PRF* are a pseudo-random generator and function respectively.

In the receiving phase, the smartphone stores:

- the EhpID of the transmitting phone;
- the BLE signal attenuation (to infer the distance between devices); and
- the day of the transmission.

[16] C Troncoso et al, 'Decentralized Privacy-Preserving Proximity Tracing' (2020) arXiv: 2005.12273, https://arxiv.org/abs/2005.12273.

It might be possible to receive more than one EphID from the same phone, depending on the duration of the contact. The smartphone also keeps a log of its own SK_t seeds from the preceding 14 days.

When a user is determined to be positive, the health authority can authorise the upload of the seed SK_t for the first day of the possible contagion window. The seed is then deleted from the phone, and the ID generation sequence starts again. This prevents the user from being trackable from the uploaded seed. With the seed for a specific day *t*, every device can compute the EphIDs for the following days with the same function used for their creation.

The back-end server collects the pairs (SK_t, *t*) uploaded by the positive users and makes them available. The phones download them and calculate the EphID of the positive user and compare it to the ones received via BLE in the preceding 14 days.[17] If the phone finds a match, the user is then alerted locally, on-device.

9.3.1.2. Privacy and Security Concerns in DP-3T

The DP-3T system ensures a high degree of privacy protection and anonymisation. The swapped keys (EphIDs) used in the data transmission of DP-3T do not reveal details about the interaction and it is therefore not possible to directly identify the two people that have come into contact. The EphIDs are unlinkable (there is no connection between them that can be inferred), and the SK_t seeds are stored only on the user's phone.

As for data minimisation, the collected IDs are kept on the central server for 14 days, after which they are deleted from the system, no longer useful for contact tracing.

As described in the DP-3T standard, the system will dismantle itself after the end of the epidemic. Infected patients will stop uploading their data to the central server, and people will stop using the app.

A malicious actor could monitor the EphID transmitted by a specific person with ad hoc Bluetooth devices strategically placed (eg in the person's workplace). If that person is then reported as positive, it could be possible to trace their movement based on the location of the Bluetooth devices. However, this is not a very effective attack, since it requires the use of multiple Bluetooth beacons, used to track the changes in ID. In recent versions of DP-3T (like the one used by Google and Apple), this risk has been further mitigated.[18]

The DP-3T system has been criticised for not preventing so-called trolling (or Sybil) attacks, where a single user creates multiple accounts and floods the system. This is feasible because there is no registration in DP-3T. PEPP-PT prevents this with a registration and a proof of work (a complex computation) that is used to delay the creation of the account.

[17] To avoid malicious users from redistributing the IDs of positive users after they are published, the phones also check that the contact has happened before the publication of the seed.

[18] Troncoso et al (n 16); S Vaudenay, 'Analysis of Dp3t – Between Scylla and Charybdis' [2020] *Infoscience*, https://infoscience.epfl.ch/record/277808.

9.3.1.3. *The Italian App: Immuni*

The Italian app Immuni is an example of the decentralised model.

The Italian ministry of health contracted the development of its contact tracing app to the Milan-based company Bending Spoons, founded in 2013 and now one of the most successful mobile developers in the world.[19] The company is one of those who started in the PEPP-PT Consortium, but pivoted to create a new standard (DP-3T) based on a decentralised model. In particular, the app uses the GAEN (Google Apple Exposure Notification) system, itself based on DP-3T, as will be expanded in section 9.3.2. Once the app was developed and active in all the Italian regions, Bending Spoons granted the government a perpetual and irrevocable licence for Immuni.[20] The documentation for the app is available in their GitHub repository,[21] making it possible to analyse the implementation.

In Italy, the app has not been very successful, despite the initial enthusiatic launch. Immuni showed problems, more of an organisational nature than a technological one. For example, people who received an at-risk contact notification were allegedly not always guaranteed sick leave while awaiting the result of the swab test, even if they were forced to stay home from work.[22]

9.3.1.4. *Data Transmission in PEPP-PT*

PEPP-PT is a centralised open protocol that uses BLE to transmit proximity data between participating devices. Unlike the decentralised approach of DP-3T, the data is analysed on a central server. Most of the information available on this protocol comes from the main implementations, the French TousAntiCOVID and the first version of the German Corona-Warn-App.[23] These systems were developed by the French Inria and German Fraunhofer, with the ROBERT and NTK implementations, respectively. We will focus on ROBERT, since it is the one that is still actively being developed.[24]

Bob and Alice have both downloaded the national app and have registered online, with some identifying data (email, phone number, etc). They generate temporary keys, and share them based on their proximity. After a positive COVID-19 test, Bob uploads onto the central server the data of his contacts of the last

[19] E Pollina, 'Italy Tests Contact-Tracing App to Speed Lockdown Exit' (*Reuters*, 2020) www.reuters.com/article/us-health-coronavirus-italy-technology-idUSKBN21Z0VJ.

[20] For Immuni, the Italian government uses a perpetual and irrevocable licence on all the code, graphics, text and documentation, granted free of charge by Bending Spoons SpA. Bending Spoons provided a documentation, design and software development service, completely free of charge and without decision-making authority or access to user data, until 13 October 2020. See also https://www.immuni.italia.it/faq.html.

[21] https://github.com/immuni-app/immuni-documentation.

[22] L Borga, 'Chi Riceve Alert Immuni Ha Diritto a Malattia, Ma Non Vale Per Tutti', https://tg24.sky.it/economia/2020/10/12/immuni-notifica-malattia-ferie-dipendenti.

[23] Germany then reimplemented the app based on the G/A API.

[24] https://github.com/ROBERT-proximity-tracing/documents/.

14 days, including the ID received from Alice. The central server then evaluates the contacts and notifies Alice if necessary.

In the description, the following terms are used:

App The specific implemented ROBERT-compatible app
Server The server managed by the data controller

The App registers itself on the upstream Server, where the permanent identifier is generated and stored in a table (*IDTable*). The Server generates Ephemeral Bluetooth Identifiers from the permanent identifier. No personal data in this phase is associated with the ID.

The messages sent by the App contain different data fields, most importantly the EBID (the ID of the other party), the time of reception and the strength of the signal (via the Bluetooth attenuation signal). All this data is kept in a local database, the *Local Proximity List*.

If a user is diagnosed as positive for COVID-19, with the necessary authorisation and consent, the App uploads the *Local Proximity List* to the Server, where the IDs contained in the *Local Proximity List* are flagged as 'exposed' in the *IDTable*. The App queries this table regularly to see if the user has been flagged and computes a risk score. If the risk is greater than the threshold, the App is notified. To enable this verification, the central server has a way of connecting the individual to the IDs he/she has transmitted.

The EBID is generated every N epochs (one epoch in this context is roughly 15 minutes) by the server, thus the App must connect to the server regularly to obtain the new list of IDs it will use in the following N epochs. The function to generate the EBID for epoch *i* is:

$$EBID_{A,i} = ENC(K_{S,i} \vee ID_A)$$

where *ENC* is a 64-bit block cipher agreed on first instance.

9.3.1.5. Privacy and Security Concerns in PEPP-PT

Like the DP-3T model, the tracing system of PEPP-PT only maintains data for a predefined number of days, and the servers will be dismantled after the end of the epidemic.

From a privacy and security standpoint, this system has been criticised for the great amount of user-identifying data that is kept on a single server. Due to the necessary identification of an individual for notification purposes, the centralised system is prone to attacks by either a third party with access to the server or a government-backed scheme. This party would be able to deanonymise the data on the server and identify directly the individual persons in a contact.

This caused a rift with some of the companies and research institutions that developed DP-3T, and is the reason for the additional data minimisation of that model.

9.3.2. The Google/Apple Implementation

The most talked about contact tracing technology is the Google/Apple application programming interface (API)-based system. To properly understand how it works, it is necessary to take a step back and understand what an API is.

9.3.2.1. What Is an API?

An API is an interaction layer between two or more programs, a set of definitions and protocols used to integrate different pieces of software. If program A needs to interact with program B, for instance to share data, it can do so via a set of precise rules that define, for instance, how the data in transit should be formatted in input and output, without needing to access the internals of either of the two programs.[25]

Another advantage that comes from having a common API is that it can be used by multiple different implementations. This is very common in computing, and has often enabled the rise of new/better software, without leaving too heavy a burden on the programmer using the API, to port the program to a new system or to address compatibility issues with previous versions. Notable examples of this are the original IBM BIOS and non-IBM machines, Unix and Linux Kernel, and mSQL and MySQL. More recently, Google used the Java APIs to simplify the development of Android apps for developers already familiar with the Java language.[26] Interoperability is a crucial part of the contact tracing system, without which the development of an app for multiple platforms (eg Apple and Android) would be significantly harder. It is thus easy to see why many countries decided to use the Google/Apple API, even those who had previously developed their own in-house apps (eg the UK, Germany).

In April 2020, during the discussion about the merits of contact tracing in the pandemic, Google and Apple decided to implement a variant of DP-3T at a low system level, with a common API. Having the implementation at system level could enhance the availability of a standard on multiple versions of the operating system (OS)[27] and could easily be made to run in the background, a functionality often suppressed for third-party apps to conserve power. These implementations are responsible for the data collection from the Bluetooth module, and the transmission to the upstream server of the health authority. The system is opt-in, and requires one of the national tracing apps to be installed, with the app providing the underlying Google/Apple implementation with the data necessary to contact the correct upstream server, and further data to determine what a contact is (different countries consider, for instance, a shorter time frame or spacial distance between users).

[25] 'What Is an API?' www.redhat.com/en/topics/api/what-are-application-programming-interfaces.

[26] Just recently, the US Supreme Court sided with Google in asserting that an API is not only fair use, but also actively a way to encourage the interoperability and lower the ceiling for developers.

[27] The minimum specifications call for iOS 12.5 from 2018 and Android M from 2015.

9.3.2.2. Security and Privacy

According to the relevant Google and Apple terms of service (ToS), the Google/Apple implementation does not collect any user-sensitive data,[28] in accordance with the DP-3T standard it is built upon. For an app to make use of the implementation and be made available on the Play Store (or Apple Store), it must minimise the data collected, not use advertising, nor collect the user-revealing keys stored locally. The data controller is the national Ministry of Health or equivalent entity. The ToS go even further, requiring that apps not access any permissions other that Bluetooth and Internet. A common misconception is that the apps use GPS location tracking, since the Location icon is enabled on Android, but they do not have the permission to use it. On Android, the ability to use Bluetooth to determine distance is under the Location tab, but the GPS system itself is not enabled.

Google and Apple have made available open source 'demo' versions of apps using the API, and many of the national implementations have been made available as open source as well, to enable further development and to encourage trust in the system.

9.3.2.3. Compatibility

Multiple European countries have introduced apps based on this system, to simplify development and guarantee interoperability. A user with the Italian app Immuni can travel to many different countries, like Germany, Ireland and Spain, without needing to install a different app.[29]

Some issues may arise from using a system that requires an OS update, since not all users of Android phones can rely on the implementation being there. As previously noted, Google released the implementation on all systems going back to 2015 (Android M). There are further issues that arise from it being included in the Google Play Services. An example of this are phones built by the Chinese Huawei, barred from using Google services by the Trump administration, which do not have access to the GAEN implementation. Another example is the open firmware community, where users typically remove the Google services for privacy concerns, or manually install versions of Android other than the official ones.

Herein lies another advantage of having an API-based system: other implementations can be used in place of the official Google/Apple one. Developers from Huawei and the open source community have built compatible implementations that do not require changes in the specific national apps.[30] The Italian app Immuni

[28] 'Google COVID-19 Exposure Notifications Service Additional Terms', https://blog.google/documents/72/Exposure_Notifications_Service_Additional_Terms.pdf.

[29] 'International Interoperability', https://github.com/minvws/nl-COVID19-notification-app-coordination.

[30] 'Nearby Service-Service Introduction', https://developer.huawei.com/consumer/en/doc/development/HMSCore-Guides-V5/contactshield--0000001057494465-V5. For the microg open source implementation, see https://github.com/microg/GmsCore/releases/tag/v0.2.12.203315.

can be installed on systems with the open source implementation, and both the German Corona-Warn-App and the Swiss LibreCHovid are available with the open source implementation included in the app itself.

All this is made possible by the fact that the API is open and well documented, and that there is an open source reference implementation available.

9.3.3. The Google/Apple API. A Quasi-monopolistic Private Infrastructure?

The Google/Apple API-based system is a very convenient proposition for countries interested in a decentralised approach to contact tracing. In the months following the release of the API, many countries implemented their first app based on it, and many more switched from an in-house system to the API-based one (eg the German Corona-Warn-App).

This is a great vote of confidence in DP-3T, Google and Apple. This concentration of apps built on the Google/Apple system can, however, be viewed as a monopolistic approach.

Both Google and Apple, in the ToS directed at app developers, state that they do not collect personal user data, and that the app data can only be shared for purposes related to the COVID response effort.[31]

This fact is corroborated by the absence in the Immuni privacy policies of any reference to data sharing and uses outside the needs of the Ministry of Health (the 'Data Controller') for the planning of the COVID response.[32]

Another example of the user-facing ToS is for the Irish app COVIDTracker, where it is stated that

> the app uses capabilities of mobile operating systems. Apple and Google have developed a method that allows specific government-only COVID-19 apps to make use of Bluetooth technology on phones that would otherwise not be available … None of the information in this app is ever shared with Apple or Google.[33]

According to some, the fact that the API is developed by Google and Apple – which together have a combined 99 per cent share of the mobile market[34] – would give them a monopoly on tracing apps, and more than that a way to determine how contact tracing apps should work. The two companies require app developers

[31] The Google ToS state that 'While end users of your App may provide personal data as part of their use of the App, you will not share this end-user personal data with Google. You may only share end-user personal data with third parties with user consent, and only as necessary for COVID-19 response efforts': 'Google COVID-19 Exposure Notifications Service Additional Terms' (n 29) 3.b.vi.

[32] 'Immuni – Privacy Notice' www.immuni.italia.it.

[33] 'StopCOVID NI – Terms & Conditions' (HSC) https://COVID-19.hscni.net/stopCOVID-ni-terms-conditions/.

[34] https://gs.statcounter.com/os-market-share/mobile/worldwide.

to accept their terms of service to use their implementation and be made available on the respective app stores. In accordance with the DP-3T definition, the Google/Apple implementation is designed to delete the IDs uploaded to the server after 14 days from the notification. It also defines the natural end of the tracing system as:

> When there are no more infections, no new keys are loaded into the central database. Since keys are deleted after 14 days, this database will automatically be empty after 14 days. When the end of the epidemic is determined, the servers can be dismantled, and Google and Apple will no longer support the API. The users will then be asked to uninstall the app.[35]

9.4. GPS versus BLE: Different Technologies for Different Purposes

The more common technology used in contact tracing is Bluetooth, and Bluetooth Low Energy (BLE) more precisely. Bluetooth seems ideal for this use, being a low consumer of power and able to determine with sufficient precision the distance between two devices. This is accomplished by sending a message and determining the attenuation with which it is received (the signal loses strength the greater the distance it must cover).[36] The Bluetooth device is not in itself directly traceable on a large scale, especially in the newer BLE standard, often used in smart devices (like bikes and scooters). To prevent intrusion in devices running BLE, the standard requires the device to have two MAC (media access control) addresses. One is fixed unique to the device and hard-coded on the BLE chip, so could be used to determine the device itself (the Bluetooth chip manufacturer needs to register with the Institute of Electrical and Electronics Engineers (IEEE)). This address is not used in transmissions, but is replaced by another, random address, not registered with the IEEE, that changes roughly every 15 minutes (for this reason, the timers for the BLE keys in DP-3T and PEPP-PT are tied to 15 minute marks).

This renders the BLE device non-traceable, since the keys are random. Thus, in DP-3T, where the system has no knowledge of the devices registered, it is not possible to trace the user. In PEPP-PT, however, this is not necessarily true, since the upstream server has knowledge of the user and his keys.

On the opposite side of the spectrum we find GPS technology. We will refer to all the different positioning systems by the GPS acronym. This is not strictly accurate, since GPS is the more common US variant, but the term is the most recognisable one.

[35] 'Exposure Notifications – Frequently Asked Questions Preliminary – Subject to Modification and Extension V1.2' 6, https://COVID19-static.cdn-apple.com/applications/COVID19/current/static/contact-tracing/pdf/ExposureNotification-FAQv1.2.pdf.

[36] A simple way to visualise this is to see that the wireless signal gets weaker the further away you are from the source antenna (router/access point).

GPS is used to get a so-called fine location, obtained through triangulation from multiple satellites. This technology is less precise in determining relative position (from another device) than the Bluetooth/BLE system. Usually GPS is enhanced on-device by snapping the position to a road, and inferring the position also from the driving direction. For this reason, when driving, it looks as if the location is very precise, even if by itself, in best case scenarios, 'GPS-enabled smartphones are typically accurate to within a 4.9 m (16 ft.) radius under open sky (view source at ION.org). However, their accuracy worsens near buildings, bridges, and trees', as defined by the US government[37] (the same applies to the other satellite systems).[38] For this reason, GPS is not an effective instrument for contact tracing. It is difficult to determine if two located positions qualify as a contact, since they do not identify spacial proximity between devices. Bob could be in a tall building, while Alice is walking on the street, and their locations would overlap. However, for these same reasons, GPS can be useful for quarantine compliance and flow modelling/ mobility reports, both for city planning and for the identification of hotspots.

GPS technology is controversial, since it can be used by both governments and providers to trace your movements. It is in fact already used, with other sources, to accumulate data used for advertisement purposes.[39]

The effectiveness of GPS traces can be enhanced in combination with other data (ID, phone numbers, facial recognition, etc), and with Bluetooth itself.[40] This is why we often find these technologies used in the more comprehensive Asian model of COVID apps (see section 9.5).

9.5. The Debate on COVID Apps between Asian and Western Countries

Most of the countries that initially deployed COVID apps were technologically advanced Asian countries like Singapore, South Korea and China.[41] Their tools are quite pervasive: their use is normally mandatory, and they often combine different

[37] https://www.gps.gov/systems/gps/performance/accuracy/.

[38] F van Diggelen and P Enge, 'The World's First GPS MOOC and Worldwide Laboratory Using Smartphones' in *Proceedings of the 28th International Technical Meeting of the Satellite Division of The Institute of Navigation* (ION GNSS+, 2015) 361, http://www.ion.org/publications/abstract.cfm?jp=p&articleID=13079.

[39] SA Thompson and C Warzel, 'Opinion – Twelve Million Phones, One Dataset, Zero Privacy' *New York Times* (New York, 19 December 2019) www.nytimes.com/interactive/2019/12/19/opinion/location-tracking-cell-phone.html.

[40] India's app Aarogya Setu, for instance, uses both BLE and GPS: https://www.mygov.in/aarogya-setu-app/.

[41] H Stevens and MB Haines, 'Tracetogether: Pandemic Response, Democracy, and Technology' (2020) 14 *East Asian Science, Technology and Society* 523; P Mozur, R Zhong and A Krolik, 'In Coronavirus Fight, China Gives Citizens a Color Code, With Red Flags' *New York Times* (New York, 1 March 2020) www.nytimes.com/2020/03/01/business/china-coronavirus-surveillance.html.

technical features (BLE, GPS, facial recognition, surveillance camera logs, etc) for different purposes in the fight against COVID (movement restriction, quarantine compliance, location tracking, and so on). In Europe, as well as in the USA, a huge debate arose on the possibility to build COVID apps that would satisfy certain ethical standards: preserving privacy and data protection, ensuring fair use and non-discrimination, limiting surveillance features.[42]

The first result of this debate was the mandate to develop contact tracing apps working on a voluntary basis with anonymised data stored for a limited time. A further line of discussion concerned the concentration of data on servers: hence the described split between centralised and decentralised systems. Most of the national contact tracing systems switched to a decentralised model, aided by the availability of the Google/Apple API in April 2020. Despite the first enthusiastic reactions, these apps have not had much success, mostly because of low adoption by citizens, who could choose whether or not to download the app.

On the other hand, apps used in Asian countries have instead shown high effectiveness. However, this comes at the price of significant restrictions to citizens' autonomy and privacy, showing the interplay of a complex surveillance system put at the service of the fight against the pandemic.

9.5.1. Asian App Clusters: China, Singapore and Others

A key feature of Asian countries' apps is the fact that they normally bring together various technological tools and public health purposes in a *single social monitoring system*. In these systems, contact tracing is only a brick in the wall.

9.5.1.1. China

China has deployed a complex system to determine movement restrictions, named Health Code.[43] Health Code collects a series of data related to people's personal features, health conditions, social encounters, etc, to determine their freedom of movement. The system flags users with three colors, corresponding to different possibilities: a green code allows citizens to move freely, yellow and red codes impose seven and 14 days of quarantine respectively. Even though little is known about this app, it seems clear that it results from a combination of tools, among which are location tracking (with GPS), quarantine compliance and symptom checking devices. The data available in this system is suspected to be shared

[42] J Morley et al, 'Ethical Guidelines for COVID-19 Tracing Apps' (2020) 582 *Nature* 29; Gasser et al (n 7); H Cho, D Ippolito and YW Yu, 'Contact Tracing Mobile Apps for COVID-19: Privacy Considerations and Related Trade-Offs', https://arxiv.org/abs/2003.11511.

[43] F Liang, 'COVID-19 and Health Code: How Digital Platforms Tackle the Pandemic in China' (2020) 6 *Social Media+ Society*, https://journals.sagepub.com/doi/full/10.1177/2056305120947657; Mozur et al (n 42).

with the police and used to limit access to certain zones with the use of facial recognition.[44]

9.5.1.2. *Singapore*

Singapore has developed a varied set of technological tools against the pandemic. The Singaporean app TraceTogether is similar to the ROBERT system, working with a user ID and the exchange of temporary keys via Bluetooth.[45] In case of a positive COVID test, the details of the contacts are uploaded to the server. The IDs of the possibly infected individuals are decrypted on the server, and they are notified, usually via a phone call, by a health professional.

To enable those without a compatible smartphone to participate in the contact tracing, the Singaporean government developed a hardware token with its own ID and Bluetooth module, which can be used without a phone.

In Singapore, the use of the TraceTogether system is technically not mandatory, but is required to enter any public space (buildings, parks, etc). To enter some public buildings, the user must also scan a QR code, which logs their presence. If a person in the building then tests positive, the others will be notified. This set of connected tools allowed Singapore to have one of the highest COVID app adoption rates, at around 70–80 per cent.[46]

9.5.1.3. *South Korea*

The South Korean tracing system is more pervasive and is the result of years of preparation. In 2015, during the MERS pandemic, the government enacted a number of laws that allowed data collection from credit cards, mobile phones and closed-circuit cameras to trace a person's movements and identify their contacts, to determine whether they might have been exposed.[47]

With the COVID pandemic, the system was used as a public monitoring and alert mechanism. A typical alert can contain the infected person's age and gender, and a detailed log of their movements down to the minute. The system works on a mandatory basis and collects data irrespective of users' consent. In March 2020, the

[44] M Wang, 'China: Fighting COVID-19 with Automated Tyranny' (Human Rights Watch, 2020) www.hrw.org/news/2020/04/01/china-fighting-COVID-19-automated-tyranny.

[45] Ministry of Health, 'Launch of New App for Contact Tracing – Factsheet on TraceTogether', www.smartnation.gov.sg/docs/default-source/press-release-materials/sndgg_tracetogether---media-factsheet.pdf.

[46] Z Huang et al, 'Awareness, Acceptance, and Adoption of the National Digital Contact Tracing Tool Post COVID-19 Lockdown among Visitors to a Public Hospital in Singapore' (2021) 27 *Clinical Microbiology and Infection* 1046, www.ncbi.nlm.nih.gov/pmc/articles/PMC7817417/.

[47] D Lewis, 'Why Many Countries Failed at COVID Contact-Tracing – but Some Got It Right' (2020) 588 *Nature* 384, www.nature.com/articles/d41586-020-03518-4; M Zastrow, 'South Korea Is Reporting Intimate Details of COVID-19 Cases: Has It Helped?' [2020] *Nature*, www.nature.com/articles/d41586-020-00740-y.

Korean authorities issued guidelines limiting the release of excessive information, after regional governments published the GPS traces of COVID-positive people. In one case, a person was wrongly accused of having an affair with his sister-in-law because their overlapping maps revealed they dined together at a restaurant.[48]

9.6. Privacy versus Effectiveness

The main concern in the European (and US) debate over COVID apps was to fashion an ethically sound device that preserved the privacy of users and guaranteed fairness of use.[49] As far as contact tracing in a strict sense is concerned, this led to the adoption of BLE technology, although a few governments (eg Bulgaria[50]) have opted for only tracking locations (not physical proximity) with GPS. Many countries have adopted the Google/Apple API to build compatible apps.

In this context, privacy issues were handled quite effectively: as we have seen, the DP-3T standard in particular offers anonymisation and minimisation of the data, states the temporal limitation of their use for COVID-related purposes and ensures their destruction after a certain time. Most European implementations (including the Google/Apple API) respect these requirements, at least according to their terms of service.[51]

Obstacles for the effectiveness of these devices have been created by different issues. The main problem seems to concern the autonomy of decision, namely the voluntary nature of the app use, as opposed to the mandatory or quasi-mandatory status of apps in Asian countries. Great attention has indeed been accorded to avoiding any kind of open or veiled coercion to use the app.[52] In fact, all European (and US) apps are voluntary based.[53] It was stated that the minimum take-up rate needed for contact tracing to work was 60 per cent of the population,[54] but this percentage has seldom been achieved. Voluntariness certainly has something to do with this. However, technical and organisational shortcomings should not be ignored. All tracing systems are imperfect, since the contacts depend on the time, whether masks are used, etc, which can lead to a number of false-positives. Moreover, several implementations of contact tracing apps experienced problems

[48] Lewis (n 47).

[49] R Klar and D Lanzerath, 'The Ethics of COVID-19 Tracking Apps – Challenges and Voluntariness' (2020) 16 *Research Ethics* 1; L Floridi, 'Mind the App – Considerations on the Ethical Risks of COVID-19 Apps' (2020) 33 *Philosophy & Technology* 167.

[50] https://virusafe.info.

[51] Most of them are available on the MIT 'COVID Tracker' database: 'A Flood of Coronavirus Apps Are Tracking Us' (n 4).

[52] Klar and Lanzerath (n 50).

[53] 'A Flood of Coronavirus Apps Are Tracking Us' (n 4).

[54] L Ferretti et al, 'Quantifying SARS-CoV-2 Transmission Suggests Epidemic Control with Digital Contact Tracing' (2020) 368 *Science*.

working with older phones.[55] The issue may be linked with the problem of digital inequality: while smartphones are rapidly entering the life of many people around the globe, still large portions of citizens do not own one (at least, not a sufficiently recent one).[56]

9.7. Conclusions

We conclude this short analysis with a few considerations on two issues. First, we examine the relations between ethical issues and technological apparatus across Asian and Western countries. Secondly, we discuss the recent evolution of COVID apps.

9.7.1. Ethically Sound Technology and Surveillance Clusters

The considerations made above show that, while each technological solution has its own scope, its potential is better revealed in a cluster of 'monitoring' technologies. Such integration is already advanced in many Asian countries. In Europe, the lack of both a centralised technological infrastructure and socio-political features offer constraints to the implementation of surveillance clusters. However, attention should not be lowered on the topic, in order to identify trends and evaluate advantages, drawbacks, and risks. For instance, 'smart cities' offer examples of the use of clustering technologies in Europe and the USA, experimenting with traffic flow monitoring to support the COVID response.[57]

As far as contact tracing is concerned, the impression is that the privacy and ethical standards advocated for, both in the USA and Europe, fell short of allowing an effective tracing mechanism. Doubts over the effective technical and organisational capacity to trace and curtail COVID have probably restrained citizens' willingness to trust these apps. The expansion of Asian apps was a big motive for investing in 'privacy preserving' apps. We can then ask ourselves whether it was right to imagine that contact tracing could be simply extrapolated from these massive surveillance mechanisms and be tailored to our 'democratic' standards.

With the help of the ambiguity of the term 'contact tracing', we seemed to forget that apps like Singapore's TraceTogether are embedded within a surveillance cluster

[55] S McLachlan et al, 'Bluetooth Smartphone Apps: Are They the Most Private and Effective Solution for COVID-19 Contact Tracing?' https://arxiv.org/abs/2005.06621.

[56] K Taylor and L Silver, 'Smartphone Ownership Is Growing Rapidly around the World, but Not Always Equally' (2019) 5 *Pew Research*, https://www.pewresearch.org/global/2019/02/05/smartphone-ownership-is-growing-rapidly-around-the-world-but-not-always-equally/.

[57] 'Smart Cities Have Responded to COVID-19' (Smart Cities Marketplace, 2020) https://eu-smart-cities.eu/news/smart-cities-have-responded-COVID-19.

guaranteeing their effectiveness. Even when some European countries integrated more functionalities into their COVID apps,[58] the absence of a comprehensive surveillance system hindered their success.

9.7.2. Present and Future of COVID Apps: From Contact Tracing to Vaccines and Travel Permits

COVID apps did not meet their original goals. Within the vaccination phase, however, these technologies have been adapted to new public health strategies.

As to contact tracing, more than one voice has been raised to remind us that this technology could still play an important role. Lower transmission rates constitute the ideal situation to implement contact tracing effectively.[59] However, since spring 2021, the topic has been set aside, public debates and governance strategies moving away from it.[60]

On the other hand, it is not clear to what extent contract tracing apps are still being used. The Italian Immuni app, for instance, is reportedly still being downloaded: however, it is not clear if it is actively being used for contact tracing.[61]

As to the new functionalities of COVID apps, the most important of these is the so-called 'green pass', also known as the COVID passport or COVID certificate. The green pass is a system for verifying COVID immunity requirements. Born within the context of an EU COVID free-travelling scheme,[62] the green pass has now been extended to domestic purposes, working as a permit for entering public places and, in an increasing number of cases, schools and workplaces. In addition to public health protection, these uses also aim at encouraging vaccination by restricting citizens' freedom of movement.[63]

[58] 'NHS COVID-19 – NHS', www.nhs.uk/apps-library/nhs-COVID-19/.

[59] D Lewis, 'Contact-Tracing Apps Help Reduce COVID Infections, Data Suggest' [2021] *Nature* 18, www.nature.com/articles/d41586-021-00451-y.

[60] For Italy, see A Cicchetti et al, 'Analisi Dei Modelli Organizzativi Di Risposta Al COVID-19' (2021) Report Alta Scuola di Economia e Management dei Sistemi Sanitari, Università Cattolica del Sacro Cuore, 57, http://www.quotidianosanita.it/allegati/allegato6584955.pdf. For the situation in the USA, see M Price, 'Contact Tracing Takes a Back Seat During Latest COVID Surge' (*AP News*, 28 August 2021) https://apnews.com/article/business-health-coronavirus-pandemic-87c3042656c6c6cc0c3464ed47737829.

[61] The usage data is available at https://github.com/immuni-app/immuni-dashboard-data. From this data it appears that the exposure notifications are decreasing rapidly.

[62] 'Proposal for a Regulation of the European Parliament and of the Council on a Framework for the Issuance, Verification and Acceptance of Interoperable Certificates on Vaccination, Testing and Recovery to Facilitate Free Movement during the COVID-19 Pandemic (Digital Green Certificate)' COM (2021) 130 final; S Palmer, 'EU Outlines Proposed COVID "Vaccine Passport" That Could Boost Travel This Summer', www.euronews.com/travel/2021/03/17/eu-plans-to-boost-summer-travel-with-its-proposal-for-a-digital-vaccine-passport.

[63] S Kamin-Friedman and MP Raz, 'Lessons from Israel's COVID-19 Green Pass Program' (2021) 10 *Israel Journal of Health Policy Research* 1, https://ijhpr.biomedcentral.com/articles/10.1186/s13584-021-00496-4#Sec6.

The green pass can be obtained with: (i) vaccination, (ii) recovery from COVID or (iii) a negative swab test. The data is encoded in a QR code, for easy access with reader apps. The QR code is a system for transmitting data encoded in an image: therefore, the green pass can be embedded either in existing COVID apps or in dedicated green pass apps.

The French COVID app TousAntiCOVID has been enhanced with a green pass, which is mandatory to enter several public places.[64] The same goes for the Italian Immuni: since October 2021, the COVID certificate in Italy has been made obligatory to access all workplaces. Singapore added the same functionality in their TraceTogether app, which is now mandatory for entering most public buildings, such as schools or government offices.[65]

Other apps have been developed for the purpose of managing green pass QR codes, with differing functionalities (some show the decoded data, like the vaccination dates). An example is the CovPass app deployed in Germany.[66] In other cases, the green pass has been integrated in a broader public service system, such as the Italian IO platform. The green pass was originally added to IO because the Italian Data Protection Authority objected to adding the functionality to the Immuni app. The Authority stated that the tracing system was developed to be agnostic to personal data, and the addition of the green pass data would have de facto annulled this premise. The Authority subsequently reversed their decision, on condition that the data management not be fully autonomous but based on manual intervention by the user.

With the help of these measures, many countries have now reopened to social life for holders of these 'passports',[67] thus relaxing the movement restrictions previously enacted in light of the pandemic.

While the green pass has allowed societies to move forward towards an 'ordinary' life, it also poses doubts from both an ethical and a legal point of view. Some have considered these movement permits to be a discriminatory measure against those who are not yet (or have refused to be) vaccinated.[68] This is also a concern for accessing the workplace.[69] Furthermore, linking such travel passes to technological means could enhance digital inequality, creating an obstacle to those who are not familiar enough with technology.[70]

[64] For details, see https://www.gouvernement.fr/info-coronavirus/pass-sanitaire.

[65] https://www.vaccine.gov.sg/health-advisory/; K Iwamoto, 'No Jab, No Entry: Singapore Highlights Rise of Vaccine Mandates' (*Nikkei Asia*, 2021) https://asia.nikkei.com/Spotlight/Coronavirus/COVID-vaccines/No-jab-no-entry-Singapore-highlights-rise-of-vaccine-mandates.

[66] https://play.google.com/store/apps/details?id=de.rki.covpass.app.

[67] Israel was one of the first: https://www.gov.il/en/departments/general/corona-certificates.

[68] https://petition.parliament.uk/petitions/569957.

[69] M Paterlini, 'COVID-19: Italy Sees Protests against Mandatory Health Passports for Workplaces' (2021) 375 *British Medical Journal*, www.bmj.com/content/375/bmj.n2575.

[70] Floridi (n 49).

The development of these e-governance measures is most likely destined to advance rapidly in our societies, and is probably going to give rise to new applications in the aftermath of the pandemic. Their design and deployment should therefore carefully balance individual rights (such as freedom of movement), safety and security needs, access to technology, privacy-oriented data management and democratic standards.[71]

9.8. Glossary

API (Application Programming Interface)

A shared language between two or more programs that need to exchange information. An API defines how the components need to communicate (question/answer) and the data format used.

An API does not include a specific implementation of either of the components, instead it just defines the transmission protocol. It is often used to enable integration with a particular software without having to open up its internals.

APIs are sometimes thought of as contracts, with documentation that represents an agreement between parties: if party 1 sends a remote request structured a particular way, this is how party 2's software will respond.[72]

BLE (Bluetooth Low Energy)

A technology developed independently from Bluetooth standards (derived from Wifi-Direct) that is intended to lower power consumption and hence running costs. BLE can communicate via radio waves point-to-point, broadcast or as part of a mesh device.

It is often used by IoT (Internet of Things) devices and personal medical equipment, like blood pressure or glucose monitors.

Bluetooth

A low-range wireless technology used to exchange data between two devices using radio waves in the globally unlicensed 2.4 GHz ISM (industrial, scientific, and medical) spectrum.

[71] Eran Fisher, *E-Governance and e-Democracy: Questioning Technology-Centered Categories* (Oxford University Press 2012).

[72] 'What Is an API?' (n 25).

The typical range is under 10 m, and occasionally up to 100 m, both for Bluetooth and BLE.

The Bluetooth and BLE standards are developed by the Bluetooth Special Interest Group.

GAEN (Google Apple Exposure Notification)

The protocol built by Apple and Google on the basis of DP-3T, which is run at the system level to make it more efficient by having the same permissions as built-in system components.

Normally, in modern smartphones, the background tasks are limited in their CPU time and usage of resources (the Bluetooth radio) to preserve battery life and to keep the device functioning

GPS (Global Positioning System)

The interconnected web of satellites used to calculate an approximate location on the world's surface.
Developed by the US government, it covers most of the world surface.
Other parallel systems exist in other regions:

Galileo – Europe
GLONASS – Russia
BeiDou – China
Navic – India
QZSS – Japan – Only an augmentation to GPS

QR Code (Quick Response Code)

A matrix barcode (it has two dimensions) that is machine-readable and is used to launch a command to a browser/application on the device used to scan it.

In can be used, for example, to log the presence of a particular device (and thus its user) in a specific venue, without having to track his whereabouts via GPS.

10

COVID-19, Tracing Apps and Big Tech: 'Can't Buy Me Love'

NICOLAS PETIT*

10.1. Introduction

Contrary to many predictions (including ours),[1] COVID-19 will not go down in history as the moment when big tech repaired their broken relationship with European policymakers.[2] Since the beginning of the pandemic, Europe has witnessed an escalation in policymakers' grievances towards big tech.[3] And the treadmill of regulation has not slowed down.[4] The European Union has recently passed unprecedented legislation that will impose asymmetric strictures on digital 'gatekeepers' business models.[5]

At a high level, this state of affairs is curious. Empirical projections show a sustained pattern of growing consumption of digital services after the pandemic.[6]

* Joint Chair in Competition Law at the Department of Law and at the Robert Schuman Centre for Advanced Studies at the European University Institute.

[1] N Petit and R Sousa, 'Opinion: COVID-19 Response Will End All the Big Tech Bashing', www.mercurynews.com/2020/04/09/opinion-COVID-19-response-will-end-all-the-big-tech-bashing/; but see also S Levy, 'Has the Coronavirus Killed the Techlash?' (*Wired*, 20 March 2020) www.wired.com/story/plaintext-has-the-coronavirus-killed-the-techlash/; 'Big Tech's COVID-19 Opportunity' *The Economist* (London, 16 April 2020) www.economist.com/leaders/2020/04/04/big-techs-COVID-19-opportunity.

[2] The EU Competition Commissioner, Margrethe Vestager, expressed skepticism on the extent of the 'restorative actions' undertook by big techs during the pandemic in the podcast episode 'Has COVID-19 Killed the Big Tech Backlash?' *The Economist* (London, 16 April 2020) www.economist.com/podcasts/2020/04/16/has-COVID-19-killed-the-big-tech-backlash.

[3] For a quick overview of the development of the relationship between Member States and big techs during the pandemic, see M Montgomery, 'How COVID-19 Is Shaping European Tech Regulation' (*Tech Stream*, 18 June 2020) www.brookings.edu/techstream/how-COVID-19-is-shaping-european-tech-regulation/.

[4] 'In 2020, Global "Techlash" Will Move from Words to Action' (*Politico*, 31 December 2019) https://www.politico.eu/article/tech-policy-competition-privacy-facebook-europe-techlash/.

[5] Commission, 'Proposal for a Regulation of the European Parliament and of the Council on contestable and fair markets in the digital sector (Digital Markets Act)' COM (2020) 842 final.

[6] For an overview, see S Kemp, 'Digital 2021: Global Overview Report' (*DataReportal*, 27 January 2021) https://datareportal.com/reports/digital-2021-global-overview-report.

A PYMNTS survey suggests that consumers and companies will keep using digital services not because they have to, but because 'they want to'.[7] Yet, policymakers interpret this as proof of how dependent consumers and companies have become on big tech.

But what is more paradoxical is elsewhere: since the pandemic, the techlash has gained force, in spite of reported big tech firms' efforts to proactively cooperate with governments in the fight against COVID-19.

In this chapter, I look in particular at how Apple and Google's efforts to assist European policymakers to supply contact tracing apps backfired; why this is paradoxical, given the substantial degree of business model adaptations that both firms initiated to cooperate with public authorities; and also why this was all quite predictable.

10.2. Techlash Reloaded

10.2.1. Action

In the early days of the pandemic, a number of governments, public health authorities and researchers across the world realised that mobile phone technology could help automate contact tracing. Manual contract tracing is costly, slow and potentially dangerous. Moreover, it is inaccurate because people exposed to COVID-19 cannot record each and every detail of their whereabouts, encounters and social interactions.[8]

In March 2020, Singapore pioneered the movement towards automated contact tracing with the Tracetogether app. Tracetogether works by performing 'Bluetooth handshakes' with nearby devices.[9] Designed to run on the foreground of mobile phones, the app was reported to drain the battery and to reduce user friendliness.[10] Tracetogether recorded bad reviews in app stores, undermining the early adoption of tracing app technology.[11]

The Singapore experience nonetheless inspired public health authorities, governments and non-governmental organisations (NGOs) of other countries to develop contact tracing applications. Across the world, consortia of research

[7] 'Millennials Will Lead the Voice Commerce Revolution' (*PYMNTS*, 19 October 2020) www.pymnts.com/news/retail/2020/millennials-will-lead-the-voice-commerce-revolution/.

[8] A brief recap of the potential of digital contact tracing is provided by RA Kleinman and C Merkel, 'Digital Contact Tracing for COVID-19' (2020) 192 *CMAJ* E653.

[9] 'App Release Notes' (TraceTogether FAQs) https://support.tracetogether.gov.sg/hc/en-sg/articles/360046481013-App-Release-Notes.

[10] H Baharudin, 'Coronavirus: Contact Tracing App Update Fixes Battery Drain in IPhones' *Straits Times* (Singapore, 7 July 2020) www.straitstimes.com/singapore/contact-tracing-app-update-fixes-battery-drain-in-iphones.

[11] 'Survey Shows People Aren't Using TraceTogether Due to It Using Too Much Battery Power' (*Goody Feed*, 15 December 2020) https://goodyfeed.com/survey-tracetogether-battery-drain/.

groups had already started working on protocols to facilitate digital contact tracing. Two dominant models emerged:

- a centralised one, which uploads all mobile devices' contact logs to a central reporting server, as well as reports of positive cases, and notifies users of possible exposure; and
- a decentralised one, which only uploads reports of positive tests on a central server and allows connected devices to download/stream the central database, identifying possible matches with contact logs that remain on the device.[12]

Amidst increased privacy concerns towards wide-scale state surveillance,[13] countries like Germany that had started to develop a centralised model reversed course.[14]

In this context, Apple and Google soon became a key part of the exposure notification discussion. Apple iPhones and Android phones jointly dominate the market for mobile phones. Allowing Bluetooth to be called in the background requires implementation of software protocols at the operating system (OS) level, which is proprietary to Apple and semi-proprietary to Google. Moreover, the two standards must detect each other easily to allow efficient exposure notification.

[12] For an accessible explanation of the two models, see C Criddle and L Kelion, 'Coronavirus Contact-Tracing: World Split between Two Types of App' (*BBC News*, 7 May 2020) www.bbc.com/news/technology-52355028. The details of the Decentralized Privacy-Preserving Proximity Tracing (DP3T) protocol, a model of decentralised protocol developed by a team of academics which inspired the Apple/Google API, including a comparison with the ROBERT centralised approach adopted by the French government, are published by C Troncoso et al, 'Decentralized Privacy-Preserving Proximity Tracing' (2020) 43 *IEEE Data Engineering Bulletin* 36. To understand the connection between the DP3T protocol and Google/Apple API, see D Leprince-Ringuet, 'The World's First Contact-Tracing App Using Google and Apple's API Goes Live', www.zdnet.com/article/the-worlds-first-contact-tracing-app-using-google-and-apples-api-goes-live/.

[13] 'Germany Flips on Smartphone Contact Tracing, Backs Apple and Google' (*Euractiv*, 27 April 2020) www.euractiv.com/section/digital/news/germany-flips-on-smartphone-contact-tracing-backs-apple-and-google/.

[14] The Czech Republic, Denmark, Italy and Lithuania undertook a similar change of direction. After announcing the developing of a centralised contact tracing app, their final release followed a decentralised protocol (European Union and Agency for Fundamental Rights, *Coronavirus Pandemic in the EU: Fundamental Rights Implications: With a Focus on Contact-Tracing Apps*, Bulletin #2 (21 March–30 April 2020); A Longo, 'L'app Immuni Cambia. Seguirà Il Modello Decentralizzato Di Apple e Google' (*Il Sole 24 Ore*, 22 April 2020) www.ilsole24ore.com/art/l-app-immuni-cambia-seguira-modello-decentralizzato-apple-e-google-ADcBF4L?refresh_ce=1; Commission, 'Mobile Applications to Support Contact Tracing in the EU's Fight against COVID-19' (June 2020) https://ec.europa.eu/health/system/files/2020-07/mobileapps_202006progressreport_en_0.pdf). Among the factors influencing their decision are the strong concerns of the national data protection authorities ('Audizione del Presidente del Garante per la protezione dei dati personali sull'uso delle nuove tecnologie e della rete per contrastare l'emergenza epidemiologica da Coronavirus', www.gpdp.it:443/web/guest/home/docweb/-/docweb-display/docweb/9308774) and the calls of the European Parliament (European Parliament Resolution on EU coordinated action to combat the COVID-19 pandemic and its consequences, 17 April 2020, P9_TA(2020)0054, available at www-europarl-europa-eu.eui.idm.oclc.org/doceo/document/TA-9-2020-0054_EN.pdf).

On 10 April 2020, Apple and Google announced a partnership to build software (application programming interfaces, APIs) into Android and iOS that would let contact tracing apps from or approved by public health authorities work reliably across Android phones and iPhones without killing battery life.[15]

Apple and Google chose a decentralised approach. Some interpreted this as an attempt to play the public opinion against public authorities willing to adopt a centralised model.[16] But, in fairness, did both companies really have a choice? As soon as Apple and Google started to work on the project, privacy concerns arose. Even if choosing a centralised approach might have been lawful under the General Data Protection Regulation standards, the reputational damage and long-term regulatory suspicions would have been broader. In fact, the choice of a decentralised approach was consistent with both companies' refusal to provide localisation data or rely on geolocalisation technology like GPS.[17]

On the same day, Apple and Google also announced that they would develop 'API-less' solutions with direct OS-level access in the future. Concretely, the idea was to allow users to opt-in for exposure notification in their device setting. The point has been to assist countries without strong technological capabilities, and boost adoption in the face of evidence that users do not download tracing apps.[18]

On 20 May 2020,[19] Apple and Google released the Google Apple Exposure Notification API release 1.3.2 for Bluetooth proximity tracing on GitHub.

10.2.2. Reaction

Many countries in Europe followed a pragmatic approach, using the Apple and Google APIs for exposure notification.[20] Two countries, the UK and France, however, crystallised opposition to big tech's tracing assistance.[21]

[15] A schematic presentation of the functioning of the Apple/Google API can be retrieved from 'Exposure Notifications: Helping Fight COVID-19', https://www.google.com/intl/en_us/COVID19/exposurenotifications/; 'Privacy-Preserving Contact Tracing – Apple and Google', https://www.apple.com/COVID19/contacttracing.

[16] France and the UK were indeed placed in the unusual position of asking for the two platforms to be less rigid regarding the measures they implemented to protect the privacy of their users. A Hern, 'France Urges Apple and Google to Ease Privacy Rules on Contact Tracing' *The Guardian* (London, 21 April 2020) www.theguardian.com/world/2020/apr/21/france-apple-google-privacy-contact-tracing-coronavirus.

[17] In this regard, note that public trust is an important asset for technology companies. In his analysis of contact tracing applications, Buzzell observes that 'The privacy preserving model serves vendor interests, allowing them to cooperate with public health authorities, thus avoiding regulatory or coercive measures, by limiting the possibility that the use of digital contract tracing apps breaks tacit or contractual agreements with their users that could damage already wavering public trust'. A Buzzell, 'Public Goods From Private Data – An Efficacy and Justification Paradox for Digital Contact Tracing' [2020] *arXiv:Computer and Society* http://arxiv.org/abs/2007.07016.

[18] Montgomery (n 3).

[19] 'Exposure Notification API Launches to Support Public Health Agencies' (*Google*, 20 May 2020) https://blog.google/inside-google/company-announcements/apple-google-exposure-notification-api-launches/.

[20] N Lomas, 'UK Gives up on Centralized Coronavirus Contacts-Tracing App – Will "Likely£ Switch to Model Backed by Apple and Google' (*TechCrunch*, 18 June 2020) https://techcrunch.com/2020/06/18/

The UK initially considered that a homemade app would be better than one based on the technology developed by Google and Apple, but reversed course in July 2020.[22] France developed its own app, and launched StopCOVID in June 2020.[23]

Two issues arose with the domestic technology approach of the UK and France. First, both countries favoured a centralised approach on the ground that this would allow more precision and rapidity in infection data collection. Both Apple and Google disagreed, arguing from the outset in favour of 'privacy by design'.[24]

Second, and perhaps more importantly, the problem with homegrown apps that did not purport to rely on the Google and Apple API is that they would not be allowed to continuously use Bluetooth in the background, limiting their efficiency. Indeed, if the device is locked or if the app is not on the foreground, the Bluetooth signal is not active. The reason for this technical restriction is to limit security breaches against users, in turn limiting the adoption of exposure notification apps.[25]

Now, these technical issues triggered acrimonious comments from British and French policy leaders.[26] The UK health secretary blamed Apple's rigidity, slamming the poor performance of the (Google/Apple) Exposure Notification (GAEN) system at distance estimation.[27] And in France, the digital minister lambasted Apple's attitude in the fight against the pandemic. The minister added 'We will remember this when the time will come'.[28]

uk-gives-up-on-centralized-coronavirus-contacts-tracing-app-will-switch-to-model-backed-by-apple-and-google/?guccounter=2.

[21] Note also that Norway and Bulgaria followed a centralised model: 'Bahrain, Kuwait and Norway Contact Tracing Apps a Danger for Privacy' (Amnesty International, 16 June 2020) www.amnesty.org/en/latest/news/2020/06/bahrain-kuwait-norway-contact-tracing-apps-danger-for-privacy/.

[22] D Sabbagh and A Hern, 'UK Abandons Contact-Tracing App for Apple and Google Model' *The Guardian* (London, 18 June 2020) www.theguardian.com/world/2020/jun/18/uk-poised-to-abandon-coronavirus-app-in-favour-of-apple-and-google-models.

[23] The app was developed through a public–private partnership involving, among the others, the firms Orange, Dassault Systèmes and Capgemini. While those companies initially started developing their proprietary app, named StopC19, they ultimately decided to join the government-led initiative. K Poireault, 'StopCOVID: l'appli française de contact tracing sera prête le 2 juin, sans Google ni Apple, annonce Cédric O' (*Industrie-techno*, 4 April 2020) www.industrie-techno.com/article/stopCOVID-attaque-de-toutes-parts-le-modele-francais-de-contact-tracing-centralise-de-plus-en-plus-esseule-en-europe.60261.

[24] Information Commissioner's Office, 'Apple and Google Joint Initiative on COVID-19 Contact Tracing Technology' (17 April 2020) https://ico.org.uk/media/about-the-ico/documents/2617653/apple-google-api-opinion-final-april-2020.pdf.

[25] Note that the issue was more relevant to Apple than Google, as the Android ecosystem allows apps to call Bluetooth functionality while running in the background.

[26] J Tapsfield, 'Apple Clashes with Matt Hancock over Tracing App Detection Claim' (*Mail Online*, 19 June 2020) www.dailymail.co.uk/news/article-8439259/Apple-hits-Matt-Hancock-claims-tracing-app-detect-distances.html.

[27] Health and Social Care Secretary Matt Hancock declared that 'as it stands, our app won't work because Apple won't change their system': 'Health and Social Care Secretary's Statement on Coronavirus (COVID-19): 18 June 2020', www.gov.uk/government/speeches/health-and-social-care-secretarys-statement-on-coronavirus-COVID-19-18-june-2020).

[28] IA Hamilton, 'France Attacked Apple for Not Helping to Build Its Contact-Tracing App' (*Business Insider*, 6 May 2020) www.businessinsider.com/france-attacks-apple-contact-tracing-app-2020-5.

There are signs that the COVID-19 exposure notification quarrel with Google and Apple left wounds. In France, the issue of tracing apps become one poster child of the fight for digital sovereignty.[29] The movement is gaining traction. In a joint op-ed published in June, top ministers, secretaries of state and officials from France, Italy, Germany, Spain and Portugal wrote that the debate over contact tracing had raised issues about 'the way Europe defines its relationship with digital global players'.[30] Since then, the discussion over 'tech sovereignty' has taken a new dimension, becoming a priority of the European Commission.[31] Even though no explicit link was made in the policy conversation with tracing apps, there are signs that the UK and French experiences have irked governments, including other countries who were faster adopters of the Google and Apple API.

10.3. No Good Big Tech Deed Goes Unpunished

To a rational eye, the mixed political reception of Apple and Google's joint contact tracing effort is a puzzle. For a number of years now, Apple and Google have been compared to monopoly, gatekeeper or systemic firms. The underlying critique is that they are said to enjoy absolute 'power' – that is, they have the ability to set their own terms towards users, workers and even governments.

Yet, if the COVID-19 tracing apps episode showed something about big tech, it is that both firms lifted proprietary design privileges and opened their software architectures to third party applications. Countries and public health authorities were left free to design their own exposure notification specifications in their apps, like distance between Bluetooth devices and duration of exposure.

Moreover, there is no debate that, at least at the highest level, both firms sided with the most privacy-friendly technological architecture, thereby implementing the social preference expressed in EU and national law.[32]

[29] S Jacob and J Lawarée, 'The Adoption of Contact Tracing Applications of COVID-19 by European Governments' (2021) 4 *Policy Design and Practice* 44. See also M Lombard-Latune, 'Appli StopCOVID: "La souveraineté est en jeu face à Apple et Google", alerte Aymeril Hoang (Conseil scientifique)' (*l'Opinion*, 26 April 2020) www.lopinion.fr/politique/appli-stopCOVID-la-souverainete-est-en-jeu-face-a-apple-et-google-alerte-aymeril-hoang-conseil-scientifique; J Darnis, 'La souveraineté technologique européenne, une réponse à la crise de la COVID-19 ?' (Fondation pour la Recherche Stratégique, 19 May 2020) www.frstrategie.org/publications/notes/souverainete-technologique-europeenne-une-reponse-crise-COVID-19-2020.

[30] S Warwick, 'Five EU States Criticize Apple and Google over Contact Tracing in Letter' (*iMore*, 27 May 2020) www.imore.com/five-eu-states-criticise-apple-and-google-imposing-technical-standards-over-contact-tracing.

[31] E Kelly, 'Decoding Europe's New Fascination with "Tech Sovereignty"' (*Science|Business*, 3 September 2020) https://sciencebusiness.net/technology-strategy-board/news/decoding-europes-new-fascination-tech-sovereignty.

[32] The European Commission also expressed some support to this approach.

But, make no mistake. The point here is not a suggestion that Apple and Google were good citizens during the COVID-19 crisis.[33] Rather, the point is that both organisations displayed relational, cooperative and adaptive behaviour that is not fully consistent with absolute 'power', 'gatekeeper' or 'monopoly' positions, and the independent, discretionary and careless behaviour that traditionally goes with it.

At this stage, it is helpful to sharpen the focus. To start with, the very idea of a technological cooperation between Apple and Google in mobile technology should leave any casual observer of the tech world in disbelief. Both firms have for years invested in building competing technological ecosystems, and are involved in head-to-head rivalry to grow their user bases.[34]

It is also interesting to observe that both Apple and Google strayed from routine corporate culture by quite a margin.

To see this, recall that Apple is one of the most secretive company in the world. It orchestrates a closed ecosystem, based on tight control of hardware components and software designs. The idea that Apple would agree to display source code or give special privilege to OS access would strike any engineer's mind as heretical. Moreover, Apple is distinctively known as a king of product execution. From this perspective, it was a rather unusual step for Apple to 'ship' iOS 14 with a partially debugged COVID-19 exposure notification setting.[35]

The same is true of Google. The tech giant's business model is one of personal data maximisation. Its ongoing acquisition of electronic wristwatch manufacturer FitBit has been criticised by many privacy regulators as an illegitimate grab of personal health data. Yet Google from the outset offered to operate in a decentralised paradigm. And it went as far as to place an advertisement for its contact tracing apps on the home page of its search engine, something that it had only exceptionally done in the past.

In this light, there is credence to the claim that big tech today are 'in a nearly impossible position in terms of almost always absorbing blame no matter what they do whenever the choices are hard'.[36]

[33] Google's former CEO and executive chairman, E Schmidt, advanced the narrative that technologists' effort to do their part amidst the pandemic is a reflection of 'the entrepreneurial, results-driven ethos of today's tech sector'. E Schmidt, 'A Real Digital Infrastructure at Last' *Wall Street Journal* (New York, 27 March 2020) www.wsj.com/articles/a-real-digital-infrastructure-at-last-11585313825. In this regard, the analysis presented here intends to present a more nuanced assessment.

[34] Rivalry between the Apple and Google ecosystems has been defined as remarkable by JC Miguel and MA Casado, 'GAFAnomy (Google, Amazon, Facebook and Apple): The Big Four and the b-Ecosystem' in M Gómez-Uranga, JM Zabala-Iturriagagoitia and J Barrutia (eds), *Dynamics of Big Internet Industry Groups and Future Trends: A View from Epigenetic Economics* (Springer International Publishing, 2016).

[35] A Khollam, 'What Is Exposure Notification in IOS 14 and How to Use It to Track COVID-19 Spread?' (*Republic World*, 2 November 2020) www.republicworld.com/technology-news/gadgets/what-is-exposure-notification-in-ios-14-and-how-to-use-it-to-track-COVID-19-spread.html.

[36] C Newton, 'Why Countries Keep Bowing to Apple and Google's Contact Tracing App Requirements' (*The Verge*, 8 May 2020) www.theverge.com/interface/2020/5/8/21250744/apple-google-contact-tracing-england-germany-exposure-notification-india-privacy.

10.4. A Self-Inflicted Wound?

Was any of this escalation of the techlash predictable?

Many observers say no. The common explanation for this new episode of the techlash is that the tracing app episode led Member States, and the EU, to suddenly realise that they had in effect abdicated their power to set technology standards to the Silicon Valley.[37]

But this rude awakening story only explains at least part of the phenomenon. In many areas of the economy, public authorities willingly delegate to the private sector the mission to set technology standards. There is no reason why this should not be the approach towards digital technologies.

Instead, a more compelling explanation consists in understanding that the underlying public policy assaults against big tech is that they increasingly compete with the classic state model for the allocation of public goods and services to society.[38] And the COVID-19 tracing app episode provides a typical case of substitution of the private sector to government authorities in a public goods situation, namely fighting a pandemic.[39]

Public goods are 'collective consumption goods' that markets traditionally undersupply, because of non-appropriable spill overs.[40] Classical economists defined public goods as defence, law enforcement or currency. In modern welfare states, they also now deemed to include education, healthcare, environmental protection or privacy.

From a pure efficiency standpoint, policymakers should welcome the emergence of big tech as suppliers of public goods, because this lowers the costs of welfare policies. To see the point, recall that many Member States would like to impose specific taxes on big tech to finance redistributive policies. Big tech's

[37] The timeliness allowed by the role of platform owners in coordinating a widely adopted standard provided in the time-pressured setting of the pandemic emergency should not, however, be underestimated. Standard setting through market competition or inclusive multi-stakeholder committees, on the contrary, proved time-consuming and inefficient. K Marhold and J Fell, 'Multi-mode Standardization under Extreme Time-Pressure – the Case of COVID-19 Contact-Tracing Apps' [2021] *R&D Management*.

[38] It is perhaps not surprising that only a few months after the release of the Apple/Google API commentators started relating it to an infrastructural power: M Veale, 'Privacy Is Not the Problem with the Apple-Google Contact-Tracing Toolkit' *The Guardian* (London, 1 July 2020) https://www.theguardian.com/commentisfree/2020/jul/01/apple-google-contact-tracing-app-tech-giant-digital-rights.

[39] The conversion of technological expertise into an advantage in the medical sector has been defined as 'governance surplus' and a transgression by big techs into the political sphere, as they set the technical conditions for the pandemic response. See T Sharon, 'Blind-Sided by Privacy? Digital Contact Tracing, the Apple/Google API and Big Tech's Newfound Role as Global Health Policy Makers' (2021) 23 *Ethics and Information Technology* 45. Similarly, Greig states that Apple is 'dictating policies to nations': P Greig, 'Contact-Tracing Apps: Apple Dictating Policies to Nations Won't Help Its EU Anti-Trust Probe' https://strathprints.strath.ac.uk/72989/1/Paul_Conversation_2020_Contact_tracing_apps_Apple_dictating_policies_to_nations_wont_help_its_EU_anti_trust_probe.html.

[40] The concept was notoriously introduced by PA Samuelson, 'The Pure Theory of Public Expenditure' (1954) 36 *The Review of Economics and Statistics* 387.

supply of public goods indirectly achieves this goal. In addition, big tech entry into public goods markets lowers the costs of political reform. Removing inefficiency in the supply of public good is a costly platform for political leaders. Big tech entry removes this moral hazard.

That said, when big tech firms provide public goods, they also enter into competition with States, decreasing the latter's legitimacy as social organisations in general and the necessity of their monopoly over taxation and regulation in particular.

This, we believe, plausibly explains public policymakers' activism against big tech firms.

Several sources of anecdotal evidence corroborate the point. First, policymakers have demonstrated resolve to nip in the bud any attempt by big tech firms to provide core public goods, like currency. Facebook's attempts to develop Libra, a cryptocurrency that would provide an alternative to existing transfer systems, is a case in point.[41]

Second, countries like France, Germany and even the UK, where the size of the 'public sector' remains substantial, have been at the forefront of the fight against big tech.[42]

Third, during the pandemic, big tech firms have also been suspected of eyeing other public goods markets, like education, with opportunism.[43]

Of course, these remarks are overly superficial. They all deserve further empirical inquiry. But there is a good ground to believe that several governments interpreted big tech's tracing app move as an illegitimate intrusion into their public goods monopoly. Had this been understood from the outset, big tech firms would perhaps have avoided offering joint technological assistance towards contact tracing, and focused their resources on less counterproductive initiatives.

[41] F Coppola, 'Libra Isn't Just a Cryptocurrency, It's a Threat to National Sovereignty' (*Wired UK*, 16 October 2019) www.wired.co.uk/article/facebook-libra-politics; T Telford, 'Why Governments around the World Are Afraid of Libra, Facebook's Cryptocurrency' *Washington Post* (Washington, DC, 12 July 2019) www.washingtonpost.com/business/2019/07/12/why-governments-around-world-are-afraid-libra-facebooks-cryptocurrency/.

[42] European Commission, Directorate General for Employment, Social Affairs and Inclusion, *A Comparative Overview of Public Administration Characteristics and Performance in EU28* (Publications Office of the European Union, 2018) https://data.europa.eu/doi/10.2767/13319.

[43] N Klein, 'How Big Tech Plans to Profit from the Pandemic' *The Guardian* (London, 13 May 2020) www.theguardian.com/news/2020/may/13/naomi-klein-how-big-tech-plans-to-profit-from-coronavirus-pandemic.

11

What Role for the Data Protection Authorities During the COVID-19 Pandemic?

MARIA MAGIERSKA*

11.1. GDPR and COVID-19: A Two-Year-Old versus a Global Health Emergency

When the World Health Organization (WHO) declared the COVID-19 outbreak a global pandemic in March 2020,[1] it was still less than two years after the General Data Protection Regulation (GDPR) had come into force in the European Union. The national data protection authorities (DPAs), controllers and processors, data subjects and consumer organisations were all focused on gradual crystallisation of the interpretation of the law and the clarification of first doubts. The authorities were in a process of learning how to exercise their new, reinforced powers and how to collaborate within the newly established cooperation and consistency mechanisms. Their main challenge was to bridge cultural and legal differences that existed under the previous legal order, including different positions of the DPAs in national administrative procedures. Controllers and data subjects were verifying in practice the strength of the regulation. It was becoming clear that the new law did not entirely solve the old problems, and even created new ones. The still unresolved issue of scarce financial and human resources of the DPAs accompanied a growing problem with effectiveness of the cross-border enforcement mechanism. The European Data Protection Supervisor (EDPS) called the GDPR on its third anniversary a child 'who must still learn to walk before it runs'.[2]

* PhD Researcher at the European University Institute, maria.magierska@eui.eu.

[1] WHO, 'WHO Announces COVID-19 Outbreak a Pandemic' (12 March 2020) www.euro.who.int/en/health-topics/health-emergencies/coronavirus-covid-19/news/news/2020/3/who-announces-covid-19-outbreak-a-pandemic.

[2] European Data Protection Supervisor, 'GDPR: A Three-Year-Old Who Must Still Learn to Walk Before It Runs' (EDPS, 25 May 2021) www.edps.europa.eu/press-publications/press-news/blog/gdpr-three-year-old-who-must-still-learn-walk-it-runs_en.

The new regulation has been under careful scrutiny from policymakers, non-governmental organisations (NGOs), academia, public institutions and the private sector.

The sudden occurrence of the pandemic came as a great shock. It required from the whole data protection sector immediate reaction and fast changes. What should have been a long, regular process of learning and adjusting became a rapid and uncoordinated sprint. EU Member States were introducing new restrictions overnight. For their citizens, it meant an abrupt switch to remote education, working from home and increased surveillance on an unprecedented scale. The DPAs, as institutions specifically envisaged to monitor the introduction of such measures, suddenly found themselves on the frontline of public attention. They had to manoeuvre between safeguarding the fundamental right to data protection and ensuring the effectiveness of the ongoing efforts to hamper the spread of the pandemic. At the same time, they were themselves struggling with the spread of the disease, switching working modes and learning to function in a new reality. The Danish DPA, for example, blamed its own secretariat for a data breach that occurred when its employers were switching to remote working and did not utilise documents properly.[3] The way the DPAs faced this unexpected challenge differed among the EU Member States and often reflected other problems relating to national enforcement of the GDPR.

In Poland, one of the first measures introduced to monitor the spread of the COVID-19 pandemic was the obligatory Public Health Passenger Locator Form (PLF), distributed on planes during international flights.[4] Passengers were asked to provide personal information, such as name, surname, sex, permanent and temporary address, and emergency contact details of another person. There was no information whatsoever about the recipient and the grounds for the collection of the data, nor on their retention. It also remained unclear whether a data subject could ever access or rectify this data.

As one of the passengers who complained about the PLF on Twitter recalled (and received a highly negative response from other users) that the aircraft crew had known only that collection was required by the Polish government. However, they were neither able to specify which ministry or institution had issued the order nor advise where to find a privacy policy.[5] Only later did data protection journalists establish that the PLFs were collected by the Warsaw Chopin Airport and subsequently transferred to the Chief Sanitary Inspectorate, as the first precaution against the spread of the pandemic.[6] The Polish DPA (UODO) in the meantime

[3] Datailsynet, 'Brud på persondatasikkerheden i Datatilsynet' (11 September 2020) www.datatilsynet.dk/afgoerelser/afgoerelser/2020/sep/brud-paa-persondatasikkerheden-i-datatilsynet.

[4] Public Health Passenger Locator Form, available www.icao.int/safety/aviation-medicine/guidelines/AvInfluenza_guidelines_app.pdf.

[5] www.twitter.com/Kpelczynska/status/1233458103967997952.

[6] S Wikariak, 'Czy Koronawirus Uchyla Przepisy RODO?' (Prawo.Gazetaprawna.Pl, 11 March 2020) www.prawo.gazetaprawna.pl/artykuly/1458883,koronawirus-a-rodo-dane-prywatnosc.html.

issued a statement arguing that the GDPR should not be an obstacle to tackling the global pandemic.[7] The DPA did not, however, address the legality of the questionnaire and its collection. Even though the PLFs were collected on a large scale for several months, no relevant information or advice was to be found on the DPA's website. Individuals seeking explanations for increased data gathering in Poland were left to rely on answers distributed by non-verified sources on social media, Internet forums and media outlets.

This early case from Poland illustrates the atmosphere around data protection during the first wave of the pandemic: the measure was introduced hastily and immediately; no sufficient information was provided to citizens or even those responsible for data collection; the DPA did not react; and the individual who voiced concerns faced hate speech on the Internet. This situation was no different from what was happening all over the EU. Governments attempted to restrain the continuous spread of the virus by hurriedly adopting measures while failing on effective communication and information. Amongst others, these included various controlling and surveilling tools: contact tracing apps, obligatory temperature checks, quarantine apps and other methods of data gathering. They were often introduced quickly and often carelessly. Their main purpose was to monitor how the virus spreads through tracing contacts between people. It required processing of robust catalogues of data, including, above all, sensitive information on a health condition. Additionally, for many of the Member States, the pandemic brought along a digitalisation of the public and private sector, through a rapid and unprecedented shift to remote education and working from home.

Although these measures are needed, they are highly intrusive on the right to privacy and the protection of personal data. The methods used raised many quandaries about the limits of the fundamental right to protection of personal data and required a proportionality test each time they were applied. The global scale and the level of intrusion provoked many experts to declare the final death of privacy and to compare the COVID-19 pandemic with the strong pro-surveillance trend after 9/11.[8] If this was true, in the EU that would also mean the end of the still nascent GDPR – which was one of the first regulations politicians called for the suspension of after the outbreak of the disease.[9]

The institutions mainly responsible for monitoring the compliance with Article 8 of the EU Charter of the Fundamental Rights (CFREU) and the GDPR are the national supervisory authorities (the DPAs). Their position in the EU legal

[7] UODO.gov.pl, 'Statement of the Polish DPA with Regard to Coronavirus (12 March 2020) www.uodo.gov.pl/pl/138/1456.

[8] N Singer and C Sang-Hun, 'As Coronavirus Surveillance Escalates, Personal Privacy Plummets' *New York Times* (New York, 23 March 2020) www.nytimes.com/2020/03/23/technology/coronavirus-surveillance-tracking-privacy.html.

[9] IAPP, 'Hungary Halts Some GDPR Rights amid COVID-19' (7 May 2020) www.iapp.org/news/a/hungary-halts-some-gdpr-rights-amid-COVID-19.

framework is unique. The Court of Justice of the European Union (CJEU) labelled the DPAs 'guardians of the fundamental right to data protection'.[10] At the same time, the GDPR gives them a wide catalogue of tasks and powers that are more similar to market regulators. As a result, many of the DPAs seem to be torn between this quasi-ombudsman role and a sectorial supervisory body. Some of them are prone to issuing fines against the private sector; others provide them with assistance.[11] This confusion seems to derive from a deeper, intrinsic misunderstanding of what the fundamental right to data protection really is and how it relates to the GDPR.[12] As Orla Lynskey argued, the EU data protection framework has a hybrid nature where both economic and right-based objectives are inextricably linked with each other.[13] This complex structure stems from the fact that the GDPR's predecessor, the Data Protection Directive, regulated internal markets and was developed before the right to data protection became an EU fundamental right.[14]

These perspectives are clearly visible in the way the DPAs' competences are constructed in the GDPR – swinging from the role of privacy protector to the role of consultant and advisor. When the COVID-19 pandemic broke out, the DPAs were in the process of learning to balance these functions. The health crisis and the unexpected measures required from them caused a sudden shift towards a role of quasi-ombudsman. For the DPAs, it was the first stress test of influence and the role they play in their respective Member States. Not everyone was ready for that.

This chapter analyses and compares the role of the EU DPAs during the pandemic. To do so, the chapter is divided into a number of parts. The first part (section 11.2) sets the scene of the issue, and explains the legal framework and the institutional structures surrounding the right to data protection and the DPAs, the European Data Protection Board (EDPB) and the EDPS. Subsequently, the second part (section 11.3) provides a general overview of the actions of the DPAs during the health crisis and their most commonly analysed topics. The chapter concludes (section 11.4) with remarks on what lessons are to be learned for the DPAs after the pandemic.

[10] Case C-518/07 *Commission v Germany* ECLI:EU:C:2010:125, [2010] ECR I-01885, para. 23.

[11] S Golla, 'Is Data Protection Law Growing Teeth? The Current Lack of Sanctions in Data Protection Law and Administrative Fines under the GDPR' (2017) 8(1) *Journal of Intellectual Property, Information Technology and Electronic Commerce Law* 70.

[12] B van der Sloot, 'Legal Fundamentalism: Is Data Protection Really a Fundamental Right?' in R Leenes et al (eds), *Data Protection and Privacy: (In)Visibilities and Infrastructures*, Law, Governance and Technology Series (Springer International Publishing, 2017).

[13] O Lynskey, *The Foundations of EU Data Protection Law* (Oxford University Press, 2015) 8.

[14] Directive 95/46/EC of the European Parliament and of the Council of 24 October 1995 on the protection of individuals with regard to the processing of personal data and on the free movement of such data (Data Protection Directive) [1995] OJ L281/31.

11.2. Should We Suspend the GDPR? DPAs, EDPB and EDPS During the Pandemic

The outbreak of the pandemic caused some voices to criticise EU laws for creating unnecessary hindrances to fighting the health crisis.[15] In their view, the right to data protection and the GDPR were a burden that slowed down implementation of preventive measures and hence caused the further spread of the disease. However, the existing EU legal framework was prepared for the exceptional case of the public health emergency.

When it comes to the legality of the processing of personal data for the purposes of monitoring the spread of COVID-19, several provisions of the GDPR have to be considered. As is explicitly confirmed by Recital 46, such processing may be regarded as necessary in order to protect the vital interests of the data subject or as necessary for the performance of a task carried out in the public interest or in the exercise of official authority vested in the controller. A similar exemption applies to special categories of data, including health data. Article 9(2)(c) allows for the processing of personal data when it is necessary 'to protect the vital interests of the data subject or of another natural person where the data subject is physically or legally incapable of giving consent'. Moreover, Article 9(2)(i) explicitly mentions 'protecting against serious cross-border threats to health' as one of the necessary reasons of public interest in the area of public health to allow processing of personal data. Hence, the GDPR was never an obstacle to combating the pandemic.

The main institutions responsible for the monitoring of the righteous application of Article 8 CFREU and the GDPR are the DPAs. Among their main tasks are promoting public awareness, advising the national parliament, government and other institutions on legislative and administrative measures relating to data protection, and monitoring relevant development of information and communication technologies and commercial practices. To that end, they wield a broad catalogue of powers, including the competence to impose administrative fines, carry out investigations in the form of data protection audits and impose temporary or definitive limitations, including a ban on processing. They may engage in legal proceedings and bring infringements to the attention of the judicial authorities. Moreover, building on the wording of Article 8 CFREU and Article 16 of the Treaty on the Functioning of the European Union (TFEU), the GDPR provides the DPAs with a large degree of independence from both internal and external influences. In the context of data processing for the purposes of the prevention of global pandemics, the role of the DPAs is essentially to monitor how the measures introduced by governments and private entities respect data protection principles. The DPAs should actively advise public institutions on the appropriate solutions and

[15] M Christofidou, N Lea and P Coorevits, 'A Literature Review on the GDPR, COVID-19 and the Ethical Considerations of Data Protection During a Time of Crisis' (2021) 30(1) *Yearbook of Medical Informatics* 226.

tools for the processing, act where there is a risk of non-compliance with Article 8 CFREU and the GDPR, inform the citizens about their rights, and issue guidelines and statements helpful in the correct application of the law. As this chapter shows, the DPAs' involvement during the global pandemic significantly varied from one Member State to another.

Although the EDPS is the institution principally responsible for monitoring compliance with the data protection laws by the EU institutions, its role has proved to be very important during the health crisis. EDPS advisory competences were strategic in developing EU-wide measures by the EU institutions. According to the provisions of Regulation 2018/1725, the European Commission is required to consult the EDPS whenever preparing or implementing acts with 'an impact on the protection of individuals' rights and freedoms with regard to the processing of personal data'.[16] The EDPS continuously provides assistance to the EU institutions. It has, for example, commented on the cross-border exchange of data between national COVID-19 contact tracing and mobile warning applications,[17] and on the proposal for a Council Directive amending Directive 2011/16/EU due to the COVID-19 pandemic,[18] and exchanged views with MEPs on the use of personal data in the fight against COVID-19.[19] Although the direct scope of the EDPS competences is limited to the EU institutions, its advisory influence on the policy-making process in the EU remains very significant.

In order to ensure the consistent application of the GDPR in the EU, the DPAs and the EDPS are obliged to cooperate within the EDPB. In the context of the COVID-19 pandemic, the EDPB's role proved to be essential in delivering guidelines, opinions and recommendations for consistent data processing throughout the pandemic. To that end, the EDPB holds, amongst others, the right to examine and issue guidelines and opinions, on its own initiative or at the request of one of its members or the Commission, on any question covering the application of the GDPR. Although these documents are not binding, they are respected by the national DPAs and considered as an important indication of how the GDPR should be interpreted and applied. The majority of the DPAs refer to guidelines issued by the EDPB on their websites or quote them in their own statements.

[16] Art 42(1) of Regulation (EU) 2018/1725 of the European Parliament and of the Council of 23 October 2018 on the protection of natural persons with regard to the processing of personal data by the Union institutions, bodies, offices and agencies and on the free movement of such data, and repealing Regulation (EC) No 45/2001 and Decision No 1247/2002/EC.

[17] EDPS, 'EDPS Comments on Cross-Border Exchange of Data between National COVID-19 Contact Tracing and Warning Mobile Applications' (9 July 2020) www.edps.europa.eu/data-protection/our-work/publications/comments/edps-comments-cross-border-exchange-data-between_en.

[18] EDPS, 'EDPS Comments on the Proposal for a Council Directive Amending Directive 2011/16/EU Due to the COVID-19 Pandemic' (1 June 2020) www.edps.europa.eu/data-protection/our-work/publications/comments/edps-comments-proposal-council-directive-amending_en.

[19] EDPS, 'Exchange of Views with the LIBE Members on the Use of Personal Data in the Fight against COVID-19' (7 May 2020) www.edps.europa.eu/data-protection/our-work/publications/speeches-articles/exchange-views-libe-members-use-personal_en.

The first document relating to the pandemic was issued by the EDPB in the press statement of the EDPB Chair, Andrea Jellinek, on the processing of personal data in the context of the COVID-19 outbreak on 16 March 2020. It was followed by a general EDPB statement on the processing of personal data in the context of the COVID-19 outbreak, published on 19 March 2020.[20] The statement reflected the main quandaries and issues that were raised by the Member States. For example, it emphasised that data protection laws 'do not hinder measures taken in the fight against the coronavirus pandemic', addressing one of the most recurring and common worries that came with the COVID-19 outbreak.[21] This left significant freedom for the DPAs, and encouraged the carrying out of ad hoc proportionality tests rather than unified solutions.

For example, the EDPB has already issued guidelines on the processing of data concerning health for the purpose of scientific research in the context of the COVID-19 outbreak[22] and guidelines on the use of location data and contact tracing tools.[23] Apart from that, it communicated several statements and opinions on the ad hoc issues that appeared during the pandemic, such as a statement on the interoperability of contact tracing applications,[24] a statement on the processing of personal data in the context of reopening the Schengen borders following the COVID-19 outbreak[25] and a statement on data subject rights in connection to the state of emergency in the Member States.[26] It is noticeable that the EDPB, while informing about its position, prefers to use short communication statements rather than produce guidelines, recommendations and opinions envisaged by the GDPR. This choice is sometimes justified and sometimes is an opportunity to avoid giving a more detailed opinion, thus allowing the DPAs more independence and flexibility to adjust to the various conditions existing in their respective Member States.

The EDPB's powers are limited. It is a networked body without strong binding competences that relies heavily on the independence of its members. In the context of the pandemic, this was a problem. When the Hungarian government

[20] (EDPB, 'Statement by the EDPB Chair on the Processing of Personal Data in the Context of the COVID-19 Outbreak' 19 March 2020) www.edpb.europa.eu/news/news/2020/statement-edpb-chair-processing-personal-data-context-COVID-19-outbreak_en.

[21] ibid 1.

[22] EDPB, Guidelines 03/2020 on the processing of data concerning health for the purpose of scientific research in the context of the COVID-19 outbreak, adopted on 21 April 2020.

[23] EDPB, Guidelines 04/2020 on the use of location data and contact tracing tools in the context of the COVID-19 outbreak, adopted on 21 April 2020.

[24] EDPB, 'Statement on the Interoperability of Contact Tracing Applications' (16 June 2020) www.edpb.europa.eu/sites/edpb/files/files/file1/edpb_statementinteroperabilitycontacttracingapps_en_0.pdf.

[25] EDPB, 'Statement on the Processing of Personal Data in the Context of Reopening the Schengen Borders Following the COVID-19 Outbreak' (16 June 2020) www.edpb.europa.eu/sites/edpb/files/files/file1/edpb_statementreopeningbordersanddataprotection_en.pdf.

[26] EDPB, 'Statement on Restrictions on Data Subject Rights in Connection to the State of Emergency in Member States' (2 June 2020) www.edpb.europa.eu/sites/edpb/files/files/file1/edpb_statement_art_23gdpr_20200602_en.pdf.

issued an act suspending GDPR data subject rights due to the state of emergency, the EDPB had no power to act other than to issue a statement.[27] The EDPB criticised Hungary by arguing that

> the mere existence of a pandemic or any other emergency situation alone is not a sufficient reason to provide for any kind of restriction on the rights of data subjects; rather, any restriction must clearly contribute to the safeguard of an important objective of general public interest of the Union or of a Member State.[28]

The clear implication of this position is that any measure restricting the provisions of the GDPR shall be necessary, proportionate and aimed directly at fighting the urgent danger to public health. Moreover, the Member States shall respect the general principles of law and the essence of the fundamental rights and freedoms.[29] As the EDPB emphasised, even the justified suspension of the GDPR data subject rights under Article 23 does not entail suspension of the fundamental right to data protection, which continues to be binding for data controllers and processors.[30] Hungary was the only Member State to introduce such an extreme measure. Although it has met with strong criticism from the EDPB and other EU institutions,[31] there was no effective legal procedure that would allow the annulment of the decree. The EDPB has no binding powers in that regard.

The EDPB remained active throughout both the first and the second wave of the pandemic, and regularly published statements and documents aimed at helping individuals, controllers, processors and governments to develop appropriate measures to fight the pandemic. It has also responded to several letters sent by MEPs or representatives of the third sector by explaining the role of data protection during the state of emergency or in the context of contact tracing apps.[32]

Although the DPAs continued to cooperate within the EDPB throughout the pandemic, on the national level they were far from being consistent in their engagement. The next part of the chapter provides an analysis that relies on publicly available documents and releases published on the websites of the EU DPAs during the initial stage of the pandemic (March–November 2020). The chapter does not intend to offer an exhaustive legal analysis of the differences

[27] Decree 179/2020 (V. 4.) Korm. rendelet a veszélyhelyzet idején az egyes adatvédelmi és adatigénylési rendelkezésektől való eltérésről (www.net.jogtar.hu/jogszabaly?docid=a2000179.kor).

[28] EDPB, 'Statement on Restrictions on Data Subject Rights' (n 26).

[29] ibid 4.

[30] ibid.

[31] S Stolton, 'EU Data Watchdog "Very Worried" by Hungary's GDPR Suspension' (*Euractiv*, 18 May 2020) www.euractiv.com/section/data-protection/news/eu-data-watchdog-very-worried-by-hungarys-gdpr-suspension/.

[32] EDPB response to Mrs Ďuriš Nicholsonová's letter on follow up questions in the fight against the COVID-19 pandemics (17 July 2020).

and similarities of the DPAs guidelines, but rather explores the way the DPAs understood their role and communicated with the public. Most of the documents were translated automatically, so it is possible to grasp the topic and general message of the source. The analysis checks the rapidity of the DPAs' reactions to the outbreak of the pandemic, their main areas of interest and their forms of communication.

11.3. Actions of the EU National Data Protection Authorities During the COVID-19 Pandemic

11.3.1. The Intensity of DPAs' Actions: Rapidity and Frequency

As Italy was the first EU country to be hit by the virus, the first DPA to issue a communication relating to the COVID-19 pandemic was the Italian Garante per la protezione dei dati personali in an official opinion published on 2 February 2020 in relation to data protection during the state of emergency.[33] Subsequently, the Polish DPA stated on 28 February 2020 that the provisions of the GDPR do not contradict the sending of messages related to the spread of the COVID-19 to mobile phone users entering Poland. It was a response to an inquiry submitted by the Ministry of Digitalization.[34]

Soon after the pandemic started, the engagement of the DPAs had significantly increased. As Figure 11.1 demonstrates, by the end of April, all the EU DPAs had published on their websites sources related to processing data during the state of the pandemic. Most of the Member States were at that time going through the first wave of the coronavirus, which often meant introducing urgent and unprecedented nationwide measures. Most of the measures were intended to monitor the movement of individuals and consisted of the deployment of digital tools aimed at tracking the spread of the disease. Such measures as obligatory temperature checks, managing quarantined individuals, communication with citizens via SMS systems and maintaining public registers of contracted people were often developed on an ad hoc basis. Their effectiveness relied on large amounts of personal data, often including health information.

[33] Garante per la protezione dei dati personali, Parere sulla bozza di ordinanza recante disposizioni urgenti di protezione civile in relazione all'emergenza sul territorio nazionale relativo al rischio sanitario connesso all'insorgenza di patologie derivanti da agenti virali trasmissibili – 2 February 2020 [9265883].

[34] Urząd Ochrony Danych Osobowych, 'UODO rozwiewa wątpliwości Ministerstwa Cyfryzacji w sprawie koronawirusa' (28 February 2020).

Figure 11.1 Initial reactions to the COVID-19 pandemic by the EU DPAs (March–November 2020)

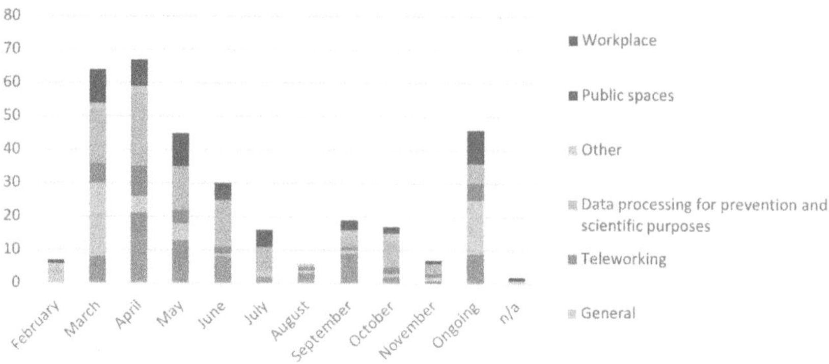

It was also the start of a shift towards the digital world, and the sudden digitalisation of work, education and daily life. In many of the Member States, this caused ramifications on an unprecedented scale, as the public sector was not at all prepared for such a revolution. Hence, the DPAs were faced with two challenges: various surveillance measures introduced by the government to stop the disease on the one hand, and individuals, data controllers and processors seeking advice in different areas of a new digital life on the other. Additionally, they were acting in an atmosphere of general fear and growing conviction that such laws as the GDPR were meant for other times and should not in any way interfere with the fight against the pandemic.

This vulnerable position of the DPAs is reflected in the tone of their first communications about the outbreak of the COVID-19 pandemic. During the first two months, almost all of the authorities issued documents explaining the relation between the GDPR and data processing during the health crisis. However, it is noticeable how differently they approached the challenge. Whereas some DPAs stated that the GDPR does not constitute an obstacle to fighting against the pandemic, other emphasised the importance of the right to data protection even in these extraordinary circumstances. In this regard, the Polish DPA reassured the public that the existing regulation would not hamper any tools that might be helpful to curb the disease.[35] Others, for example the French DPA, from the very beginning put an emphasis on respect for the fundamental right to data protection and the provisions of the GDPR also during the time of emergency.[36]

As Figure 11.2 demonstrates, during the first months of the pandemic, Slovenia, France and Germany (without including the regional DPAs) were among the Member States that published the highest number of sources relating to COVID-19

[35] UODO, 'Oświadczenie Prezesa UODO w sprawie koronawirusa' (12 March 2020) www.uodo.gov.pl/pl/138/1456.

[36] CNIL, 'Crise sanitaire: audition de Marie-Laure DENIS, Présidente de la CNIL, devant la commission des lois|CNIL', www.cnil.fr/fr/crise-sanitaire-audition-de-marie-laure-denis-presidente-de-la-cnil-devant-la-commission-des-lois.

on their websites. They assisted individuals and communicated in the form of communications, official documents, guidelines and other actions. While France and Germany are the Member States with traditionally strong data protection cultures, it is interesting to observe the extraordinary involvement of the Slovenian DPA. Slovenia remains the last EU Member State that has not yet fully implemented the GDPR into its legal order. Its DPA is currently unable to issue administrative fines and has to resort to non-binding opinions and answers to inquiries.[37]

Figure 11.2 Number of COVID-19 sources on the EU DPAs websites per country (March–November 2020)

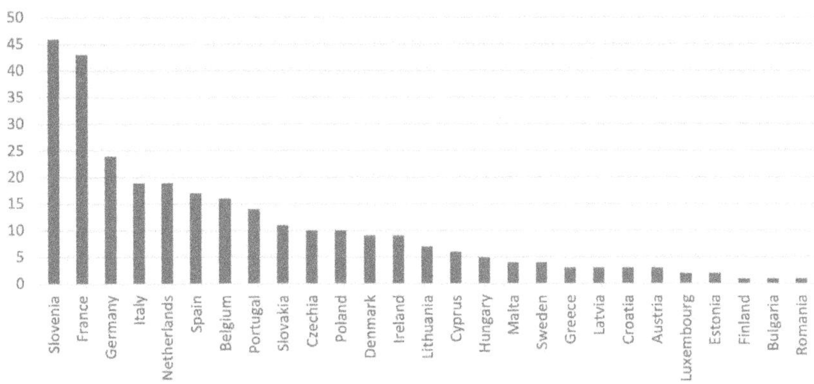

Countries with a small number of pandemic-related items on their websites may differ in their content. For example, although both the Finnish and the Austrian DPAs have issued only two entries on the subject of COVID-19, they both consist of the well-developed Q&A section that is constantly updated and addresses various issues that are relevant for the measures introduced in the respective Member State.[38] On the other hand, the Croatian and Estonian DPAs published only a few releases on selected, specific issues, such as data protection while working from home or contact tracing apps, without any general information on functioning of the GDPR during the health crisis.

The Bulgarian and Romanian DPAs were the least active DPAs in the EU with regard to communicating about the pandemic with the public. In the case of Bulgaria, for a long time there was no information whatsoever on the website about the COVID-19 pandemic or the processing of data in the context of the disease.[39] There was only a short notification that the DPA was switching to remote work because of the spread of the coronavirus. The DPA only mentioned the pandemic in

[37] HU Vrabec, 'GDPR Implementation Series · Slovenia: Introduction to the Most Recent Public Draft of the GDPR Implementing Law' (2020) 6(1) *European Data Protection Law Review* 121.

[38] Österreichische Datenschutzbehörde, Information der Datenschutzbehörde zum Coronavirus (COVID-19), www.dsb.gv.at/download-links/informationen-zum-coronavirus-COVID-19-.html; Office of the Data Protection Ombudsman (F), Usein kysyttyä koronaviruksesta ja tietosuojasta, www.tietosuoja.fi/koronavirus.

[39] Commission for Personal Data Protection (BG), www.cpdp.bg/index.php.

its newsletters, the earliest issued in May 2020. In December 2021, the DPA introduced a special category on its website relating to the pandemic, but it concerned mostly measures introduced within its premises. In the case of Romania, the DPA limited itself to publishing general information on GDPR provisions and the legal basis for data processing for prevention and scientific purposes.[40]

It is noticeable that gradually the number of sources diminished to the extent that the ones relating to general COVID issues almost disappeared. Instead, attention switched towards specific topics, such as contact tracing and quarantine apps, remote education and working from home. This evolution is easily explained by the fact that since March 2020 many of the questions had already been addressed and solved. In 2021 there was a significant rise in the number of sources relating to EU Digital COVID Certificates and the different verification procedures implemented among the Member States. The DPAs remain active to react to any new problems that may arise.

11.3.2. Communicating with the Public: An Official Document or a Blog Post?

The GDPR obliges supervisory authorities to, amongst other things, promote public awareness and understanding of the risks, rules, safeguards and rights in relation to the processing of data. Moreover, in accordance with national laws, they shall provide advisory assistance to the national parliament, the government and other institutions on legislative and administrative measures relating to data protection. These two tasks were of exceptional importance during the COVID-19 pandemic. Individuals were seeking information about functioning in the new reality and governments were introducing new, often very data-driven measures targeting the spread of the pandemic. The DPAs should be there for them and to fulfil the roles of advisor and protector. Once again, the mission was understood differently across the EU, in terms of forms of communications and providing assistance to individuals. When it comes to forms of communication, the DPAs would use one of the following:

(a) official documents (eg an official opinion on a contact tracing app);
(b) blog posts – information published directly on the website (eg FAQs, blog posts);
(c) guidelines – documents with detailed guidelines concerning a specific subject (eg guidelines on remote education for schools and educators); or
(d) other actions – lectures, speeches in parliament, presence in the media.

[40] The National Supervisory Authority for Personal Data Processing, 'Prelucrarea datelor privind starea de sănătate' (18 March 2020) www.dataprotection.ro/index.jsp?page=Prelucrarea_datelor_privind_starea_de_sanatate&lang=en.

Figure 11.3 Forms of communication by the EU DPAs on their websites during the COVID-19 pandemic (March–November 2020)

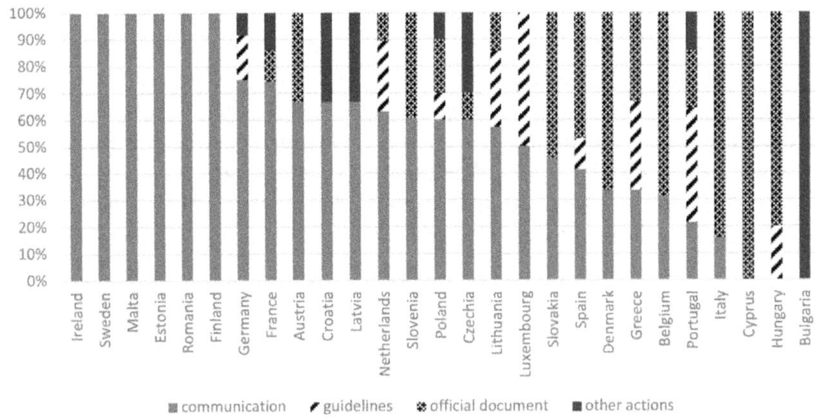

Until December 2021, 15 of the EU DPAs launched on their websites easily accessible categories or sub-pages dedicated specifically to data processing connected to the COVID-19 pandemic. This form of communication is the most readable and user-friendly for interested individuals, data processors and controllers, as it is easy to find, short and addresses specific issues. The official answer to any question relating to data processing may be quickly found through a web search. There, individuals and any other interested parties could find all information concerning data processing in the context of the pandemic. For example, when the PLFs were still applicable, information about their legality could have been found in the special section on the website of the Austrian DPA (contrary to, as mentioned above, the Polish DPA, which had not provided any assistance on that matter). These sections are usually updated on an ongoing basis. Often, they have a form of simple Q&A or blog posts, sometimes divided into sub-categories.

Even though these forms of communication are usually very simple and concise, their role is crucial. It allows data subjects, processors and controllers to be easily informed about their rights and obligations during the pandemic. Taking into account the wide spread of fake news and the dynamic changes in laws during the pandemic, this form of communication by national authorities is very important. Hence, the fact that most of the DPAs preferred to publish their opinions and answers directly on their websites and within specially dedicated categories is highly valuable. Unfortunately, not all of the authorities introduced this form of communication with citizens and stakeholders. Instead, they resorted to official documents or refused to take any action at all.

Official documents are equally significant, as they are often evidence of DPAs' key actions both as a regulator and as a quasi-ombudsman. They usually comprise statements and declarations where the DPAs inform about their binding position or opinion on a certain issue. For example, the DPAs may decide to suspend the contact tracing app for failing to meet the provisions of the fundamental right to data protection. That was the case of the French app StopCOVID, which was initially declared by the DPA to be non-compliant with the GDPR.[41] The DPA may also issue an official opinion for controllers on how to process certain data – for example, for employers gathering information about an employee contracted with the virus, or for restaurants collecting contact details of their clients. The authority may also assess the validity of a measure introduced by the government. For example, the Italian DPA favoured certain technical rules for the implementation of electronic administrative proceedings in the Italian courts.[42] The publication of such documents on the website also shows the level of transparency in the DPAs office.

The vast number of diverse measures implemented resulted in several decisions against public and private controllers. For example, the Portuguese DPA fined a municipality €2500 for sharing on its Facebook page information about a couple that contracted COVID-19 in March 2020.[43] The Hungarian DPA fined the District Office of Budapest Government Office for transferring health data to general practitioners without any additional safeguards.[44] The Danish DPA recommended that a company carrying out COVID-19 tests on children prepare a privacy policy in the form of a pamphlet.[45] Finally, the French DPA prohibited the use of drones by the police to monitor compliance with lockdown measures.[46] These decisions should be considered important steps in development of GDPR enforcement in the EU, as Member States still differ in their rules governing data processing within the public sector.

The importance of communication with the public is shown in an example of the Polish DPA. Despite numerous controversies and doubts about Polish contact tracing and quarantine apps,[47] the DPA did not issue any relevant communication on its website. The most popular, and a relatively reliable, source assessing their legality (other than the government's website[48]) was a blog post prepared by a privacy NGO.[49] Only there might one find evidence that the Polish DPA was

[41] CNIL, Decision MED-2020-015, 15 July 2020.

[42] Garante per la protezione dei dati personali, Decision No 88/2020, 19 May 2020.

[43] CNPD, Decision Deliberação 548/2021, 27 April 2020.

[44] Nemzeti Adatvédelmi és Információszabadság Hatóság, Határozatok/Végzések – BFKH XI. kerületi Hivatalánál bekövetkezett egészségügyi adatokat érintő adatvédelmi incidens és adatbiztonságihiányosságok,www.naih.hu/hatarozatok-vegzesek/file/354-bfkh-xi-keruleti-hivatalanal-bekovetkezett-egeszsegugyi-adatokat-erin.

[45] Datatilsynet, 'Tilsyn med iagttagelse af oplysningspligten ved hurtigtest i grundskolen' (21 September 2021) www.datatilsynet.dk/afgoerelser/afgoerelser/2021/sep/tilsyn-med-iagttagelse-af-oplysningspligten-ved-hurtigtest-i-grundskolen-.

[46] CNIL, Délibération SAN-2021-003, 12 January 2021.

[47] NAIH, 'Határozatok/Végzések – BFKH XI. kerületi Hivatalánál bekövetkezett egészségügyi adatokat érintő adatvédelmi incidens és adatbiztonsági hiányosságok', www.naih.hu/hatarozatok-vegzesek/file/354-bfkh-xi-keruleti-hivatalanal-bekovetkezett-egeszsegugyi-adatokat-erinto-adatvedelmi-incidens-es-adatbiztonsagi-hianyossagok.

[48] ProteGO Safe, Gov.pl, www.gov.pl/web/koronawirus/protegosafe.

[49] Panoptykon, ProteGO Safe: instalować czy nie, https://panoptykon.org/czy-instalowac-protego-safe.

consulted during the process of deployment of the contact tracing application and that the authority sent a formal letter to the ministry about it. Unfortunately, no communication or document about this can be found on the DPA's website.

On the other side of the scale is the French DPA, which prepared a very readable and accessible website devoted specifically to COVID-19.[50] It is updated regularly and comprises information on various subjects, from the most general ones, such as GDPR application, to data processing during health crises and to such detailed issues as data processing in the context of sport associations and COVID-19. Moreover, the DPA has transparently informed the government and the parliament about its actions concerning contact tracing apps and prepared a separate communication with questions and answers addressed to individuals.[51]

Analysis of the types of sources that are issued by the DPAs shows different approaches towards their role in the EU, demonstrated in Figure 11.3. Some of them treat each act of communication as an official document and publish it with a designated number and a seal; others prefer to issue more direct and informal blog posts. In that regard, it is noticeable how differently accessibility and transparency are understood across the EU.

11.3.3. DPAs During the COVID-19 Pandemic: Guarding Specific Areas

As shown in Figures 11.4 and 11.5, DPAs focused attention on several subjects, reflecting the main issues that occurred during the outbreak of the COVID-19 pandemic:

(a) general – providing general information on the GDPR during the pandemic;
(b) contact tracing and quarantine apps – sources relating to the contact tracing and quarantine monitoring apps;
(c) safety measures in public spaces – sources on data processing in public spaces (airports, restaurants, buildings, etc);
(d) data processing for prevention and scientific purposes – sources on data processing by health, security and municipal authorities;
(e) data processing in the workplace – sources on the rights and obligations of employers and employees with regard to the processing of health data in the workplace;
(f) working from home – sources on remote working, videoconferencing and digitalisation of work;
(g) remote education – sources on remote education and guidance for schools, teachers and parents;

[50] CNIL, 'Coronavirus (COVID-19) | CNIL', www.cnil.fr/fr/coronavirus-COVID-19.

[51] CNIL, 'L'application mobile StopCOVID en questions' (5 June 2020) www.cnil.fr/fr/lapplication-mobile-stopCOVID-en-questions.

(h) vaccination – sources on data gathering around vaccination campaigns, including EU Digital COVID Certificates and verification procedures; and
(i) other – sources on other issues (eg cybercrimes during the pandemic).

The scope of the DPAs' interest is irregular and there are visible divergences among them. Some of the DPAs, such as the Romanian and Bulgarian, limited themselves to providing general information about the GDPR during the pandemic. Others usually also commented on other questions that were important during the health crisis, such as specific measures introduced by the governments, data processing in the workplace or deployment of contact tracing apps. Germany, Spain, France and the Netherlands were among the countries with DPAs that provided information in almost all of the above-mentioned categories. On the other hand, Estonia, Romania and Bulgaria published the least thematically diverse documents on their websites. Lack of any communication on such issues as remote education, home office or processing data in the workplace would signal resignation from the role of promoter of data protection in the daily lives of individuals. Hence, it is noteworthy that the vast majority of the DPAs provided assistance in at least three different categories.

Apart from several cases with evenly distributed information, usually there was one category that significantly dominated in each country. For example, for the Cypriot DPA, education was the most important field of interest, whereas the Irish DPA focused on data processing in the workplace. For the Danish DPA, the most central issue was data processing for prevention and scientific purposes. The majority of its sources in that category in 2020 concerned the legality of data transfers from public health institutions to universities for research. In 2021, the DPA issued several decisions against institutes that failed to comply with data protection laws while carrying out COVID-19 tests.

Figure 11.4 EU DPAs websites during the COVID-19 pandemic: topics per country (March–November 2020)

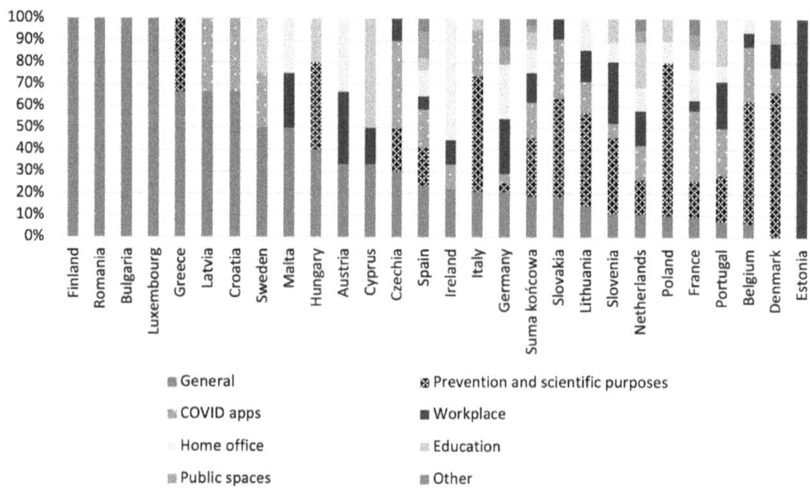

A dominant category may indicate how the DPA understands its role. If the authority limited itself to providing only basic information about the GDPR, then this might suggest that it does not consider itself an appropriate institution to react in more challenging situations. Instead of monitoring emerging surveillance laws and restrictions in the Member States and fulfilling their advisory role, some of the DPAs remained silent or continued doing their work outside of the context of the COVID-19 pandemic. They usually limited themselves to explaining the legality and conditions of various restrictions, such as the collection of PLFs at airports or the mass testing. They commented on such issues as using public registers to identify citizens in order to distribute to them surgical masks, or the lawfulness of data processing for research purposes.

In the most extreme cases, they were acting as enablers for the governments, rather than their independent supervisors. For example, the Greek DPA issued guidelines in favour of obligatory governmental SMS permits to leave the house.[52]

Sometimes, this might even have included violation of the rule of law. This was the case in annulled postal elections in Poland, which resulted in the unlawful processing of vast amounts of personal data by the national post. The DPA issued a statement where it had refused to act on that matter. This decision was later revoked by the court and declared a serious violation of the principles of administrative procedure.[53]

The scope of the engagement of DPAs in the monitoring of measures was often dependent on the national laws that regulate rules of data processing by the public sector, but also data protection cultures in the respective Member States. For example, the Italian and French DPAs both communicated about their advisory role in the development of contact tracing apps or were asked to authorise the introduction of respective measures. Others, such as the Bulgarian or Romanian DPA, seem to have been much less involved in governmental cooperation.

Figure 11.5 EU DPAs webistes during the COVID-19 pandemic: main areas of interest (March–November 2020)

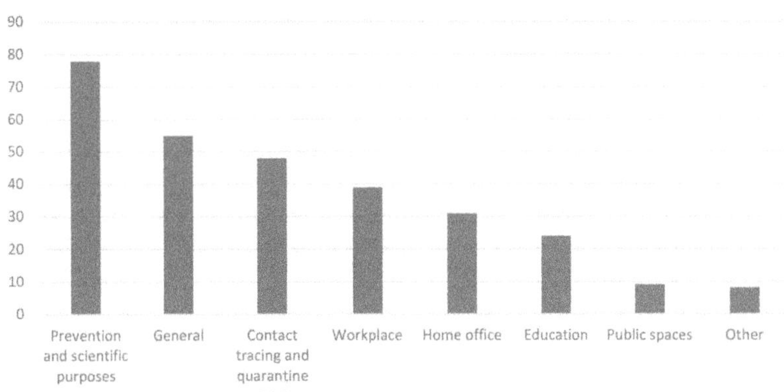

[52] N Vavoula, 'The COVID-19 Pandemic as a Stress Test on the Right to Protection of Personal Data: The Case of Greece' (eucrim – The European Criminal Law Associations' Forum, 2021) https://doi.org/10.30709/eucrim-2021-018.

[53] Wyrok Wojewódzkiego Sądu Administracyjnego w Warszawie II SA/Wa 1635/20.

11.4. Lessons (Not) Learned? EU Digital COVID Certificate

During the first months of the pandemic, the EU DPAs reacted in an uncoordinated way, as the outbreak of the disease was unprecedented and came at the least favourable time. However, it is noticeable that they are gradually learning how to cooperate and use their powers fully.

On 1 July 2021, the EU Digital COVID Certificate Regulation, which allowed for EU-wide verification of vaccinated individuals, came into force.[54] The EDPB and the EDPS contributed to the legislative procedure by issuing on 31 March 2021 a joint opinion on the proposal for a Digital Green Certificate.[55] The authorities expressed their views on aspects relating to the protection of personal data, underlining that it is necessary to ensure in the regulation consistency and compliance with the application of the GDPR and thus to respect provisions of Article 8 CFREU and Article 16 TFEU.[56] They highlighted that the Member States should comply with the general principles of effectiveness, necessity and proportionality whenever introducing new measures involving data processing.[57] The DPAs also called for more specific provisions on purposes, scope and retention of data processed within the Green Digital Certificate, as well as for the introduction of both online and offline variants of the certificate to ensure sufficient inclusion. Additionally, they advocated for an enhanced monitoring system that would ensure compliance with the GDPR.

In the meantime, many of the EU Member States introduced obligatory certificates to be presented whenever entering public spaces such as restaurants, hairdressers or theatres. In others, the use of certificates was left to the discretion of employers or business owners. The DPAs actively coordinated deployment of these measures. For example, the Italian DPA imposed a temporary limitation of processing on the Mitiga Italia app, which had been used to verify vaccination certificates of people entering stadiums.[58] The DPA also warned the Campania Region that its verification system had failed to comply with data protection laws.[59]

[54] Commission, 'EU Digital COVID Certificate', www.ec.europa.eu/info/live-work-travel-eu/coronavirus-response/safe-COVID-19-vaccines-europeans/eu-digital-COVID-certificate_en.

[55] EDPB-EDPS Joint Opinion 04/2021 on the Proposal for a Regulation of the European Parliament and of the Council on a framework for the issuance, verification and acceptance of interoperable certificates on vaccination, testing and recovery to facilitate free movement during the COVID-19 pandemic (Digital Green Certificate), 31 March 2021.

[56] ibid 5, 9.

[57] ibid 12.

[58] EDPB, 'Italian DPA: Processing Limitation on a COVID19-Related App ("Mitiga")' (4 June 2021) www.edpb.europa.eu/news/national-news/2021/italian-dpa-processing-limitation-COVID19-related-app-mitiga_en.

[59] EDPB, 'Italian DPA: The Italian SA Issues a Warning to the Campania Region' (26 May 2021) www.edpb.europa.eu/news/national-news/2021/italian-dpa-italian-sa-issues-warning-campania-region_en.

The Bulgarian DPA promoted the use of EU Digital Certificates in its Member State, advising employers how to introduce the measure in a workplace.[60]

While some of the DPAs explained the importance and applicability of the certificates, others focused on stressing their discretionary nature. To that end, the Polish DPA declared that entities obliged to comply with limiting the number of persons are not eligible to request from them disclosure of information on vaccination but, rather, this might be presented only at the individual's initiative.[61]

Although the DPAs are now more engaged in cases related to the COVID-19 pandemic and have worked together on the joint opinion for the EU Digital COVID Certificate, divergences among them continue. Only some of the DPAs are actively consulted by their governments and transparently communicate about it to the public. Others prefer either to focus on non-pandemic related issues or to issue opinions in line with governmental policies. It is also noticeable that some of the DPAs' websites are less accessible than others: information is hard to find or is dispersed among different sections. Discrepancies are significant and should be worrying, as they are evidence of uneven standards of data protection in the EU. Lack of consistent action harms individuals and controllers, and weakens the already flawed enforcement system of the GDPR.

11.5. Conclusions

The outbreak of the global pandemic has demonstrated how fragile the fundamental right to data protection is, and how easy it is to renounce its provisions during an emergency. The DPAs, the EDPS and the EDPB are the sole institutions responsible for monitoring whether the measures introduced by governments and the private sector are compliant with the GDPR and Article 8 CFREU. Thus, it is necessary that they act consistently and proactively through advising national institutions and reacting in cases where there is a significant danger to the protection of personal data and the right to privacy.

As the preliminary results of the analysis show, actions of the DPAs differed among the EU Member States – some of them were more prone to act, while others were limited to issuing one or two releases on the general basis of data processing during the pandemic. Only some of the DPAs took an active part in the development of the contact tracing and quarantine apps or reacted immediately to the surveillance measures introduced by the respective governments. In some of the Member States, individuals may easily find detailed information and advice

[60] DataGuidance, 'Bulgaria: Processing of Personal Data Concerning Vaccinations and the EU Digital COVID-19 Certificate' (1 November 2021) www.dataguidance.com/opinion/bulgaria-processing-personal-data-concerning.

[61] UODO, 'Wyłączenia zaszczepionych z limitu osób na imprezach' (23 June 2021) www.uodo.gov.pl/pl/138/2088.

provided to them by their supervisory authorities; in others, they should rely solely on their own knowledge or search through unreliable sources on the Internet.

The COVID-19 pandemic was a stress test for the DPAs and proved how differently they perceive their role depending on their Member State. It seems that at least some of them failed their citizens. Instead of acting within their competences and taking advantage of the impressive scope of independence they were bestowed, they limited themselves to be another public institution closed because of the lockdown. Following the omnipresent belief that more surveillance is necessary to curb the pandemic, they resigned from their functions in order not to hamper the fight against the disease. What they have not taken into account is that there is no evidence that such intrusive measures are indeed effective and that their role is precisely to monitor that. It was to avoid the second wave of pro-surveillance obsession that occurred after 9/11 that such authorities as the DPAs had been established and the fundamental right to data protection had been introduced.

The existence of the EDPB helps the DPAs to strengthen their involvement. Within a transnational network with a strong level of independence, they may exchange and unify their views and separate from the respective national governments. Without this common platform, some of the emerging threats to data protection could have not been addressed at all, particularly by the national DPAs. Even within its limited scope of binding powers, the EDPB's role is unprecedented.

Tackling the pandemic is a crucial goal of the Member States, but it should be done without the complete sacrifice of fundamental rights. There is a possible risk of mass surveillance staying with us after the epidemic, especially in those Member States in which there is an observable rise in the autocratic ambitions of their governments. The EU legal system envisages institutions that have all the powers to prevent that from happening. It is now their role to make proper and effective use of their competences.

12

Keeping the Internet Safe During and after the Pandemic: Dealing with the Rise of Cybercrime in the EU

SARAH TAS*

12.1. Introduction

Albert Einstein once said that 'in the midst of every crisis, lies great opportunity'.[1] Years later, these words resonate and perfectly apply to this chapter, intended to discuss the European Union's cybercriminal landscape during the pandemic. This chapter will show that the opportunities in this area are dual. First, there is the possibility for cybercriminals to exploit the COVID-19 health crisis and the shift to the digital sphere for criminal purposes. Second, there is a chance for the EU to learn from the crisis, reflect on its own shortcomings in dealing with it and develop new rules ensuring a safe cyberspace.

The COVID-19 pandemic became a major issue in the EU in March 2020, when the first lockdown was imposed in Italy.[2] The subsequent progressive shift from the physical to the digital world, through home schooling, remote working and virtual socialising, represented a driver of the increased cybercrime rate.[3] Cybercriminals preyed on societal vulnerabilities and various attempts of cybercrimes were witnessed in the EU. Examples include the malware attack in March 2020 on the Brno Hospital in Czech Republic, which had severe consequences for Czech public health.[4] Computers were shut down and the hospital was forced to postpone urgent surgeries and reroute patients. Next, there was a cyber mask

* PhD Researcher at the European University Institute.

[1] P Liao, *Post-9/11 Historical Fiction and Alternate History Fiction: Transnational and Multidirectional Memory* (Springer Nature, 2020). See also ch 3 in this book by F de Abreu Duarte.

[2] Agenzia ANSA, 'Era il 9 marzo 2020, Conte e l'annuncio del lockdown – VIDEO – Cronaca' (*ANSA.it*, 5 March 2021) www.ansa.it/sito/notizie/cronaca/2021/03/05/marzo-2020-conte-e-lannuncio-del-lockdown-video_732532d9-77c0-4ff8-9172-8112d3778392.html.

[3] A Georgiadou, S Mouzakitis and D Askounis, 'Working from Home during COVID-19 Crisis: A Cyber Security Culture Assessment Survey' [2021] *Security Journal* 1.

[4] Europol, 'Pandemic Profiteering: How Criminals Exploit the COVID-19 Crisis' (2020).

fraud scheme that affected Germany.[5] German health authorities contracted two sales companies to procure 15 million euros' worth supplies of face masks and ended up ensnared in an elaborate international scam. Finally, in 2021, a Dutch data scandal came out.[6] A widespread trade in personal data of Dutch COVID-19 tests subject had been discovered and data (home addresses, telephone numbers, date of birth …) was sold on various instant message apps. Many more examples exist, related to frauds, scams and fake medical messages. What emerges from these examples is that there has been a tangible spike in cyber criminality linked to the pandemic and the numerous lockdowns.

This chapter discusses this phenomenon of the rise of cybercrime linked to the pandemic in the EU. It shows that the pandemic brought along significant changes to the cybercriminal landscape and the EU approach. The aim is to examine the role of the EU in the area, and the influence the pandemic had on the EU with regard to future legislative and policy developments.

In doing so, the chapter starts by shedding light on the notion of 'cybercrime' and on the interconnectedness of the ideas of cybercrime and cybersecurity. As no consensus exists on the notion of cybercrime, the chapter seeks to offer a new definition that emerges from various documents and applies to COVID-19 research. Once the correlation between cybercrime and cybersecurity is established, the chapter dives into the analysis of EU cybercrime during and after the pandemic, focusing on the one hand on the criminal landscape, and on the other hand on the EU monitoring mechanisms related to it. It has been commonly acknowledged that criminals exploited the pandemic to increase cybercrimes. This chapter will show that while new narratives and techniques appeared, the cybercriminal landscape did not significantly change. The EU played an essential role in monitoring the rise of cybercrime during the pandemic. It is thanks to the constant reporting of EU bodies that the issues were put in the spotlight and potential weaknesses appeared. The last section, thus, focuses on the lessons learnt from the pandemic in cybercrime and the steps taken by the EU in the area of cybercrime.

12.2. Towards an Interconnectedness of Cybercrime and Cybersecurity to Ensure a Safe Cyberspace

In the past years, European societies have become increasingly dependent on the Internet. While this digital world brings benefits, it also comes along with criminal threats.[7] Ten years ago, cybercrime was already mentioned as one of the main

[5] 'Unmasked: International COVID-19 Fraud Exposed', www.interpol.int/News-and-Events/News/2020/Unmasked-International-COVID-19-fraud-exposed.

[6] 'Dutch Data Scandal: Illegal Trade of COVID-19 Patient Data | Privacy-Ticker.Com' (*Privacy Ticker*, 19 February 2021) www.privacy-ticker.com/dutch-data-scandal-illegal-trade-of-COVID-19-patient-data/.

[7] C Verleysen, 'Theoretical Paper – Cybercrime: A Theoretical Overview of the Growing Digital Threat' (European Crime Prevention Network, 2016) Theoretical Paper Series.

crime threats Europe was facing.[8] This remains true today and has been a top priority during the pandemic. It is essential to clarify the concept of cybercrime before analysing it with regard to the pandemic. What arises from the analysis is that the concepts of cybercrime and cybersecurity are very closely intertwined, and have been particularly so during the health crisis.

12.2.1. Defining Cybercrime: Broad or Narrow Notion?

As of today, there is no universally agreed definition of the notion of cybercrime.[9] It is used as a container concept that encompasses a range of criminal activities that use information and communication technologies.[10] Various interpretations of cybercrime are found in the literature. Casey defines cybercrime as a computer-related offence, in which networks as well as computers may play an instrumental part.[11] Wall goes further by creating categories based on the transformative aspect of the crime, meaning that he looks at how the technologies transformed the crime. According to Wall, there are three types of cybercrimes: traditional crimes, in which a computer had been used (fraud); hybrid crimes, for which technologies created new opportunities (global frauds); and true cybercrimes, which were created by the Internet (spam, phishing).[12] Grabosky follows the same path but uses different categories: conventional crimes, committed with computers; attacks on computer networks; and conventional criminal cases in which digital evidence exists.[13] Thus, the majority of academics agree on a correlation between cybercrime and computer-related offences, meaning offences committed in the virtual world.[14] However, no common categorisation has been developed. Conceptually, the notion of cybercrime is distinct from the concept of cybersecurity. Cybersecurity also lacks a consistent definition in the literature.[15] Cybersecurity has in the past been associated either with data security or with network and information security.[16] However, the practice shows that it encompasses both aspects. No reference was made to cybercrime in the conceptualisation of cybersecurity.

[8] Council of the European Union. General Secretariat of the Council, *Internal Security Strategy for the European Union : Towards a European Security Model* (Publications Office of the European Union, 2010) https://data.europa.eu/doi/10.2860/87810.

[9] M Yar, 'The Novelty of 'Cybercrime': An Assessment in Light of Routine Activity Theory' (2005) 2 *European Journal of Criminology* 407.

[10] D Wall, 'What Are Cybercrimes?' (2004) 58 *Criminal Justice Matters* 20.

[11] E Casey, *Handbook of Computer Crime Investigation – Forensic Tools and Technology* (Academic Press, 2001).

[12] Wall (n 10).

[13] P Grabosky, 'The Global Dimension of Cybercrime' (2004) 6 *Global Crime* 146.

[14] N Robinson and others, 'Feasibility Study for a European Cybercrime Centre' (RAND Corporation, 2012).

[15] 'Definition of Cybersecurity – Gaps and Overlaps in Standardisation' (ENISA, 2015) V1.0.

[16] A Kasper and A Antonov, *Towards Conceptualizing EU Cybersecurity Law* (Zentrum für Europäische Integrationsforschung, Rheinische Friedrich-Wilhelms Universität, 2019).

While a legal definition of cybercrime exists in national criminal law, there is no consensus on the concept at the European and international levels. What can be observed instead is a patchwork of different definitions and categorisations. At the international level, the first legal instrument that officially dealt with the fight against cybercrime is the Council of Europe Cybercrime Convention of 2001.[17] The Convention was set up to harmonise computer-related criminal law offences and procedural legislation on electronic evidence.[18] It is a key instrument for combating cybercrime. In the Convention, cybercrime was broadly defined to include (i) core computer-related offences (illegal access, illegal interception, data and system interferences, and misuse of data); (ii) other computer-related offences (forgery and fraud); (iii) content-related offences (child pornography); and (iv) offences related to infringements of copyright and related rights. The Convention does not refer to cybersecurity aspects, nor to attacks against network and information systems. Thus, cybersecurity and cybercrime remain two distinct entities in the international sphere.

The interconnectedness between cybercrime and cybersecurity started to appear on the European level. The EU measures adopted in cyberspace revolved around three areas: the critical infrastructure protection (cybersecurity), cybercrime and cyberdefence (the protection of the cyberspace with regard to military actions).[19] Thus, separated policy and legislative instruments are taken within these different pillars. However, while cyberdefence essentially remains an exclusive category, an overlap exists between the two others.[20] The concept of cybersecurity refers to the actions and safeguards taken to protect the cyberspace, notably from threats that affect the network and information systems.[21] It forms an integral part of cybercrime, and the European Commission already recognised the importance of network security in the fight against cybercrime in 2001.[22] Vice versa, in its cybersecurity strategy of 2013, the Commission also emphasised the need to reduce cybercrimes, and the link between cybercrime and cybersecurity incidents.[23] The two concepts need to go hand in hand to ensure a safe cyberspace. In its 2013 strategy, the Commission developed

[17] Convention on Cybercrime 2001.

[18] A Nunzi, 'Cybercrime – A New Challenge for the European Union' (2012) 83 *Revue internationale de droit pénal* 289.

[19] H Carrapico and A Barrinha, 'The EU as a Coherent (Cyber)Security Actor?' (2017) 55 *Journal of Common Market Studies* 1254.

[20] G Christou, 'The European Union and Cybercrime' in G Christou (ed), *Cybersecurity in the European Union: Resilience and Adaptability in Governance Policy* (Palgrave Macmillan, 2016).

[21] Joint Communication to the European Parliament, the Council, the European Economic and Social Committee and the Committee of the Regions, 'Cybersecurity Strategy of the European Union: An Open, Safe and Secure Cyberspace' (2013).

[22] Communication from the Commission to the Council, the European Parliament, the economic and social Committee and the Committee of the Regions, 'Creating a Safer Information Society by Improving the Security of Information Infrastructures and Combating Computer-Related Crime' (2001).

[23] Joint Communication (n 21).

three categories of cybercrime – traditional offences (fraud, forgery, identity theft), content-related offences (child pornography, incitement to racial hatred) and offences unique to computers and information systems (attacks against information system and denial of service).[24] While regulated in separate policy and legal instruments, cybercrime and cybersecurity remain very closely interlinked. Europol's European Cybercrime Centre (EC3), which is the main body dealing with the issue of cybercrime in the EU, focuses on cybersecurity aspects, alongside traditional cybercrimes.[25] In fact, in its 'Internet Organized Crime Threat Assessment' of 2020, it emphasised this correlation.[26]

This chapter takes a singular approach to cybercrime, defining it as a crime committed using a computer or network and information systems. The core idea is that cybercrime, and the fight against it, includes both the traditional concept of cybercrime and the broader phenomenon of cybersecurity. In fact, cybersecurity strategies are vital to reducing the risk of cybercrime. This chapter bases itself on the Commission's categorisation, mentioned above,[27] which divides cybercrime in three categories: (i) traditional offences (or computer-related offences); (ii) offences unique to computers and information systems (or high-tech crimes); and (iii) content-related offences. This interconnectedness between cybercrime and cybersecurity is key to analysing the cybercriminal landscape and has been essential in the reporting of the pandemic.

12.2.2. Intertwining Cybercrime and Cybersecurity During the Pandemic

As shown above, the connection between these two areas is not new and has been emphasised on numerous occasions by the EU. The intertwinement became evident in the reporting during the pandemic, when actors of the cybersecurity sector cooperated with actors of the cybercrime one. This link has been expressed in a Joint Statement made by the EU: 'The European Commission, ENISA [European Network and Information Security Agency], CERT-EU 9 [Computer Emergency Response Team for the EU Institutions, bodies and agencies] and Europol [European Union Agency for Law Enforcement Cooperation], among others, will continue to monitor the situation and coordinate as appropriate to insure a safer cyberspace for the EU and the world.'[28]

[24] ibid.

[25] Europol, 'European Cybercrime Centre – EC3', www.europol.europa.eu/about-europol/european-cybercrime-centre-ec3.

[26] Europol, 'Internet Organised Crime Threat Assessment (IOCTA) 2020' (2020).

[27] Joint Communication (n 21).

[28] Commission, 'Coronavirus Outbreak – Joint Statement European Commission, ENISA, CERT-EU and Europol' (20 March 2020) https://ec.europa.eu/digital-single-market/en/news/coronavirus-outbreak-joint-statement-european-commission-enisa-cert-eu-and-europol.

One EU institution (the Commission), two EU agencies (Europol and ENISA) and one EU body (CERT-EU) are continuously monitoring and reporting on the cybercriminal situation in the EU. While the Commission has competences in both cybercrime and cybersecurity,[29] it is not the case for the others. ENISA is the EU Agency for Cybersecurity and, as such, its main task is to ensure the security of network and information systems and a high level of cybersecurity in the EU.[30] CERT-EU also focuses on the cybersecurity side of EU institutions, bodies and agencies, and aims at ensuring a high level of network and information security policy.[31] Europol, on the other hand, initially deals with cybercrime matters.[32] It notably developed the EC3, specialised in cybercriminality. Even within each monitoring body, the interrelationship manifests itself in the overlap that may exist between cybercrime and cybersecurity. This is noticeable, for example, in the reporting of the EC3, which also touches upon cyberattacks to network and information systems, and specifically mentions the cybersecurity ecosystem.[33]

This intertwinement is also visible at both the national and international levels. In the reporting of cybercrimes in EU Member States, different actors play a role: law enforcement authorities, which deal with cybercrimes in the field; and national competent authorities, which focus on the security of network and information systems. To get the overall picture of the cybercriminal landscape, both must be considered. Again, when analysing the reporting of the Federal Office for Information Security in Germany (cybersecurity body)[34] or of the national Agency for the Security of Information Systems in France, the overlap between the two areas is evident.[35] In the reports, the bodies are as much concerned with computer-related offences as with cybersecurity attacks. At the international level, the main body that plays a role is the International Criminal Police Organisation, Interpol.[36] It essentially deals with cybercrimes, but the overlap is again visible, since the reporting also includes details on attacks on network and information systems, and thus cybersecurity issues.

The focus of this chapter is the role of the EU in dealing with the rise of cybercrime. However, the deep intertwinement between cybersecurity and cybercrime

[29] E Fahey, 'The EU's Cybercrime and Cyber-Security Rulemaking: Mapping the Internal and External Dimensions of EU Security' (2014) 5 *European Journal of Risk Regulation* 46.

[30] Regulation (EU) 2019/881 of the European Parliament and of the Council of 17 April 2019 on ENISA (the European Union Agency for Cybersecurity) and on information and communications technology cybersecurity certification and repealing Regulation (EU) No 526/2013 (Cybersecurity Act) [2019] OJ L151/15.

[31] 'CERT-EU News Monitor', https://cert.europa.eu/cert/plainedition/en/cert_about.html.

[32] Regulation (EU) 2016/794 of the European Parliament and of the Council of 11 May 2016 on the European Union Agency for Law Enforcement Cooperation (Europol) and replacing and repealing Council Decisions 2009/371/JHA, 2009/934/JHA, 2009/935/JHA, 2009/936/JHA and 2009/968/JHA [2016] OJ L135/53.

[33] Europol, 'Internet Organised Crime Threat Assessment 2021' (2021).

[34] Federal Office for Information Security, 'The State of IT Security in Germany in 2020' (2020).

[35] ANSSI, 'Cybersécurité: Face Aux Risques, Les Françaises et Français Attendent Des Solutions plus Accessibles' (2020) Cybermois.

[36] Interpol, 'Global Landscape on COVID-19 Cyberthreat' (2020).

aspects indicates that they must be studied together when looking at the cybercriminal landscape during the pandemic.

12.3. Monitoring the Rise of Cybercrimes During the Pandemic: Was the EU Fit for Purpose?

EU Commissioner for Home Affairs Ylva Johansson stated that 'the coronavirus pandemic has slowed many aspects of our normal lives. But it has unfortunately accelerated criminal activity.'[37] Thus, while the world was on pause and subject to lockdown measures, the cybercriminals only increased their activities. This section analyses the current cybercriminal landscape and the EU response to its increase.

12.3.1. COVID-19 Pandemic and Cybercrime in the EU: Evolution or Revolution?

The pandemic prompted an unprecedented shift from the physical to the digital world,[38] which led to an increase in cybercrimes in the EU. This is true for the three categories of cybercrimes listed by the European Commission above.

First, computer-related offences increased during the pandemic due to the rise in frauds and forgeries. This includes the distribution of substandard and counterfeit goods,[39] such as medical devices and fake Corona cures.[40] During a global operation carried out by Interpol, with the support of Europol and national law enforcement authorities, more than 37,000 unauthorised and counterfeit medical products sold online were seized.[41] It also encompasses an increase in pandemic-related fraud and scam schemes, notably investment scams in stocks related to COVID-19 and supply scams.[42] France, for example, reported a large increase in scams, and shut down seven fake websites that advertised selling masks and hydroalcoholic gel.[43]

[37] J Leyden, 'Cyber Scams and Ransomware Booming amid COVID-19 Lockdowns – Europol' (*The Daily Swig*, 6 October 2020) https://portswigger.net/daily-swig/cyber-scams-and-ransomware-booming-amid-COVID-19-lockdowns-europol.

[38] Economist Intelligence Unit, 'Digitalisation Surges in Europe during the Pandemic' (10 February 2021) www.eiu.com/n/digitalisation-surges-in-europe-during-the-pandemic/.

[39] Europol, 'Internet Organised Crime' (n 33).

[40] Europol, 'Rise of Fake 'Corona Cures' Revealed in Global Counterfeit Medicine Operation' (21 March 2020) www.europol.europa.eu/newsroom/news/rise-of-fake-%E2%80%98corona-cures%E2%80%99-revealed-in-global-counterfeit-medicine-operation.

[41] ibid.

[42] Europol, 'Pandemic Profiteering' (n 4).

[43] S Bernard, 'Coronavirus : les gendarmes font fermer sept sites frauduleux de vente en ligne' (7 April 2020) www.gendinfo.fr/enquetes/2020/coronavirus-les-gendarmes-font-fermer-sept-sites-frauduleux-de-vente-en-ligne.

Second, high-tech crimes linked to network and information systems also peaked during the COVID-19 crisis and became more sophisticated.[44] The increase concerned malware and ransomware attacks, notably in the health sector. Examples of this have been mentioned in the introduction of this chapter (Brno University Hospital).[45] A cyberattack was also reported by the European Medicines Agency with the object of accessing documentation related to the vaccines.[46] In addition to this, phishing attacks also increased with COVID-19 and affected not just the financial sector, but also individuals.[47] Examples of phishing were observed in France through fake medical messages requesting the individual to click on fraudulent links to receive reimbursement for medical treatment. The aim was to trick receivers into clicking on the malicious links to download malware onto their computer or mobile phone.[48]

Third, an increase was also observed on content-related crimes, particularly with regard to child sexual exploitation online.[49] Since children were increasingly on the Internet, they became more vulnerable to sexual exploitation online. Criminals were also spending more time at home and consequently there was a rise in individuals searching for content online.[50]

The increase in cybercrime is commonly agreed upon. However, it is unclear whether one can talk about a new landscape or whether the landscape has essentially remained the same. The crimes that emerged during the pandemic are based on traditional forms of cybercrimes that already existed before, such as fraud, scams and malware attacks. There has, however, been a change in their narratives. During the pandemic, cybercriminals preyed on societal vulnerabilities and developed Corona-related crimes, such as masks scams, fake Corona cure scams and phishing attempts linked with COVID test results. Most of the cybercrimes during the pandemic were related to the health crisis, and the scenario for cybercrime was adapted to COVID-19.[51] New vector attacks also appeared, due to the extension of the targets of cybercrime. Companies had to embrace cloud services due to the increase in remote working, and employees were using insecure personal smartphones and computers, which opened the way for various cybercriminal acts.[52] In addition, cybercriminals also changed their approach

[44] Europol, 'Beyond the Pandemic – What Will the Criminal Landscape Look like after COVID-19?' (30 April 2020) www.europol.europa.eu/newsroom/news/beyond-pandemic-what-will-criminal-landscape-look-after-COVID-19.

[45] Europol, 'Pandemic Profiteering' (n 4).

[46] A Gryszczyńska, 'The Impact of the COVID-19 Pandemic on Cybercrime' (2021) 69 *Bulletin of the Polish Academy of Sciences Technical Sciences* 3.

[47] European Cyber Security Organisation, 'ESCO Barometer 2020: "Cybersecurity in Light of COVID-19"' (2020).

[48] ENISA, 'Understanding and Dealing with Phishing during the COVID-19 Pandemic', www.enisa.europa.eu/news/enisa-news/understanding-and-dealing-with-phishing-during-the-COVID-19-pandemic.

[49] Europol, 'IOCTA 2020' (n 26).

[50] ibid.

[51] Gryszczyńska (n 46).

[52] ibid.

and increasingly used social engineering techniques, which proved highly effective in the health crisis.[53] They notably impersonated government organisations and national health institutions to offer support or information on COVID-19.[54] Generally, one cannot say that there has been a real revolution of the cybercriminal landscape, but there has been an evolution of it, and particularly of its narrative, focusing on the COVID-19 context, and of its techniques.

With regard to the post-pandemic situation, it is difficult to offer a definite assessment yet, as it is unclear when the 'post-COVID world' will start. However, there is one certainty: the new cyberthreats that appeared during the pandemic will continue to hit Europe, and the situation will not return to the pre-pandemic status.[55] In fact, the techniques developed during the pandemic will continue to be used and the critical infrastructures targeted by cybercriminals will continue to be targeted afterwards.[56] With the new vaccination campaigns, Europol noted that it is expected that vaccine-specific cybercrime and cyberattacks on pharmaceutical research will appear.[57] Finally, the prolonged pandemic put a heavy burden on the national economies. Since cybercrime is a highly dynamic domain, crime may adapt to the potential economic crises that will follow. It is crucial to analyse the EU's response to it, to identify the shortcomings and to tackle cybercrimes more effectively in the future.

12.3.2. The Role of the EU in Monitoring and Facing the Increase of Cybercrimes

Two functions of the EU have been observed: (i) the reporting and monitoring functions; and (ii) a more active participatory role of Europol.

12.3.2.1. The Monitoring and Reporting Functions

The first section of this chapter mentioned the monitors of the EU, namely the European Commission, ENISA, Europol and CERT-EU.[58] A more thorough analysis of these different actors shows the essential role of the EU in the reporting of the situation.

The Commission repeatedly reported on the rise of cybercrime during the COVID-19 crisis, through press releases, reports and conferences. In this regard,

[53] J Hakmeh et al, 'The COVID-19 Pandemic and Trends in Technology' [2021] *Research Paper International Security Programme* 48.

[54] E Ventrella, 'Privacy in Emergency Circumstances: Data Protection and the COVID-19 Pandemic' (2020) 21 *ERA Forum* 379.

[55] C Gow, 'Learning the Lesson to Build Europe's Cyber Resilience' (*Euractiv*, 2 June 2021) www.euractiv.com/section/digital/opinion/learning-the-lesson-to-build-europes-cyber-resilience/.

[56] Europol, 'European Union Serious and Organised Crime Threat Assessment' (2021).

[57] ibid.

[58] Commission, 'Coronavirus Outbreak' (n 28).

Commissioner Johansson participated in various conferences, in which she referred to two types of cybercrimes.[59] These are, on the hand, the traditional cybercrimes, such as fraud, ransomware and child sexual exploitation, and on the other hand, the development of new forms of crimes that adapted to the virus and exploited the fear of people and the lack of medical equipment. The Commission's reports essentially dealt with online scams and frauds.[60] ENISA extensively reported on cybersecurity issues. It notably developed reports on the cybersecurity trends and published news item focusing on specific sectors, such as the health sector, or specific crimes, such as phishing.[61] CERT-EU also continuously assessed cybersecurity aspects during the pandemic and addressed potential threats that affected the interests of EU institutions, bodies and agencies.[62] It notably mentioned the risk of cyberattacks on the European Medicine Agency to get sensitive information. Europol was probably one of the most active agencies in the area. It provided up-to-date situational pictures of the criminal landscape during the crisis and published regular reports. These reports were either of a general nature, on the development of cybercrime,[63] or more specific, on sexual exploitation online,[64] or on counterfeits and substandard goods crimes.[65] It also published the Internet organised crime threat assessment, in which Europol assessed the cybercriminal landscape in relation to the pandemic.[66]

Next to these reporting functions, these actors also went further in their monitoring by offering recommendations and guidance. In this regard, the Commission issued recommendations on a common Union toolbox for the use of technology and data to combat and exit from the pandemic.[67] ENISA published tips for a secure use of the Internet and protection against cyberattacks,[68] and CERT-EU issued cybersecurity guidance.[69] Finally, Europol participated in the publication

[59] Bruegel, 'Tackling the Rise of Cybercrime amid COVID-19 with Ylva Johansson' (7 May 2020) www.bruegel.org/events/tackling-the-rise-of-cybercrime-amid-COVID-19-with-ylva-johansson/.

[60] Commission, 'Escroqueries liées au COVID-19', https://ec.europa.eu/info/live-work-travel-eu/consumer-rights-and-complaints/enforcement-consumer-protection/scams-related-COVID-19_fr.

[61] ENISA, 'Understanding and Dealing with Phishing' (n 48).

[62] CERT-EU, 'Threat Landscape Report' (2021) 1.

[63] Europol, 'Pandemic Profiteering' (n 4).

[64] Europol, 'Exploiting Isolation: Offenders and Victims of Online Child Sexual Abuse during the COVID-19 Pandemic' (2020).

[65] Europol, 'Viral Marketing – Counterfeits, Substandard Goods and Intellectual Property Crime in the COVID-19 Pandemic' (2020).

[66] Europol, 'IOCTA 2020' (n 26).

[67] Commission Recommendation (EU) 2020/518 of 8 April 2020 on a common Union toolbox for the use of technology and data to combat and exit from the COVID-19 crisis, in particular concerning mobile applications and the use of anonymised mobility data [2020] OJ L114/7.

[68] ENISA, 'Top Ten Cyber Hygiene Tips for SMEs during COVID-19 Pandemic' (2 June 2020) www.enisa.europa.eu/news/enisa-news/top-ten-cyber-hygiene-tips-for-smes-during-COVID-19-pandemic.

[69] Commission, 'CERT-EU Issued Cyber Security Guidance in the Context of the Coronavirus Outbreak' (26 March 2020) https://ec.europa.eu/digital-single-market/en/news/cert-eu-issued-cybersecurity-guidance-context-coronavirus-outbreak.

of a guide for parents and carers on how to ensure a safe cyberspace for their children during the pandemic.[70] Europol's role goes well beyond reporting, since it has a dual role in the fight against cybercrime – a monitoring one and an active, participatory one.

12.3.2.2. Towards a More Active Role from Europol

Next to its classical function of monitoring, Europol plays an active role in the fight against cybercrime, through EC3. The aim of the Centre was to become the focal point in the EU's fight against cybercrime. The Centre strongly supports cross-border investigations, as well as the exchange of information. During the pandemic, Europol participated in and facilitated numerous investigations. One of them, Operation Pangea, concerned cybercrime of counterfeit goods, and notably hygienic products.[71] The operation was coordinated by Interpol and included 90 other countries alongside Europol, and resulted in numerous arrests and seizures of unauthorised and counterfeit medical devices. Another example is Operation Aphrodite, which brought together Europol and 21 countries to target counterfeit goods trafficking and fake COVID-19 medical equipment.[72]

In addition to the investigations it participates in, Europol also developed campaigns to support criminal investigations. This is visible in the fight against child sexual exploitation online.[73] Europol developed the 'Trace an Object' campaign, aimed at identifying sexual offenders and victims through object recognition on pieces of content.[74]

Finally, Europol is also an active member of the EU Law Enforcement Emergency Response Protocol adopted by the Council in December 2018. The idea is to provide law enforcement authorities with support on major cross-border cyberattacks (rapid assessment, secure and timely sharing of information, effective coordination of international aspects of investigations).[75]

However, even though various actors continuously reported on the increase of cybercrime during the pandemic, and participated in the fight against it, the efforts made in the EU were insufficient. The COVID-19 pandemic highlighted and exacerbated pre-existing shortcomings that prevented the EU from being capable of keeping a safe cyberspace.

[70] Australian Government, eSafety Commissioner and Europol, 'COVID-19 Global Online Safety Advice for Parents and Carer' (2020).

[71] Europol, 'Pandemic Profiteering' (n 4).

[72] Europol, 'No Safe Market for Fakes: 21 Countries Target Illegal Goods in Europe-Wide Sting' (25 September 2020) www.europol.europa.eu/newsroom/news/no-safe-market-for-fakes-21-countries-target-illegal-goods-in-europe-wide-sting.

[73] Europol, 'Exploiting Isolation' (n 64).

[74] Europol, 'Stop Child Abuse – Trace an Object', www.europol.europa.eu/stopchildabuse.

[75] Europol, 'Pandemic Profiteering' (n 4).

12.3.3. Lessons Learnt from the Pandemic: Shortcomings of the EU in Fighting Cybercrime

The growth of cybercrimes during the pandemic highlighted existing but also new issues in the fight against cybercrime.[76] Overall, what arose is that the current cybercrime and cybersecurity legal framework is for the most part outdated, especially during and after the pandemic. Table 12.1 below provides some of the legal instruments pertaining to these two areas.

Table 12.1 The current EU legal framework on cybercrime and cybersecurity

Cybercrime	Cybersecurity
Child sexual abuse Directive 2011/93/EU Directive 2013/40/EU on attacks against information systems Proposal for e-Evidence Regulation Europol Regulation 2016/794 Directive (EU) 2019/713 on combating fraud and counterfeiting of non-cash means of payment	NIS Directive 2016/1148/EU (network and information systems) Cybersecurity Act Regulation 2019/881/EU (regarding ENISA)

In addition to these instruments, the General Data Protection Regulation could be added to both categories, since it permits harmonisation of cybersecurity and cybercrime policy through the protection of personal data against unauthorised and unlawful access.[77] With the pandemic, it became clearer that most of these legal instruments are outdated and the issues were put back on the agenda.[78] The current legal framework no longer meets the needs of the area. Three specific limits were highlighted by the pandemic: (i) the lack of cooperation; (ii) the difficult exchange of information and electronic evidence; and (iii) the security of network and information systems.

The first limit in the area is the lack of cooperation among different actors. The most visible gap is between the private and the public sector. Nowadays, cooperation does exist, but it remains largely insufficient. In principle, Europol is, for example, not allowed to directly process personal data from private parties.[79] The data needs to be received via a national unit or a state with which Europol concluded an agreement or for which an adequacy decision has been taken. Exceptions to this rule exist but remain very limited. The pandemic showed once

[76] Europol, 'IOCTA 2020' (n 26).

[77] S De Schrijver and J Van Loon, 'The Upcoming Changes to the EU's Cybersecurity Framework – Technology – European Union' (*Mondaq*, 22 June 2021) www.mondaq.com/security/1082026/the-upcoming-changes-to-the-eu39s-cybersecurity-framework.

[78] H Carrapico and B Farrand, 'Discursive Continuity and Change in the Time of COVID-19: The Case of EU Cybersecurity Policy' (2020) 42 *Journal of European Integration* 1111.

[79] Regulation (EU) 2016/794 (n 32).

again that working with the private sector is essential.[80] In fact, private entities store a vast amount of data that becomes essential in criminal investigations. This is notably the case of banks that process information on financial operations that may be linked to cybercrime, or Internet companies that have data that may concern content-related cybercrime. It is thus essential to strengthen the public–private relationship, but also the cooperation amongst law enforcement authorities and with international partners. In fact, since cybercrime knows no border, various actors can become involved and support might be needed from different law enforcement authorities, as well as international partners.[81]

The second limit is closely related to the first one and concerns the exchange of information and electronic evidence across borders, as well as encryption that protects sensitive data and prevents access to it. This challenge was already observed pre-pandemic, but it increased significantly during it. In fact, it is extremely difficult for law enforcement authorities to access and gather relevant data for criminal investigations. This is even more true for encrypted data, or data on encrypted networks.[82] Thus, there is an insufficient exchange of information between national authorities, and between the public and the private sector, which further complicates the fight against cybercrime.

The third limit concerns the security of network and information systems. The pandemic emphasised the lack of secure IT systems in the EU and the need to introduce stricter cybersecurity measures. Europol noted that cybersecurity measures were insufficient, which facilitated the emergence of cybercrimes.[83] Many IT systems were brought to a complete halt due to cyberattacks, for example in the health sector.[84] Much effort is needed in this regard to ensure a safe cyberspace.

Overall, the EU is still lacking a coordinated response to cybercrime issues, and in particular to large-scale cyberattacks. Only with joint efforts with partners and changes can the EU be at the forefront of digital resilience and the fight against cybercrime.

12.4. Getting Ready for a Post-pandemic World: Stronger Efforts from the EU?

The COVID-19 pandemic played an essential role in highlighting the existing gaps in cybercrime, as well as new ones. The fight against cybercrime became one of

[80] Carrapico and Farrand (n 78).

[81] Europol, 'IoT Cybersecurity: Webinar Series to Tackle Security Challenges of IoT', www.europol.europa.eu/newsroom/news/iot-cybersecurity-webinar-series-to-tackle-security-challenges-of-iot.

[82] Europol, 'COVID-19 Sparks Upward Trend in Cybercrime', www.europol.europa.eu/newsroom/news/COVID-19-sparks-upward-trend-in-cybercrime.

[83] Europol, 'IOCTA 2020' (n 26).

[84] E Saeva, 'Cybersecurity and the EU: Lessons from the COVID-19 Crisis' (*Crossroads Europe*, 6 October 2020) https://crossroads.ideasoneurope.eu/2020/10/06/cybersecurity-and-the-eu-lessons-from-the-COVID-19-crisis/.

the priorities of the EU, and its institutions were forced to take actions to ensure a safe cyberspace. The measures developed were essentially based on the existing philosophy; however, the pandemic also triggered and accelerated the development of new innovative solutions.

12.4.1. Towards Stronger Efforts on the EU Level: Old Wine in a New Bottle?

Several developments and proposals have been put on the table. However, they are built on existing institutional structures and legal frameworks. Several proposals have been made in three EU strategies developed during the pandemic: the EU Security Union Strategy (July 2020),[85] the EU Strategy for a More Effective Fight against Child Sexual Abuse (July 2020)[86] and the EU's Cybersecurity Strategy for the Digital Decade (December 2020).[87]

Two general legislative changes can be mentioned. First, the proposal for the NIS 2 (Network and Information Systems) Directive is a readaptation of the NIS Directive. It is an important step towards a united and harmonised response to cyberattacks.[88] In fact, it obligates more entities and sectors to adopt measures that increase the level of cybersecurity in the EU, such as critical medical devices, public administration and food supply manufacturers.[89] It thus broadens the scope of the Directive, but remains an evolution based on the same core elements, namely cross-border cooperation, security requirements, incident reporting and preparedness.[90] Second, the proposal for an interim Regulation on the processing of personal data and other data to combat child sexual exploitation online.[91] The aim is to ensure that online communication services continue to process data that enables the detection of child sexual abuse online. The Parliament adopted the proposal in July 2021.[92]

[85] Commission, 'EU Security Union Strategy: A New Security Ecosystem' (24 July 2020) https://ec.europa.eu/commission/presscorner/detail/en/ip_20_1379.

[86] Communication from the Commission to the European Parliament, the Council, the European economic and social Committee and the Committee of the Regions, 'EU Strategy for a More Effective Fight against Child Sexual Abuse' (2020).

[87] Joint Communication to the European Parliament and the Council, 'The EU's Cybersecurity Strategy for the Digital Decade' (2020).

[88] Gow (n 55).

[89] Commission, 'Proposal for a Directive of the European Parliament and of the Council on measures of high common level of cybersecurity across the Union, repealing Directive (EU) 2016/1148 2020', COM (2020) 823 final.

[90] Gow (n 55).

[91] Commission, 'Proposal for a Regulation of the European Parliament and of the Council on a temporary derogation from certain provisions of Directive 2002/58/EC of the European Parliament and of the Council as regards the use of technologies by numberindependent interpersonal communications service providers for the processing of personal and other data for the purpose of combatting child sexual abuse online', COM (2020) 568 final.

[92] 'Texts Adopted – Use of Technologies for the Processing of Data for the Purpose of Combating Online Child Sexual Abuse (Temporary Derogation from Directive 2002/58/EC) ***I – Tuesday, 6 July 2021', www.europarl.europa.eu/doceo/document/TA-9-2021-0319_EN.html.

Developments and additions were also made to the existing institutional structure, whether through legislative changes or simple additions. The main proposal made was the amendment of Europol's Regulation.[93] The proposal was published in December 2020 and included various changes. Among them were the possibility for Europol to process large and complex datasets, the strengthening of Europol's role in research and innovation, the possibility for the agency to enter data into the Schengen Information System, and the strengthening of the cooperation with third countries and with private parties.[94] These two last points are the most relevant for this chapter, and should allow Europol to effectively fight cybercrime. In addition, Europol also launched an innovative new decryption platform at the end of December 2020 based on the old Regulation.[95] This platform will strengthen Europol's ability to decrypt information lawfully obtained in an investigation and will enhance the agency's support to Member State investigations, notably in the fight against online child sexual abuse.[96]

These changes highlight the following points. There is a strong need to increase cooperation on different levels, which is what the Commission aims to improve with its proposed changes. Thus, the public–private partnership shall improve in the future, as well as the cooperation with international parties, strongly encouraged by the Commission.[97] The Commission also pushed for extended collaboration between the two key agencies in the field – Europol and ENISA – in Europol's amendments,[98] but also in the adoption of the latest ENISA Regulation.[99] This, once again, confirms that cybersecurity and cybercrime are highly intertwined. The Commission emphasised this need for strong overlap between the two sectors, particularly in the revision of the NIS Directive, which notes the importance of the role of Europol and the EC3 as observer in cybersecurity matters.[100]

Changes have been made to the EU policy and legal framework in cybercrime. However, the majority of them are more an evolution than a revolution. They follow the old philosophy, but adapted to the current situation. Furthermore, some changes had already begun before the pandemic. The COVID-19 crisis allowed the

[93] Commission, 'Proposal for a Regulation of the European Parliament and of the Council amending Regulation (EU) 2016/794, as regards Europol's cooperation with private parties, the processing of personal data by Europol in support of criminal investigations, and Europol's role on research and innovation', COM (2020) 796 final.

[94] N Vavoula and V Mitsilegas, 'Strengthening Europol's Mandate: An Appraisal of the Commission's Proposal to Amend Regulation (EU) 2016/784 (Europol Regulation)' (*EU Law Analysis*, 29 July 2021) <http://eulawanalysis.blogspot.com/2021/07/strengthening-europols-mandate.html.

[95] Europol, 'Europol and the European Commission Inaugurate New Decryption Platform to Tackle the Challenge of Encrypted Material for Law Enforcement Investigations', www.europol.europa.eu/newsroom/news/europol-and-european-commission-inaugurate-new-decryption-platform-to-tackle-challenge-of-encrypted-material-for-law-enforcement.

[96] ibid.

[97] Commission, 'Proposal for a Regulation' (n 93).

[98] ibid.

[99] Regulation (EU) 2019/881 (n 30).

[100] Commission, 'Proposal for a Directive' (n 89).

issues to come into the spotlight and for reforms to be accelerated. In fact, since cybercrimes rapidly multiplied, EU actions had to accelerate. The pandemic did, however, also trigger some new developments.

12.4.2. COVID-19 as a Trigger for Developments in the EU's Response to Cybercrime

While most of the developments followed an old approach and focused on the adaptation of existing legal and institutional structures, some brought the creation of new bodies. The pandemic also pushed for debated changes that might not have been adopted in the same way without the sense of urgency brought along by the pandemic.

As to the first aspect, the Commission has mentioned three potential bodies that could appear in the coming years. Within the EU Cybersecurity Strategy, the Commission mentioned first the creation of a network of Security Operations Centres that should be powered by artificial intelligence and take on the role of a 'cybersecurity shield'.[101] It should be able to detect cyberattack at an early stage. Second, the creation of a Joint Cyber Unit, which 'would serve as a virtual and physical platform for cooperation for the different cybersecurity communities in the EU, with a focus on operational and technical coordination against major cross border cyber incidents and threats'.[102] The platform should allow participants to support each other by sharing expertise to be aware of and prepared for the cybersecurity situation and to be able to offer a coordinated response and recovery. Thus, while the EC3 has become the focal point of the fight against cybercrime in the EU, the Joint Cyber Unit aspires to become the EU hub for cybersecurity operational cooperation. This Joint Cyber Unit was also referred to in the EU Security Union Strategy, which once again confirms the overlap between cybersecurity and cybercrime.[103] Finally, within the EU Strategy against Child Sexual Exploitation Online, the Commission mentioned the potential development of a European Centre aimed at preventing child sexual abuse.[104] The Centre would coordinate the prevention and investigation of child abuse and offer support to the victims. It should directly receive reports from private companies on child sexual abuse in the EU and accelerate their processing.[105] While these structures would be newly established, the idea of their creation did not appear with the pandemic. The idea had already emerged at an earlier stage. The Joint Cyber Unit, for example, is built

[101] Joint Communication, 'The EU's Cybersecurity Strategy for the Digital Decade' (n 87).
[102] ibid.
[103] Commission, 'EU Security Union Strategy' (n 85).
[104] Communication, 'EU Strategy for a More Effective Fight' (n 86).
[105] Commission, 'Fighting Corona-Crime and Cyber-Crime' (7 April 2020) https://ec.europa.eu/commission/commissioners/2019-2024/johansson/blog/fighting-corona-crime-and-cyber-crime_en.

on the Recommendation on a Coordinated Response to Incidents and Crises, the so-called Blueprint of 2017.[106]

The second change that the pandemic triggered was the push for the rapid adoption of debated changes in the EU decision-making landscape. While it was necessary to readapt the existing legal frameworks, the pandemic shall not justify dubious practices. The best example of a legislation pushed by the pandemic is the amendment of Europol. Strengthening the powers of Europol and modifying its legal framework quickly became necessary, so the process started and developed rapidly. The Inception Impact Assessment was launched in May 2020, the proposal by the Commission in December 2020, the trialogue work between the Commission, the Council and the European Parliament started at the end of October 2021 and Commissioner Johansson stated that she hopes that the Regulation is adopted by the end of 2021.[107] This has not been the case, but a provisional agreement between the Council Presidency and the European Parliament was reached on 1 February 2022,[108] and adoption is expected in the following months. The drafting of the proposal took less than a year and its adoption will last a year and a half. This rapid legislative process is a matter of concern for two reasons.

The first reason is that the proposal came around one and a half years before the planned evaluation of Europol by the Commission, which would have included details on the agency's impact, effectiveness, efficiency and working practices.[109] While an inception impact assessment was launched by the Commission, with public consultation,[110] it can in no way replace the knowledge acquired by a thorough evaluation made by the Commission. MEP Clare Daly stated at the Joint Parliamentary Scrutiny Group on Europol's 9th Meeting that they 'were asked to legislate blind here'.[111] In fact, the European Parliament must decide on the amendments without a clear and detailed overview of the issues at stake. The risk is in setting a precedent where legislative processes can be rushed, and legally mandated evaluation simply skipped.

The second reason is that the rushed measures concerned highly contentious topics, such as the direct cooperation of Europol with private parties. The Commission requested a study to be made on this aspect – it is the only area of the Regulation that was subject to legally mandated evaluation.[112] However, this

[106] Commission, 'Joint Cyber Unit', https://digital-strategy.ec.europa.eu/en/policies/joint-cyber-unit.

[107] Multimedia Centre, '9th Meeting of the Joint Parliamentary Scrutiny Group (JPSG) on Europol', https://multimedia.europarl.europa.eu/en/9th-meeting-of-joint-parliamentary-scrutiny-group-jpsg-on-europol_20211025-1645-COMMITTEE-LIBE_vd.

[108] Council of the EU, 'Europol: provisional agreement between the Council presidency and the European Parliament on the agency's new mandate' (2022) www.consilium.europa.eu/en/press/press-releases/2022/02/01/europol-provisional-agreement-between-council-presidency-and-european-parliament/.

[109] C Riehle, 'Commission Proposes Europol Reform' (*eucrim*, 12 February 2021) https://eucrim.eu/news/commission-proposes-europol-reform/.

[110] DG Home European Commission, 'Inception Impact Assessment – Europol Regulation' (2020).

[111] Multimedia Centre (n 107).

[112] Milieu Consulting, 'Study on the Practice of Direct Exchanges of Personal Data between Europol and Private Parties' (2020) Final Report HOME/2018/ISFP/FW/EVAL/0077.

study has several shortcomings and does not offer a complete picture of the issues at stake. It notably fails to address independent judicial control, and the positions of national data protection authorities and private parties.[113] According to the proposal from the Commission, Europol shall be able to directly receive personal data from private parties on a more regular basis, ask Member States to request private parties to share additional information and inform private parties of missing data.[114] This strongly encourages public–private partnerships and makes Europol a focal point for collecting this data.[115] However, this direct exchange of personal data between private parties and Europol is highly contentious, and deserves proper attention.[116] Some argue that this exchange goes against fundamental rights, the principle of the rule of law and European procedural safeguards.[117] For such a topic, mulitiple aspects need to be considered, namely detailed rules on the duties, on the nature of the private parties, on the relevant safeguards and on the involvement of supervisory authorities in this regard.[118] The rush to adopt the Regulation, especially in a post-pandemic context, should not circumvent the ordinary procedures and negatively affect fundamental rights.

12.5. Conclusion

This chapter has analysed the effects of the pandemic on the EU cybercriminal landscape and the EU's response to it. During the COVID-19 pandemic, a rise of cybercrimes was reported because of a shift from the physical to the digital world. As a result, the issue of cybercrime was placed back at the heart of the discussion and became a key priority of the EU. This chapter has shown that while there was a clear increase in cybercrime, the pandemic did not completely change the landscape. It only triggered evolution, through a clear change of narrative and the use of new techniques. The EU played a key role during the crisis, in monitoring and supporting individuals and companies, especially Europol, in actively participating in the fight against cybercrime. However, as also shown by this chapter, the EU did not have sufficient tools to be able to face the situation that changed at an exponential rate. It thus became the upmost necessity to come up with new solutions. The Commission developed several strategies and came up with new proposals. These ideas were essentially based on old, existing legal instruments,

[113] W Van Ballegooij, 'Revision of the Europol Regulation' (European Parliamentary Research Service, 2021) Briefing – Implementation Appraisal.

[114] Commission, 'Proposal for a Regulation' (n 93).

[115] Vavoula and Mitsilegas (n 94).

[116] S Eskens, 'New and Extensive Data Processing Powers Proposed for Europol' (*European Law Blog*, 30 July 2021) https://europeanlawblog.eu/2021/07/30/new-and-extensive-data-processing-powers-proposed-for-europol/.

[117] EDRI, 'Recommendations on the Revision of Europol's Mandate' (2021).

[118] Vavoula and Mitsilegas (n 94).

but the Commission also developed innovative solutions for new bodies. While the pandemic was not the only trigger for EU actions in this area, it did play a strong role of accelerator. In fact, it highlighted the existing gaps and pushed the EU to act and update the current instruments. Acting to ensure a safe cyberspace is a noble cause and deserves special attention, but it is essential to ensure that the new measures adopted are followed by specific safeguards and that the pandemic does not allow the EU institutions to circumvent and push aside any potential obstacle. Finally, the chapter has repeatedly emphasised the interconnectedness between cybercrime and cybersecurity, whether it is in the reporting of cybercrime during the pandemic or in the proposed solutions to the shortcomings. It is essential to consider the two aspects jointly to ensure a safe cyberspace, and while the EU is increasingly noting this overlap, it still adopts separate legal instruments. The future will show whether cybercrime, as predicted, will continue to increase, and whether the legal instruments proposed by the Commission will be adopted and ensure a safer cyberspace. It is paramount for the EU to be at the forefront of this issue, but it should remain within the realm of the law.

INDEX

www.ingramcontent.com/pod-product-compliance
Ingram Content Group UK Ltd.
Pitfield, Milton Keynes, MK11 3LW, UK
UKHW022222151225
9585UKWH00003B/114

9 781509 955985